WHO'S WHO IN
THE WRITERS' UNION
OF CANADA

WHO'S WHO IN THE WRITERS' UNION OF CANADA

A DIRECTORY OF MEMBERS

Published by the Writers' Union of Canada

Copyright © The Writers' Union of Canada 1988
24 Ryerson Avenue, Toronto, Ontario   M5T 2P3

Canadian Cataloguing in Publication Data:

Writers' Union of Canada
    Who's who in the Writers' Union of Canada

3rd ed.
Previous editions published under title: The Writers' Union of Canada :
a directory of members.

ISBN 0-9690796-2-1

1. Writers' Union of Canada – Directories.   2. Authors, Canadian
(English) – 20th century – Biography.*   3. Canadian literature (English) –
20th century – Bio-bibliography.*   I. Title. II. Title: The Writers' Union of
Canada : a directory of members.

PS8081.W74 1988   C810'.9'0054   C88-093698-3
PR9189.6.W74 1988

The purpose of The Writers' Union of Canada is to unite Canadian writers for the advancement of their common interests. These interests include: the fostering of writing in Canada; relations with publishers; exchange of information among members; safeguarding the freedom to write and publish; and the advancement of good relations with other writers and their organizations in Canada and all parts of the world.

(from the Writers' Union of Canada constitution)

PREFACE

If anybody had told me, a quarter of a century ago, that it would be possible to publish a directory containing the names of 586 Canadian writers, all of whom have at least one published book in print, I would have thought him (or even her) demented.

Well, here is that directory – the third that the Writers' Union of Canada has produced. The first, published in 1977, contained 205 names of professional book writers. The second, published in 1981, contained 322 names. Even as I write this, our third edition is in danger of becoming out-of-date. For the Writers' Union of Canada now numbers over 600 and it's still growing.

When the Union was founded in 1973 it was clear that writing in Canada was coming of age. But who could have imagined the strides that we would make in fifteen years?

We set out to try to improve the writers' position in Canada – with publishers, government, booksellers and buyers; to increase literacy; to promote the increased library holdings of books by Canadian authors; to promote the study of Canadian literature in schools.

Our goal remains the same: the care and feeding of the literary community. But on the way to that goal, we've had some signal successes. These include:

- The adoption, in 1976, of publishers' guidelines for multiple submissions by authors to help market their work more efficiently; and the adoption of a model trade book contract that includes, among other innovations, a royalty of ten percent as a minimum standard for trade books.
- The implementation, in 1978, of a schedule "C", which stops foreign publishers from dumping remaindered copies of foreign editions of Canadian-authored books on the Canadian market.
- The institution by Canada Council, in 1984, of a program of grants for non-fiction writers.
- And – perhaps the most significant success of all – the adoption, in 1986, of a Public Lending Right by which Canadian writers are paid annually for the use of their books in the libraries.

As these lines are written, the Union is leading the fight against the government's censorship bill, C-54. It is taking measures to upgrade the book pages of Canadian newspapers and to increase the coverage given to Canadian books. It is working to update Canada's notoriously antiquated copyright act, and to establish a working plan to compensate writers for work reproduced by mechanical means. As well, it has launched a campaign to ensure that women writers receive equal treatment from universities, libraries, book pages and government agencies.

Any writer who has published at least one trade book of fiction, non-fiction or poetry in the last seven years (or whose work is still in print) is eligible to join The Writers' Union of Canada. Fully 605 have already done so; 586 of these are in this reference work, which is now widely used by teachers, librarians, reading and lecture series sponsors, journalists and others.

A quarter of a century ago such a directory would not have been possible. This newest edition suggests the extent to which we have really come of age.

Pierre Berton
Chairman

ACKNOWLEDGMENTS

We gratefully thank the Directory Committee for their contribution of judgement, expertise and time: Joan Clark (Chair); Susan Kerslake; Jillian Dagg; Bryna Barclay; and Robert Bringhurst.

We are grateful to all members who undertook the laborious task of compiling their entries.

Special thanks go to Valerie Frith for editing, Shaun Oakey for proofreading, Jodi Franklyn for cover design concept and Anthony Schatzky for inputting the text.

The Writers' Union of Canada acknowledges with thanks funding assistance from The Canada Council; the Ontario Ministry of Culture and Communications, Dr. Lily Munro, Minister; the Department of Communications; Alberta Culture; and the Saskatchewan Arts Board.

MARK ABLEY

Born in England, May 13, 1955. Grew up in Lethbridge and Saskatoon. Learned more about writing in four years in the Saskatoon Poetry Group than from six years of analysing literature at the University of Saskatchewan (B.A.) and Oxford (M.A.). Researcher, CBC-TV Drama, 1978-79; full-time writer since 1979. A once and future poet, now writing prose in Montreal. Also edit and occasionally broadcast. Contributing editor to Saturday Night.

Selected Publications:

The Parting Light (Selected Writings of Samuel Palmer): (ed.), Manchester and New York, Carcanet, 1985. ISBN 0-85635-619-0
Beyond Forget (Rediscovering the Prairies): Vancouver, Douglas & McIntyre, 1986. ISBN 0-88894-520-5

Awards: Rhodes Scholarship, 1975. Fiona Mee Award (Literary Journalism), 1980. Eric Gregory Award, Society of Authors (U.K.), 1981.

Comments: *"Beyond Forget* is astonishing in its freshness and precision — and impressive in its implied doggedness." — Kenneth McGoogan, *Calgary Herald*

"Beyond Forget is the record of an inner journey as well as an actual one. It's a superior species of travel book, the kind of informed personal journalism in which The New Yorker specializes. Abley brings to his task a fine sensitivity, a solid literary background and a questing intelligence." — William French, *Globe and Mail*

"Abley brings humility and curiosity to the West. His spare descriptions and honest prose achieve an epic rhythm worthy of his theme. In *Beyond Forget* the breath of the divine spirit is still felt." — Ronald Wright, *The Reader*

Mailing Address: c/o TWUC, 24 Ryerson Avenue, Toronto, Ontario M5T 2P3

EDNA ALFORD

Born in Turtleford, Saskatchewan, November 19, 1947. Raised and educated in Saskatoon. Lived in Calgary 14 years where I co-founded and co-edited Dandelion magazine. I now live near Livelong, Saskatchewan.

Selected Publications:

A Sleep Full of Dreams: Lantzville, Oolichan, 1981. ISBN 0-88982-013-7
The Garden of Eloise Loon: Lantzville, Oolichan, 1986. ISBN 0-88982-080-5

Awards: Gerald Lampert Award Co-winner, 1981

Readings, Lectures & Workshops: Often read at universities and high schools. Have taught creative writing (fiction and poetry) at Mount Royal College, Calgary; The Okanagan School of the Arts, Penticton; and the Saskatchewan Summer School of the Arts, Fort San, Saskatchewan. Readings, workshops, etc. may be booked through TWUC.

Mailing Address: Box 179, Livelong, Saskatchewan S0M 1J0 *or* c/o TWUC, 24 Ryerson Avenue, Toronto, Ontario M5T 2P3

BEVERLEY ALLINSON

Born in Australia, April 17, 1936. Arrived in Canada in 1969. Writer, photographer, teacher. Founding collective member of Broadside magazine.

Selected Publications:

Mandy and the Flying Map: Toronto, Scholastic, 1973. ISBN 0-590-71045-1
Mumbles and Snits: Toronto, Women's Press, 1975. ISBN 0-88961-022-4
All Aboard! (A Cross-Canada Adventure): (with Barbara O'Kelly), Toronto, Greey de Pencier, 1979. ISBN 0-919872-44-1

Readings, Lectures & Workshops: Regularly conduct workshops, partnering adolescents with primary-aged children. Currently developing intergenerational writing programme for senior citizens and school students.
Mailing Address: 231 Concord Avenue, Toronto, Ontario M6H 2P4

SIDNEY ALLINSON

 Born in Durham, England. Served with the RAF. Canadian citizen in 1956. Worked as a newspaper reporter, advertising copywriter, movie scriptwriter/producer and creative director of an international advertising agency. Now freelance full time as a business communications consultant, book author, magazine writer and public speaker. Past national Vice-President, Canadian Authors Association. Currently publications editor, Royal Canadian Military Institute.

Selected Publications:

Season for Homicide: Houston, Lone Star, 1972. (no ISBN)
Make Money Fast as a Ghostwriter: Cobalt, Highway Book Shop, 1977.
   ISBN 0-88954-122-1
The Bantams (The Untold Story of World War I): Oakville, Mosaic, 1983.
   ISBN 0-88962-191-8
Jeremy Kane: Toronto, Salvo, 1987. ISBN 0-921289-00-6

   Comments: Works in progress: The Spitsbergen Commando, a novel linking Canadians in World War II with the present day; and How Sleep the Brave: 75 Years of the Commonwealth War Graves Commission.
   Readings, Lectures & Workshops: Frequently present seminars at universities and writers' workshops. Give lectures on writer's craft, freelancing, business communications and military history.
   Mailing Address: 24 Ravencliff Crescent, Agincourt, Ontario M1T 1R8

DORIS ANDERSEN

Born February 6, 1909, in Tanana, Alaska, after a 100-mile trip by dog team along the frozen Yukon River from the Indian village of Mouse Point to Tanana. B.A., University of British Columbia, 1929; B.S.L.S., University of Washington, 1930. Worked in Ottawa, Seattle and Vancouver. Retired as Branch Head, Vancouver Public Library, 1974. Married George C. Andersen, 1929. Children: Deirdre, Richard and David. Six grandchildren and three great grandchildren.

Selected Publications:

Blood Brothers: Toronto, Macmillan, 1967. ISBN 0-7705-1156-2
Ways Harsh and Wild: Vancouver, J.J. Douglas, 1973. ISBN 0-88894-027-0
Slave of the Haida: Toronto, Macmillan, 1974. 0-7705-1633-5 (trade ed.),
     ISBN 0-7705-1699-8 (educ. ed.)
Evergreen Islands (The Islands of the Inside Passage): Sidney, Gray's, 1979./
     Vancouver, Whitecap, 1985. ISBN 0-88826-084-9
The Columbia is Coming!: Sidney, Gray's, 1982. ISBN 0-88826-094-6
To Change the World (A Biography of Pauline Jewett): Toronto, Irwin, 1987.
     ISBN 0-7725-1567-0

  Readings, Lectures & Workshops: Readings, talks and workshops in many B.C. towns in the Peace River district, Mackenzie district, Okanagan district, Vancouver Island and Greater Vancouver.
  Mailing Address: 1232 Esquimalt Avenue, West Vancouver, British Columbia V7T 1K3

MARGUERITE ANDERSEN

Born in Germany. Grew up in Berlin. Youngest of the three daughters of a very fine woman and her husband, a professor, writer, politician and founding member of the German Writers' Union, the Schriftstellerschutzverband. Lived, studied, taught and wrote in Germany, Austria, France, England, Tunisia, Ethiopia, the U.S. and Canada. Professor of French Studies at the University of Guelph. Live in Toronto. Two sons, one daughter. Six granddaughters, one grandson.

Selected Publications:

Paul Claudel et l'Allemagne: Ottawa, Editions de l'Universite d'Ottawa, 1965. ISBN 0-7766-4203-0
Mother Was Not a Person: Montreal, Black Rose, 1974. ISBN 0-919618-00-6
De memoire de femme: Montreal, Quinze, 1982. ISBN 2-89026-313-4
L'Autrement pareille: Sudbury, Prise de Parole, 1984. ISBN 0-920814-63-8

Awards: Prix du Journal de Montreal, 1983
Comments: Write the Chronique page in Poetry Canada. Co-editor, Resources for Feminist Research/Documentation sur la recherche feministe.
Member of Amnesty International and PEN Canada. I write mainly in French and am a member of the Union des ecrivains quebecois.
Numerous poems, short stories, book reviews, T.V. scripts and articles, mostly in French.
Mailing Address: c/o TWUC, 24 Ryerson Avenue, Toronto, Ontario M5T 2P3

6

ALLAN ANDERSON

Born in Calgary, Alberta, in 1915, when it was still a real cowtown. Lived in Montreal, 1926-42. Honours in English and Economics at McGill (studied under Stephen Leacock, incredible experience!). Freelance broadcaster, CBC, 1949-78, hosting public affairs programmes and taping documentaries all over Canada. Became oral historian in 1977 and have edited two huge local histories, working on a third, making ten books in all. My wife, Betty, saved my skin, helping with every book. Have five children.

Selected Publications:

Remembering the Farm: Toronto, Macmillan 1977. ISBN 0-7705-1572-X
Greetings from Canada: (with Betty Tomlinson), Toronto, Macmillan, 1978. ISBN 0-7705-1736-6
Postcard Memories of Muskoka: (with Ralph Beaumont), Erin, Boston Mills, 1979. ISBN 0-919822-86-X
Salt Water, Fresh Water: Toronto, Macmillan, 1979. ISBN 0-7705-1819-2
Roughnecks and Wildcatters: Toronto, Macmillan, 1981. ISBN 0-7715-9496-8
Remembering Leacock: Ottawa, Deneau, 1983. ISBN 0-88879-093-7

Comments: "There's a flavour of unvarnished truth about this book . . . If culture is the simple act or art of living, then this book shows that it is alive and well in rural Canada." – Harry Boyle, *Canadian Reader* (on *Remembering the Farm*)
"Anderson's third oral history is a winner!" – *Ottawa Citizen* (on *Roughnecks and Wildcatters*)

Readings, Lectures & Workshops: For seven years I have taught a creative writing class at Tottenham, Ontario. We have published three anthologies; class members' ages range from 13 to 78 years.

Mailing Address: RR 3, Tottenham, Ontario L0G 1W0

BETTY TOMLINSON ANDERSON

Born in Stratford, Ontario, in 1923. Now living in rural setting near Tottenham (40 miles north-west of Toronto). Grew up in beauteous Stratford before heading for McMaster University. An English course and extracurricular activities led to extended career in radio broadcasting from 1944-78 (commentator and producer), mainly with CBC, in Ontario, Alberta and Manitoba. Since 1977, I've teamed with my husband, Allan Anderson, to work on all his books and to co-author Greetings from Canada and to co-edit Tecumseth Township: The Unforgettable Past.

Selected Publications:

Greetings from Canada: (with Allan Anderson), Toronto, Macmillan, 1978. ISBN 0-7705-1736-6

Tecumseth Township (The Unforgettable Past): Corporation of the Township of Tecumseth, 1984. ISBN 0-919303-91-9

Comments: "There I was, preparing to be bored with *Greetings from Canada* – an album of unique postcards from the Edwardian era, 1900-1916 – rapidly the boredom left me, as I found this a delightful, unusual book – informative, educational, full of history and geography, and very important, lots of fun." – *Victoria Times Colonist*

Readings, Lectures & Workshops: Since 1975, Allan Anderson and I have been giving lectures on Edwardian Canada based on our postcards of that period. We have made our own slides of the cards and lectured in many Ontario communities, large and small, and also in major cities in Manitoba, Saskatchewan, Alberta and British Columbia.

Mailing Address: RR 3, Tottenham, Ontario L0G 1W0

DORIS ANDERSON

Born in Calgary, Alberta. B.A. from the University of Alberta, 1945. Came to Toronto immediately and held a number of extremely dull jobs in the dregs of publishing. Wrote short fiction one glorious year in the U.K. and France. Joined Chatelaine in sales promotion in 1951. Seven years later made editor. President of the Canadian Advisory Council and National Action Committee on the Status of Women. Currently a columnist for the Toronto Star.

Selected Publications:

Two Women: Toronto, Macmillan, 1979. ISBN 0-7705-1653-X
Rough Layout: Toronto, McClelland & Stewart, 1981. ISBN 0-7710-0742-6

Awards: Officer of the Order of Canada. Member, News Hall of Fame. Woman of Distinction, YWCA Award, 1983. Constance E. Hamilton Award for the City of Toronto.
Mailing Address: c/o TWUC, 24 Ryerson Avenue, Toronto, Ontario M5T 2P3

JAN ANDREWS

Born in England in 1942, married and came to Canada in 1963. Spent four years in Saskatoon and now live in Ottawa. Specialise in writing for children, creating dramatic montages and designing and organising projects and events with a multicultural focus. Have two children, three foster children and an addiction to hiking, canoeing, skiing and wilderness adventures of various kinds.

Selected Publications:

Fresh Fish . . . and Chips: Toronto, Women's Press, 1973. (no ISBN)
Ella, an Elephant, un Elephant: Montreal, Tundra, 1976. ISBN 0-88776-063-5
The Dancing Sun: (ed.), Victoria, Press Porcepic, 1979. ISBN 0-88878-196-2
Very Last First Time: Toronto, Groundwood, 1985. ISBN 0-88899-043-X

Awards: Shortlisted, Ruth Schwartz Award, 1986. Canada Council Children's Literature Award, 1986.

Readings, Lectures & Workshops: Read regularly and give creative writing workshops in elementary and junior-high schools. Provide general workshops on children's literature and teach creative writing for educators. Received two Ontario Arts Council Artists in the Schools grants for longer-term work with selected classes. I welcome this type of activity.

Mailing Address: 444 Athlone Avenue, Ottawa, Ontario K1Z 5M7

BRUCE ARMSTRONG

Montreal-born with Nova Scotia roots. Travelled across Canada and in the Yukon and NWT as a broadcaster, magician, actor and lecturer. Five years in Toronto in TV, stage and commercials. Moved to Halifax. Past 20 years include writing radio and TV scripts, hosting own TV series. A published poet, now working on new non-fiction and fiction projects. Past President of the Writers' Federation of Nova Scotia.

Selected Publications:

Sable Island: Toronto, Doubleday, 1981. ISBN 0-385-13113-5

Awards: Evelyn Richardson Memorial Literary Award, 1982

Comments: "Bruce Armstrong has written and put together the Sable Island book with the sensitivity and artistry of a poet." – *Evelyn Richardson Memorial Trust Selection Committee*

"Beautifully written." – Alden Nowlan, *Atlantic Advocate*

"A loving and enchanting profile of the island." – *Toronto Star*

"Armstrong writes luminous prose." – Helen Delaney, *Midland Free Press*

"This is such a book as quickens dreams." – M. Allen Gibson, *Halifax Mail-Star*

"In an age of specialization, this writer and performer is an imaginative, inventive, enterprising generalist, drawing from all aspects of the arts." – Basil Deakin, *Halifax Mail-Star*

Readings, Lectures & Workshops: Read and give presentations in universities, schools and libraries, as well as workshops on journal keeping, Sable Island slide shows and classes on magic and its history. May be booked through TWUC.

Mailing Address: c/o TWUC, 24 Ryerson Avenue, Toronto, Ontario M5T 2P3

SUSAN ATKINSON-KEEN

Born and raised in Montreal. Educated as a geologist 1967-76: B.Sc. (Sir George Williams), M.Sc. (Acadia), Research (Johns Hopkins). Spent ten years working as a field geologist from Newfoundland to British Columbia, Iceland, Scotland and the central Appalachians. Now live in Halifax, Nova Scotia, with husband, three children and various small animals. Turned to fiction writing in 1981. Creator of the Adventures of Broughton Bear series; titles listed below.

Selected Publications:

One Thing Leads to Another: Toronto, Greey de Pencier, 1985. ISBN 0-920775-13-6
Lost and Found: Toronto, Greey de Pencier, 1985. ISBN 0-920775-12-8
A Whole Day of Surprises: Toronto, Greey de Pencier, 1985. ISBN 0-920775-11-X
Fun Times: Toronto, Greey de Pencier, 1985. ISBN 0-920775-09-8
Unexpected Wonders: Toronto, Greey de Pencier, 1985. ISBN 0-920775-10-1
A Dream Becomes Real: Toronto, Greey de Pencier, 1985. ISBN 0-920775-08-X

Awards: Red Cross Story Contest, 1960, Honourable Mention (Gr. 4)
Readings, Lectures & Workshops: Part of the Nova Scotia writers-in-the-schools programme. Give readings from the Broughton Bear series, accompanied by nature talk, slides and hands-on nature props (from porcupine quills to cattail fluff).
Mailing Address: c/o TWUC, 24 Ryerson Avenue, Toronto, Ontario M5T 2P3 *or* 1591 Chestnut Street, Halifax, Nova Scotia B3H 3S9

MARGARET ATWOOD

I was born in Ottawa, Ontario, in 1939 and have been writing – poetry, fiction, non-fiction prose, children's books – since 1956. Attended the University of Toronto and Harvard University; both long ago. Canoe in summer, hibernate in winter and live with novelist Graeme Gibson, our daughter, his two sons and two collective cats, in Toronto.

Selected Publications:

The Edible Woman: Toronto, McClelland & Stewart, 1969. ISBN 0-7710-9193-1

Power Politics: Toronto, Anansi, 1971. ISBN 0-88784-020-5

Survival: Toronto, Anansi, 1972. ISBN 0-88784-713-7

Surfacing: Toronto, McClelland & Stewart, 1972. ISBN 0-7710-0822-8

Lady Oracle: Toronto, McClelland & Stewart, 1976. ISBN 0-7710-0815-5

Life Before Man: Toronto, McClelland & Stewart, 1979. ISBN 0-7710-0807-4

Bluebeard's Egg: Toronto, McClelland & Stewart, 1983. ISBN 0-7710-0808-2

Bodily Harm: Toronto, McClelland & Stewart, 1981. ISBN 0-7710-0812-0

Interlunar: Toronto, Oxford, 1984. ISBN 0-19-54051-3

The Handmaid's Tale: Toronto, McClelland & Stewart, 1985. ISBN 0-7710-2115-6

Selected Poems II: Toronto, Oxford, 1986. ISBN 0-19-540561-7

Awards: Governor General's Awards, 1966 and 1986. Welsh Arts Council International Writer's Prize, 1982. Los Angeles Times Prize for Fiction, 1986.

Mailing Address: c/o Oxford University Press, 70 Wynford Drive, Don Mills, Ontario M3C 1J9

IVAN AVAKUMOVIC

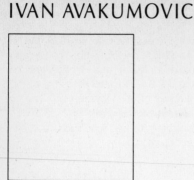

Selected Publications:

The Anarchist Prince (A Biographical Study of Peter Kropotkin): (with George Woodcock), London, Boardman, 1950. (no ISBN)

History of the Communist Party of Yugoslavia: Aberdeen, Aberdeen UP, 1964. (no ISBN)

The Communist Party of Canada (A History): Toronto, McClelland & Stewart, 1975. ISBN 0-7710-0980-1

Socialism in Canada (A Study of the CCF-NDP in Federal and Provincial Politics): Toronto, McClelland & Stewart, 1978. ISBN 0-7710-0978-X

The Doukhobors: (with George Woodcock), Toronto and New York, Oxford, 1968./Ottawa, Carleton, 1977. ISBN 0-7710-9807-3

Mailing Address: History Dept., University of British Columbia, Vancouver, British Columbia V6T 1W5

JAMES BACQUE

Selected Publications:

The Lonely Ones: Toronto, McClelland & Stewart, 1969. (no ISBN)
A Man of Talent: Toronto, New Press, 1972. ISBN 0-88770-154-X
Big Lonely: Toronto, McClelland & Stewart, 1978. ISBN 0-7710-9258-X
The Queen Comes to Minnicog: Toronto, Macmillan, 1979. ISBN 0-7715-
9488-7

Mailing Address: c/o TWUC, 24 Ryerson Avenue, Toronto, Ontario
M5T 2P3

DON BAILEY

Born in Toronto, October 7, 1942. I'm told I have several brothers, maybe even a sister. My father was overseas fighting someone. He was killed and my mother split, leaving us kids with my grandmother. At two I was placed in an orphanage. Shortly thereafter I was adopted by a nice middle-class family, and I lived with them until I was 13. I couldn't stand the quiet of their lives so I left and went looking for the action. Still looking. Now living in Winnipeg. I am co-owner of Real Special Productions. We have just completed a half-hour drama entitled All Sales Final.

Selected Publications:

My Bareness is Not Just My Body: Fredericton, Fiddlehead, 1971. ISBN 0-919196-79-9
If You Hum Me a Few Bars I Might Remember the Tune: Ottawa, Oberon, 1973. IBSN 0-88750-083-8
In the Belly of the Whale: Ottawa, Oberon, 1974. IBSN 0-88750-103-6
Making Up: Ottawa, Oberon, 1979. ISBN 0-88750-372-1
Swim For Your Life: Ottawa, Oberon, 1984. ISBN 0-88750-546-5
Casual Encounters: Ottawa, Oberon, 1986.
How Will We Know When We Get There: Oakville, Mosaic, 1986.

Comments: Writing is a process that helps me know what I know. About myself, the world I live in and the people who inhabit that world. Once I know what I know I can never unknow it although I may forget things. But to know what I know makes me feel more keenly alive and curious to explore further into what I don't know. And there is so much I don't know. To know what I know provides the flickering candle of faith into that vast dark place of the unknown.

Readings, Lectures & Workshops: I have participated in artists-in-the-schools programmes.

Mailing Address: 8th Floor, 139 Roslyn Road, Winnipeg, Manitoba R3L 0G7

JOHN BALLEM

Born in New Glasgow, Nova Scotia. I now live in Calgary, Alberta, where I am a senior partner with the law firm Ballem, McDill, MacInnes and Eden. B.A., M.A., LL.B. (Dalhousie); LL.M. (Harvard); Q.C. Married Grace Louise Flavelle; three children, Flavelle, Mercedes and John. Pilot, Fleet Air Arm of the Royal Navy, 1944-45. Work in progress: Wildcatters (a novel).

Selected Publications:

The Devil's Lighter: Toronto, General, 1973. ISBN 0-7736-0025-6

The Judas Conspiracy: Toronto, Musson, 1976. ISBN 0-7737-0028-5
(Reissued as Alberta Alone: Toronto, General, 1981. ISBN 0-7736-7016-5)

The Moon Pool: Toronto, McClelland & Stewart, 1978. ISBN 0-7710-1004-4

Sacrifice Play: New York, Fawcett, 1981. ISBN 0-449-14381-3

The Marigot Run: New York, Ballantine, 1983. ISBN 0-449-12535-1

The Dirty Scenario: Toronto, General, 1984. ISBN 0-7736-0035-3

Oilpatch Empire: Toronto, McClelland & Stewart, 1985. ISBN 0-7710-1052-4

The Oil and Gas Lease in Canada: (Second Edition), Toronto, University of Toronto Press, 1985. ISBN 0-8020-2550-1

Mailing Address: 40th Floor, West Tower, 150-6 Avenue S.W., Calgary, Alberta T2P 3Y7

BYRNA BARCLAY

Conceived in a tent on a Swedish homestead near Livelong, Saskatchewan. Born under a hair dryer at Marvel Beauty School, Saskatoon. B.A. (English) University of Saskatchewan, 1961. Former children's librarian, puppeteer and social worker. One-time research writer for the Federation of Saskatchewan Indians and instructor in Indian Studies at the Wascana Institute of Applied Arts and Science, Regina. Former president of the Saskatchewan Writers Guild and vice-chair of the Saskatchewan Arts Board, 1982 to present. Raised two children and one lawyer husband to Queen's Bench. Write full-time in Regina.

Selected Publications:

Summer of the Hungry Pup: Edmonton, NeWest, 1981. ISBN 0-920316-19-0

The Woman Who Talks to Canada Geese in *Saskatchewan Gold*: Moose Jaw, Coteau, 1982.

From the Belly of a Flying Whale in *More Saskatchewan Gold*: Moose Jaw, Coteau, 1984.

The Last Echo: Edmonton, NeWest, 1985. ISBN 0-920316-94-8

Greenhouse for Maureen in *The Old Dance*: Moose Jaw, Coteau, 1986.

Awards: Saskatchewan Culture and Youth Novel Competition, 1977-78. Saskatchewan Writers Guild Literary Competition (Short Story and Poetry), 1978.

Comments: *The Last Echo* "should be of interest in senior high school English classes where it will stand with other very good literature whether Canadian or otherwise." – *Reviewing Librarian*, 1986

"Her characters would be happy rubbing shoulders with the Kashubian peasant woman in Grass's The Tin Drum." – *Victoria Times Herald*

"I have never read a novel where the voice is so true, the history so complete and the detail so correct." – Patrick Lane

Readings, Lectures & Workshops: I have extensive experience in all of these fields and have led fiction and poetry workshops for writers.

Mailing Address: 6 Hogarth Place, Regina, Saskatchewan S4S 4J8

JOAN BARFOOT

Born and raised in Owen Sound, Ontario. Graduated with a B.A. in English from the University of Western Ontario, 1969. Reporter for various newspapers, including the Owen Sound Sun-Times, the Windsor Star, the Toronto Sun and currently the London Free Press part-time (job sharing with another reporter).

Selected Publications

Abra: Toronto, McGraw-Hill Ryerson, 1978. ISBN 0-07-082740-0
Dancing in the Dark: Toronto, Macmillan, 1982. ISBN 0-7715-9723-1
Duet for Three: Toronto, Macmillan, 1985. ISBN 0-7715-9680-4

   Awards: Books in Canada First Novel Award, 1978
   Comments: "A marvellous book about mutual dependence written in Barfoot's tense and urgent style." – *London Sunday Times*
   "An immensely touching and acute tale of the sad and terrible delicacy of family ties and the wounding price of isolation." – *Kirkus Reviews*
   "Poignant and gratifying." – *Publishers Weekly*
   "Predictable, banal plot . . . strikingly unoriginal novel . . . " – *Books in Canada*
   Readings, Lectures & Workshops: Reads occasionally at libraries and galleries. May be contacted for readings through TWUC or Macmillan of Canada.
   Mailing Address: 286 Cheapside Street, London, Ontario N6A 2A2

JOYCE BARKHOUSE

Born Joyce Killam, third child of a country doctor in the Annapolis Valley of Nova Scotia. Taught elementary school before marriage to Milton Barkhouse in 1942 (d.1968). Lived in Halifax, Charlottetown and Montreal. Life-long writer of fiction and non-fiction, progressing from stories in church papers to publication of six books 1974-1986 and from articles in local newspapers to the New York Times.

Selected Publications:

Anna's Pet: (with Margaret Atwood), Toronto, James Lorimer, 1980. ISBN 0-88862-249-X
Abraham Gesner: Toronto, Fitzhenry & Whiteside, 1980. ISBN 0-88902-673-4
The Witch of Port Lajoye: Charlottetown, Ragweed, 1983. ISBN 0-920304-26-5
A Name for Himself (The Biography of Thomas Head Raddall): Toronto, Irwin, 1986. ISBN 0-7725-1566-2

Awards: Cultural Life Award, Cultural Federations of Nova Scotia, 1982. First prize, Children's Booklength Fiction, Writers Federation of Nova Scotia Competition, 1979.
Comments: "Barkhouse's writing is clear and moving." – Nancy Robb, *Quill & Quire*
"Your storytelling from *The Witch of Port Lajoye* captivated everyone present." – Hope Bridgewater, *Halifax City Regional Library*
"The book is written for youth, but adults will learn much from it . . . " – *Calgary Herald*
Readings, Lectures & Workshops: I give readings and talks regularly in Nova Scotia schools and libraries. Writer-in-the-Community in Halifax 1983. On tour in Manitoba for The Children's Book Centre, 1984.
Mailing Address: 719-1472 Tower Road, Halifax, Nova Scotia B3H 4K8

MICHAEL BARNES

Born in London, England, the only child of George and Elsie Barnes. Canada-bound 1956, citizen 1961. Lived since in such places as Biscotasing, Sudbury, Wawa, Lively, Moose Factory and Cochrane. Now make my home in gold-mining town of Kirkland Lake. B.A. (Western 1964), M.Ed. (Toronto 1971). Have been teacher, now school principal. Wife Joan (nee Wyatt); children Stephen, Alison and Wesley. Have a special interest in northern Canada and this gives background to work. Lecture on creative writing and northern history. Will be a full-time writer July 1, 1990, D.V.

Selected Publications:

Fortunes in the Ground: Erin, Boston Mills, 1986. ISBN 0-919783-52-X
Link with a Lonely Land: Erin, Boston Mills, 1985. ISBN 0-919783-36-8
Gateway City: North Bay, Chamber of Commerce, 1982. ISBN 0-9690991-1-8
Police Story: Toronto, Scholastic, 1981. ISBN 0-590-71032-X
The Town That Stands on Gold: Cobalt, Highway Book Shop, 1978. ISBN 0-88954-093-4

Comments: Author of 16 other books written since 1971, which I am too shy to mention, although one was *Monster From the Slimes*. Contributed to and co-authored a series of school reading texts for Nelson Canada. Produced six readers with a Northern Ontario background for slow learners. Worked for various newspapers.
Mailing Address: Box 243, Kirkland Lake, Ontario P2N 2L9

TED BARRIS

Born in Toronto, July 12, 1949. Now living in Edmonton. Married to Jayne MacAulay; two daughters, Quenby and Whitney. Hold a B.A.A. from Ryerson, 1971. Have worked as a free-lance writer and broadcaster in Ontario, Saskatchewan and Alberta for 20 years. Currently regular Infotape commentator and host of two regional weekly series, one on CBC TV, the other on CBC Radio. Regular contributor to western periodicals.

Selected Publications:

Fire Canoe (Prairie Steamboat Days Revisited): Toronto, McClelland & Stewart, 1977. ISBN 0-7710-1025-7

Positive Power (The Story of the Edmonton Oilers): Edmonton, Executive Sport Publications, 1982. ISBN 0-019035-13-2

Rodeo Cowboys (The Last Heroes): Saskatoon, WP Prairie Books, 1985. ISBN 0-88833-161-4

Awards: White Owl Conservation Award, Montreal, 1972. International Billboard Radio Documentary Award, New York, 1978. Prix Anik Award for Entertainment Programming, Toronto, 1981. Golden Sheaf Award, Yorkton Film Festival, 1985.

Comments: President of ACTRA Writers Guild of Alberta
Member of Writers Guild of Alberta
Member of Chair for Deafness Studies, University of Alberta
Alberta Heritage Society member

Mailing Address: 7132-85 Street, Edmonton, Alberta T6C 3A7

JACK BATTEN

Fifty-four years old. Torontonian. Arts and law degrees from University of Toronto. Staff writer at Maclean's and managing editor at Saturday Night in the 1960s. Jazz reviewer at the Globe and Mail in 1970s. Movie reviewer on CBC radio. Sixteen books; sports, history, legal subjects, biography. Radio drama and young adult fiction. Crime novel coming in 1987. Maybe it represents a personal wave of the future.

Selected Publications

The Leafs in Autumn: Toronto, Macmillan, 1975. ISBN 0-7705-1315-8
Canada Moves Westward: Toronto, Natural Science of Canada, 1977. ISBN 0-9196-4420-1
Lawyers: Toronto, Macmillan, 1980. ISBN 0-7715-9568-9
Tie-Breaker: Toronto, Clarke Irwin, 1984. ISBN 0-7720-1448-5
Judges: Toronto, Macmillan, 1986. ISBN 0-7715-9729-0

Awards: Gold Award, International Radio Festival of New York
Mailing Address: 41 Salisbury Avenue, Toronto, Ontario M4X 1C5

NANCY BAUER

Born north of Boston, July 7, 1934. Hold a B.A. from Mount Holyoke College. Immigrated to Fredericton with husband, Bill, and three children in 1965. Edited N.B. Chapbooks, 1967-82. Began Maritime Writers Workshop, 1975. Member, Ice House Gang, 1967-84. Writer in Residence at the Cape Cod Writers Conference in 1983 and at Bemidji State University in 1987. Write art and literary journalism in addition to fiction.

Selected Publications:

Flora, Write This Down: Fredericton, Fiddlehead/Goose Lane, 1982. ISBN 0-86492-030-X
Wise-Ears: Ottawa, Oberon, 1985. ISBN 0-88750-586-4

Awards: CBC Literary Competition, Second Prize (Short Story), 1982
Comments: "Bauer displays a delicacy of emotion and tone, which permits her to capture those elusive properties, simplicity and feeling without bathos." – *University of Toronto Quarterly*
"*Wise-Ears* is distinguished by the natural flow of events and words – by a style perhaps unmatched in Canadian fiction for convincingness and low-keyed humour since the publication of . . . The Stone Angel." – *The Fiddlehead*
Readings, Lectures & Workshops: Have read from my novels and led workshops around the Maritimes. Have taught writing at UNB. Lecture on the contemporary art and literature of New Brunswick.
Mailing Address 252 Stanley Street, Fredericton, New Brunswick E3B 3A3

BOB BEAL

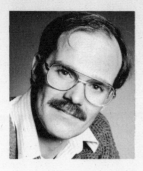

Born in Toronto, May 21, 1949, and lived in Lindsay and Peterborough, Ontario, before first moving west in 1970. Hold a B.A. in political science from Trent University. Former reporter and editor with Cranbrook (B.C.) Townsman, Calgary Herald and Edmonton Journal. Now a graduate student in history at the University of Alberta, Edmonton, and writing journalism and narrative history. (Most significant recent research is on the trade in buffalo robes.) Aim to present scholarly historical research and analysis in a popular narrative framework.

Selected Publications:

Prairie Fire (The 1885 North-West Rebellion): (with Rod Macleod), Edmonton, Hurtig, 1984. ISBN 0-88830-262-2

War in the West (Voices of the 1885 Rebellion): (ed. with Rudy Wiebe), Toronto, McClelland & Stewart, 1985. ISBN 0-7710-8973-2

Comments: "Prodigiously researched, swiftly moving and capably crafted, *Prairie Fire* draws readers into complex events without oversimplifying them." – *Globe and Mail*

"An almost unique blend of the best of modern scholarship and popular history." – *Canadian Book Review Annual*

Readings, Lectures & Workshops: Frequently read, lecture and give seminars on Western Canadian history, journalism and writing non-fiction.

Mailing Address: 7212-114 Street, Edmonton, Alberta T6G 1M4

JENNY BECK

Born in Fort William, Ontario, November 6, 1947, I have lived most of my life in Northwestern Ontario. After graduating from Lakehead University in 1969, I hitch-hiked through parts of Europe, the Middle East and South America and worked at an eclectic assortment of jobs. I have two children and make my home in Thunder Bay. Hold a B.A. in anthropology and a B.Ed. from Lakehead University.

Selected Publications:

A World of Dragons: Moonbeam, Penumbra, 1982. ISBN 0-920806-40-6

Awards: City of Thunder Bay Award, 1984

Comments: "The story is well written, richly imaginative and warm with the personalities of the children who are its main characters." – *Federation of Women Teachers' Association of Ontario (FWTAO) Newsletter*

Readings, Lectures & Workshops: Read to classes of primary and junior level school children and talk about the process of writing. Readings may be booked through TWUC.

Mailing Address: c/o TWUC, 24 Ryerson Avenue, Toronto, Ontario M5T 2P3

BERNIE BEDORE

Born March 3, 1923, at Crow Lake, Ontario. Grew up in the Ottawa Valley. Served in the Royal Naval Fleet Air Arm. Worked in Ontario Tourism for 23 years. Created mythical character Joe Mufferaw: a salute to true man Joseph Montferrand. Created other Ottawa Valley mythology. Live between Arnprior and Renfrew. Retired, live in the country quiet. Write and tell stories now mostly.

Selected Publications:

Tall Tales of Joe Mufferaw: Toronto, Amethyst, 1979. ISBN 0-920474-12-8
Scotty the Pike: Toronto, Amethyst, 1979. ISBN 0-920474-20-9
Wonder Things: Arnprior, Mufferaw Enterprises, 1985. ISBN 0-920837-00-X

Awards: Golden Poetry Awards (three), World of Poetry, (Sacramento, California)

Comments: "Jokes, legends, facts and fantasies flow effortlessly in the Irish lilt of the Ottawa Valley. Through his stories, plays, poems and books, Bernie brings to life an era of Valley life now long since past. Bedore has become the official storyteller and ambassador of The Valley, he himself has emerged as a hero and a legend." – Margaret Breen, *Discovery Magazine*

Readings, Lectures & Workshops: Tell stories and read regularly at schools. Give after-dinner speeches on special occasions. Tell of the Valley on tours. Write for regional newspapers and other publications.

Mailing Address: Box 111, Arnprior, Ontario K7S 3H2 *or* c/o TWUC, 24 Ryerson Avenue, Toronto, Ontario M5T 2P3

VEN BEGAMUDRE

 Born March, 1956, in Bangalore, India. Moved to Canada at age six. Also lived in Mauritius and the U.S. Studied public administration in Ottawa and Paris; graduated with honours from Carleton University. Visited Regina for one month and liked the people so much I moved there. Now a policy analyst with the provincial government. Member of the Bombay Bicycle Club prose group and former member of the writers' guild executive. Live with artist Shelley Sopher.

Selected Publications:

Sacrifices: Erin, Porcupine's Quill, 1986. ISBN 0-88984-071-7
Mosaic in *More Saskatchewan Gold*: Regina, Coteau, 1984. ISBN 0-919926-38-X
Fire Mountain or Amar's Gift in *Prairie Jungle*: Regina, Coteau, 1985. ISBN 0-919926-45-2
A Promise We Shall Wake in the Pink City After Harvest in *The Old Dance*: Regina, Coteau, 1986. ISBN 0-919926-56-8

Awards: Saskatchewan Literary Awards (Short Fiction), 1980 and 1986. Culture and Recreation Award (Full-length Children's Manuscript), 1980.
Readings, Lectures & Workshops: University of Regina extension classes, W.C. How Enrichment Centre workshops, public-school and high-school workshops and occasional readings.
Mailing Address: 2265 Garnet Street, Regina, Saskatchewan S4T 3A1

HENRY BEISSEL

Author of more than 20 books of poetry, plays, prose and translations. Came to Canada in 1951 from Germany. Studied philosophy in London (UK) and literature at the University of Toronto. Founder and editor of the controversial Edge (1963-70). My work has been translated into many languages, including Chinese and Finnish. Plays are produced internationally. Inook premiered at the Stratford Festival (1973). Currently Professor of English at Concordia University, Montreal.

Selected Publications:

Face on the Dark: Toronto, New Press, 1970. ISBN 0-88770-066-7
Inook and the Sun: Toronto, Gage, 1973. ISBN 0-7715-9979-X
The Salt I Taste: Montreal, D.C. Books, 1975. ISBN 0-919-688-06-3
Under Coyote's Eye: Dunvegan, Quadrant, 1979. ISBN 0-86495-002-0
Kanada, Romantik & Wirklichkeit: Innsbruck, Pinguin Verlag, 1981.
   ISBN 3-7016-2101-2
Cantos North: Moonbeam, Penumbra, 1982. ISBN 0-920806-41-4
Season of Blood: Oakville, Mosaic, 1984. ISBN 0-88962-272-8
New and Selected Poems: Oakville, Mosaic, 1987.

   Awards: Epstein Award, 1958. Davidson Award, 1959. DAAD Fellowship, 1977.
   Comments: "The Canadian Imagination . . . is a reality. Henry Beissel finds its constant source of strength and renewal in the wonder of our northland . . . this epic is the first to see it in its entirety, as a matrix which binds the whole together in a national mythology." – F.R. Scott
   Readings, Lectures & Workshops: Co-founder of the Concordia University Creative Writing programme and its director for five years.
   Mailing Address: P.O. Box 339, Alexandria, Ontario K0C 1A0

MARY LILE BENHAM

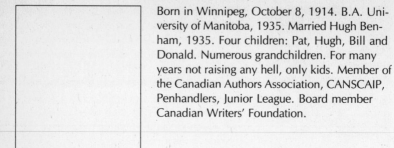

Born in Winnipeg, October 8, 1914. B.A. University of Manitoba, 1935. Married Hugh Benham, 1935. Four children: Pat, Hugh, Bill and Donald. Numerous grandchildren. For many years not raising any hell, only kids. Member of the Canadian Authors Association, CANSCAIP, Penhandlers, Junior League. Board member Canadian Writers' Foundation.

Selected Publications:

The Manitoba Club 1874-1974: Manitoba Club, 1974. (no ISBN)
Winnipeg: (with George Mitchell), Winnipeg, City of Winnipeg, 1974. ISBN 0-9690482-0-3
Nellie McClung: Toronto, Fitzhenry & Whiteside, 1975. ISBN 0-88902-219-4
Paul Kane: Toronto, Fitzhenry & Whiteside, 1977. ISBN 0-88902-233-X
La Verendrye: Toronto, Fitzhenry & Whiteside, 1977. ISBN 0-88902-676-9
Once More Unto the Breach: St. George's Church, 1982. ISBN 0-919673-25-2

Awards: YWCA Woman of the Year (Arts), 1984. Hon. Mention Manitoba Historical Society, 1983. Writers' Digest, 1980. Cross-Canada Writers' Quarterly (poem), 1984. CAA - Manitoba (poem), 1985.
Comments: Judge CAA national and regional contests frequently.
Readings, Lectures & Workshops: Often speak to school children on writing and Manitoba history. Speaker (among many) at Canadian Conference of Teachers of English on biography in the classroom.
Mailing Address: 249 Waverley Street, Winnipeg, Manitoba R3M 3K4

EUGENE BENSON

Born in Northern Ireland, July 6, 1928. M.A.
(Western), Ph.D. (Toronto). Currently professor
of English at the University of Guelph. Married
Renate Niklaus in 1968; two children, Ormonde
and Shaun. President (1971-72) and Director
(1968-86) of the Guelph Spring Festival. Chairman of The Writers' Union of Canada (1983-
84), Co-President (1984-85) and Vice-President
(1985-) of PEN, English Canada. Hobbies
include tennis and sailing.

Selected Publications:

Encounter (Canadian Drama in Four Media): Toronto, Methuen, 1973. ISBN
0-458-90970-X
The Bulls Of Rhonda: Toronto, Methuen, 1976. ISBN 0-458-9130-3
Power Game (The Making of a Prime Minister): Toronto, NC Press, 1980.
ISBN 0-919601-09-X
J.M. Synge: London, Macmillan, 1980. ISBN 0-7171-1243-8

Comments: Three Quebec plays translated by Renate Benson and Eugene
Benson have been published in Canada's Lost Plays, (ed. A. Wagner,
Toronto, CTR, 1982). I have written the libretti for three operas performed at
the Stratford Festival, the Guelph Spring Festival and by the Canadian Opera
Company. I have had four plays broadcast on radio. I edit the journal Canadian Drama/L'Art dramatique canadien, and I have published extensively
in scholarly journals. In 1985 I was awarded (with L.W. Conolly) a grant to
edit the forthcoming Oxford Companion to Canadian Theatre (1988).

Readings, Lectures & Workshops: I have lectured widely in Canada, the
U.S., Australia, New Zealand and Ireland. In 1986 I was invited by the Vice-
Chancellors of the Universities of New Zealand to lecture at five universities
there on modern Anglo-Irish literature and Canadian drama.

Mailing Address: Department of English, University of Guelph, Guelph,
Ontario N1E 2P9

STEVEN BENSTEAD

Born in London, England, October 28, 1951. Landed in Canada, January, 1958. It was cold even then. B.A., University of Winnipeg, 1974. Have metamorphosed into a bookseller.

Selected Publications:

The Wooing of a Lady: Winnipeg, Queenston House, 1978. ISBN 0-919866-28-X

> **Comments:** "Different and worth reading." – *London Free Press*
> A "sureness of touch in the elegant prose." – *Winnipeg Free Press*
> **Readings, Lectures & Workshops:** Run a monthly workshop under the auspices of the Canadian Authors Association.
> **Mailing Address:** 467 Inkster Boulevard, Winnipeg, Manitoba R2W 0K6

CONSTANCE BERESFORD-HOWE

Born in Montreal, now living in Toronto. B.A. (McGill University), 1945, M.A. (McGill), 1946, Ph.D. (Brown University) 1950. Lecturer, Associate Professor, McGill, 1948-70. Professor of English, Ryerson Polytechnical Institute since 1971. Married Christopher Pressnell, 1961; one son, Jeremy. Member of PEN.

Selected Publications:

The Unreasoning Heart: New York, Dodd Mead, 1946. ISBN 0-7705-1731-5 (Macmillan edition)
Of This Day's Journey: New York, Dodd Mead, 1947. (no ISBN)
The Invisible Gate: New York, Dodd Mead, 1949. (no ISBN)
My Lady Greensleeves: New York, Ballantine, 1955. (no ISBN)
The Book of Eve: Toronto, Macmillan, 1973. ISBN 0-7705-0888-X
A Population of One: Toronto, Macmillan, 1976. ISBN 0-7705-1575-4
The Marriage Bed: Toronto, Totem, 1982. ISBN 0-00-222198-5
Night Studies: Toronto, Macmillan, 1985. ISBN 0-7715-9681-2

Awards: Dodd, Mead Intercollegiate Literary Fellowship, 1945. Canadian Booksellers Award, 1973.
Comments: Listed in Who's Who in Canada, The Dictionary of National Biography, The International Who's Who, The Oxford Companion to Canadian Literature, Who's Who in America, etc. etc.
Readings, Lectures & Workshops: For the last 16 years, I have given innumerable readings in the Toronto area, Vancouver, Winnipeg, Montreal, Saskatoon, Timmins et al.
Mailing Address: 16 Cameron Crescent, Toronto, Ontario M4G 1Z8

PIERRE BERTON

Born in Whitehorse, Yukon, July 12, 1920. Schooled in Dawson and Victoria, British Columbia. Graduated, University of British Columbia, Arts, 1941. Worked Klondike mining camps, summers 1937 to 39. News-Herald, Vancouver, 1939-41 (reporter, news desk, city editor). Army service February 1941 to October 1945. (Lieutenant Infantry instructor; Captain GSO3I, RMC, Intelligence School.) Vancouver Sun 1945-47 as reporter, deskman. Maclean's Magazine, 1947-58 (managing editor). Toronto Star, 1958-62 (columnist, associate editor). Freelance since.

Selected Publications:

The National Dream: Toronto, McClelland & Stewart, 1970. ISBN 0-7710-1326-4

The Last Spike: Toronto, McClelland & Stewart, 1971. ISBN 0-7710-1327-2

Klondike: Toronto, McClelland & Stewart, 1972. ISBN 0-7710-1283-7

My Country: Toronto, McClelland & Stewart, 1976. ISBN 0-7710-1393-0

The Wild Frontier: Toronto, McClelland & Stewart, 1978. ISBN 0-7710-1360-4

The Invasion of Canada: Toronto, McClelland & Stewart, 1980. ISBN 0-7710-1235-7

Flames Across the Border: Toronto, McClelland & Stewart, 1981. ISBN 0-7710-1244-6

Why We Act Like Canadians: Toronto, McClelland & Stewart, 1982. ISBN 0-7710-1363-9

The Promised Land: Toronto, McClelland & Stewart, 1984. ISBN 0-7710-1243-8

Vimy: Toronto, McClelland & Stewart, 1986. ISBN 0-7710-1339-6

Awards: Three Governor General's Awards (Non-Fiction). Stephen Leacock Medal. Companion, Order of Canada

Mailing Address: RR 1, Kleinburg, Ontario L0J 1C0

LITA-ROSE BETCHERMAN

Combine careers of labour arbitrator and author. Hold Ph.D. from the University of Toronto and have lectured in history at Carleton University. Formerly director of Ontario Women's Bureau. Was member of the Ontario Human Rights Commission, Ontario Press Council, Education Relations Commission, Judicial Council of Ontario and a vice-chairman of the Ontario Labour Relations Board.

Selected Publications:

The Swastika and the Maple Leaf (Fascist Movements in Canada in the Thirties): Toronto, Fitzhenry & Whiteside, 1975. ISBN 0-88902-122-8

The Little Band (The Clashes between the Communists and the Political and Legal Establishment in Canada, 1928-1932): Ottawa, Deneau, 1982. ISBN 0-88879-071-6

Comments: *The Swastika and the Maple Leaf* a Book-of-the-Month Club Alternative Choice.

"It's strong evocative stuff, a necessary reminder of how things were only forty years ago, and I recommend it highly." – Mordecai Richler, *Saturday Night*.

"*Swastika* performs a useful service by recalling for Canadians one of the dark corners of the country's history." – *Time*

"No one who reads *The Little Band* will ever subscribe to the old canard that the Canadian past is dull." – *Globe and Mail*

Mailing Address: RR 1, Richmond Hill, Ontario L4C 4X7

SANDRA BIRDSELL

I was born in Hamiota, Manitoba, in 1942. Besides my two collections of stories, I am a playwright and film script writer. I live in Winnipeg and am currently at work on a novel.

Selected Publications:

Night Travellers: Winnipeg, Turnstone, 1982. ISBN 0-88801-072-9
Ladies of the House: Winnipeg, Turnstone, 1984. ISBN 0-88801-092-3

Awards: Robert Kroetsch Scholarship, Saskatchewan Arts Board, 1982. Gerald A. Lampert Award, League of Canadian Poets, 1984. National Magazine Award for Fiction, 1984.

Comments: "Birdsell revives the joy of finding new talent." – William French, *Globe and Mail*

"It is a thrill to discover a great new talent. Sandra Birdsell is here to stay." – W.P. Kinsella, *The Reader*

Mailing Address: 755 Westminster Avenue, Winnipeg, Manitoba R3G 1A5

ANN BLADES

Born in Vancouver, British Columbia, November 16, 1947. Now living in Crescent Beach, British Columbia. Elementary school teacher from 1967 to 1971. Registered nurse (summers only) 1974 to 1980. Have painted with watercolours, with no formal art training, since 1959. Currently illustrating children's books and doing paintings for the Bau Xi Gallery in Vancouver and Toronto.

Selected Publications:

Mary of Mile 18: Montreal, Tundra, 1971. ISBN 0-88776-025-2
A Boy of Tache: Montreal, Tundra, 1973. ISBN 0-88776-023-6
The Cottage at Crescent Beach: Toronto, Magook, 1977. ISBN 0-88869-000-2
Jacques the Woodcutter: (with Michael Macklem), Ottawa, Oberon, 1977. ISBN 0-88750-239-3
A Salmon for Simon: (with Betty Waterton), Vancouver, Douglas & McIntyre, 1978. ISBN 0-88894-168-4
By the Sea (An Alphabet Book): Toronto, Kids Can', 1985. ISBN 0-919964-74-5

Awards: CACL Book Of The Year, 1972. Canada Council Children's Literature Award (Illustration), 1979. Amelia Francis Howard-Gibbon Award, 1979. Elizabeth Mrazik-Cleaver Canadian Picture Book Award, 1986.

Mailing Address: 2150 Alexandra Street, Crescent Beach, British Columbia V4A 3A9

MARIE-CLAIRE BLAIS

Born in Quebec City, 1939. Studied at Laval University. Began to publish poems, short stories and then a novel, Mad Shadows, in 1959. Went to France on a fellowship. Then in 1963 went to the U.S. with two Guggenheim Fellowships. Stayed there until 1971 and then lived in Brittany for a few years. I am now living in Canada in the Cantons de l'Est. I have written 31 books. Most of them have been translated into English and as many as 16 other languages.

Selected Publications:

Mad Shadows: Toronto, McClelland & Stewart, 1960. ISBN 0-7710-7032-8
A Season in the Life of Emmanuel: New York, Farrar, Straus, Giroux, 1966. (no ISBN)
Durer's Angel: Vancouver, Talon, 1976. ISBN 0-88922-103-0
Nights in the Underground: Toronto, General, 1979. ISBN 0-7736-7032-7
Deaf to the City: Toronto, Lester & Orpen Dennys, 1981. ISBN 0-919630-56-1
Manuscripts of Pauline Archange: Toronto, McClelland & Stewart, 1982. ISBN 0-7710-9178-8
Anna's World: Toronto, Lester & Orpen Dennys, 1984. ISBN 0-88619-058-4

Awards: Prix de la langue francaise, 1959. Prix France-Quebec, 1964. Prix Medicis, 1966. Prix Belgique Canada, 1970. Prix du Gouverneur General (twice).

Readings, Lectures & Workshops: Read regularly at universities in Canada, France, Germany and the U.S. and recently was invited to Russia and Israel.

Mailing Address: Baker Road, Kingsbury, Quebec J0B 1X0

MARY BLAKESLEE

Born in Calgary and raised in British Columbia. A social worker for many years and also worked as a curriculum consultant with Manitoba Department of Education. In Calgary, where I make my home, I have hosted a public affairs television broadcast and have been a radio broadcaster. I live with my husband, Clem, and gigantic cat, Samantha, in a suburb of Calgary where I write full time. My love of cooking and my experience in a wheelchair led to my first book.

Selected Publications:

Wheelchair Gourmet: Toronto, General, 1981. ISBN 0-7736-0086-8
It's Tough to Be a Kid: Toronto, Scholastic, 1983. ISBN 0-590-71177-6
Halfbacks Don't Wear Pearls: Toronto, Scholastic, 1986. ISBN 0-590-71682-4
Edythe with a "Y": Toronto, Scholastic, 1987. ISBN 0-590-71680-8
Outa Sight: Toronto, Scholastic, 1987. ISBN 0-590-71376-0

Comments: "Blakeslee's talent and ability to identify with children have brought her remarkable success." – *Calgary Herald*
"Wheelchair cooker a surefire winner." – *Victoria Times-Colonist*
"When kids read her verses they can't help but laugh at themselves. She writes hard cold facts on what being a kid is really like." – *Calgary Sun*
Readings, Lectures & Workshops: Read regularly in Alberta schools. Teach poetry writing on a bi-weekly basis at a Calgary elementary school.
Mailing Address: 1306-2010 Ulster Road, Calgary, Alberta T2N 4C2

ELLA BOBROW

Born in the Ukraine on December 12, 1911. Studied trade and commerce as well as music. Have lived in Toronto since 1950. Worked as an accountant until 1973, while devoting free time to writing and translating, poetry, prose, essays and reviews, published by the Russian periodical press in Canada, the U.S., Austria, Argentina and France. Write in Russian, English and German.

Selected Publications:

Irina Istomina: Oakville, Mosaic, 1980. ISBN 0-88962-125-X (cloth), ISBN 0-88962-124-X (paper)
The Three Brave Snowflakes: Oakville, Mosaic, 1982. ISBN 0-88962-204-3
Autumnal Cadenza: Oakville, Mosaic, 1985. ISBN 0-88962-282-5
Die Drei Tapferen Schneeflocken: Ottawa, Les Editions du Vermillon, 1986. (no ISBN)

Comments: My own Russian and German translations of my books have been published in Canada and abroad. Forthcoming from Albatros of Paris is I. Odoevzeva, Poetess, Prosaist, Memorialist.

Member of PEN since 1979 and the League of Canadian Poets.

Listed in The Dictionary of International Biography (20th Edition), The World Who's Who of Women (1985).

Readings, Lectures & Workshops: Have lectured in Toronto, Montreal, Washington, Los Angeles, Syracuse, St. Petersburg and Rio on the poetry of Dimitry Klenovsy, the image of Russia in the works of her poets, the poetry and prose of Irina Odoevzeva. Readings may be booked through TWUC.

Mailing Address: 14 Gooch Court, Toronto, Ontario M6S 2N8

FRED BODSWORTH

Born in Port Burwell, Ontario, a fishing port on Lake Erie. Worked in tobacco fields and on towing tugs. Now live in Toronto. Reporter for the St. Thomas Times-Journal, 1940-43. Reporter and editor, Toronto Star, 1943-47. Staff writer, Maclean's, 1947-55. Free-lance writer since. President of the Federation of Ontario Naturalists, 1964-67. Have organised and led ornithological tours around the world.

Selected Publications:

The Strange One: Toronto, McClelland & Stewart, 1959. ISBN 0-7710-1856-8
The Sparrow's Fall: Toronto, Doubleday, 1967. (no ISBN)
The Pacific Coast: Toronto, Natural Science of Canada, 1970. ISBN 0-9196-4403-1
The Atonement of Ashley Morden: Toronto, McClelland & Stewart, 1977. ISBN 0-7710-9253-9
Last of the Curlews: Toronto, Scholastic, 1985. ISBN 0-590-71603-4.

Awards: Rothman's Merit Award for Literature, 1974. Doubleday Canadian Novel Award, 1967.

Comments: "No other Canadian writer can match Bodsworth's ability to bring alive details of the natural world . . . He imbues biologically authentic descriptions of nature with tremendous narrative power . . . (Has) the knack of balancing scientific objectivity with narrative excitement." – John Moss in *A Reader's Guide to the Canadian Novel*

"In the context of Canadian literature, Bodsworth is one of the leading traditional novelists." – James R. Stevens in *Contemporary Novelists of the English Language*

Mailing Address: c/o TWUC, 24 Ryerson Avenue, Toronto, Ontario M5T 2P3

ALICE BOISSONNEAU

Born in Walkerton, Ontario. Later employed in social work; first in Toronto, then in Vancouver, mainly in rehabilitation programmes for general and provincial mental hospitals. While engaged in this, wrote a number of short stories, published in the Canadian Forum and Alphabet magazine and heard on CBC Radio's Anthology. Married in 1961, I spent six years travelling in a trailer around northern Ontario, during the clement months, while my husband worked at land-use research.

Selected Publications:

The McCrimmons in *Stories from Ontario*: Toronto, Macmillan, 1974. ISBN 0-7705-1068-X

Eileen McCullough: Toronto, Simon and Pierre, 1976. ISBN 0-88924-052-3

Comments: *Eileen McCullough* was a finalist in Books in Canada First Novel Competition and the City of Toronto Book Awards in 1977. Fragments of it were interpreted as found poetry by Colleen Thibaudeau in Un Dozen (Black Moss Press, 1984). *The McCrimmons* was used in the Metropolitan Toronto Library's sesquicentennial celebration.

Readings, Lectures & Workshops: Scarborough Branch, Toronto Public Library, 1978. University of Western Ontario, 1978. Various readings by Colleen Thibaudeau, with thanks, London, Ontario, 1982. Cannington Public Library, 1984.

Mailing Address: Cannington, Ontario L0E 1E0

ROO BORSON

Born on January 20, 1952, in Berkeley, California; immigrated to Canada in 1974. B.A., Goddard College, Vermont; M.F.A. in creative writing, University of British Columbia. Writer of poetry and occasional prose. Have been employed in a range of occupations, from building drift chambers to teaching creative writing. Live in Toronto.

Selected Publications:

A Sad Device: Dunvegan, Quadrant, 1981. ISBN 0-86495-011-X
The Whole Night, Coming Home: Toronto, McClelland & Stewart, 1984.
   ISBN 0-7710-1579-8
The Transparence of November/Snow: (with Kim Maltman), Kingston,
   Quarry, 1985. ISBN 0-919627-30-7

Awards: CBC Literary Competition, First Prize (Poetry), 1982
Comments: "She may well be the first major poet to emerge in Canada in the 80s." — *Maclean's*
"Borson's power is in some ways the most deeply poetical of all. There are moments when she absorbs one totally, dissolving the conventional distinctions between body, mind, and heart." — *Globe and Mail*
"The sort of poetry that reminds city dwellers that we ought to be able to look up to the sky at night and still see stars." — *Vancouver Sun*
Poems appear in The Norton Introduction to Poetry, The New Oxford Book of Canadian Verse and The New Canadian Poets (M & S).
Readings, Lectures & Workshops: Have given readings and workshops across Canada and in the U.S.
Mailing Address: c/o TWUC, 24 Ryerson Avenue, Toronto, Ontario M5T 2P3

LYNNE BOWEN

Born in Indian Head, Saskatchewan, August 22, 1940. Raised in Alberta, blossomed in B.C. Trained as a public health nurse at the University of Alberta. Having acquired "something to fall back on" (i.e. a sensible career and an educated husband), began to study history. M.A. in Western Canadian History from the University of Victoria. Live in Nanaimo with aforementioned husband and three children who randomly appear and disappear.

Selected Publications:

Boss Whistle: Lantzville, Oolichan, 1982. ISBN 0-88982-041-4

Awards: British Columbia Book Award, 1983. Canadian Historical Association Certificate of Merit, 1984.

Comments: " . . . magnificent and feeling recalling of the generations-long saga of the mines" – *Vancouver Sun*

"lively and well-researched narrative" – *Canadian Historical Association Newsletter*

Articles include *The Great Vancouver Island Coal Miners' Strike, 1912-14* in Journal of the West (Vol. XXIII), *The Coal Miners of Vancouver Island Remember* in Canadian Oral History Journal (Vol. 6: 1983) and *King of the Castle* in Horizon Canada (Vol. 6, No. 72: 1986).

Readings, Lectures & Workshops: Lectures and readings at universities, colleges, high schools, museums, or wherever "two or three are gathered . . ."

Mailing Address: 4982 Fillinger Crescent, Site 51, Nanaimo, British Columbia V9S 5N7

MARILYN BOWERING

Born in Winnipeg, April 13, 1949, and brought up in Victoria, B.C. First book published 1973. Studied at the University of Victoria and the University of British Columbia, for a B.A. and an M.A. Have worked as a teacher, in advertising and marketing and as a book editor. Instructor in creative writing at the University of Victoria 1982-86. After living and working in various parts of Canada and Europe, now live in Sooke, B.C.

Selected Publications:

The Killing Room: Victoria, Sono Nis, 1977. ISBN 0-919462-37-5
Many Voices: (co-editor with David Day), Vancouver, J.J. Douglas, 1977. ISBN 0-88894-134-X
The Visitors Have All Returned: Toronto, Press Porcepic, 1979. ISBN 0-88878-164-4
Sleeping with Lambs: Toronto, Press Porcepic, 1980. ISBN 0-88878-180-6
Giving Back Diamonds: Toronto, Press Porcepic, 1982. ISBN 0-88878-200-4
The Sunday Before Winter: Toronto, General, 1984. ISBN 0-7736-1153-3
Winter Harbour: Staffordshire, Johnston Green, 1987.

Awards: National Magazine Award
Comments: "One has the sense of walking in a fascinating mind, but also of perceiving through a subtle and highly tuned sensibility." – George Woodcock
"Marilyn Bowering's poetry . . . reflects a completeness and understanding only possible in the finest art." – Robin Skelton
"A clear voice – lyric soprano – and singing *such* songs: difficult, frightening, fragile. But all glistening like wet stones, the wings of insects, scissors." – P.K. Page
Readings, Lectures & Workshops: Readings, lectures etc. may be booked through TWUC.
Mailing Address: c/o 3777 Jennifer Road, Victoria, British Columbia V8P 3X1

RICK BOWERS

Born on Prince Edward Island in 1955. I attended Summerside High School and Dalhousie University, and have taught at the University of British Columbia as well as at the University of Calgary.

Selected Publications:

The Governor of Prince Edward Island: Porters Lake, Pottersfield, 1986. ISBN 0-919001-31-9

Comments: "Bowers . . . writes of Prince Edward Islanders unable to handle their lives as well as he can handle sentences." — *Toronto Star*

Mailing Address: c/o English Department, University of Calgary, Calgary, Alberta T2N 1N4

J. PATRICK BOYER

 I grew up in my family's weekly newspaper office where I instinctively learned that until a story has been written, it hasn't happened. I have worked as journalist in Ontario, Quebec and Saskatchewan. I hold an honours degree in economics and political science from Carleton University; an M.A. in Canadian history and a law degree, both from the University of Toronto. I was elected to Parliament in 1984.

Selected Publications:

Political Rights (The Legal Framework of Elections in Canada): Toronto, Butterworths, 1981. ISBN 0-409-81601-9

Lawmaking by the People (Referendums and Plebiscites in Canada): Toronto, Butterworths, 1982. ISBN 0-409-81602-7

Money and Message (The Law Governing Election Financing, Advertising, Broadcasting and Campaigning in Canada): Toronto, Butterworths, 1983. ISBN 0-409-81603-5

Election Law in Canada (The Law and Procedure of Federal, Provincial and Territorial Elections): 2 vols., Toronto, Butterworths, 1987. ISBN 0-409-81600-0

Comments: "Patrick Boyer in his comprehensive work has given for the first time a thorough exposition of the legal machinery concerning the democratic process as it is designed to fulfil its purposes in Canada" – Hon. James C. McRuer

"Canadians involved in the working of democracy – and many beyond Canada – will have reason to be grateful to Mr. Boyer." – Prof. David Butler

Readings, Lectures & Workshops: Occasionally quote from my own books in Parliament!

Mailing Address: 2583 Lakeshore Boulevard West, Etobicoke, Ontario M8V 1G3

KARLEEN BRADFORD

Born in Toronto. Went with parents to Argentina at age nine and lived there until returning to Canada to take a B.A. in English at the University of Toronto. Married to James Bradford, a Foreign Service Officer with the Canadian Government, so spend most of my time travelling from one country to another and writing. Now living in Bonn, West Germany, with youngest son, Christopher, one dog and three cats. Two older children back in Canada.

Selected Publications:

Wrong Again, Robbie: (originally published in 1977 as A Year for Growing), Toronto, Scholastic, 1983. ISBN 0-590-71312-4
The Other Elizabeth: Toronto, Gage, 1982. ISBN 0-7715-7004-X
I Wish There Were Unicorns: Toronto, Gage, 1983. ISBN 0-7715-7005-8
The Stone in the Meadow: Toronto, Gage, 1984. ISBN 0-7715-7014-7
The Haunting at Cliff House: Toronto, Scholastic, 1985. ISBN 0-590-71517-8
The Nine Days Queen: Toronto, Scholastic, 1986. ISBN 0-590-71617-4

Awards: First prize, CommCept Canadian KidLit Novel Contest, 1979. First prize, Juvenile Short Story, Canadian Authors Association Prose Competition (Ottawa Branch), 1978. Second prize, Juvenile Short Story, Canadian Authors Association Prose Competition (Ottawa Branch), 1984.

Comments: "*The Nine Days Queen* has just enough historical detail to make it spicy but arranged in such a way as not to interfere with the story. It contains romance, tragedy and fun. I am sure that once you have read this book you will want to keep on reading about the kings and queens in the 16th century." – Sarah Hentschel, 14 years old

Readings, Lectures & Workshops: Available for readings and workshops in schools and libraries, when in Canada.

Mailing Address: c/o TWUC, 24 Ryerson Avenue, Toronto, Ontario M5T 2P3

THECLA JEAN BRADSHAW

Born in Toronto. Second child of Harry Marshall Robbins. Daughters Mary Oliarnyk and Carol Rey. Deceased husband Harry Bradshaw. A.T.C.M. from the Royal Conservatory of Music, Toronto. Special interest: Indian people of Manitoba and Saskatchewan. Feature-story writer and editorialist: stories and photos in the Winnipeg Free Press, Winnipeg Tribune, Western Catholic Press, Montreal Star and Indian Record as well as union and trade publications. Travel stories: Singapore, South Africa, South America and the West Indies in Toronto Telegram. Co-founder and editor of The Northian Magazine, for teachers across northern Canada in Indian, Inuit schools.

Selected Publications:

Mobiles: Toronto, Ryerson, 1956. (no ISBN)
Here We Are, Where Do We Go (The Indian Child and Education): (with Andre Renaud), Canadian Home and School and Parent-Teacher Fed., 1967. (no ISBN)
A Cree Life (The Art of Allen Sapp): (with John Ansen Warner), Vancouver, Douglas & McIntyre, 1978. ISBN 0-88894-149-8
Poverty and Public Education in *The Best of Times, The Worst of Times*: Toronto, Holt Rinehart & Winston, 1972. (no ISBN)
Since Demolished in *Spirit of Canada*: Toronto, Canadian Authors Assoc., 1977. (no ISBN)

Awards: Canadian Women's Press Club Memorial Award, Editorial Column, 1968

Comments: My papers are in the Provincial Archives of Manitoba. Reviews of and articles about my work have appeared in the Winnipeg Tribune (Dec. 14, 1955), Winnipeg Free Press (Feb. 11, 1956), the University of Toronto Quarterly (April, 1956), CBC Times (March-April, 1962), The Northian Magazine (Vol. 6, No. 2) and The Brandon Sun (January 12, 1974). In other media, I have worked documentaries such as We're Still in Treaty with the Indians, Three Children of the Trapline, and By Instinct a Painter.

Mailing Address: c/o TWUC, 24 Ryerson Avenue, Toronto, Ontario M5T 2P3

MAX BRAITHWAITE

Born in Nokomis, Saskatchewan, December 7, 1911. Educated in Saskatchewan. Seven years teaching in that province. Joined RCNVR in 1942. Discharged, 1945, with rank of Lt. Cmdr. Became full-time free-lance writer in 1946, writing radio plays, magazine articles, screenplays and books. Married Aileen Treleaven, 1935. Five children, 12 grandchildren. Have lived in Streetsville, Ontario, and Orangeville, Ontario, and now live on Brandy Lake in Muskoka. Have written 25 books as well as radio dramas and screenplays.

Selected Publications:

Why Shoot The Teacher: Toronto, McClelland & Stewart, 1965. ISBN 0-7710-1599-2

The Night We Stole the Mountie's Car: Toronto, McClelland & Stewart, 1971. ISBN 0-7710-1603-4

A Privilege and a Pleasure: Vancouver, Douglas & McIntyre, 1973. ISBN 0-88894-040-8

The Hungry Thirties: Toronto, McClelland & Stewart, 1977. ISBN 0-919644-25-2

The Commodore's Barge is Alongside: Toronto, McClelland & Stewart, 1979. ISBN 0-7710-1610-7

Lusty Winter: Toronto, McClelland & Stewart, 1979. ISBN 0-7704-1558-X

McGruber's Folly: Toronto, McClelland & Stewart, 1981. ISBN 0-7710-1613-1

All the Way Home: Toronto, McClelland & Stewart, 1986. ISBN 0-7710-1612-3

Awards: Leacock Medal for Humour, 1972

Comments: "Thoroughly enjoyable . . one of the few true humorists in Canada" — *Montreal Star*

Mailing Address: Box 163, Port Carling, Ontario P0B 1J0

VICTORIA BRANDEN

Hold a B.A. from the University of Alberta and an M.A. from the University of Toronto. Worked for some years in publishing and journalism; returned to university on death of husband and taught for 15 years at various high schools and colleges. During this period wrote many short stories and articles as well as scripts for both radio and television. Currently working on a murder mystery for Macmillan and on a television script with peace theme.

Selected Publications:

Mrs. Job: Toronto, General, 1981. ISBN 0-7736-7008-4
Understanding Ghosts: London, Gollancz, 1980. ISBN 0-575-02623-5
Flitterin' Judas: Toronto, McClelland & Stewart, 1985. ISBN 0-7710-1508-9

Awards: Hamilton Canadian Club Award (Service to Literature). Canadian Women's Press Club Award (Comedy Writing).
Readings, Lectures & Workshops: Hamilton Public Library, June 1986. Women's World Trade Fair, Convention Centre, Hamilton, November 1986.
Mailing Address: 65 Wellington Street, Box 581, Waterdown, Ontario LOR 2H0

MARIANNE BRANDIS

Born in the Netherlands. Have lived in British Columbia and Nova Scotia as well as Ontario. Degrees from McMaster University in Hamilton, Ontario. After having experimented with other literary forms, I now concentrate on novels for adults and young adults. Teach English at Ryerson Polytechnical Institute.

Selected Publications:

This Spring's Sowing: Toronto, McClelland & Stewart, 1970. (no ISBN)
A Sense of Dust: Carlisle, Brandstead Press, 1972. (no ISBN)
The Tinderbox: Erin, Porcupine's Quill, 1982. ISBN 0-88984-064-4
The Quarter-Pie Window: Erin, Porcupine's Quill, 1985. ISBN 0-88984-085-7

Awards: Saskatchewan Library Association (Young Adult Book), 1986
Comments: "Detail by glittering detail, Emma's life, the routine, the hundreds of tasks that make up her daily existence, are observed and recorded in rich and precise prose." – Wynne-Jones, *Globe and Mail* (on *The Quarter-Pie Window*)
"*The Quarter-Pie Window* . . . has about it a pleasant and vigorous plainness . . . A straightforward story, humanely and well told." – *Toronto Star*
Readings, Lectures & Workshops: Gives readings and lectures at schools, libraries, etc.
Mailing Address: 108 Isabella Street, Apt. 505, Toronto, Ontario M4Y 1N9

BRIAN BRETT

Born in Vancouver, 1950. Author of five books of poems and prose poems. I have just completed a novella about termites called The Fungus Garden and have been working on a four-volume novel about the Queen Charlotte Islands, Clouds & Rain, for the last 11 years. I live with my family in White Rock, where I cultivate my garden and create ceramic forms.

Selected Publications:

Monster: White Rock, White Rhino, 1975. (no ISBN)
Fossil Ground At Phantom Creek: Vancouver, Blackfish, 1976. (no ISBN)
Smoke Without Exit: Victoria, Sono Nis, 1984. ISBN 0-919203-25-6
Evolution in Every Direction: Saskatoon, Thistledown,1987. ISBN 0-920633-32-3

Comments: "His work can sing . . ." — *Pacific Northwest Review*
"He has a strong poetic voice and his imagery is superb." — *Spotlight*
"Brian Brett is one of those rare poets who can turn sound into mythology." — *Poetry Canada Review*

Readings, Lectures & Workshops: Inaugurated the Poetry in the Schools workshops throughout the lower mainland of B.C. in the early 1970s. Since then, I have given readings and workshops across Canada, including a national tour sponsored by the League of Canadian Poets.

Mailing Address: 971 Kent Street, White Rock, British Columbia V4B 4S9

ELIZABETH BREWSTER

 Born in Chipman, New Brunswick, August 26, 1933. Educated at the University of New Brunswick, University of Toronto Library School, Radcliffe (Harvard), King's College (London) and Indiana University. Have lived and worked in Victoria, Kingston, Ottawa and Edmonton. Since 1972 have been a member of the English Department of the University of Saskatchewan, Saskatoon.

Selected Publications:

It's Easy To Fall On The Ice: Ottawa, Oberon, 1977. ISBN 0-88750-247-4
The Way Home: Ottawa, Oberon, 1982. ISBN 0-88750-427-2
Digging In: Ottawa, Oberon, 1982. ISBN 0-88750-446-9
A House Full Of Women: Ottawa, Oberon, 1983. ISBN 0-88750-486-8
Selected Poems: (2 vols.), Ottawa, Oberon, 1985. ISBN 0-88750-595-3
   (vol.1), ISBN 0-88750-598-8 (vol.2)

Awards: E.J. Pratt Award (Poetry), University of Toronto. President's Medal (Poetry), University of Western Ontario.

Comments: "It is in skillful and stoic objectivity that Brewster excels. In it, the strength of her stories lies." – H.R. Percy, *Atlantic Provinces Book Review*

"The stories will please anyone who accepts the ordinariness of Brewster's world, and who sees in it the fusion of universal concerns (love, loneliness, memory, imagination) with the particularities of a certain time and place." – Cathy Matyas, *Books in Canada*

Readings, Lectures & Workshops: Have frequently given readings and taken part in workshops.

Mailing Address: Department of English, University of Saskatchewan, Saskatoon, Saskatchewan S7N 0W0

ROBERT BRINGHURST

I was born in Los Angeles in 1946, immigrated with my parents to Canada in 1952 and spent most of my childhood in western Alberta. Later spent a decade as a student and wanderer in the 1960s manner, worked as a dragoman in Palestine, law clerk in Panama and taught writing and literature at the University of British Columbia for three years. I now write and scavenge full time.

Selected Publications:

Bergschrund: Victoria, Sono Nis, 1975. ISBN 0-919462-14-6

The Beauty of the Weapons (Selected Poems 1972-82): Toronto, McClelland & Stewart, 1982. ISBN 0-7710-1660-3

Visions (Contemporary Art in Canada): (ed.), Vancouver, Douglas & McIntyre, 1983. ISBN 0-88894-392-X

Ocean/Paper/Stone: Vancouver, William Hoffer, 1984. ISBN 0-91975-807-X

The Raven Steals the Light: (with Bill Reid), Vancouver, Douglas & McIntyre, 1984. ISBN 0-88894-447-0

Tending the Fire: Vancouver, Alcuin Society, 1985. ISBN 0-919026-14-1

The Blue Roofs of Japan: Mission, Barbarian Press, 1986. ISBN 0-7710166-1-1

Pieces of Map, Pieces of Music: Toronto, McClelland & Stewart, 1986. ISBN 0-7710-1661-1

Comments: "A sense of shared responsibility and shared fate burns through this book (*The Beauty of the Weapons*)." – *New York Times*

"He is without a doubt a major poet, not only in the context of Canadian letters, but in that of all writing of our time." – Robin Skelton, *Poetry*

Readings, Lectures & Workshops: Frequently work with Ojibwa and Cree writers in northern Ontario. Have lectured on Canadian literature and art in Europe, Australia, New Zealand, Fiji and Japan as well as North America.

Mailing Address: Box 280, Bowen Island, British Columbia V0N 1G0 *or* c/o TWUC, 24 Ryerson Avenue, Toronto, Ontario M5T 2P3

RON BROWN

A bona fide Toronto-bred "Boomer": obtained a Masters in community planning before banishing self to jungles of South America. Happily designed jungle towns in a place later made famous by Jonestown. Returned to Canada to make Canadians aware of their historic landscapes through books and articles on ghost towns and backroads.

Selected Publications:

Ghost Towns of Ontario (Vol. 1): Toronto, Cannonbooks, 1978. ISBN 0-9691210-2-4
Ghost Towns of Ontario (Vol. 2): Toronto, Cannonbooks, 1983. ISBN 0-9691210-1-6
Backroads of Ontario: Edmonton, Hurtig, 1984. ISBN 0-88830-238-X
Ontario Ghost Towns and Scenic Backroads Atlas: Toronto, Cannonbooks, 1985. ISBN 0-9691210-4-0

Comments: "An excellent guide to some of Ontario's fascinating secondary roads" — *The Toronto Star* (on *Backroads of Ontario*)
"So get hold of this book. Use it to plan an excursion to one or more of the ghost towns. Frankly I can't think of a more enjoyable family outing. Or a more vivid history lesson." — Peter Martin, *CBC* (on *Ghost Towns of Ontario*)
Readings, Lectures & Workshops: In addition to the usual after-dinner circuit, teach a ghost town course to selected paying adults in East York.
Mailing Address: 267 Dewhurst Boulevard, Toronto, Ontario M4J 3K9

HARRY BRUCE

Born in Toronto, July 8, 1934, son of poet, novelist and newspaperman Charles Bruce and Agnes King Bruce. Married Penny Meadows, Toronto. We have two sons, one daughter and two grand-daughters. After 30 years of writing reports, articles, columns and essays for newspapers, magazines, CBC radio – and non-fiction trade books – received honorary degree, Doctor of Civil Laws, from the University of King's College, Halifax, in May, 1985. Live in Halifax and Port Shoreham, N.S.

Selected Publications:

Lifeline (The Story of the Atlantic Ferries and Coastal Boats): Toronto, Macmillan, 1977. ISBN 0-7705-1608-4

R.A. (The Story of R.A. Jodrey, Entrepreneur): Toronto, McClelland & Stewart, 1979. (o/p)

Each Moment As It Flies: Toronto, Methuen, 1984. ISBN 0-458-98170-2

The Man and the Empire (Frank Sobey): Toronto, Macmillan, 1985. ISBN 0-7715-9834-3

Movin' East: Toronto, Methuen, 1985. ISBN 0-458-9967-0X

Awards: ACTRA Nellie (Radio Drama), 1977. Evelyn Richardson Memorial Literary Award (Non-Fiction), 1978. National Business Book Award, 1986.

Comments: "A journalistic marriage of virtue to perfection." – William French, *Globe and Mail*

"The great theme of Harry Bruce's remarkable career is the fragility and brevity of human life, and our duty to cherish the life we are given." – Robert Fulford, *Saturday Night*

"Harry Bruce might well be the most versatile essayist in Canada." – Michael Carin, *The Montreal Gazette*

Readings, Lectures & Workshops: Book through TWUC.

Mailing Address: 1510 Lilac Street, Apt. 22, Halifax, Nova Scotia B3H 3W3 *or* RR 1, Mulgrave, Nova Scotia B0E 2G0

SHARON ANNETTE BUTALA

Born in Nipawin, Saskatchewan, August 24, 1940. The second of five daughters. Educated in small towns. Attended St. Mary's School, Saskatoon Technical Collegiate and the University of Saskatchewan, all in Saskatoon. Taught English and art, then became a special education teacher and consultant. Married in 1961. A son born in 1964. Divorced in 1975. Remarried in 1976. Live with husband on a ranch in southwestern Saskatchewan.

Selected Publications:

Coming Attractions: (ed.) (with David Helwig), Ottawa, Oberon, 1983. ISBN 0-88750-497-3
Country of the Heart: Saskatoon, Fifth House, 1984. ISBN 0-920079-05-9
Queen of the Headaches: Regina, Coteau, 1985. ISBN 0-919926-48-7
The Gates of Sun: Saskatoon, Fifth House, 1986. ISBN 0-920079-20-2

    Awards: Saskatchewan Writers Guild Long Fiction Award, 1982. Saskatchewan Writers Guild Major Drama Award, 1985. Governor General's Award (Short list), 1986.
    Comments: Contributor to Saskatchewan Gold (Regina, Coteau, 1982); More Saskatchewan Gold (Regina, Coteau, 1984); Double Bond (Saskatoon, Fifth House, 1984).
    Readings, Lectures & Workshops: Have read in many prairie towns and most cities as well as in British Columbia and Ontario. Invited to take part in Sechelt Festival of the Written Arts, the NeWest Institute Symposium, and the International Symposium on Saskatchewan Writing.
    Mailing Address: Box 428, Eastend, Saskatchewan S0N 0T0

EILEEN CADE-EDWARDS

Born and educated in London, England. After living in Thunder Bay for several years, my husband and I moved to London, Ontario, where we have lived for more than 30 years. We have four grown sons and two young granddaughters. I began writing extensively for publications in Canada, the U.K. and the U.S. after my sons graduated from the "extensive care" stage. Now I mainly write for children.

Selected Publications:

Squirrel in My Tea Cup!: Ottawa, Borealis, 1981. ISBN 0-88887-037-X
The Starling Summer: Toronto, Three Trees, 1986. ISBN 0-88823-110-5

Comments: "This is a delightful tale . . . the style is humorous and light . . . The adventures of the boy and his pet are interesting and well written . . . Should appeal to the 7-12 age group." – *The London Free Press* (on *Squirrel in My Teacup!*)
"This charming story provides enjoyable reading." – *Canadian Materials*
"Pupils and teachers alike, appreciate her family-centered stories and the heart-warming way in which she handles the relationships between children and their pets." – Jean Blair Simms, *Celebrating Canadian Children's Literature*

Readings, Lectures & Workshops: Have given numerous readings and informal talks at public schools. Readings etc. may be booked through TWUC.

Mailing Address: 353 Byron Boulevard, London, Ontario N6K 2L6

BARRY CALLAGHAN

Born in Toronto, 1937. Professor at York University, Atkinson College, 1966-; gambler and gad-about, 1960-; literary editor, Toronto Telegram, 1966-71; producer and war correspondent, CBC Public Affairs, 1968-71; commentator, CTV network, 1976-1982; founder and editor, Exile: A Literary Quarterly, 1972-; founder and editor, Exile Editions, 1975-.

Selected Publications:

The Hogg Poems and Drawings: Toronto, General, 1978. ISBN 0-7736-0066-3
The Black Queen Stories: Toronto, Lester & Orpen Dennys, 1982. ISBN 0-919630-24-3
As Close As We Came: Toronto, Exile Editions, 1982. ISBN 0-920428-44-4
Lords of Winter and of Love (Canadian Love Poems): Toronto, Exile Editions, 1984. ISBN 0-920428-53-3

Awards: National Magazine Awards, 1977, 78, 79, 80, 83, 84, 85. University of Western's Ontario President's Medal for Excellence in Journalism, 1979, 1985. CBC Literary Competition (Fiction), 1985.
Comments: "*The Hogg Poems* is a most remarkable book. Hogg is a major breakthrough in modern Canadian poetry." – Yehuda Amichai
"Poems of a rare loyalty to poetry, that international conspiracy against darkness, a rare joy over *le mot juste*." – Josef Skvorecky
"*The Black Queen* is a must for all who are interested in the finest of contemporary North American writing." – Joyce Carol Oates
"*As Close As We Came* comes to resonate with repeated rereading, and becomes a poignant drama of the precariousness of life in a world devoted to death." – Northrop Frye
Readings, Lectures & Workshops: Some readings, some talks, but not sought on any regular basis.
Mailing Address: 69 Sullivan Street, Toronto, Ontario M5T 1C2

GINA CALLEJA

Illustrator/Author. Studied Fine Art at Reading University and the Slade School of Fine Art, London University. Have illustrated for many publishers. Interest in literature for small children led to production of picture book, Tobo Hates Purple. Work in progress on other projects.

Selected Publications:

Tobo Hates Purple: Toronto, Annick,1983. ISBN 0-920236-49-9

Awards: Canada Council Children's Literature Awards (Honourable Mention, Illustration), 1984

Comments: "*Tobo Hates Purple* presents Tobo's reluctance to accept being purple . . . coping with difference of colour is handled allegorically or in fantasy. One is led further to speculate on the use of colour symbolism in literature . . . After trying every colour, Tobo, with the help and kindness of his friend, Mina, decides to accept himself as purple. Mina's love and sympathy conquer Tobo's despair." – *Canadian Children's Literature*

Readings, Lectures & Workshops: Two readings in Montreal libraries in 1984. Two readings in Toronto libraries in 1986.

Mailing Address: 156 Kingsdale Avenue, Willowdale, Ontario M2N 3W7

JUNE CALLWOOD

Journalist. Founding member and past chair (1979) of TWUC.

Selected Publications:

Love, Hate, Fear, Anger: Toronto, Doubleday, 1964. (no ISBN)
The Law Is Not For Women: (with Marvin Zuker), Toronto, Copp Clark, 1973. (no ISBN)
Portrait of Canada: Toronto, Doubleday, 1981. ISBN 0-385-05746-6
Emma: Toronto, Stoddard,1984. ISBN 0-7737-2026-X
Emotions: Toronto, Doubleday, 1986. ISBN 0-385-05746-6
Twelve Weeks In Spring: Toronto, Lester & Orpen Dennys, 1986. ISBN 0-88619-115-7

Awards: B'nai Brith Woman of the Year, 1969. City of Toronto Award of Merit, 1974. Member, Order of Canada, 1978. Canadian News Hall of Fame, 1984. Officer, Order of Canada, 1986. YWCA Woman of Distinction, 1986.
Mailing Address: 21 Hillcroft Drive, Islington, Ontario M9B 4X4

SILVER DONALD CAMERON

 I have written seven books, about forty radio dramas, several TV scripts and innumerable magazine stories. Executive director of the Cape Breton Arts Institution (Centre Bras D'Or), vice-chairman of Magi Corporation and President of my own company (Paper Tiger Enterprises). I live in D'Escousse, Nova Scotia, with my wife Lulu Terrio-Cameron, one son, one cat and a cruising sailboat.

Selected Publications:

The Education of Everett Richardson: Toronto, McClelland & Stewart, 1977. ISBN 0-7710-1845-2

Seasons in the Rain: Toronto, McClelland & Stewart, 1978. ISBN 0-7710-1847-9

Dragon Lady: Toronto, McClelland & Stewart, 1980; Seal, 1981. ISBN 0-7710-1833-9

The Baitchopper: Toronto, Lorimer, 1982. ISBN 0-88862-599-5

The Schooner (Bluenose I and Bluenose II): Toronto, Seal, 1984. ISBN 0-7704-1861-9

Comments: I'm a journeyman writer; after 15 years of full-time writing, I'm able to work in many fields. For money, I write briefs, software manuals, business plans, press releases and brochures. I write books and stories for love. Alas, I am eclectic to a fault. In one month, I may write about sex therapy, nuclear power, sailboats and economic development as well as writing a comic radio drama and speaking about computers and writing. I have no niche. I confuse my readers. But I'm happy.

Readings, Lectures & Workshops: I do them all the time, to all kinds of ages and groups. Comedy, pathos, national issues, deep thought, whatever you like. Quality custom workmanship. Rates on request.

Mailing Address: D'Escousse, Nova Scotia B0E 1K0

MARGARET CAMPBELL

A New Zealander by birth, Canadian by choice, I have also lived in Thailand and Malaysia. A former university teacher, I now work as an editor and writer. Married with three children and one Saluki.

Selected Publications:

From the Hands of the Hills: Hong Kong, Media Transasia, 1978. ISBN 962-7024-01-5
Guide To The Best Restaurants of Greater Vancouver, Vancouver Island and Whistler: Vancouver, Soules, 1986. ISBN 0-919574-56-4

Comments: From the Hands of the Hills is a detailed study of the hand-made artifacts of six culturally and linguistically unique nomadic groups from the mountains of southern Asia. Short pieces of fiction are interwoven with the factual text to convey the context of ritual and belief that surrounds these artifacts, and the book is extensively illustrated with colour and black and white photos.

Mailing Address: 4605 Glenwood Avenue, North Vancouver, British Columbia V7R 4G6

DAVID CARPENTER

I was born in Edmonton, moved to Saskatoon and was discovered on a slush pile by Tecca Crosby of Saturday Night. I teach English for a living, write fiction, play the five-string banjo as well as anyone on Osler Street and consider myself an excellent fisherman. My writing is done in monasteries, haunted houses, bug-infested rooms, log cabins and Toronto.

Selected Publications:

Jokes for the Apocalypse: Toronto, McClelland & Stewart, 1985. ISBN 0-7710-1908-4
Jewels: Erin, Porcupine's Quill, 1985. ISBN 0-88984-073-3

Comments: Forthcoming: God's Bedfellows (Toronto, McClelland & Stewart, 1988).
Readings, Lectures & Workshops: Read regularly at universities and coffee houses; give talks about writing; may be booked through Canada Council or TWUC.
Mailing Address: 1324 Osler Street, Saskatoon, Saskatchewan S7N 0V2

JEAN-GUY CARRIER

Raised in Ontario and Quebec, I've earned a livelihood as a journalist and communications specialist, mostly with public organisations. I am most proud to have remained a socialist and a writer.

Selected Publications:

My Father's House: Ottawa, Oberon, 1974. ISBN 0-88750-116-8
Family: Ottawa, Oberon, 1977. ISBN 0-88750-225-3
A Cage of Bone: Ottawa, Oberon, 1978. ISBN 0-88750-287-3
The Trudeau Decade: Toronto, Doubleday, 1979. ISBN 0-385-15543-3

Mailing Address: 920 Chemin Cook, Aylmer, Quebec J9H 5C9

NORMA CHARLES

Born in Ste. Boniface, Manitoba, May 10, 1940. Graduated from the University of British Columbia in 1961 and have taught all grades from one to ten. Currently employed as teacher-librarian at Van Horne, in Vancouver, and writing as much as possible. Four children, two sons and two daughters.

Selected Publications:

See You Later Alligator: Toronto, Scholastic, 1974. (no ISBN)
Amanda Grows Up: Toronto, Scholastic, 1976. (o/p)

   Comments: "Highly enjoyed by four to seven year olds as a read-aloud . . . Parents were also very enthusiastic about the book. A sure favourite . . ." – *Children's Choices of Canadian Books*, Volume 2
   Readings, Lectures & Workshops: Read often and conduct workshops in schools and at Young Writers' Conferences.
   Mailing Address: 1844 Acadia, Vancouver, British Columbia V6T 1R3

ANN CHARNEY

Born in Poland in 1940. Educated at McGill University and the Sorbonne in Paris. M.A. in French Literature. Member of l'Union des ecrivains quebecois, PEN and PWAC. Columnist for Maclean's and contributor to the Op-Ed page of the Toronto Star.

Selected Publications:

Dobryd: Toronto, New Press, 1973. (no ISBN)

Awards: National Magazine Award (Gold Medal). National Magazine Award (Finalist, Short Story). Chatelaine Fiction Contest (First Prize). Okanagan Short Fiction Award.

Comments: "Ann Charney has a unique talent, and a singular intelligence. Her book is marked by freshness, sagacity, emotional truth and a complete lack of sentimental cheating." – John Richmond, *Montreal Star*

"Her book is a tour de force, a tale told with great force and simplicity." – Norman Ward, *Maclean's*

"The honesty of *Dobryd* sets it apart from the mainstream of war novels. In time it will take its place as one of the truly significant insights into the effects of war on the people it touches." – Richard Sparks, *Books in Canada*.

"One of the best books on European destiny in our century." – *Stuttgarter Zeitung*

Articles have appeared in Saturday Night, Canadian Forum, Chatelaine, Ms, Weekend, Today and The Canadian.

Short fiction in Ms, Chatelaine, Canadian Author and Bookman, Descant.

Mailing Address: 3620 Marlowe Avenue, Montreal, Quebec H4A 3L7

LAURENCE CHERNIAK

Born in Canada. Writer, actor and painter. I speak many languages as a result of having lived and travelled extensively throughout the world. Have been interviewed by Newsweek, Time/ Life, Honolulu Star, the Maui News, Penthouse, InternationalTimes and HomeGrown and others in Germany, Holland, Italy and Canada. Have been given permanent exhibition space for my photographic journalism on ethnobotanical pharmacology at Germany's Koln Museum, Boston's Harvard University and San Francisco's Fitz Hugh Ludlow Library.

Selected Publications:

The Great Books of Hashish (Book One): Berkeley, And/Or Press. ISBN 0-915904-40-3
The Great Books of Cannabis (Book Two): New York, Cherniak. ISBN 0-911093-03-6

Comments: "An outstanding photographic study of the various uses of Cannabis." – *Journal of Ethnopharmacology*
"Cherniak's unique contribution is that after fifteen years of traveling the 'Hashish Trail' he presents us not only with pictures of hashmaking the likes of which the world has never seen, but also with something infinitely more valuable: an understanding of humanity. Cherniak records nothing less than a phenomenon of human consciousness kept secret from the world at large."
– Michael Aldrich, Curator, Fitz Hugh Ludlow Memorial Library
"I know of no other book presenting this information . . . The volume indeed is a priceless reference for libraries, researchers, novices, and enthusiasts . . ." – Richard Evans Shultes, Director, Botanical Museum, Harvard University
Readings, Lectures & Workshops: Have given readings, lectures, slide shows and workshops at dozens of universities, libraries and bookstores in the U.S. May be booked through TWUC.
Mailing Address: c/o TWUC, 24 Ryerson Avenue, Toronto, Ontario M5T 2P3

LESLEY CHOYCE

Born in Riverside, New Jersey, March 21, 1951, and attended Rutgers University, Montclair State College and the City University of New York before finding my way to a civilised life on the Eastern Shore of Nova Scotia in 1979. Now a Canadian citizen, I teach at Dalhousie University; run Pottersfield Press; host a TV show; write novels, short stories and drama; and surf year round at Lawrencetown Beach.

Selected Publications:

Eastern Sure: Halifax, Nimbus, 1981. ISBN 0-920852-08-4
Fast Living: Fredericton, Fiddlehead, 1982. ISBN 0-86492-026-1
Billy Botzweiler's Last Dance: Toronto, blewointment, 1984. ISBN 0-88971-099-6
Conventional Emotions: St. John's, Creative, 1985. ISBN 0-920021-27-1
The End of Ice: Fredericton, Fiddlehead, 1985. ISBN 0-86492-054-7
The Dream Auditor: Charlottetown, Ragweed, 1986. ISBN 0-920304-63-X
The Top of the Heart: Saskatoon, Thistledown, 1986. ISBN 0-920633-12-9

Awards: Writers' Federation of Nova Scotia Literary Competition (Novel and Short Fiction). Pierian Spring Editor's Award for Poetry.
Comments: "Choyce has a feeling for the young and the dispossessed, for the terrible angst of adolescence and the rituals of rebellion." – William French, *Globe and Mail*
"Taut dialogue, memorably exact phrasing, and marvelously inventive throwaway lines . . . one of Canada's most accomplished younger writers." – Reynold Stone, *Atlantic Provinces Book Review*
Readings, Lectures & Workshops: Have read in libraries, schools, shopping malls and universities from New York City to Labrador to Vancouver.
Mailing Address: R.R. 2, Porters Lake, Nova Scotia B0J 2S0

DELWIN MARK CLARK

Born in St. John's, Newfoundland, November 20, 1937. Family migrated to Canada about six years later. When Newfoundland joined Confederation in 1948, my dreams of returning to the homeland became dreams of freeing the homeland eventually from Liberal-Conservative oppression. Both parents died before this could be realised, however, leaving me to bear the torch should it become necessary.

Selected Publications:

Inside Shadows: Toronto, McClelland & Stewart, 1973. ISBN 0-7710-2136-4
The Sunshine Man: New York, St. Martin's Press, 1978. ISBN 0-312-77580-8
The Sunshine Man: Toronto, McClelland & Stewart, 1977. ISBN 0-7710-2148-8
Wild Rose: Toronto, McClelland & Stewart, 1982. ISBN 0-7710-2119-4

Awards: Capilano Review Short Story Contest
Comments: "Who?" – Nearly everyone in Canada, except immediate family
"I meant to read your book, but it's out at the Library." – Immediate family
"The bookstore never heard of it." – Close friend
"Do you have a copy I could borrow?" – Another close friend
Readings, Lectures & Workshops: Lead a few workshops from time to time for local prison. Played softball with the convicts, too.
Mailing Address: 46998 Prairie Central Road, RR 1, Chilliwack, British Columbia V2P 6H3

JOAN CLARK

Born in Liverpool, Nova Scotia, October 12, 1934. Raised in Nova Scotia and New Brunswick. Attended Acadia University and the University of Alberta. Taught school intermittently in various places for five years. Co-founded and co-edited Dandelion magazine for six years. Three children. Married to Jack Clark. Full-time writer. Now living in St. John's, Newfoundland.

Selected Publications:

From a High Thin Wire: Edmonton, NeWest, 1982. ISBN 0-920316-51-4
The Leopard and the Lily: Lantzville, Oolichan, 1984. ISBN 0-88982-078-2
Wild Man of the Woods: Toronto, Penguin, 1985. ISBN 0-670-8015-5
The Hand of Robin Squires: Toronto, Penguin, 1986. ISBN 0-14-031905-0
The Moons of Madeleine: Toronto, Penguin, 1987. ISBN 0-670-81284-6

Readings, Lectures & Workshops: Have read extensively, particularly to children. Will continue to read, give workshops, informal talks.
Mailing Address: c/o TWUC, 24 Ryerson Avenue, Toronto, Ontario M5T 2P3

STEPHEN CLARKSON

Educated in history and languages at Toronto, philosophy and economics at Oxford and political science at the Sorbonne where I earned my doctorate. I have professed political economy at the University of Toronto since 1964. I specialise in Canadian politics and Canadian-American relations, topics on which I have published several books and scores of articles. I am married to Christina McCall with whom I am writing a book on the end of the Trudeau era.

Selected Publications:

Visions 2020 (Fifty Canadians in Search of a Future): (ed.), Edmonton, Hurtig, 1970. ISBN 0-88830-033-6
City Lib (Parties and Reform): Toronto, Hakkert, 1972. ISBN 0-88866-510-3
The Soviet Theory of Development (India and the Third World in Marxist-Leninist Scholarship): Toronto, University of Toronto Press, 1978. ISBN 0-8020-5391-2
Canada and the Reagan Challenge (Crisis and Adjustment, 1981-85): Toronto, Lorimer, 1985. ISBN 0-88862-791-2

Awards: John Porter Award (Social Science), Canadian Anthropology and Sociology Association, 1984
Comments: "Clarkson has brilliantly dissected the bilateral relationship and produced a thorough, penetrating analysis." – Lawrence Martin, *Globe and Mail* (on *Canada and the Reagan Challenge*)
"Raises a number of disconcerting and searching questions concerning the future of Canada." – George Rawlyk, *Kingston Whig-Standard*
Readings, Lectures & Workshops: Often speak to organisations both large (the Canadian Clubs of Canada) and small (Science for Peace) on topics like free trade and star wars.
Mailing Address: 44 Rosedale Road, Toronto, Ontario M4W 2P6

MATT COHEN

Born in Kingston, Ontario, December 30, 1942. B.A. from the University of Toronto, 1965. Lecturer in religion, McMaster University, 1967-68. Writer-in-residence, University of Alberta, 1975-76. Visiting Professor of Creative Writing, University of Victoria, 1979-80. Writer-in-residence, University of Western Ontario, 1981. Visiting professor, University of Bologna, 1986.

Selected Publications:

The Disinherited: Toronto, McClelland & Stewart, 1974. ISBN 0-7710-9221-0

Wooden Hunters: Toronto, McClelland & Stewart, 1975. ISBN 0-7710-9265-2

The Colours of War: Toronto, McClelland & Stewart, 1977. ISBN 0-7710-2175-0

The Sweet Second Summer of Kitty Malone: Toronto, McClelland & Stewart, 1979. ISBN 0-7710-2221-2

Flowers of Darkness: Toronto, McClelland & Stewart, 1981. ISBN 0-7710-2235-2

The Expatriate: Toronto, General/New Press, 1982. ISBN 0-7736-7018-1

Cafe le Dog: Toronto, McClelland & Stewart, 1983. ISBN 0-7710-2179-8

The Spanish Doctor: Toronto, McClelland & Stewart, 1984. ISBN 0-7710-2239-9

Nadine: New York, Viking, 1986. ISBN 0-670-81083-5

Mailing Address: c/o TWUC, 24 Ryerson Avenue, Toronto, Ontario M5T 2P3

ROBERT J. COLLINS

Born and raised on a farm near Shamrock, Saskatchewan. RCAF in World War II. Graduated in journalism, University of Western Ontario, 1950. Since then: the London Free Press, western editor of Maclean's, editor of the Imperial Oil Review, editor of Toronto Life. Now a roving editor for Reader's Digest and adjunct professor in the University of Western Ontario's Graduate School of Journalism.

Selected Publications:

The Age of Innocence: Toronto, NSL, 1977. ISBN 0-9196-4419-8
A Voice from Afar: Toronto, McGraw-Hill Ryerson, 1977. ISBN 0-07-082536-X
Butter Down the Well: Saskatoon, Prairie Books, 1980. ISBN 0-88833-060-X
The Mystery at the Wildcat Well: Toronto, Seal, 1981. ISBN 0-7704-1684-5
One Thing for Tommorrow: (with J.R. Brack), Saskatoon, WP Prairie Books, 1981. ISBN 0-88833-080-4
The Long and the Short and the Tall: Saskatoon, WP Prairie Books, 1986. ISBN 0-88833-187-8
The Holy War of Sally Ann: Saskatoon, WP Prairie Books, 1986. ISBN 0-88833-158-4

Awards: Twenty-five for writing and editing, including the President's Medal, National Magazine Awards, 1978
Comments: "Crackles with vitality and good humour." – *Books in Canada*
"It's Collins' writing style, tight and flowing, that works the magic."
– *Ottawa Citizen*
Readings, Lectures & Workshops: Read occasionally at public schools, high schools and libraries. Lecture on non-fiction writing.
Mailing Address: 300 Airdrie Road, Toronto, Ontario M4G 1N3

JAN CONN

I grew up in Asbestos, a small mining town in southern Quebec. I have a B.Sc. in Biology from Concordia University and an M.Sc. in Entomology from Simon Fraser University. Just completing a Ph.D. in Cytotaxonomy (black flies) at the University of Toronto. My field work requires frequent trips to Central and South America, where some of my poetry is written. Working on a new manuscript of poetry as yet untitled.

Selected Publications:

Red Shoes in the Rain: Fredericton, Fiddlehead, 1984. ISBN 0-86492-025-3
The Fabulous Disguise of Ourselves: Montreal, Vehicule, 1986. ISBN
  0-919890-75-X

Comments: Memberships: Entomological Society of Canada, Entomological Society of America, Society for the Study of Evolution, League of Canadian Poets. Five scientific papers published in refereed journals, and one patent from M.Sc.; two papers in progress from Ph.D. research. Also enthusiastic amateur photographer.

Readings, Lectures & Workshops: Read regularly at universities and other venues. Have led workshops in high schools.

Mailing Address: 54 Beatrice Street, Toronto, Ontario M6J 2T3

GREGORY M. COOK

Born in Yarmouth, Nova Scotia, during World War II. Hold an M.A. (English) from Acadia University. Worked as a reporter, lecturer and administrator (of the Writers' Federation of Nova Scotia). A member of the Evelyn Richardson Memorial Literary Trust, the Nova Scotia Coalition on Arts and Culture, PEN, the League of Canadian Poets and the Writers' Development Trust. I live near Wolfville, Nova Scotia.

Selected Publications:

Love from Backfields: St. John's, Breakwater, 1980. ISBN 0-919948-89-8
Love en Route: Fredericton, Fiddlehead, 1983. ISBN 0-86492-034-2
Love in Flight: Charlottetown, Ragweed, 1985. ISBN 0-920304-42-7

Comments: "An unpretentious writer, a fine craftsman, a consummate poet." – Ann Munton, *The Dalhousie Review*
"Cook has created a fine sense of landscape and family history that allows us to transcend pain and vulgarity." – Linda Rogers, *Canadian Literature*
"The poems suggest a debate between war and peace, and between the position that some fights – like the Second World War – must be fought, and that which says any preparation for warfare is intolerable." – Fraser Sutherland, *Globe and Mail*

Readings, Lectures & Workshops: Have read, as invited, in schools, libraries, art galleries, universities, legion halls, on CBC radio and bandstands, dance halls, theatres, provincial parks and museums in Canada, the U.S. and Europe.

Mailing Address: c/o TWUC, 24 Ryerson Avenue, Toronto, Ontario M5T 2P3

HUGH COOK

Born in The Hague, The Netherlands, I grew up in Vancouver and now live in Hamilton, Ontario, where I am a professor of English at Redeemer College. My stories have been published in numerous Canadian literary journals; I am frequently asked to read to audiences.

Selected Publications:

Cracked Wheat and Other Stories: Oakville, Mosaic, 1985. ISBN 0-88962-265-5

Comments: "One of the finest collections of the past years." – *Globe and Mail*

"The best stories . . . find a poise among the demands of poetry, narrative, and meaning . . . It catches, as the best short fiction does, the poetry of the real." – *Toronto Star*

"What the author seems adept in is the creation of story elements. We find evocative descriptions, carefully drawn details, and poignant moments." – *Books in Canada*

"*Cracked Wheat* is a solid, enjoyable collection of stories." – *Choice*

"The canon of Canadian literature has been enriched by this volume." – *The Ottawa Citizen*

Readings, Lectures & Workshops: I often read at universities, schools and churches. I also conduct fiction writing workshops. All may be arranged directly or through TWUC.

Mailing Address: 67 Trevi Road, Hamilton, Ontario L9B 1B3

LYN COOK

Born in the country near Weston, Ontario, on May 4, 1918. Now live in Scarborough. University of Toronto B.A., B.L.Sc. Married Robb Waddell in 1949. Two children, Christopher and Deborah. Librarian, Toronto Public Libraries, 1941-42. Military service, RCAF (WD), 1942-46. Children's librarian in Sudbury, Ontario, 1946-47. Writer, director, narrator children's radio show, A Doorway in Fairyland, 1947-52. Creative drama teacher, New Play Society Theatre School, 1956-65. Pre-school story hour, monthly festivals, Scarborough Public Libraries, 1962-76.

Selected Publications:

The Road to Kip's Cove: Toronto, Macmillan, 1961. ISBN 0-7705-0061-7
Toys from the Sky: Toronto, Clarke Irwin, 1972. ISBN 0-7720-0568-0
Pegeen and the Pilgrim: Toronto, Macmillan, 1972. ISBN 0-7705-0986-X
Jolly Jean-Pierre: Toronto, Burns & MacEachern, 1973. ISBN 0-88768-43-7
The Magical Miss Mittens: Toronto, Macmillan, 1974. ISBN 0-7705-1209-7
The Bells on Finland Street: Toronto, Macmillan, 1978. ISBN 0-7705-1702-1
Samantha's Secret Room: Toronto, Scholastic, 1978. ISBN 0-590-71428-7
A Treasury for Tony: Cobalt, Highway Book Shop, 1980. ISBN 0-88954-224-4
Sea Dreams: Hantsport, Lancelot, 1981. ISBN 0-88999-155-3
The Secret of Willow Castle: Camden East, Camden House, 1984. ISBN 0-920656-30-7

Awards: Vicky Metcalf Award, 1978
Readings, Lectures & Workshops: Workshops and readings for children, teachers and librarians.
Mailing Address: 72 Cedarbrae Boulevard, Scarborough, Ontario M1J 2K5

ANN COPELAND

Born in Hartford, Connecticut, educated in Connecticut and New York. Ph.D. in English from Cornell University. Have taught literature and fiction writing at colleges and universities in the U.S. and Canada: Indiana University Northwest, Linfield College (Oregon), University of Idaho (distinguished visiting fiction writer), College of Idaho, Mt. Allison University. Live in Sackville, New Brunswick, where I write full time.

Selected Publications:

At Peace: Ottawa, Oberon, 1978. ISBN 0-88750-270-9
The Back Room: Ottawa, Oberon, 1979. ISBN 0-88750-307-1
Earthen Vessels: Ottawa, Oberon, 1984. ISBN 0-88750-522-8

Readings, Lectures & Workshops: Read occasionally at universities and libraries. Give workshops on fiction.
Mailing Address: Box 1450, Sackville, New Brunswick E0A 3C0

KAZIMIERA JANINA (JEAN) COTTAM

 Born in Poland on April 23, 1930, and arrrived in Canada on February 4, 1949. Hold a B.A. from Sir George Williams University and an M.A. and a Ph.D. in East European History from the University of Toronto. Now reside in a suburb of Ottawa, where I am employed full time as editor/translator and write part time.

Selected Publications:

Soviet Airwomen in Combat in WWII: Manhattan, Kan., MA/AH Publishing, 1983. ISBN 0-89126-118-4

The Golden-Tressed Soldier: Manhattan, Kan., MA/AH Publishing, 1983. ISBN 0-89126-119-2

In the Sky Above the Front: Manhattan, Kan., MA/AH Publishing, 1984. ISBN 0-89126-126-5

The Girl from Kashin: Manhattan, Kan., MA/AH Publishing, 1984. ISBN 0-89126-128-1

Awards: Birks Medal and Lieutenant-Governor of Quebec Medal for History, 1964. Kosciuszko Foundation Doctoral Dissertation Award, 1972. Foundation for the Advancement of Canadian Letters and Periodical Distributors of Canada Award, 1983.

Comments: "A marvelous example of serious, problem-oriented scholarship." – *Austrian History Yearbook*

"Solid, perceptive, and sometimes brilliant study." – *American Historical Review*

"A military history that is also a valuable contribution to women's history . . . Her effort certainly proves that the two fields are not mutually exclusive, but rather, when properly melded, form a new area for exciting historiographical advances." – *Minerva*

Mailing Address: c/o TWUC, 24 Ryerson Avenue, Toronto, Ontario M5T 2P3

JANICE COWAN

Born in Hampshire, England, on New Year's Day, 1941. Trained as a journalist on various newspapers then moved to Australia to work as a writer for the Australian Broadcasting Commission. Married Ian Cowan from Ottawa in 1966 and moved to Canada. Worked for CTV, taught journalism at community colleges and worked for the Miramichi Leader in New Brunswick and Der Kanadier in Germany. Have three children, Hamish, Kyra and Angus.

Selected Publications:

Maple Island Mystery: Ottawa, Borealis, 1976. ISBN 0-919594-59-X
The Mystery of Castle Hotel: Ottawa, Borealis,1978. ISBN 0-919594-56-5
Secret of Ivy Lea: Ottawa, Borealis, 1981. ISBN 0-88887-055-8
The Mystery on the Miramichi: Ottawa, Borealis, 1985. ISBN 0-88887-04-0

Comments: "Ninety per cent of the children who read the book liked it." — *Children's Choice of Canadian Literature*, Vol. 2 (on *The Mystery of Castle Hotel*)

"The *Secret of Ivy Lea* . . . excels as an adventure story . . . and . . . the portrayal of a very close and fun loving family whose affection for one another . . . provides emotional depth." — *Canadian Literature*

Readings, Lectures & Workshops: Have toured schools in Lahr, Baden and Heidelberg, West Germany; Brunssum, Holland; New Brunswick, Ontario and Manitoba. Taught The Art of Writing Children's Mysteries to grades five and six for the East York School Board. Readings may be booked through TWUC.

Mailing Address: c/o Borealis Press, 9 Ashburn Drive, Ottawa, Ontario K2E 6N4

SAROS COWASJEE

 Born in India on July 12, 1931, I hold an M.A. from Agra University (India) and a Ph.D. from Leeds University (U.K.). Before coming to Regina, in 1963, I worked as an assistant editor with Times of India Press, Bombay, for two years. I have been a professor of English at the University of Regina since 1971 and have held visiting appointments at the University of California (Berkeley) and the University of Aarhus in Denmark.

Selected Publications:

Sean O'Casey (The Man Behind the Plays): Edinburgh, Oliver & Boyd, 1963. (no ISBN)
Goodbye to Elsa: Toronto, New Press, 1974. ISBN 0-88770-206-6
Modern Indian Short Stories: (ed.), New Delhi, Oxford, 1982. ISBN 0-19-561563-8
Stories from the Raj: (ed.), London, Bodley Head, 1982. ISBN 0-370-30456-X
More Stories from the Raj and After: (ed.), London, Grafton, 1986. ISBN 0-586-06526-1
When the British Left: New Delhi, Arnold-Heinemann, 1987.

Comments: "A novel typical of our times. A book by turns disturbing, startling and vastly amusing." – G. Wilson Knight (on *Goodbye to Elsa*)

"Saros Cowasjee has rendered us a great service by disinterring these stories and bringing so many of these writers out of an undeserved obscurity." – Paul Theroux (on *Stories from the Raj*)

Readings, Lectures & Workshops: Have given lectures and readings extensively in Canada, the U.K., France, Denmark, Australia, India, Singapore and Fiji.

Mailing Address: Dept. of English, University of Regina, Saskatchewan S4S 0A2

SONIA CRADDOCK

Born in England and emigrated to Saskatchewan as a teenager. B.A., University of British Columbia, 1972. M.Ed., University of British Columbia, 1976. D. Ed. (Language Education), University of British Columbia, 1982. Have been a pre-school teacher, an elementary teacher and a university lecturer. At present I teach and write in Vancouver.

Selected Publications:

The TV War and Me: Toronto, Scholastic, 1981. ISBN 0-590-71065-6
The Treasure Hunt: Toronto, Gage, 1984. ISBN 0-7715-7011-2
You Can't Take Micky!: Toronto, Scholastic, 1986. ISBN 0-590-71613-1

Readings, Lectures & Workshops: Readings and workshops in elementary schools and libraries. Lectures on children's literature and the importance of Canadian children's literature in the classroom.

Mailing Address: c/o TWUC, 24 Ryerson Avenue, Toronto, Ontario M5T 2P3

SUSAN (S.M.) CREAN

Born in Toronto, February 14, 1945. Studied art history at the University of Toronto (B.A., M.A.), in France and in Italy. Returned to Canada in 1970. Freelanced as a researcher, cultural policy critic and university lecturer. Associate producer for CBC-TV Current Affairs (A Question of Country, 1980; There Never Was an Arrow, 1979) and part of the CBC-2 project team. Member of the This Magazine editorial collective since 1979. Live in South Riverdale.

Selected Publications:

Who's Afraid of Canadian Culture: Toronto, General, 1976. ISBN 0-7736-1010-7

Two Nations: (with Marcel Rioux), Toronto, Lorimer, 1983. ISBN 0-88862-382-8

Newsworthy (The Lives of Media Women): Toronto, Stoddart, 1985. ISBN 0-7737-0081-1

Readings, Lectures & Workshops: Frequent commentator and speaker on cultural politics and feminist issues. Presented a course on Women in Politics at the University of Prince Edward Island's Political Studies Department, 1985. Distinguished Visitor, Department of Political Science, University of Alberta, 1986.

Mailing Address: c/o TWUC, 24 Ryerson Avenue, Toronto, Ontario M5T 2P3

ANNE INNIS DAGG

I was born and grew up in Toronto. I studied biology at the University of Toronto and since then have researched the behaviour of the giraffe and the camel in Africa. I analysed the locomotion of large mammals for my Ph.D. (1967) from the University of Waterloo. I am now academic director of the Independent Studies Program at the University of Waterloo. My current research area centres on feminism.

Selected Publications:

Mammals of Waterloo and South Wellington Counties: (with C.A. Campbell), Waterloo, Otter, 1972. (no ISBN)

Canadian Wildlife and Man: Toronto, McClelland & Stewart, 1974. ISBN 0-7710-2520-3

Mammals of Ontario: Waterloo, Otter, 1974. ISBN 0-9690963-1-3

The Giraffe (Its Biology, Behavior and Ecology): (with J.B. Foster), New York, Van Nostrand, 1976. ISBN 0-442-22431-1

Running, Walking and Jumping (The Science of Locomotion): London, Francis and Taylor, 1977. ISBN 0-85109-530-5

Wildlife Management in Europe: Waterloo, Otter 1977. ISBN 0-9690963-4-8

Camel Quest (Research on the Saharan Camel): Toronto, York, 1978. ISBN 0-920424-10-4

Harems and Other Horrors (Sexual Bias in Behavioral Biology): Waterloo, Otter, 1983. ISBN 0-9690963-7-2

The Fifty Per Cent Solution (Why Should Women Pay for Men's Culture?): Waterloo, Otter, 1986.

Comments: "I enjoyed this small book tremendously." — Fay Nemani, Canadian Woman Studies (on *Harems and Other Horrors*).

"This is an excellent book, which I recommend if only for sheer reading pleasure." — Valerius Geist (on *Natural History of The Camel*).

Mailing Address: 81 Albert Street, Waterloo, Ontario N2L 3S6

JILLIAN DAGG

Born Jillian Fayers in Walton-on-Thames, Surrey, England, on January 28, 1944. Moved to Winnipeg, Manitoba, at the age of 13. From 1970 to 1975 travelled in England and Canada. Now residing in Burlington, Ontario.

Selected Publications:

Rain Lady: (wa Faye Wildman), New York, Silhouette, 1980. ISBN 0-671-57029-3

A Race for Love: (wa Faye Wildman), New York, Silhouette, 1980. ISBN 0-671-57048-X

Whispers of the Heart: (wa Jillian Fayre), New York, Simon & Schuster, 1981. ISBN 0-671-43867-0

Lovesong: (wa Faye Wildman), New York, Silhouette, 1983. ISBN 0-671-53626-5

Passion's Glow: (wa Marilyn Brian), New York, Berkley, 1984, ISBN 0-515-06946-9

The Fletcher Legacy: (wa Faye Wildman), New York, Silhouette, 1984. ISBN 0-671-57307-1

Readings, Lectures & Workshops: Occasionally teach fiction-writing workshops. Will also do consultation with a single writer.

Mailing Address: c/o TWUC, 24 Ryerson Avenue, Toronto, Ontario M5T 2P3

DANIEL GEORGE DANCOCKS

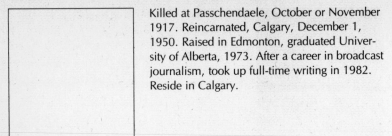

Killed at Passchendaele, October or November 1917. Reincarnated, Calgary, December 1, 1950. Raised in Edmonton, graduated University of Alberta, 1973. After a career in broadcast journalism, took up full-time writing in 1982. Reside in Calgary.

Selected Publications:

In Enemy Hands: Edmonton, Hurtig, 1983. ISBN 0-88830-240-1
Sir Arthur Currie: Toronto, Methuen, 1985. ISBN 0-458-99560-6
Legacy of Valour: Edmonton, Hurtig, 1986. ISBN 0-88830-305-X

  Awards: Alberta Culture Award (Non-Fiction), 1983
  Comments: "Dancocks has managed the remarkable feat of rendering a fascinating story boring. I thought that it might have been an accident: apparently it was on purpose." – Desmond Morton, *Books in Canada*.
  Readings, Lectures & Workshops: Ready, willing and possibly able.
  Mailing Address: 114-433 Pinestream Place N.E., Calgary, Alberta T1Y 3A5

LOIS E. DARROCH

Born in Toronto. Primary school education in a one-room school at Wolverton, Ontario. Secondary, at Humberside Collegiate in Toronto. B.A. in English and History, 1933; M.A. in English, 1943 (Toronto). Taught high school. Married Camillo Milani in 1945; one daughter, Cristine. Supported progressive and peace movements. Self-published first biography. Made profit. With publication of first novel, 1985, could be called the Grandma Moses of Canadian literature.

Selected Publications:

Robert Gourlay, Gadfly (Forerunner of the Rebellion in Upper Canada 1837): Willowdale, Ampersand, 1971. ISBN 0-9690442-0-8

Bright Land (A Warm Look at Arthur Lismer): Toronto and Vancouver, Merritt Publishing, 1981. ISBN 0-920886-07-08

Maria Morca's Belly Dance Kit (History and Basic Course): (ed.) Toronto, Anthony Perris Associates, 1975. (no ISBN)

Four Went to the Civil War: Kitchener, McBain, 1985. ISBN 0-902469-01-9

Awards: Canadian Literature Club, 1942. Canadian Women's Press Club, 1943.

Readings, Lectures & Workshops: Burlington Arts and Letters Club, Harbourfront, Queen's University Extension, Toronto Heliconian Club, York Pioneer Society, et al.

Mailing Address: 2009-33 Elmhurst Avenue, Willowdale, Ontario M2N 6G8

ROBERTSON DAVIES

Born in 1913, educated in Canada and at Oxford; until 1940 an actor in London; for two years literary editor of Saturday Night; for 20 years Master of Massey College in the University of Toronto. During this time published novels, plays and criticism, as listed elsewhere. For further details see the Oxford Companion to Canadian Literature.

Selected Publications:

World of Wonders: Toronto, Macmillan, 1975. ISBN 0-7705-1419-0
One Half of Robertson Davies: Toronto, Macmillan, 1977. ISBN 0-7705-1579-7
The Enthusiasms of Robertson Davies: Toronto, McClelland & Stewart, 1979. ISBN 0-7710-2565-3
Robertson Davies (The Well-Tempered Critic): Toronto, McClelland & Stewart, 1981. 0-7710-2567-X
The Rebel Angels: Toronto, Macmillan, 1981. ISBN 0-7715-9556-5
High Spirits: Toronto, Penguin, 1982. ISBN 0-14-00-6505-9
The Mirror of Nature: Toronto, University of Toronto Press, 1983. ISBN 0-8020-6536-8
What's Bred in the Bone: Toronto, Macmillan, 1985. ISBN 0-7715-9684-7
The Papers of Samuel Marchbanks: Toronto, Irwin, 1985. ISBN 0-7725-1539-5

Awards: The Stephen Leacock Medal (Humour), 1955. Governor General's Award (Fiction), 1973. City of Toronto Book Award, 1986. Toronto Arts Awards, Lifetime Achievement Award, 1986.
   Mailing Address: 4 Devonshire Place, Toronto, Ontario M5S 2E1

DAVID DAY

Born in 1947 in Victoria, British Columbia, and raised on Vancouver Island. Worked for five years as a logger in British Columbia. Taught in Greece for one year and worked for a Toronto publisher for one year before turning to writing as a full-time profession. Have published books in such diverse areas as poetry, fiction, natural history, fantasy, ecology and mythology. My books have sold 500,000 copies in 20 countries and seven languages.

Selected Publications:

The Burrough Bestiary: London, New English Library, 1978.
A Tolkien Bestiary: Madeira Park, Harbour, 1970. ISBN 0-920080-47-2
The Scarlett Coat Serial: Victoria, Press Porcepic, 1981. ISBN 0-88878-135-0
The Doomsday Book of Animals: Toronto, Wiley, 1981. ISBN 0-471-799944-0
Castles: Toronto, McGraw-Hill Ryerson, 1984.
The Emperor's Panda: Toronto, McClelland & Stewart, 1986. ISBN 0-7710-2573-4
Gothic: Toronto, Exile, 1986.
The Whale War: Vancouver, Douglas & McIntyre, 1987. ISBN 0-88894-485-5

Comments: "Day is a poet whose first commitment is to words . . . his poems attack each of our senses with equal vitality and power." – Susan Musgrave, *Victoria Times*
"David Day's writing is wonderfully lucid . . . pure story-telling at its finest." – Gwendolyn MacEwen, *Books in Canada*
"Haunting, bittersweet meditations." – *Maclean's*.
"David Day weaves a spell . . . makes me believe." – Stephen R. Donaldson, *New York Times*
"A magical touch . . . brilliantly lucid." – Ted Hughes
Mailing Address: c/o TWUC, 24 Ryerson Avenue, Toronto, Ontario M5T 2P3

SHIRLEY DAY

Born in Toronto, October 12, 1931. Educated at Memorial Public School in Weston, Ontario; Weston Collegiate; and the Ontario College of Art. Painter and illustrator for 25 years. Writer for five years. One husband (Arthur). Four daughters (Susan, Nancy, Jennifer and Sandy). Live at the Beach in Toronto.

Selected Publications:

Ruthie's Big Tree: Toronto, Annick, 1982. ISBN 0-920236-35-9
To the End of the Block: (with bp Nichol), Windsor, Black Moss, 1984.
    ISBN 0-88753-119-0
Waldo's Back Yard: Toronto, Annick, 1984. ISBN 0-920236-73-1
The Red Apples: (with Marion Mineau), Windsor, Black Moss, 1986. ISBN
    0-88753-140-7

Readings, Lectures & Workshops: Readings and workshops for primary and junior grades may be booked through TWUC.
Mailing Address: c/o TWUC, 24 Ryerson Avenue, Toronto, Ontario M5T 2P3

JAMES DEAHL

Born in Pittsburgh, Pennsylvania, December 5, 1945. Came to Canada in May 1970 and became a citizen in 1981. I live in Toronto and am married to the painter Gilda Mekler. Father of Sarah Deahl. Have been a hard-rock miner, steel-mill labourer, college teacher and financial analyst. Currently edit poetry for Unfinished Monument Press. Serve on the board of directors of the Workers' Educational Association of Canada.

Selected Publications:

Real Poetry: Toronto, Unfinished Monument, 1981. ISBN 0-920976-30-1
In the Lost Horn's Call: Toronto, Aureole Point, 1982. ISBN 0-919915-00-0
No Cold Ash: Victoria, Sono Nis, 1984. ISBN 0-919203-23-X
Blue Ridge: Toronto, Aureole Point, 1985. ISBN 0-919915-06-X
Into This Dark Earth: (with Raymond Souster), Toronto, Unfinished Monument, 1985. ISBN 0-920976-27-1
A Stand of Jackpine: (with Milton Acorn), Toronto, Unfinished Monument, 1987. ISBN 0-920976-31-X

Awards: Mainichi Award (First), 1985
Comments: "His poems have a quiet strength, are restrained, and show his powers of keen observation: the still eye sees deeply." – Laurence Hutchman, *Waves*
"Deahl's work is laid out like a painting, and its energy is generated by contrasts of colours and images apposed on the 'canvas'." – Noah Zacharin, *Rubicon*
Readings, Lectures & Workshops: Read poetry and lecture on literature at universities and high schools in Canada and the U.S.
Mailing Address: Box 909, Adelaide Street Station, Toronto, Ontario M5C 2K3

WILLIAM H. DEVERELL

Born in Regina in 1937, I began my writing career as a journalist, working for several newspapers across Canada and for Canadian Press in Montreal, while studying for my law degree. I have had a law practice in Vancouver since 1964 and am currently practising in Victoria. Former President of the British Columbia Civil Liberties Association. Books have been published in Canada, the U.S. and U.K. and translated into numerous foreign languages. I've written five screenplays and created the CBC-TV series Street Legal.

Selected Publications:

Needles: Toronto, McClelland & Stewart, 1979. ISBN 0-7710-2727-3
High Crimes: Toronto, McClelland & Stewart, 1981. ISBN 0-7710-273-2
Mecca: Toronto, McClelland & Stewart, 1983. ISBN 0-7710-2666-8
The Dance of Shiva: Toronto, McClelland & Stewart, 1984. ISBN 0-7710-2665-X

Awards: Seal First Novel Award, 1979. Periodical Distributors of Canada (Book of the Year), 1981.
Readings, Lectures & Workshops: Canada Council readings.
Mailing Address: N. Pender Island, British Columbia V0N 2M0

MARY DI MICHELE

Born in Italy, August 6, 1949, immigrated to Canada in 1955, I now live in Toronto. B.A., Toronto, 1972; M.A., Windsor, 1974. Poetry editor for Toronto Life (1980-82) and Poetry Toronto (1983-1985). Review and write for Books in Canada, Poetry Canada Review and other literary periodicals.

Selected Publications:

Tree of August: Toronto, Three Trees, 1978. ISBN 0-88823-003-6
Bread and Chocolate: Ottawa, Oberon, 1980. ISBN 0-88750-370-5
Mimosa and Other Poems: Oakville, Mosaic, 1981. ISBN 0-88962-132-2
Necessary Sugar: Ottawa, Oberon, 1983. ISBN 0-88750-508-2
Anything is Possible: (ed.), Oakville, Mosaic, 1984. ISBN 0-88962-251-1
Immune to Gravity: Toronto, McClelland & Stewart, 1986. ISBN 0-7710-2823-7

Awards: CBC Literary Competition, 1st prize (Poetry), 1980. National Magazine Award (Silver), 1982. Air Canada Writing Award, 1983.

Comments: "Feminine, tough, ironic, and unsentimental . . . striking images and sharp insights . . ." – *The Canadian Forum*

"With impressive skill, di Michele turns her hand to a range of ideas and emotions, accompanied by vividly physical images, that are often both contemporary and timeless." – *Books in Canada*

Readings, Lectures & Workshops: Visiting lecturer, Banff Centre, summer 1983. Humber College, writing workshop, spring 1985. University of Toronto, writer-in the-schools programme, February 1987. Readings in high schools, universities across Canada and in Italy.

Mailing Address: 680 Queen's Quay West, #522, Toronto, Ontario M5V 2Y9

JILL DOWNIE

Born in Georgetown, Guyana, and educated in Great Britain and the Channel Islands. Hold a B.A. (Honours) in languages from Bristol University. Immigrated to Canada in 1966 and settled in Burlington, Ontario, in 1971 with my husband, son and daughter and two stepsons. Besides writing full time, I teach Hathayoga and perform in community theatre.

Selected Publications:

Turn of the Century: New York, Avon, 1982. ISBN 0-380-80861-7
Angel in Babylon: Toronto, PaperJacks, 1984. ISBN 0-7701-0293-X
Dark Liaisons: Toronto, PaperJacks, 1985. ISBN 0-7701-0340-5
Mistress of Moon Hill: PaperJacks, 1985. ISBN 0-7701-0424-X

Comments: "(*Turn of the Century*) moves out of the range of the trivial romance and becomes one of those books that lives and lingers in the mind – more, Jill Downie, more!" – L.M., *West Coast Review of Books*
"(In *Mistress of Moon Hill*) Ms. Downie places the reader in the searing, steaming jungles as easily as she evokes the damp chill of England." – *Romantic Times*
"Writers like Jill Downie could give historical romance a good name – (she) combines impeccable research, several strong, unconventional characters, a social conscience." – Marg Langton, *Burlington Post*
Readings, Lectures & Workshops: Readings and lectures at universities, book clubs, university women's clubs and Canadian Authors Association branch meetings. May be booked through TWUC.
Mailing Address: 3129 Centennial Drive, Burlington, Ontario L7M 1B8

MARY ALICE DOWNIE

Born in Illinois, grew up in Toronto and graduated in English. Then the usual range of jobs:
steno pool, editorial assistant, publicity manager
for publisher. In 1959, married John Downie
and moved to Pittsburgh where I wrote film and
book reviews and had two daughters, Christine
and Jocelyn. In 1962 the family moved to
Kingston where we may stay. Alexandra was
born in 1967. Now I write and edit full time.

Selected Publications:

Honor Bound: (with John Downie), Toronto, Oxford, 1971. ISBN 0-19-
540192-1
Dragon on Parade: Toronto, Peter Martin, 1974. ISBN 0-88778-106-3
And Some Brought Flowers: (with Mary Hamilton), Toronto, University of
Toronto Press, 1980. ISBN 0-8020-2363-0
Jenny Greenteeth: Toronto, Kids Can, 1984. ISBN 0-919964-58-3
Alison's Ghosts: (with John Downie), Toronto, Nelson, 1984. ISBN 0-17-
602085-3
The New Wind Has Wings: (with Barbara Robertson), Toronto, Oxford,
1984. ISBN 0-19-54031-9

Awards: CBC Literary Competition, (with John Downie), second prize,
children's story.
Readings, Lectures & Workshops: Have given readings, lectures and
workshops across the country from Prince Edward Island to British Columbia.
May be booked through the TWUC.
Mailing Address: 190 Union Street, Kingston, Ontario K7L 2P6

BRIAN DOYLE

Born in Ottawa, living in Ottawa, staying in Ottawa. Not moving. Not going anywhere. Not budging. In Ottawa, in the backyard, awaiting.

Selected Publications:

Hey Dad: Toronto, Groundwood, 1978. ISBN 0-88899-005-7
You Can Pick Me Up At Peggy's Cove: Toronto, Groundwood, 1979. ISBN 0-88899-003-0
Up to Low: Toronto, Groundwood, 1982. ISBN 0-88899-017-0
Angel Square: Toronto, Groundwood, 1984. ISBN 0-88899-034-0

Awards: Canadian Library Association (Book of the Year), 1984
Comments: "Once you put one of his books down you just can't pick it up again!" – Gene Rheaune, *Ontario Human Rights Commission*
Readings, Lectures & Workshops: Get him out of the backyard, he'll do almost anything.
Mailing Address: 539 Rowanwood Avenue, Ottawa, Ontario K2A 3C9

JAN DRABEK

Born in Czechoslovakia, May 5, 1935. Came to Canada in 1965 after 17 years in the U.S., India, Austria and Germany. Received a B.A. in English Literature from the American University in Washington, D.C. Taught high school in Vancouver for ten years where I now write full time.

Selected Publications:

Blackboard Odyssey: Vancouver, J. J. Douglas, 1973. ISBN 0-88894-039-4
Whatever Happened to Wenceslas?: Toronto, Peter Martin, 1975. ISBN 0-88778-209-4
Melvin the Weather Moose: Toronto, Holt Rinehart & Winston, 1976. ISBN 0-03-923887-3
Report on the Death of Rosenkavalier: Toronto, McClelland & Stewart, 1977. ISBN 0-7710-2880-6
The Lister Legacy: Toronto, General, 1980. ISBN 0-7701-0178-X
The Statement: Toronto, Musson/General, 1982. ISBN 0-7737-0055-2

Comments: ". . . displays a hair trigger sensitivity to the nuances of conversation, an ability to create human characters in a few lines." – *Globe and Mail* (on *Whatever Happened to Wenceslas?*)
"He does more . . . than just entertain. He is interested in the effects of tyranny . . . and the reaction to oppression." – *Winnipeg Free Press*
Readings, Lectures & Workshops: Read regularly across Canada; lecture on the search for peace and the writer's place in it. Teach writing at places like the Banff School of Fine Arts and co-ordinate workshops, among them How To Use Family History as Resource Material in Writing. May be booked through TWUC.
Mailing Address: 3330 W. King Edward, Vancouver, British Columbia V6S 1M3

SHARON DRACHE

Born (Sharon Abron) in Toronto, March 22, 1943, the only child of Edythe (nee Levinter) and Murray Abron. B.A. University of Toronto, 1965. Diploma in Child Study, University of Toronto, 1966. Special student in the Department of Religion, Carleton University, 1974-1978. Married Arthur Barry C. Drache in December, 1965; four children, Deborah, Ruth, Joshua and Mordecai. Now reside in Ottawa.

Selected Publications:

Jeremiah Proosky in the Dancing Sun: Victoria, Press Porcepic, 1981. ISBN 0-88878-196-2

The Mikveh Man and Other Stories: Toronto, Aya, 1984. ISBN 0-920544-37-1

Comments: "An outstanding talent, puckish and surrealistic with overtones of Kafka." – Arnold Ages, *Western Jewish Bulletin*

"Drache's uses of fantasy call to mind I.B. Singer." – Miriam Waddington, *Globe and Mail*

"Rare combination of fantasy, humour and compassion." – Lea Abramowitz, *Jerusalem Post*

Readings, Lectures & Workshops: Often read at bookstores, service clubs and book clubs. Readings booked through the Canada Council or TWUC.

Mailing Address: 19 Clemow Avenue, Ottawa, K1S 2B1

STAN DRAGLAND

Born in Calgary, Alberta, December 2, 1942. Educated at the University of Alberta and Queen's University. Teacher of English at the University of Western Ontario since 1971. Summers on Depot Creek near Bellrock north of Kingston, Ontario.

Selected Publications:

Wilson MacDonald's Western Tour: Toronto, Coach House, 1975. (no ISBN)
Peckertracks: Toronto, Coach House, 1978. ISBN 0-88910-136-1
Simon Jesse's Journey: Toronto, Groundwood, 1983. ISBN 0-88899-025-1
Journeys Through Bookland and Other Passages: Toronto, Coach House, 1984. ISBN 0-88910-278-3

Mailing Address: 47 Briscoe Street West, London, Ontario N6J 1M7

LESLIE DREW

Born and grew up in the Kootenays but I've lived in other regions of British Columbia during a 30-year career as a reporter and editor for daily newspapers. Articles on B.C. historical and native Indian subjects have been published in national magazines.

Selected Publications:

Argillite (Art of the Haida): (with Douglas Wilson), Vancouver, Hancock House, 1980. ISBN 0-88839-037-8

Haida (Their Art and Culture): Vancouver, Hancock House, 1982. ISBN 0-88839-132-3

Comments: "Co-operating in a manner that should be standard for books on ethnic art, but is not . . . The book is a must for collectors of Northwest Coast carving . . . Students of Northwest Coast culture and aesthetics will find this volume valuable as source material . . ." – *Choice*

"A thorough discussion . . . an impressive look into a nearly forgotten world." – *Oregonian*

"By far the most definitive book on argillite carving that has yet appeared." – *Alaska Magazine*

"A dazzling document of Indian culture." – *Vancouver Sun*

Mailing Address: RR 2, 4491 Creighton Road, Duncan, British Columbia V9L 1N9

WAYLAND DREW

Born in Oshawa, Ontario, December 9, 1932. B.A. in English Language and Literature from the University of Toronto (1957). Live with my wife, Gwen, in Bracebridge, Ontario, where I teach English full time at Bracebridge and Muskoka Lakes Secondary School.

Selected Publications:

The Wabeno Feast: Toronto, Anansi, 1973. ISBN 0-88784-425-1
Superior (The Haunted Shore): (with Bruce Littlejohn), Toronto, Gage, 1975. ISBN 0-7715-9320-1
Browns' Weir: (with Gwen Drew), Ottawa, Oberon, 1983. ISBN 0-88750-475-2
A Sea Within (The Gulf of St. Lawrence): (with Bruce Littlejohn), Toronto, McClelland & Stewart, 1984. ISBN 0-7710-5318-5
The Erthring Cycle: New York, Doubleday, 1986. [Published as separate titles by Del Rey/Ballantine Books, The Memoirs of Alcheringia (1984), The Gaian Expedient (1985), The Master of Norriya (1986).]

Comments: "A powerfully realized indictment of civilized man . . . an intensely readable and remarkably effective piece of fiction." — *The Windsor Star* (on *The Wabeno Feast*)

"Some coffee table books are as readable as they are good looking. A season's sample: Best of the lot is *Superior: The Haunted Shore*, a photo-and-text tribute to the raw beauty of the largest and least despoiled Great Lake." — *Time*

"A poem in prose that is a joy to read." — *Arts Atlantic* (on *Browns' Weir*)

"A master of many levels, his history becomes parable, his stories of people long dead become poetry." — *Globe and Mail* (on *A Sea Within*)

"A common enough scenario in sf, but Drew infuses it with drama, eloquence, and passion." — *Locus* (on *The Erthring Cycle*)

Mailing Address: c/o TWUC, 24 Ryerson Avenue, Toronto, Ontario M5T 2P3

MARGARET DRURY-GANE

Toronto-born of British immigrants, two brothers. Oakwood Collegiate Institute then every university course I could cram in while working as an Eaton's copy writer. Married, four children. Mixed short fiction and journalism almost equally until my first novel was published. Second novel, Blissland, is nearly finished. A third, untitled, perking close behind.

Selected Publications:

Parade on an Empty Street: Toronto, Clarke Irwin, 1979. ISBN 0-7720-1169-9

Comments: Insight pieces for Saturday Night, Chatelaine, Weekend (contributing editor), The Canadian and Maclean's. Ten short stories, originally in magazines, soon to be published in collected form.

Mailing Address: c/o TWUC, 24 Ryerson Avenue, Toronto, Ontario M5T 2P3

FRANCES DUNCAN

Born in Vancouver, British Columbia; lived in Saskatchewan and Ontario; now living in Vancouver. B.A. (English and Psychology) University of British Columbia, 1962; M.A. (Psychology), 1963. Worked as a Clinical Psychologist in the Greater Vancouver area 1963-73. Began writing fiction in 1973. Have two daughters, Kelly, b. 1967; Kirsten b. 1968.

Selected Publications:

Cariboo Runaway: Toronto, Burns & MacEachern, 1976. ISBN 0-88768-4
The Toothpaste Genie: Toronto, Scholastic, 1981. ISBN 0-590-71090-7
Dragonhunt: Toronto, Women's Press, 1981. ISBN 0-88961-068-1
Finding Home: New York, Avon, 1982. ISBN 0-380-80143-4
Kap-Sung Ferris: Toronto, Macmillan, 1982. ISBN 0-7715-9606-5

Awards: Greater Vancouver Library Federation Award; 1982, 1983. Surrey Book of the Year Award, 1983.

Comments: "An important work, one which challenges the conventions of Canadian literature, books 'about' women, and realist literature in general." — *Broadside*

"Astonishing, hilarious, touching, and properly inevitable. Duncan's style has an easy page-turning momentum, her ear is faultless and her sensibilities very fine." — *Writers' Quarterly*

"Gracefully written, characters are believable . . . events well-plotted." — *Newsday*

Readings, Lectures & Workshops: Read regularly in schools, libraries and universities. Have been writer-in-residence, editor, creative writing instructor. May be booked through TWUC.

Mailing Address: c/o TWUC, 24 Ryerson Avenue, Toronto, Ontario M5T 2P3

HELEN H.B. DUNCAN

Born in St. Mary's, Ontario. B.A. in French from the University of Toronto and the Sorbonne. B.Sc. in Library Science from the Pratt Institute in Brooklyn. Columbia University Writer's Workshop with Helen Hull. Employed by the Brooklyn Museum of Art in Prospect Park as art librarian and by the NYC office of Reader's Digest as art librarian and art researcher. Forthcoming: Across the Bridge (Simon & Pierre, Toronto).

Selected Publications:

The Treehouse: Toronto, Simon & Pierre, 1975. ISBN 0-88924-040-X
Kate Rice, Prospector: Toronto, Simon & Pierre, 1984. ISBN 0-88924-134-1

Comments: "Her portrait (Kate Rice) is wonderfully balanced by Duncan's lively evocation of the milieu in which Kate lived." – *Globe and Mail*
"Kathleen Rice was assuredly an extraordinary Canadian. Few other University of Toronto gold medallists . . . can have turned to prospecting and trapping in Northern Manitoba as she did from 1911-1941." – *Toronto Star*
Readings, Lectures & Workshops: Lectured at the Canadian Library Association's Conference in Toronto in 1986. Available for readings.
Mailing Address: 7 Relmar Road, Toronto, Ontario M5P 2Y4

SONJA DUNN

Writer, actress, former teacher, television performer and producer. Toronto-born. I found
rhythm in words during my many years of
working with children and teachers as a drama
consultant. Hold B.A. and M.Ed. degrees and
have given keynote addresses and workshops
internationally. My TV show, Sonja Dunn
and Company, broadcast out of Sudbury, has
reached most of Northern Ontario for 20 years.
Volunteer work for Cable 10, Etobicoke: a storytelling show, Sonja's Story Tree, and an adult
show, Books Alive. Freelance for the National
Film Board. Articles have appeared in Sudbury
Star, Drama Contact and Canadian Children's
Literature, among other publications.

Selected Publications:

Butterscotch Dreams: Toronto, Pembroke, 1987. ISBN 0-921217-07-2

Comments: "Sonja Dunn is a happening. Through a mesmerising variety
of genres she enchants and enthralls with a myriad of exciting ways to inte-
grate curriculum through storytelling, puppetry, writing and fine literature."
– *Scarborough and East York Region*
"With a guitar slung over her shoulder, a song in her heart, and a story
for every occasion, Dunn spreads her brand of joy for children." – *Toronto
Star*
Poetry, songs and chants published in anthologies from Gage, Doubleday
and Holt Rinehart & Winston (Impressions Big Book 1 and 2, 1987).
President of CANSCAIP (The Canadian Society of Children's Authors,
Illustrators and Performers) as well as Vice President of CODE (The Council
of Drama Education).
Readings, Lectures & Workshops: Read, perform and lead workshops at
schools, universities, libraries and community events. Storytelling and drama
workshops for educators. Have Story Skirt will travel.
Mailing Address: 401-355 Mill Road, Etobicoke, Ontario M9C 1Y6

BETTY DYCK

Born in Port Arthur, Ontario, May 28, 1932. Now living in Winnipeg. Began writing in 1970. As a freelancer was on editorial staff of Mennonite Mirror for ten years, wrote a family life column for the Prairie Messenger for three years, edited a small magazine, published numerous other articles and poems. Member of Canadian Authors Association since 1973. Associate Member, League of Canadian Poets since 1980. Married, with three children and one grandchild.

Selected Publications:

Ignace (A Saga of the Shield): (with Elinor Barr), Winnipeg, Prairie, 1979. ISBN 0-919576-14-1
Hugging the Meridian, Macdonald (A Manitoba Municipal History, 1881-1981): Macdonald, Municipality of Macdonald, 1981. ISBN 0-88925-237-8

Awards: Kathleen Strange Memorial Award (Service to the Manitoba Branch of CAA), 1976. Honorable Mention, Margaret McWilliams competition (Local History). Manitoba Historical Society Award, 1982. Allan Sangster Award (Service to CAA National), 1986.

Readings, Lectures & Workshops: Have conducted workshops on researching and writing history, under the auspices of the Manitoba Branch of the Canadian Authors Association in conjunction with the provincial Ministry of Culture.

Mailing Address: 11 Tahoe Bay, Winnipeg, Manitoba R2J 2W3

DOROTHY HARLEY EBER

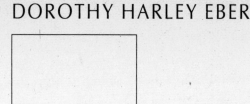

Selected Publications:

The Computer Centre Party (Canada Meets Black Power): Tundra, 1968. (no ISBN)

Pitseolak (Pictures Out Of My Life): Toronto, Oxford, 1971. ISBN 0-19-540191-3

People From Our Side (An Eskimo Life Story In Words And Photographs): (with Peter Pitseolak), Edmonton, Hurtig, 1975. ISBN 0-88830-090-5

Peter Pitseolak's Escape From Death: (ed.), Toronto, McClelland & Stewart, 1977. ISBN 0-7710-3030-4

Genius At Work (Images of Alexander Graham Bell): New York, Viking, 1982. ISBN 0-670-27389-9

Mailing Address: Apt. 1001, 1455 Sherbrooke Street West, Montreal, Quebec H3G 1L2

YEHUDA ELBERG

Born in Poland, May 15, 1912. Education: Rabbinical ordination, textile engineering. Participated in Warsaw-Ghetto underground. Came to the U.S. in 1948; Canada in 1956. Now living in Montreal.

Selected Publications:

On the Tip of A Mast: New York, Shulsinger, 1974.
Scattered Stalks: Montreal, Shula, 1976.
Belev Yam: Tel Aviv, Eked, 1978.
Tales: Tel Aviv, World Council for Jewish Culture, 1980.
The Empire of Kalman the Cripple: Tel Aviv, Israel Book, 1983.
In Clay Houses: Tel Aviv, Israel Book, 1985.

Awards: I.I. Segal Prize, 1975. Weislitz Prize, Australia, 1975. Gonopolsky Prize, Paris, 1977. Manger Prize, Tel Aviv, 1977. Wisenberg Prize, Congress for Jewish Culture, New York 1985.

Comments: "Y.E.'s work has the stamp of authenticity. . . . He writes with a rare, poetic realism . . . Picture follows picture, each more dramatic than the other . . ." – Elie Wiesel, *Algemeiner Journal*

Readings, Lectures & Workshops: Lecture tours in the U.S., 1950-1956; Australia in 1981 and South America in 1985.

Mailing Address: 1745 Cedar Avenue, Apt. 608, Montreal, Quebec H3G 1A7

SARAH ELLIS

Born in Vancouver, May 19, 1952, and still live there. B.A. and M.L.S. from the University of British Columbia, M.A. from Simmons College, Boston. I write a column on Canadian children's books for Hornbook magazine. Work as a librarian and teach the occasional course on children's literature and librarianship when not writing. Interested in storytelling and early music.

Selected Publications:

The Baby Project: Toronto, Groundwood, 1986. ISBN 0-88899-047-2

   Comments: "Ellis writes with a confident, original and authentic voice." – *Globe and Mail*
   "The Baby Project . . . is bright, funny, timely and touching." – *Quill & Quire*
   Readings, Lectures & Workshops: Readings in schools and libraries as well as Young Writers' Conferences.
   Mailing Address: 303 - 2350 West 1st Avenue, Vancouver, British Columbia V6K 1G2

FRANK ETHERINGTON

Born in England, came to Canada in 1967. Journalist. Currently living in Kitchener and working as assistant city editor with the Kitchener-Waterloo Record. Have written stories and plays for children since 1979 and produced material for children between five and 15.

Selected Publications:

The Spaghetti Word Race: Toronto, Annick, 1981. ISBN 0-920236-11-1
Those Words: Toronto, Annick, 1981. ISBN 0-920236-42-1
The General: Toronto, Annick, 1983. ISBN 0-920236-54-5
When I Grow Up Bigger Than Five: Toronto, Annick, 1986. ISBN 0-920303-48-X

Awards: Nineteen Western Ontario newspaper awards in various categories. Honourable Mention, National Newspaper Award.

Comments: The General, now in play form, is produced by Theatre Direct (Canada) in Toronto; also in film-slide version from the National Film Board. Theatre Direct is producing my new play, The Snake Lady, in 1987. These plays go into schools throughout Ontario. I have written a song to use with my most recent book. (I sing and play guitar.)

Readings, Lectures & Workshops: In schools, libraries and bookstores across Canada.

Mailing Address: 140 Water Street South, Kitchener, Ontario N2G 1Z5

CHAD ARTHUR EVANS

Born in Victoria, British Columbia, July 11, 1951. B.A. in English Literature from the University of Victoria; an M.A. in Drama from the University of Toronto. Resided in Australia from 1982 to 1986. Now repatriated, with dual citizenship, I write part time in Victoria.

Selected Publications:

Frontier Theatre (A History of Nineteenth-Century Theatrical Entertainment in the Canadian Far West and Alaska): Victoria, Sono Nis, 1983. ISBN 0-919203-26-4

Comments: "He is a highly competent stylist. This is a remarkable book in every respect." — *Theatre History Studies*

"It would be difficult to imagine how the book could be improved stylistically . . . A landmark achievement in the history of theater in North America." — *Choice*

A Woman for Hanging, a full-length play, was produced by the University of Adelaide, South Australia, July 1986. Currently working on a screenplay adaptation of an unpublished novel for a Vancouver film production company. I have written numerous government publications pertaining to heritage conservation and interpretation.

Mailing Address: c/o V. Evans, #103-1400 Newport Avenue, Victoria, British Columbia V8S 4E9

DOROTHY FARMILOE

Born in Toronto, raised in Windsor, seasoned in the North. M.A. University of Windsor, 1969. Teacher of English, St. Clair College, Windsor, 1969-78. Now live in Elk Lake, Ontario, where I publish and edit The Elk Lake Explorer when I'm not gardening, splitting wood, skiing or shovelling snow. Write and paint in my spare time.

Selected Publications:

Adrenalin of Weather: Toronto, York, 1978. ISBN 0-920424-06-6
How to Write a Better Anything: Windsor, Ont., Black Moss, 1979. ISBN 0-88753-085-3
Words for my Weeping Daughter: Moonbeam, Penumbra, 1981. ISBN 0-920806-08-2
Isabella Valancy Crawford (The Life And Legends): Ottawa, Tecumseh, 1983. ISBN 0-919662-65-X
Elk Lake Lore and Legend: Little Current, Plowshare, 1984. (no ISBN)

Readings, Lectures & Workshops: May be booked through TWUC.
Mailing Address: P.O. Box 94, Elk Lake, Ontario P0J 1G0

CLIFF FAULKNOR

Born in Vancouver, British Columbia, March 3, 1913, now living in Calgary, Alberta. B.S.A. University of British Columbia, 1949; A.A.C.I., Calgary 1976. War service as a marine diesel engineer with Army Water Transport, 1939-45. University student, 1945-49. B.C. Land Inspector, 1949-54. Freelance writer then associate editor for Country Guide, 1954-75. Land appraiser, 1975-78. Member Alberta Land Compensation Board since 1978. Married Elizabeth Sloan, 1943. Two children, Stephen (lawyer) and Noreen (teacher-housewife).

Selected Publications:

The Romance of Beef: Winnipeg, Public Press, 1966. (no ISBN)
The Smoke Horse: London, Dent, 1968. ISBN 0-460-05709-X
West To Cattle Country: Toronto, McClelland & Stewart, 1975. ISBN 0-7710-3106-8
Pen and Plow: Winnipeg, Public Press, 1976. (no ISBN)
Turn Him Loose!: Saskatoon, WP Prairie Books, 1977. (o/p)
Alberta Hereford Heritage: Calgary, Alberta Hereford Assoc., 1981. ISBN 0-969096-50-X
Johnny Eagleclaw: Edmonton, LeBel, 1982. ISBN 0-920008-24-0

Awards: Little Brown Award, 1964. Vicky Metcalf Award, 1979. Canadian Farm Writers Awards; 1961, 68, 69, 73, 74, 75.

Comments: For 11 years I wrote a national column under the pseudonym Pete Williams. My work has been used extensively in elementary and high-school texts. Archival material in The Kerlan Collection (Research Center for Children's Books) at the University of Minnesota. Also personal papers, tear sheets and unpublished manuscripts with the University of Calgary.

Mailing Address: 2919-14th Avenue N.W., Calgary, Alberta T2N 1N3

BRIAN FAWCETT

Born in Prince George, British Columbia, in 1944 and have lived in Vancouver since 1966. Colourful occupations: forest service cruiser, truckdriver, university teacher in federal penitentiaries and urban planner. Colour: fond of impersonating other writers. Best sandlot baseball catcher/writer in Canada.

Selected Publications:

My Career with the Leafs and Other Stories: Vancouver, Talon, 1982. ISBN 0-88922-199-5

Aggressive Transport: Vancouver, Talon, 1982. ISBN 0-88922-187-1

Capital Tales: Vancouver, Talon, 1984. ISBN 0-88922-221-5

The Secret Journal of Alexander Mackenzie: Vancouver, Talon, 1985.

Cambodia (A Book For People Who Find Television Too Slow): Vancouver, Talon, 1986. ISBN 0-88922-237-1

Awards: Senior Sixer, 1st Prince George Cub Pack, 1955. (Free of significant artistic awards and positions of authority since.)

Comments: "These are not ordinary tales. Brian Fawcett has recreated — in microcosm — all our collective childhoods with a deft touch, light heart and humorous style." — *Toronto Star* (on *My Career with the Leafs & Other Stories*)

"Reading *Capital Tales* is like sparring with a skilled prize fighter. Again and again Fawcett aims for the head with acuity and precision . . . Fawcett knows his world. Though these are tales of violence and of crippling ideologies out of control, they are also tales of hope." — *Canadian Book Review Annual*

Mailing Address: 936 East 13th Avenue, Vancouver, British Columbia V5T 2L6

TED FERGUSON

Born in Victoria, British Columbia. Became full-time writer 15 years ago. Have published four non-fiction books, had 30 TV-radio dramas produced (four on CBC Morningside) and written articles for, among others, Canadian Business, Reader's Digest, Equinox and Toronto Life. Now live in Toronto.

Selected Publications:

A White Man's Country: Toronto, Doubleday, 1975. ISBN 0-385-11400-1
Kit Coleman (Queen of Hearts): Toronto, Doubleday, 1978. ISBN 0-385-13447-9
Desperate Siege: Toronto, Doubleday, 1980. ISBN 0-385-14694-9
Sentimental Journey: Toronto, Doubleday, 1985. ISBN 0-385-23252-7

Awards: Alberta Non-Fiction Book Award, 1980. IBAC Silver Leaf (Magazine Article of Year), 1985.

Comments: "A brisk and vivid account." – *Toronto Star* (on *Desperate Siege*)

"Gripping, well-researched." – *Hamilton Spectator*

"One of the year's ten best Canadian books." – *Maclean's* (on *Kit Coleman: Queen of Hearts*)

"A must for all true lovers of railway lore." – *Vancouver Sun* (on *Sentimental Journey*)

Readings, Lectures & Workshops: Have conducted many writing seminars and workshops for colleges, high schools and private groups, such as the Canadian Authors Association. Last speech: Toronto Women's Press Club.

Mailing Address: Apt. 423, 680 Queen's Quay West, Toronto, Ontario M5V 2Y9

TREVOR FERGUSON

Born November 11, 1947, in Ontario. Removed to Montreal at the age of three. Left home early. At 14, deported from the U.S. (Suspicious activity). Drifted to northwest. Heavy equipment operator. The 70s: odd jobs. Then drove a cab by night, writing by day. The 80s: writing. New novel, The Kinkajou, finished fall, 1986. A chapter appeared in The Malahat of June 1986 as First Flames. Frequent contributor to the book pages of the Montreal Gazette. Still living in Montreal with my wife, Lynne. Love her and love my work.

Selected Publications:

High Water Chants: Toronto, Macmillan, 1977. ISBN 0-7705-1568-1
Onyx John: Toronto, McClelland & Stewart, 1985. ISBN 0-7710-3126-2

Comments: "Delightfully idiosyncratic. Ferguson writes as if he were on a wild binge . . . determined to compensate us for all the tidily assembled and yet . . . lifeless novels we've read in the last ten years." – Ken Adachi, *Toronto Star* (on *Onyx John*)

"*Onyx John* took my breath away . . . It is funny and moving . . . it is beautifully written. It is very intelligent, and behind all the entertainment, the marvellous pyrotechnical display, it is an authentic and serious work of art. It is about huge things like magic, love, and guilt. And Ferguson's energy, his narrative drive, is simply dazzling. From Halifax to Victoria, we should all be saying, 'Hats off!' " – Constance Rooke, *The Malahat Review*

"Blackly comic . . . *Onyx John* is funny, tragic, crazy, clever, offensive, erotic, exciting, provocative . . ." – *Winnipeg Free Press*

"An unbuttoned portrait of our times . . . a rollicking binge of a book . . . the novel works, because it never stops humming as fervent fiction."
– *Montreal Gazette*

Readings: May be booked through TWUC.

Mailing Address: c/o Lucinda Vardy Agency, 297 Seaton Street, Toronto, Ontario M5A 2T6

DOUG FETHERLING

Born April 23, 1949. Studied or worked in New York, London, Vancouver and (currently) Toronto. Employed variously as a journalist and as a publisher's editor. Married.

Selected Publications:

The Five Lives of Ben Hecht: Toronto, Lester & Orpen, 1977. ISBN 0-919630-85-5

A George Woodcock Reader: (ed.), Ottawa, Deneau, 1980. ISBN 0-88879-035-X

Variorum (New Poems and Old 1965-1985): Toronto, Hounslow, 1985. ISBN 0-88882-083-6

The Blue Notebook (Reports On Canadian Culture): Oakville, Mosaic, 1986. ISBN 0-88962-320-1

Moving Towards the Vertical Horizon: Toronto, Subway Books, 1986. (no ISBN)

Comments: "A unique consiousness." – Norman Snider, *Globe and Mail*
"Fetherling seldom loses sight of his dream of organic community. His vision is humanist to the core." – Terry Whelan, *Canadian Literature*
"A fine poet and biographer and one of our most talented and perceptive literary journalists . . . devotedly civilized and urbane." – Ken Adachi, *Toronto Star*
"Fetherling is a poet to return to again and again because each reading will uncover new subtleties and pleasures." – Robin Skelton, *Quill & Quire*
Mailing Address: Box 367, Station F, Toronto, Ontario M4Y 2L8

TIMOTHY FINDLEY

Born in Toronto, October 30, 1930. Secondary education terminated by illness in grade 10. Thereafter studied acting in Toronto and London, England. Consequently, professional actor 1950-1962 in Canada, the U.S. and U.K. Professional writer from 1962 to present. Playwright-in-Residence, National Arts Centre, Ottawa, 1974-75; Writer-in-Residence at the University of Toronto, 1979-80; Trent University, 1984; University of Winnipeg, 1985. D. Litt (Hon) Trent University, 1982, and the University of Guelph, 1984. Officer, Order of Canada, 1985.

Selected Publications:

Can You See Me Yet?: Vancouver, Talon, 1977. ISBN 0-88922-119-7
The Wars: Toronto, Penguin, 1978. ISBN 0-14-005011-6
Famous Last Words: Toronto, Penguin, 1982. ISBN 0-14-006268-8
The Last of the Crazy People: Toronto, Penguin, 1983. ISBN 0-14-006846-5
Dinner Along the Amazon: Toronto, Penguin, 1984. ISBN 0-14-007304-3
Not Wanted on the Voyage: Toronto, Penguin, 1985. ISBN 0-14-000306-X
The Butterfly Plague: (revised), Toronto, Penguin, 1986. ISBN 0-14-007305-1
The Telling of Lies: Toronto, Viking/Penguin, 1986. ISBN 0-670-81206-4

Awards: Governor General's Award (Fiction), 1977. City of Toronto Book Award, 1977. Periodical Distributors of Canada Author of the Year, 1983. CBA Author of the Year, 1984. CNIB Talking Book of the Year Award, 1986.

Readings, Lectures & Workshops: Innumerable readings across Canada, in the U.K., Australia, New Zealand and the U.S. Enquiries c/o TWUC or The Colbert Agency.

Mailing Address: c/o Nancy Colbert, The Colbert Agency, 303 Davenport Road, Toronto, Ontario M5R 1K5

ESTHER LEE SOKOLOV FINE

Born in 1941 in inner-city Detroit, daughter of Eugene and Bertha, sister of Joe. B.A., University of Michigan; M.Ed., Ontario Institute for Studies in Education. Immigrated to Canada mid-1960s. Now an inner-city elementary teacher researching collaborative writing with adolescents and working on doctoral thesis in this field. Live in Toronto with 17-year-old daughter Keira and step family, Adrian, Jill and Andrew Adamson. Have publishing company, esPress Canada. Planning more books for, by and about young people.

Selected Publications:

I'm a Child of the City: Toronto, Kids Can, 1973./Rhino, 1979. ISBN 0-920978-01-0

The Double Mirror: Toronto, Kids Can, 1973. (o/p)

The Mushrooming House: Toronto, Kids Can, 1974. (o/p)

We Make Canada Shine: (ed.), Toronto, Lorimer, 1980. ISBN 0-88862-289-9

Awards: Hopwood Award (Fiction), University of Michigan, 1968

Comments: Founding editor of Roll Call, the Toronto Teachers Federation Newspaper (1978-83); contributing editor for Mudpie magazine (1981-85) and founding editor of First Edition, a tabloid of children's writing.

Readings, Lectures & Workshops: Led a Young Authors' Workshop for the Toronto Board of Education in May, 1983. Lectured the Toronto Council for Teachers of Language Arts in April, 1986. Available for readings and collaborative writing workshops in schools, libraries, bookstores and at conferences.

Mailing Address: 138 Keewatin Avenue, Toronto, Ontario M4P 1Z8

JUDYLAINE FINE

I live in Toronto where I have been a freelance writer and journalist for 16 years. I am the editor of Feeling Good, an educational publication of the Canadian Cancer Society that is distributed to 500,000 school children, and the founder and executive vice-president of the Back Association of Canada. I also write a food column for Flare magazine and raise prize-winning lilies.

Selected Publications:

Afraid To Ask (A Book For Families To Share About Cancer): Toronto, Kids Can, 1984. ISBN 0-919964-79-6
Your Guide To Coping With Back Pain: Toronto, McClelland & Stewart, 1985. ISBN 0-7710-3139-4

Comments: "Amazingly lucid descriptions . . . clearer and more thorough than those in many medical textbooks (but) without the medical jargon the language is fully comprehensible to a non-medical person." – *Canadian Medical Association Journal*
"A calm, useful book." – *New York Times Book Review*
"Fine's gift for simile helps answer . . . scientific puzzlements." – *Kirkus Reviews*
"Afraid to Ask is a book badly needed." – *Healthsharing*
Readings, Lectures & Workshops: Readings and lectures for high schools and community groups on the subjects of back pain and cancer as well as the role of our health-care system. May be booked through the Back Association of Canada. (416) 967-4670.
Mailing Address: 83 Cottingham Street, Toronto, Ontario M4V 1B9

JOAN FINNIGAN (MACKENZIE)

 Born and raised in Ottawa, Ontario. Attended Lisgar Collegiate, Carleton and Queen's. Husband, Dr. Charles Grant MacKenzie, died in 1965. Since then continuous freelance writing for the National Film Board, the CBC and book publishers; poetry, short stories, screenplays, history, biography, oral history, humour and literary history. Three children: Dr. Jonathan MacKenzie, Ottawa; Roderick MacKenzie, lawyer, McCarthy & McCarthy, Toronto; Martha (Mrs. Louis Vezina), teacher, Ottawa. Permanent address is Hartington, Ontario, but Winter Works address is Aylmer, Quebec.

Selected Publications:

Entrance to the Greenhouse: Toronto, Ryerson, 1968. ISBN 0-7700-0256-0
It Was Warm and Sunny When We Set Out: Toronto, Ryerson, 1970. ISBN 0-7700-0313-3
I Come From the Valley: Toronto, NC Press, 1976. ISBN 0-919600-55-7
Kingston (Celebrate This City): Toronto, McClelland & Stewart, 1976. 0-7710-3162-0
Some of the Stories I Told You Were True: Ottawa, Deneau, 1981. ISBN 0-88879-066-X
Look! The Land is Growing Giants: Montreal, Tundra, 1983. ISBN 0-88776-151-8
Laughing All the Way Home: Ottawa, Deneau, 1984. ISBN 0-88879-103-8
Legacies, Legends and Lies: Toronto, Deneau, 1985. ISBN 0-88879-120-8

Awards: President's Medal (Poetry), University of Western Ontario, 1969. Philemon Wright Award (Ottawa Valley History), 1983. The first Ottawa-Carleton Literary Award, 1985.

Readings, Lectures & Workshops: So numerous that I don't keep track.

Mailing Address: 59 Broad Street, Aylmer, Quebec J9H 4H7 (Winters)

PEGGY FLETCHER

Artist-Writer. Born in St. John's, Newfoundland, in 1930. Married to John Drage, poet. Five daughters. Editor of Mamashee. Taught writing and visual arts at the University of Western Ontario in 1981. Entrepreneur. Co-own studio at Reeces Corners. Member of the Artists Workshop (WITs), Sarnia. Published in little mags. Write for CBC. Completed three novels. Working on another. Guard privacy. Celebrate life. Survive.

Selected Publications:

The Hell-Seekers: Fredericton, Fiddlehead, 1971. ISBN 0-919196-64-3
Impulse on the Run: Cornwall, Vesta, 1976. ISBN 0-919806-08-02
When the Moon is Full: Cornwall, Vesta, 1977. ISBN 0-919806-28-7

Awards: Canadian One Act Play Competition (Third Prize), 1983
Readings, Lectures & Workshops: Poetry readings in Sarnia, London, Windsor, Collingwood, Edmonton and Halifax. Workshops and lectures on creative writing in Sarnia, Ontario.
Mailing Address: RR 1, Wyoming, Ontario N0N 1T0

HELEN FORRESTER (JUNE BHATIA)

Born in Hoylake, Cheshire, England, June 6, 1919. Now reside in Edmonton, Alberta. Fifteen years in business and social work, 36 years as a writer.

Selected Publications:

Most Precious Employee: London, Robert Hale, 1976. ISBN 0-7091-5173-X
Twopence To Cross The Mersey: London, The Bodley Head, 1979. ISBN 0-370-30196-X
Minerva's Stepchild: London, The Bodley Head, 1979. ISBN 0-370-30197-8
Liverpool Daisy: London, Robert Hale, 1979. ISBN 0-7091-7731-3
By The Waters Of Liverpool: London, The Bodley Head, 1981. ISBN 0-370-30909-X
Lime Street At Two: London, The Bodley Head, 1981. ISBN 0-370-30886-7
The Latchkey Kid: London, Robert Hale, 1985. ISBN 0-7090-2156-9
Thursday's Child: London, Collins, 1985. ISBN 0-00-222963-3

Awards: Hudson's Bay Co. Beaver Awards, 1970 and 1977. Honoured by City of Edmonton for distinguished contribution to the literary life of the city, 1977. Alberta Achievement Award for Literature, 1979. Alberta Culture Award (Non-fiction), 1986.

Comments: All my books, except for *Most Precious Employee*, are available in paperback from Collins-Fontana as of 1987.

Readings, Lectures & Workshops: Innumerable.

Mailing Address: c/o TWUC, 24 Ryerson Avenue, Toronto, Ontario M5T 2P3

JANET FOSTER

Born in Ottawa. Danced professionally with the National Ballet of Canada. Graduated Toronto and York universities with B.A., M.A. and Ph.D. in Canadian history. Television writer and co-host of 25 one-hour wilderness specials. Nature photographer and author of non-fiction books, articles and stories for adults and children. Based in Toronto and working full time as a photographer, film maker and writer.

Selected Publications:

To the Wild Country: Toronto, Van Nostrand Reinhold, 1975. ISBN 0-442-29947-8

Working for Wildlife: Toronto, University of Toronto Press, 1978. ISBN 0-8020-5399-8

A Cabin Full of Mice: Toronto, Greey de Pencier, 1980. ISBN 0-919872-49-2

The Wilds of Whip-poor-will Farm: Toronto, Greey de Pencier, 1982. ISBN 0-919872-79-4

Adventures in Wild Canada: (with John Foster), Toronto, McClelland and Stewart, 1984. ISBN 0-7710-3191-2

Comments: Writings and stories are all based on personal explorations in Canada's wilderness regions and true life encounters with wildlife. Readings are accompanied by a variety of slide programmes suitable for all ages from kindergarten to adults.

Readings, Lectures & Workshops: A professional still photographer, specialising in nature and wildlife, I give many public slide lectures to adult audiences as well as special programmes based on wildlife experiences and writings to elementary and high-school children. Lectures may be booked through TWUC.

Mailing Address: c/o TWUC, 24 Ryerson Avenue, Toronto, Ontario M5T 2P3

TONY FOSTER

Born in Winnipeg in 1932; schools in Canada, the U.S., England. Ph.D. in Economics from the University of Mexico, 1959. Merchant seaman, RCAF, US Special Forces, Korean War: crop-duster, bush, airline and executive pilot (13,000 flying hours). Smuggler, Latin American revolutionary; CEO several U.S., Canadian and international companies; served time in Latin American, U.S. and Canadian prisons. Began writing in jail at Terminal Island, California, 1976. Full-time fiction, non-fiction, screenplay and script writer.

Selected Publications:

By Pass: Toronto, Methuen, 1983. ISBN 0-458-96080-2
The Money Burn: Toronto, Methuen, 1984. ISBN 0-458-98150-8
Heart of Oak: Toronto, Methuen, 1985. ISBN 0-458-80130-5
A Coeur Ouvert: St. Laurent, P.Q., Trecarre, 1985. ISBN 2-89249-095-2
Meeting of Generals: Toronto, Methuen, 1986. ISBN 0-458-80520-3
Sea Wings: Toronto, Methuen, 1986. ISBN 0-458-80410-X
Rue Du Bac: Toronto, Methuen, 1987. ISBN 0-458-99860-5
Muskets to Missiles: Toronto, Methuen, 1987. ISBN 0-458-81220-X

Awards: Canadian Authors Association Award (Non-Fiction), 1987. Evelyn Richardson Memorial Prize (Non-Fiction), 1987.

Comments: Script credits include Green for the Grass, The Rockford Files, Streets of San Francisco, The Eagle and the Crown, The Sound and the Silence and for CBC radio drama Mabel Bell (a ten-part series, 1985) and A Lady with Style (a five-part series, 1985).

Readings, Lectures & Workshops: Occasional lecturer at Dalhousie University. Regional elementary, junior-high and high-school appearances. Workshops on script writing (TV, film, radio).

Mailing Address: 67 Briarwood Crescent, Halifax, Nova Scotia B3M 1P2

EDITH FOWKE

Born in Lumsden, Saskatchewan, of Irish parents. Took B.A. and M.A. in English at the University of Saskatchewan. Wrote many scripts on folk songs and folklore for CBC radio. Collected folksongs and children's lore, mainly in Ontario. Produced eight records of songs by traditional singers. Joined York University as an English professor to teach folklore.

Selected Publications:

Sally Go Round the Sun: Toronto, McClelland & Stewart, 1969. ISBN 0-7710-3165-3

Folklore of Canada: Toronto, McClelland & Stewart, 1976. ISBN 0-7710-3202-1

Folktales of French Canada: Toronto, NC Press, 1979. ISBN 0-919601-61-8

A Bibliography of Canadian Folklore in English: Toronto, University of Toronto Press, 1981. ISBN 0-8020-2394-0

Riot of Riddles: Toronto, Scholastic, 1982. ISBN 0-590-71092-3

Songs and Sayings of an Ulster Childhood: (with Alice Kane), Toronto, McClelland & Stewart, 1983. ISBN 0-7710-3210-2

Lumbering Songs from the Northern Woods: Toronto, NC Press, 1985. ISBN 0-920053-51-3

Explorations in Canadian Folklore: (ed.), Toronto, McClelland & Stewart, 1985. ISBN 0-7710-1909-2

Tales Told in Canada: Toronto, Doubleday, 1986. ISBN 0-385-25109-2

The Penguin Book of Canadian Folk Songs: Toronto, Penguin, 1986. ISBN 0-14-070842-1

Awards: Canadian Children's Librarians Award (Book of the Year), 1970. Order of Canada, 1978. Vicky Metcalf Award, 1985. Honorary degrees from Trent, Brock and York universities.

Mailing Address: 5 Notley Place, Toronto, Ontario M4B 2M7

MARIAN FOWLER

Born in Newmarket, Ontario; graduated in 1951 with a B.A. in English and the Governor General's Gold Medal from the University of Toronto. Married, 1953; divorced, 1971. Ph.D. in English, University of Toronto, 1970. Taught at Atkinson College, York University, Toronto, 1970-82. Now write full time, spending summer months in a country house near Shelburne, Ontario, and winter months abroad, usually in London.

Selected Publications:

The Embroidered Tent (Five Gentlewomen in Early Canada): Toronto, Anansi, 1982. ISBN 0-88784-091-4
Redney (A Life of Sara Jeannette Duncan): Toronto, Anansi, 1983. ISBN 0-88784-099-X
Below the Peacock Fan (First Ladies of the Raj): Toronto, Viking/Penguin, 1987. ISBN 0-670-80748-6

Awards: Canadian Biography Award, Association for Canadian Studies
Comments: "One of Canada's best biographers." – *Edmonton Journal*
"Fowler is both scholarly and tart, with demure but irrepressible wit."
– *Maclean's*
"Fowler's scholarship is impeccable, but she also allows her intuition to flourish. The combination is rare and admirable." – *Ottawa Citizen*
Readings, Lectures & Workshops: Lectures and readings abroad include: the Italian Association for Canadian Studies Annual Symposium, Sicily, 1983; the Canadian Academic Centre, Rome, 1983; the Edinburgh University, 1983; and the British Association for Canadian Studies, Birmingham, England, 1984.
Mailing Address: Kilmara, RR 2, Lisle, Ontario L0M 1M0

DIANE FRANCIS

 Born in Chicago, Illinois, November 14, 1946, and immigrated to Canada in 1966. After a business career and staying at home to raise two children, I became a journalist in 1976. Now a columnist and broadcaster, I live in Missis-sauga, Ontario.

Selected Publications:

Controlling Interest (Who Owns Canada?): Toronto, Macmillan, 1986. ISBN
 0-7715-9744-4

Awards: Royal Bank Business Feature Award, 1982. Canadian Petroleum
Association Energy Writing Awards, 1983, 84, 86.
Comments: "I like this book because it is needed and should be read by
Canadians everywhere." – Eric Kierans, *Montreal Gazette*
"Diane Francis' book, which describes the causes and effects of corporate
concentration in Canada, may well be the most important book about Cana-
dian business in a decade." – Andrew Allentuck, *Quill & Quire*
"As a polemicist, Francis has few peers." – Rod McQueen, *Canadian
Business*
Mailing Address: c/o TWUC, 24 Ryerson Avenue, Toronto, Ontario
M5T 2P3

WOLFGANG E. FRANKE

 Born in Horstmar, Germany, in 1915. Sold my first story at age 15 in Kiel. Studied and worked in 23 countries. Survived four years in communist camps in the Balkans (1945-49). Got hooked on Canada in 1951. Hold a B.A. from the University of Toronto and an M.Sc. from the University of Ottawa.

Selected Publications:

Goldenrod: Toronto, Trans-Canada, 1983. ISBN 0-920966-21-7
The Baltimore Connection: Toronto, Williams-Wallace, 1984. ISBN 0-88795-032-9

Comments: "A wholesome story of young love triumphing over the odds of family, church and society prejudice. A good addition to the ranks of light fiction by Canadian authors." – *Winnipeg Free Press*

"Franke is most effective in the characterisation of strong, positive and determined young people; he is also able to convey the strength of their feelings, and to sympathise with their difficulties when confronted with the juggernaut of an unbending educational system." – *Toronto Star*

"A compassionate and honest narrative." – *Kingston Whig-Standard*

"The main theme of the book is intriguing: the protaganist is ordered to take on the identity of a dead American airman who has the same name. Thus disguised, the young Alex Ripley is handed the job of assassinating an intrepid British agent. The almost father-son relationship that develops between the two men is well handled, forging an affection that later becomes the youth's lifeline." – Sidney Allinson, *Canadian Book Review Annual* (on *The Baltimore Connection*)

"A strikingly new voice in Canadian literature." – Prof. H. Froeshle
Mailing Address: 302 Ellerslie Avenue, Willowdale, Ontario M2R 1B7

BILL FREEMAN

Born in London, Ontario, October 21, 1938. Raised in a school teachers' family in London. After high school, lived and worked in Alberta and England. Returned to Canada in 1961. Graduated from Acadia University, Wolfville, Nova Scotia, in 1964. Since then a varied career as a social worker, graduate student, community activist, teacher, trade union militant and writer. Received an M.A. in Sociology in 1970, and a Ph.D.in Sociology in 1979, both from McMaster University in Hamilton. Lived in Hamilton from 1965 to 1976 and Montreal from 1976 to 1986. Currently living on Ward's Island in Toronto. Father of four children.

Selected Publications:

Shantymen of Cache Lake: Toronto, Lorimer, 1975. ISBN 0-88862-091-8
Last Voyage of the Scotian: Toronto, Lorimer, 1976. ISBN 0-88862-113-2
Cedric and the North End Kids: Toronto, Lorimer, 1978. ISBN 0-88862-177-9
Their Town (The Mafia, the Media and the Party Machine): (with Marsha Hewitt), Toronto, Lorimer, 1979. ISBN 0-88862-266-X
1005 (Political Life in a Local Union): Toronto, Lorimer, 1981. ISBN 0-88862-550-2
Harbour Thieves: Toronto, Lorimer, 1984. ISBN 0-88862-747-5

Awards: Canada Council Children's Literature Award, 1976. Vicky Metcalf Award (A Body of Work), 1984.

Readings, Lectures & Workshops: I have had a wide experience as a writer, lecturer and teacher. Not only will I read from my books to young people in elementary schools but I like to talk to audiences about the way fiction can make historical periods come alive.

Mailing Address: 16 Third Street, Ward's Island, Toronto, Ontario M5J 2B2

DORIS CAVELL FRENCH (SHACKLETON)

Born in Saskatchewan in 1918 (consequently a broad education but no university degrees). Moved to Ottawa in 1944. Worked from 1936 on as a waitress, teacher, sales clerk, political writer, political organiser, broadcaster (CBC Ottawa), editor (Statistics Canada, Health & Welfare, et al.) and author. Ran twice as NDP federal candidate. Councillor, Township of Gloucester, 1976-78. Married first, Rob French; second, Philip Shackleton.

Selected Publications:

Ask No Quarter: (with Margaret Stewart), Toronto, Longmans, 1959. (no ISBN)
Faith, Sweat and Politics: Toronto, McClelland & Stewart, 1962. (no ISBN)
High Button Bootstraps: Toronto, Ryerson, 1968. (no ISBN)
Tommy Douglas: Toronto, McClelland & Stewart, 1975. ISBN 0-7710-8116-2
Powertown: Toronto, McClelland & Stewart, 1977. ISBN 0-7710-8100-6

    Comments: Contributed to The Clear Spirit (Twenty Canadian Women and Their Times), (University of Toronto Press, 1966). Recent short stories include The Small House in The Antigonish Review, No. 62-63, 1985.
    Forthcoming: Ishbel and the Empire, Biography of Lady Ishbel, Countess of Aberdeen.
    Shorter published work, fiction as well as non-fiction.
    Mailing Address: Box 29, RR 5, Gloucester, Ontario K1G 3N3

MARK FRUTKIN

Ottawa writer, editor and journalist. I have published two books of poetry and two books of fiction in Canada, England and Holland. Poetry has been translated into Hindi and Punjabi and published widely in India. Studied with Allen Ginsberg, John Ashbery and Robert Duncan. Have written on art and books for the Canadian Forum, the Ottawa Citizen, Harper's and others. Fiction and poetry have been published widely in Canadian journals.

Selected Publications:

Opening Passages: Ottawa, Bakti Press, 1977. ISBN 0-9690736-0-7
The Growing Dawn: Dunvegan, Quadrant, 1984. ISBN 0-86495-023-3
The Alchemy of Clouds: Fredericton, Fiddlehead, 1985. ISBN 0-86492-060-1

Comments: "Alchemy exists in his ability to open our eyes to the commonplace" – *Toronto Star* (on *The Alchemy of Clouds*)
"Brilliant tight poems." – *Poetry Canada Review*
"The story of Marconi has been written before but never quite with the same daring and invention." – Peter Gzowski, *Morningside* (on *The Growing Dawn*)

Readings, Lectures & Workshops: Have read widely in Canada and India (available for readings anytime). Also have done performance art and performance poetry, as well as art installations. Currently, Editor of CARFAC News, the national magazine of Canadian Artists' Representation.

Mailing Address: 15 Heney Street, Ottawa, Ontario K1N 5V5

MARY BEACOCK FRYER

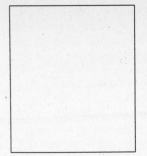

Born in Brockville, Ontario, a city started by United Empire Loyalists following the American Revolution. This helps explain my preoccupation with Ontario's founders. Hold a B.A. in geography from the University of Toronto and an M.A. in historical geography from Edinburgh University. Live in Toronto, but do most of my writing in the summer at a cottage in the Thousand Islands.

Selected Publications:

King's Men (The Soldier Founders of Ontario): Toronto, Dundurn, 1980. ISBN 0-919670-51-2
The Rideau (A Pictorial History of the Waterway): (with A.G. Ten Cate), Brockville, Besancourt, 1981. ISBN 0-920032-04-4
Escape (Adventures of a Loyalist Family): Toronto, Dundurn, 1982. ISBN 0-919670-60-1
Lives of the Princesses of Wales.: Toronto, Dundurn, 1983. ISBN 0-919670-68-7
Allen Maclean (Portrait of an 18th Century Career Soldier): Toronto, Dundurn, 1987. ISBN 1-5502-009-9

Comments: "Mary Fryer . . . has made a valuable contribution to a clearer understanding of our country's origins." — Robert Duffy, *Toronto Star*
"No one who reads *Escape* could afterwards fail to detect the human dramas between the lines of the historical accounts of the European settlements of Ontario." — *St. Catharines Standard*
Readings, Lectures & Workshops: Have read in elementary and secondary schools around Ontario and Prince Edward Island. Have lectured to historical and genealogical societies.
Mailing Address: Apt. 107, 335 Lonsdale Road, Toronto, Ontario M5P 1R4

PRISCILLA GALLOWAY

Author, teacher and grandmother, I have lived and worked in Metro Toronto since 1953, with scuba excursions to points south. Born in Montreal in 1930, I lived in Victoria and Ottawa as well as northern mining towns before settling in Toronto. Although I write mostly for children, my Ph.D. study examined sexism in school English programmes. With early retirement after three decades in public education, I am exploring the delights and vicissitudes of full-time authorship.

Selected Publications:

What's Wrong With High School English? . . . It's Sexist, Un-Canadian, Outdated: Toronto, OISE, 1980. ISBN 0-7744-0197-4

Good Times, Bad Times, Mummy and Me: Toronto, Women's Press, 1980. ISBN 0-88961-066-5

Timely and Timeless (Contemporary Prose): (ed.), Toronto, Clarke Irwin, 1983. ISBN 0-7720-1409-4

When You Were Little and I Was Big: Toronto, Annick, 1984. ISBN 0-920236-84-7

Jennifer Has Two Daddies: Toronto, Women's Press, 1985. ISBN 0-88961-095-9

Comments: "Gimlet-eyed and devastating." – Michele Landsberg, *Women And Children First*

"Priscilla Galloway has captured the anomalous feelings of a child about her working mother without being moralistic or pedantic." – Robert Munsch, *Canadian Children's Literature*

"A trail-blazer." – John Brown, *Christchurch (New Zealand) Star*

Readings, Lectures & Workshops: I work with librarians, teachers and parents across Canada to celebrate Canadian books for young people. I've also led workshops helping others to improve and market their own writing. May be booked through TWUC.

Mailing Address: 12 Didrickson Drive, North York, Ontario M2P 1J6

GEORGE GALT

Born in Winnipeg, Manitoba, in 1948. Lived in Montreal until 1970, then in Ottawa, Greece and North Fredericksburgh County near Napanee, Ontario. Have written for Saturday Night, Books in Canada, Canadian Geographic and Canadian Heritage.

Selected Publications:

Trailing Pythagoras: Dunvegan, Quadrant, 1982. ISBN 0-86495-016-0
Whistle Stop (A Journey Across Canada): Toronto, Methuen, 1987. ISBN 0-458-80510-6

Comments: *"Trailing Pythagoras* is a fascinating account of travels in the Aegean, which is also a series of meditations and reflections upon Greek history and the Greek character." – *Malahat Review*
"That little gem of a book." – George Woodcock, *Ottawa Citizen*
Mailing Address: c/o TWUC, 24 Ryerson Avenue, Toronto, Ontario M5T 2P3

LAWRENCE GARBER

Born in Toronto, Ontario, May 24, 1937. Now residing in London, Ontario. Ph.D. (1973), University of Toronto. Associate Professor (English), University of Western Ontario. My academic career has been broken intermittently by European travel and residences abroad (Paris, Spain, Italy). Married Carole Soskin in 1967; one daughter, Jennifer. My work is mainly of a fantasist or international nature; inevitably comic.

Selected Publications:

Tales from the Quarter: Toronto, Peter Martin, 1969. (no ISBN)
Circuit: Toronto, Anansi, 1970. ISBN 0-88784-414-6
Visions Before Midnight in *Penguin Book Of Canadian Short Stories*: Toronto, Penguin, 1980. ISBN 0-14-00-5673-4
Sirens and Graces: Toronto, Stoddart, 1983. ISBN 0-7737-0069-2

Comments: "Garber is one of the few Canadian writers to have successfully combined experimentalism with realism." — Wayne Grady, *The Penguin Book of Canadian Short Stories*
Mailing Address: 199 Regent Street, London, Ontario N6A 2G9

JOE GARNER

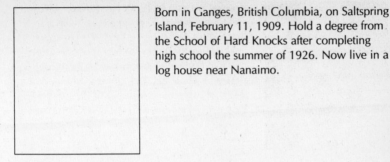

Born in Ganges, British Columbia, on Saltspring Island, February 11, 1909. Hold a degree from the School of Hard Knocks after completing high school the summer of 1926. Now live in a log house near Nanaimo.

Selected Publications:

Never Fly Over an Eagles Nest: Lantzville, Oolichan, 1980. ISBN 0-88982-035-X

Never a Time to Trust: Nanaimo, Cinnabar, 1984. ISBN 0-9691343-1-2

Mailing Address: Box 392, Nanaimo, British Columbia V9R 5L3

GREG GATENBY

Born in Toronto in 1950. Graduated from Glendon College, York University with a B.A. (English) in 1972. Since 1975 I've been the artistic director of the reading series and International Festival of Authors at Harbourfront. Active in whale and dolphin research and conservation. Executive member of PEN and the Writers' Development Trust. Live, with pride, in Toronto.

Selected Publications:

Whale Sound: Vancouver, Douglas & McIntyre, 1977. ISBN 0-88894-135-8
The Salmon Country: Windsor, Black Moss, 1981. ISBN 0-88753-045-1
Growing Still: Windsor, Black Moss, 1981. ISBN 0-88753-075-3
Whales (A Celebration): Toronto, Lester & Orpen Dennys, 1983. ISBN 0-13-951723-5

Awards: Jerusalem Book Fair Art Book Prize, 1983/84
Comments: "A number of poems in *Growing Still* are vital and alive . . . he is in good company: F.R. Scott and Irving Layton . . . " – Judith Fitzgerald, *Quill & Quire*
"*Whale Sound* . . . is a splendid, moving and very beautiful book." – Margaret Laurence, *Toronto Star*
"*Whales: A Celebration* is . . . a lavish, artistic tribute to all cetacea." – *New York Times Book Review*
Readings, Lectures & Workshops: Read and lecture regularly at universities and literary festivals around the world.
Mailing Address: Harbourfront Reading Series, 410 Queen's Quay West, Toronto, Ontario M5V 2Z3

TONY GERMAN

Born in Ottawa in 1924, schooled there and at Trinity College School, Port Hope, then to sea in the Canadian Navy during WW II. Left the Navy in 1966 after commanding three ships and started my own business. Director of Development at Ashbury College, 1972-77. With my wife, Sage, I live in the Gatineau Hills. We have four children and a growing number of grandchildren.

Selected Publications:

Tom Penny: Toronto, McClelland & Stewart, 1977. ISBN 0-7710-3265-X
River Race: Toronto, McClelland & Stewart, 1979. ISBN 0-88778-194-2
Tom Penny and the Grand Canal: Toronto, McClelland & Stewart, 1982.
   ISBN 0-7710-3260-9
A Breed Apart: Toronto, McClelland & Stewart, 1985. ISBN 0-7710-3266-8

  Comments: "German writes fast-paced adventure tales with attractive (at least partly because they are fallible) adolescent heroes, but what distinguishes the stories is the quality of the historical research. German is writing fiction but he is doing it within an authentic framework, one that gives flavour and verve to his narrative." – Sandra Martin, *Globe and Mail*
  "German's tight prose and his handling of dialects and characters recall the traditions of Stevenson and Twain." – *Quill & Quire*
  Readings, Lectures & Workshops: I enjoy reading to young people age nine through high school. Have given courses on writing at the University of Ottawa, Continuing Education, 1983-85; and workshops on aspects of history and writing.
  Mailing Address: Kingsmere, Old Chelsea, Quebec J0X 2N0

C.H. (MARTY) GERVAIS

I am a poet, playwright, journalist and the publisher of Black Moss Press. I have won numerous journalism awards and have travelled extensively throughout the world. My plays have toured Ontario theatres. I hold an M.A. in English from the University of Windsor where I studied creative writing under Morley Callaghan.

Selected Publications:

The Rumrunners: Toronto, Firefly, 1980. ISBN 0-920668-08-9
Into a Blue Morning: Toronto, Hounslow, 1982. ISBN 0-88882-063-1
Letters from the Equator: Moonbeam, Penumbra, 1986. ISBN 0-920806-87-2

Awards: Western Ontario Newspaper Awards; 1983, 1984, 1985
Comments: Profiled in Books in Canada (January-February, 1985) and Writer's Quarterly (Fall 1985).
Readings, Lectures & Workshops: Read regularly at universities and colleges and lecture on the prohibition period at service clubs and genealogical societies. May be booked through TWUC.
Mailing Address: 1939 Alsace Street, Windsor, Ontario M8W 1M5

CAROLE GIANGRANDE

 Born in Mount Vernon, New York, January 20, 1945. Came to Canada in 1962 to attend the University of Toronto. Hold a B.A. and an M.A. in Political Science. Besides writing books, short articles and book reviews, I have had extensive experience as a broadcast journalist for CBC Radio, where I have worked both full time and freelance since 1973. I now live and write in Cobourg, a quiet town on the shores of Lake Ontario.

Selected Publications:

The Nuclear North (The People, the Regions, and the Arms Race): Toronto, Anansi, 1983. ISBN 0-88784-136-8
Down To Earth (The Crisis in Canadian Farming): Toronto, Anansi, 1985. ISBN 0-88784-147-3

Comments: "*The Nuclear North* is one of the most readable, thoughtful and comprehensive overviews of the Canadian uranium and weapons connection ever published." – *Saskatoon Star-Phoenix*
"A readable, sensitive portrayal of the people behind the bombs." – *Toronto Star*
"*Down To Earth* is not a book for everyone . . . only those who eat." – *Kingston Whig-Standard*

Readings, Lectures & Workshops: I enjoy giving talks, lectures and workshops on agricultural concerns, peace and disarmament issues and writing and broadcasting skills.

Mailing Address: 545 Lakeshore Road, Cobourg, Ontario K9A 1S4

GRAEME GIBSON

Born in London, Ontario, in 1934, I have lived in various parts of Canada, in Australia, England, France, Germany, Mexico, Scotland and the U.S. I now live in Toronto.

Selected Publications:

Eleven Canadian Novelists: Toronto, Anansi, 1973. ISBN 0-88784-615-7
Perpetual Motion: Toronto, McClelland & Stewart, 1982. ISBN 0-7710-3291-9
Five Legs/Communion: Toronto, McClelland & Stewart, 1983 (first published 69/71). ISBN 0-7710-9328-4

Awards: First recipient of the Canada/Scotland Fellowship
Comments: Active in cultural politics since the early 70s, I was one of the organisers of TWUC and its chairman in 1974-75. As chairman of the Union I was a founding member of the Book and Periodical Development Council and was that group's chairman in 1975. I am also active in PEN and the Writers' Development Trust.
Readings, Lectures & Workshops: I have conducted workshops at the University of Guelph, York University, Port Townsend and Aspen, Colorado. I was writer-in-residence at the Universities of Ottawa and Waterloo and have read from my work in Europe, Latin America, India and Australia as well as across Canada and in the U.S.
Mailing Address: c/o TWUC, 24 Ryerson Avenue, Toronto, Ontario M5T 2P3

WILLIAM MORRISON GIBSON

Born in Scotland in 1916. Graduated as a physician, September, 1939 (Glasgow University). Served with the British Army as a medical officer, 1940-1946. Worked as a G.P. in England, 1946-1955. Emigrated to Okotoks, Alberta, in 1955 with my wife Janet (also a doctor) and Catriona, our daughter. In 1971 was appointed professor and head of the division of family practice at the University of Calgary. Retired in 1978 and have since written three books.

Selected Publications:

One Man's Medicine: Toronto, Collins, 1981. ISBN 0-00-216831-6
A Doctor in the West: Toronto, Collins, 1983. ISBN 0-00-217119-5
A Doctor's Calling: Vancouver, Douglas & McIntyre, 1986. ISBN 0-88894-521-3

Awards: Fellow, College of Family Physicians of Canada 1977. Hon. Doctor of Laws, University of Calgary 1986.

Comments: My special interests have been family or general practice, for the last ten years as teacher as well as practitioner. I think it is fair to claim that I was a pioneer in the use of medical hypnosis.

Readings, Lectures & Workshops: I have lectured on various medical subjects at Canadian, British, American and New Zealand universities and was a visiting professor in New Zealand in 1977.

Mailing Address: Site 292, RR 2, Courtney, British Columbia V9N 5M9

MICHAEL A. GILBERT

 Born in Brooklyn, New York, October 31, 1945. Received a B.A. from Hunter College, City University of New York, 1966. Attended State University of New York/Buffalo until moving to Canada in 1968. Received a Ph.D. in philosophy from the University of Waterloo, 1973. After teaching at the University of Toronto for two years, received an appointment at York University where I am now associate professor of philosophy and sometime teacher of creative writing.

Selected Publications:

How To Win an Argument: New York, McGraw-Hill, 1979. ISBN 0-07-023215-6

Office Party: New York, Simon & Schuster/Pocketbooks, 1981. ISBN 0-671-45524-9

Yellow Angel: New York, Simon & Schuster/Pocketbooks, 1985. ISBN 0-671-54425-X

Awards: Best All-Around Camper, Toro Hill Lodge Day Camp, 1952

Comments: "A neatly written little book . . . a commentary on the human way of thought." – *Vancouver Sun* (on *How to Win an Argument*)

"Psychologically astute probing of moral gray areas." – *Library Journal* (on *Office Party*)

"Psychologically sound and compelling." – *Publishers Weekly*

"One of the most enjoyable reads to come off the presses in quite some time." – *Calgary Herald* (on *Yellow Angel*)

Readings, Lectures & Workshops: In addition to fiction readings and talks on the art of argument, I offer workshops on conflict and negotiation.

Mailing Address: 70 Withrow Avenue, Toronto, Ontario M4K 1C9

PHOEBE GILMAN

I grew up in New York City and studied at Hunter College and the Art Students' League in Manhattan. I lived in Europe and Israel for some years before coming to Canada in 1972. My work has been exhibited in galleries here and around the world. An instructor at the Ontario College of Art, I am currently making up stories and pictures from my studio/home in Toronto.

Selected Publications:

The Balloon Tree: Toronto, Scholastic, 1984. ISBN 0-590-71410-0
Jillian Jiggs: Toronto, Scholastic, 1985. ISBN 0-590-71548-8
Little Blue Ben: Toronto, Scholastic, 1986. ISBN 0-590-71692-1

Readings, Lectures & Workshops: Lead workshops on writing and illustrating picture books. Will gladly speak to groups about the evolution of a picture book and/or picture-book maker. Like to read and speak to young audiences.

Mailing Address: 30 Edgemore Drive, Toronto, Ontario M8Y 2N2

JOAN GIVNER

Born in Manchester, England, in 1936. B.A. and Ph.D. from the University of London; M.A. from Washington University, St. Louis, Missouri. Married; two grown children; professor of English, University of Regina. Editor of Wascana Review. Writer of biography and fiction; currently at work on the life of the Canadian novelist Mazo de la Roche.

Selected Publications:

Katherine Anne Porter (A Life): New York, Simon & Schuster, 1982.
Tentacles of Unreason: University of Illinois, 1985.
Katherine Anne Porter in Conversation: (ed. and introd.), University of Mississippi, 1987.

   Readings, Lectures & Workshops: Readings of my own fiction. Lectures on biography and feminist criticism; workshops in biography and short-story writing.
   Mailing Address: Dept. of English, University of Regina, Saskatchewan S4S 0A2

DOUGLAS GLOVER

Born in 1948. Hold an M.Litt. from Edinburgh University and M.F.A. from the Iowa Writers Workshop. At various times a lecturer in philosophy at the University of New Brunswick, a reporter and editor on several daily newspapers including the Star-Phoenix in Saskatoon and the Montreal Star, First Novels columnist at Books in Canada. Now write full time, using the family farm in Waterford, Ontario, as home base.

Selected Publications:

The Mad River: Windsor, Black Moss, 1981. ISBN 0-88753-080-X
Precious: Toronto, Seal, 1984. ISBN 0-7704-1840-6
Dog Attempts to Drown Man in Saskatoon: Vancouver, Talon, 1985. ISBN 0-88922-228-2

Awards: Canadian Fiction Magazine Annual Contributor's Prize, 1984. Finalist in Books in Canada First Novel Contest, 1985. Literary Press Group Writer's Choice Award, 1986.

Comments: "Some masterpiece must eventually come from a writer who writes so well." – Anne Montagnes, *Globe and Mail*

"Everything one wants in a literary entertainment: pace, verve, snappy dialogue, witty, intelligent narration, and, of course, mystery and suspense." – Paul Wilson, *Books in Canada*

"A very nervy writer, the kind who does not play safe . . . " – Ken Adachi, *Toronto Star*

Readings: Occasional.
Mailing Address: RR 1, Waterford, Ontario N0E 1Y0

MARTYN N. GODFREY

I was born in Birmingham, England. Came to Canada at age eight and grew up in various areas of Toronto. My interests range from Shakespeare to Spiderman and from Wagner to Heavy Metal. Before becoming a full-time juvenile and YA writer in 1985, I taught junior high-school in Ontario and Alberta. I have also lived in the North and am dedicated to saving the land as a refuge for blood-sucking insects.

Selected Publications:

The Vandarian Incident: Toronto, Scholastic, 1981. ISBN 0-590-71080-X
Alien Wargames: Toronto, Scholastic, 1984. ISBN 0-590-71224-1
Spin Out: Toronto, Collier-Macmillan, 1984. ISBN 0-02-947170-2
Here She Is – Ms. Teeny-Wonderful: Toronto, Scholastic, 1985. ISBN 0-590-71482-1
Ice Hawk: Toronto, Collier-Macmillan, 1985. ISBN 0-02-947310-1
Plan B is Total Panic: Toronto, Lorimer, 1986. ISBN 0-88862-850-1
The Last War: Toronto, Collier-Macmillan, 1986. ISBN 0-02-947380-2
It Isn't Easy Being Ms.Teeny-Wonderful: Toronto, Scholastic, 1986. ISBN 0-590-71674-3
Wild Night: Toronto, Collier-Macmillan, 1987. ISBN 0-02-947420-5
Rebel Yell: Toronto, Collier-Macmillan, 1987. ISBN 0-02-947410-8

Awards: Vicky Metcalf Award (Outstanding Children's Short Story), 1984
Comments: "Godfrey writes in a fast moving style that is sure to appeal to students." – *The Reviewing Librarian*
"Loaded with humour." – *Quill & Quire*
Readings, Lectures & Workshops: School readings and workshops for teachers and writers. May be booked directly or through TWUC.
Mailing Address: 54, 2703-79 Street, Edmonton, Alberta T6K 3Z6

DONALD R. GORDON

Born September 14, 1929, educated at Queen's University, the University of Toronto and the London School of Economics. CBC European correspondent, 1956-63. Academic (political science and communications) at the University of Calgary and University of Waterloo, 1963-81. Writer and consultant (CBC, CRTC et al.) since 1981. Live and work in Waterloo basement awash in memories and neat ideas. Member of the Royal Commission on the Status of Women in Canada, 1967.

Selected Publications:

Language Logic and the Mass Media: Toronto, Holt Rinehart & Winston, 1966. (no ISBN)
The New Literacy: Toronto, University of Toronto Press, 1971. ISBN 0-8020-1775-4
Fineswine: Kitchener, McBain, 1984. ISBN 0-9691607-4-7
The Rock Candy Bandits: Kitchener, McBain, 1984. ISBN 0-9691607-5-5
S.P.E.E.D.: Kitchener, McBain, 1985. ISBN 0-920469-00-0

Comments: "A gift for lively turns of phrase and for terse comic description . . . refreshingly different." – *Toronto Star* (on *Fineswine*)
"A racy tongue-in-cheek account of kinky sex and power plays . . . about the Ottawa scene." – *Canadian Press* (on *S.P.E.E.D.*)
"A great Canadian." – Patrick Watson
Readings, Lectures & Workshops: Have lectured extensively on non-fiction media writing. Will talk on the media and human survival. Also good at unprincipled, amoral ad copy.
Mailing Address: 134 Iroquois Place, Waterloo, Ontario N2L 2S5

LEROY GORMAN

Born in Smiths Falls, Ontario, August 7, 1949, and raised on a farm near Merrickville. Hold a B.A. in English and political science from Carleton and a B.Ed. from Queen's. Live in Napanee with my wife, Sheila, and our children Lori, Kimberly and Sean. Teach emotionally disturbed adolescents at South Cottage Regional School in Kingston.

Selected Publications:

If I Could Trust The Moon: London, Killaly, 1977. ISBN 0-920438-00-8
Only Shadflies Have Come: Oneonta, N.Y., Swamp, 1979.
Whose Smile the Ripple Warps: Toronto, Underwhich, 1980.
Cutout Moons: Battle Ground, Ind., High/Coo Press, 1980.
Wind in the Keys: Battle Ground, Ind., High/Coo Press, 1980.
Heart's Garden: Montreal, Guernica, 1983. ISBN 0-919349-45-5
Beautiful Chance: London, South Western Ontario Poetry, 1984. ISBN
    0-919139-20-5
Bendings: Toronto, Curvd H & Z, 1984.
Bad News: Sterling, Virg., Mockersatz Zrox, 1986.

Awards: First Place, Cthulhu Calls Science Fiction Poetry Contest, 1979. Creative Writing Award (Staff), Prison Arts Foundation, 1978. Cicada Prize, Haiku Society of Canada, 1979. Second Prize, Mya Pasek Award, St. Louis Poetry Center, 1985.

Comments: "Major poet in the maturing field of Canadian haiku poetry." — *Cross-Canada Writers' Quarterly*

"A man in touch with both sides of his brain." — *Frogpond*

Readings, Lectures & Workshops: Readings and workshops for schools and universities. Have lectured on motivating students to write poetry and on writing and understanding haiku. Exhibit visual poetry.

Mailing Address: c/o TWUC, 24 Ryerson Avenue, Toronto, Ontario M5T 2P3

PAUL GOTTLIEB

Born in Budapest, Hungary, years ago. Punned my way to Montreal in 1957. Now a Torontonian, I discovered this city is ravine mad. B.A. and M.A. from Sir George Williams University. Taught at Concordia and Ryerson. Now head of the media writing programme at Sheridan College in Oakville, Ontario. Married to Erika Gottlieb, Ph.D., teacher at Seneca College and author of Lost Angels of a Ruined Paradise (Sono Nis, 1981). Son, Peter, and daughter, Julia, also in the same boat.

Selected Publications:

Agency: Toronto, Musson, 1974. ISBN 0-7737-0015-3

Awards: More than 25 Canadian and international creative awards for television and print advertising.

Comments: Columnist for Playback and Marketing magazines and contributor to Toronto Life. Numerous screenplays for various Canadian and U.S. feature film producers including In Praise of Older Women based on Stephen Vizinczey's novel.

Agency was filmed in Montreal by RSL Films with Robert Mitchum and Saul Rubinek in 1980.

Work in progress for Key Porter Books, Toronto: Adventures in the Message Parlour.

"During the editing of A la Recherche du Temps Perdus, Marcel Proust kept making last-minute changes in the galleys, calling on his editor in the middle of the night and generally being a nuisance. Exasperated, his editor finally cried out, 'Will no one rid me of this meddlesome Proust?' " – P.G.

"When reality intrudes on theory, it's detail wagging the dogma." – P.G.

Readings, Lectures & Workshops: Read regularly, lecture daily, work and shop when necessary.

Mailing Address: c/o TWUC, 24 Ryerson Avene, Toronto, Ontario M5T 2P3

WILLIAM GOUGH

Born in Halifax, Nova Scotia, August 24, 1945. Raised and educated all over Newfoundland. In addition to books, mainly known as a television producer and writer. Producer of numerous shows including Charlie Grant's War and The Marriage Bed. Co-writer with Anna Sandor of nine episodes of Seeing Things. Writer of many other television scripts. Married to Anna Sandor; one daughter, Rachel Alice Sandor-Gough. Two other children, Jim and Sarah, from a previous marriage.

Selected Publications:

Maud's House: St. John's, Breakwater, 1984. ISBN 0-919519-54-7
The Proper Lover: Toronto, Hounslow, 1986. ISBN 0-88882-089-5

Awards: As a film producer include Actra, Bijou, Genie, Prix Anik (twice) and the Chris Plaque (twice).
Comments: "The richness of language . . . is in Gough's literary blood." — Michael Harris, *Globe and Mail*
"Gough . . . combines poetic language and a style so filmic that every scene has dimension and reality." — Linda Spalding, *Canadian Forum*
"*Maud's House* is a wonderful book, a treat to read . . ." — Peter Gard, *St. John's Evening Telegram*
Readings, Lectures & Workshops: Lectured at the Summer Institute of Film in Ottawa. Have given various library readings, Harbourfront, etc. Available for workshops, especially on film writing.
Mailing Address: 514 Castlefield Avenue, Toronto, Ontario M5N 1L6

ALLAN GOULD

Born in Detroit, Michigan (to Canadian parents), on April 22, 1944; have an M.A. in English from New York University, and a Ph.D. from York University, Toronto, on the theatre criticism of Nathan Cohen, 1977. Have taught at York, Guelph, the University of Toronto and the Ontario College of Art. Lecture across North America on humour, satire, literature, history and ethics. Have written for and performed on numerous Canadian radio and TV programmes, including Morningside, Sunday Morning, Canada AM, Take 30, King of Kensington and Thrill of a Lifetime. Live in Toronto with (brilliant teacher) wife, son and daughter.

Selected Publications:

The Unorthodox Book of Jewish Records and Lists: (with Danny Siegel), Edmonton, Hurtig, 1982. ISBN 0-88830-222-3

The Toronto Book: Toronto, Key Porter, 1983. ISBN 0-919493-06-8

Air Fare (The Entertainers Entertain): Toronto, CBC Enterprises, 1984. ISBN 0-88794-157-5

The Top Secret Tory Handbook: (with Graham Pilsworth), Toronto, Lester & Orpen Dennys, 1984. ISBN 0-88619-066-5

Letters I've Been Meaning To Write: Toronto, Fitzhenry & Whiteside, 1986. ISBN 0-88902-964-4

The New Entrepreneurs (80 Successful Business Stories): Toronto, Seal, 1986. ISBN 0-7704-2092-3

Comments: "Gould is one of my favorite Toronto writers; he's funny, with a delicious, demented sense of humour." – *Toronto Star*

"Who else can make tourist books, cook books, even business books, hysterically funny, witty, breezy, delightful to read? And who else can churn them out so quickly and so well?" – Ann Gould, mother of Allan Gould (Author's note: Thanks, mom. But what have you done for me lately?)

Readings, Lectures & Workshops: I speak (and teach) frequently across Canada and the U.S. on how humour and political satire work.

Mailing Address: 31 Glen Rush Boulevard, Toronto, Ontario M5N 2T4

ED GOULD

Born on Sunset Boulevard in lovely downtown Turner Valley, Alberta. Travelled widely. Lived in London, England. Entered business and broadcasting. Succumbed to writing bug after many years as a reporter and editor for newspapers and Canadian Press. Wrote my first book on Saltspring Island during the hippie era. After three years as a Swivel Servant, I returned to writing in Victoria where many ancient people are retired and living with their grandparents.

Selected Publications:

Bridging the Gulf: Saanichton, Hancock, 1975. ISBN 0-919654-35-5
Logging (British Columbia's Logging History): Saanichton, Hancock, 1975. ISBN 0-919654-44-4
Oil (The History of Canada's Oil and Gas Industry): Saanichton, Hancock, 1976. ISBN 0-919654-55-X
Ralph Edwards of Lonesome Lake: Saanichton, Hancock, 1979. ISBN 0-919654-74-6
Intimacy Through Cookery: (with Dolores Gould), Victoria, Cappis, 1982. ISBN 0-919763-04-9
Tut, Tut, Victoria!: Victoria, Cappis, 1983. ISBN 0-919763-06-5

Awards: Media Club of Canada First Prize (Best Feature Newspaper Article), 1973
Comments: "Hilarious" – Joey Slinger, *Victoria Times*
"For light, fun-reading and hearty laughs, we recommend this book."
– Alec Merriman, *Daily Colonist*
"A delightful spoof." – Alex MacGillivray, *Vancouver Sun*
Readings, Lectures & Workshops: Have lectured on using the library and creative journalism as well as readings at libraries and galleries.
Mailing Address: 1119 Oscar Street, Victoria, British Columbia V8V 2X3

TERRY GOULD

Born in 1949 in New York City where I made a minor impression as a Broadway actor and child model before going on to work as a cab driver and lifeguard at Coney Island. Graduated from City University of New York at 21, married painter Leslie Hoffman and moved to northern British Columbia where we homesteaded a wilderness of 160 acres and built a two-storey log home that we still live in. Work as a brakeman, teacher, father and writer, and travel with my family each winter to hot places.

Selected Publications:

How the Blind Make Love: Vancouver, Orca Sound, 1984. ISBN 0-920616-36-4

    Comments: So It's My Fault? and The Payment of Little Debts appeared in The Malahat Review, 1980; The Jewish Giant in Riverrun, 1980.
    Awards: First Prize, Riverrun Short Story Contest, 1981
    Readings, Lectures & Workshops: Regular on the National Book Festival circuit in B.C. Give regular creative writing workshops to teachers and students, elementary through high school.
    Mailing Address: RR 1, Telkwa, British Columbia V0J 2X0

KATHERINE GOVIER

Born in Edmonton in 1948, I left Alberta to go to graduate school at York University in Toronto in 1971, 'round about the time when everyone went west. M.A. in English, 1972, then a career as a magazine writer. This was when we had lots of good magazines to write for. Gradually made the shift to all fiction and a little teaching. Live in Toronto except for stints in London, England, and Washington, D.C. Married with two children.

Selected Publications:

Random Descent: Toronto, Macmillan, 1979. ISBN 0-7705-1719-6
Going Through the Motions: Toronto, McClelland & Stewart, 1982. ISBN 0-7710-3416-4
Fables of Brunswick Avenue: Toronto, Penguin, 1985. ISBN 0-14-007578-X
Between Men: Toronto, Penguin, 1987. ISBN 0-670-81499-7

Awards: National Magazine Award, 1980
Comments: Short fiction in anthologies and periodicals in Canada and the United Kingdom.
Readings, Lectures & Workshops: Taught creative writing at York University from 1982 to 1986.
Visiting Fellow, School of English, Leeds University, England, 1986-87.
Mailing Address: c/o TWUC, 24 Ryerson Avenue, Toronto, Ontario M5T 2P3

DOROTHY GRANT

Born in Guelph, Ontario. Early education in England. Later educated in Canada. No degree. Married to Gerry Grant, Alderman. Live in Cornwall, Ontario. Currently working on a novel, Dialogue Through Oblivion.

Selected Publications:

The Shifting Change: Philadelphia, Dorrance, 1973. ISBN 0-8059-1846-9
Go Ask the Mole: Cornwall, Ont., Vesta, 1975. ISBN 0-919806-05-8
Double Exposure: Toronto, Amethyst, 1979. ISBN 0-9690055-0-4

Comments: "A moving look at humanity and its idiosyncrasies; behind its surface simplicity lies a complex and touching look at life." *– Quill & Quire* (on *Double Exposure*)

"While to some readers, it may be mildly reminiscent of a Canadian Peyton Place most will respond keenly to Ms. Grant's characters. The book is refreshing in its lack of trivial detail." *– Canadian Author and Bookman* (on *Go Ask the Mole*)

Short stories and poems have appeared in the Canadian Forum, the Fiddlehead and in Seaway Valley Poets (Vesta, 1975).

Mailing Address: 204 Riverdale Avenue, Cornwall, Ontario K6J 2K2

JANET GRANT

Born in Toronto in 1957, one of five children. Learned to keep out of trouble by playing competitive tennis. Grew up in historic Thornhill, Ontario. Received Hon. B.A. in English Literature from the University of Sussex, England. Developed several business courses in Vancouver and Toronto.

Selected Publications:

Canadian All 5 (Portraits of Our People): Toronto, Methuen, 1985. ISBN 0-458-99060-4

Canadians All 6 (Portraits of Our People): Toronto, Methuen, 1986. ISBN 0-458-80030-9

Comments: Currently running my own writing and course design business in Toronto, Better Brains. I also tutor adolescents in writing skills. Member of the Canadian Society of Children's Authors, Illustrators and Performers.

Readings, Lectures & Workshops: Occasionally lead workshops in writing skills that focus on organization of material and developing the writer's own style. Workshops may be booked through TWUC.

Mailing Address: c/o TWUC, 24 Ryerson Avenue, Toronto, Ontario M5T 2P3

BARBARA GREENWOOD

Born in Toronto in 1940, earned a B.A. from the University of Toronto and taught elementary school for several years. Now divide my time between writing and teaching creative writing as part of school enrichment programmes. Currently I am working on another YA historical novel and writing a book-review column for Kids Toronto. 1983-85 president of CANSCAIP (The Canadian Society of Children's Authors, Illustrators and Performers).

Selected Publications:

A Question of Loyalty: Toronto, Scholastic, 1984. ISBN 0-590-71450-3

Awards: Vicky Metcalf Award (Short Story), 1982

Comments: *A Question of Loyalty*, a YA adventure story set during the Mackenzie Rebellion of 1837, was shortlisted for the Saskatchewan Library Association's Young Book Award and is currently being used in many grade eight classrooms as part of the history programme. Short stories and articles have appeared in anthologies and magazines.

Readings, Lectures & Workshops: Read in libraries, elementary schools and high schools to both English and history classes. Give workshops on creative writing from grades four to high school and PD day talks on how to motivate the student writer. Adult workshops on writing for the children's market. May be booked through TWUC.

Mailing Address: 59 Leacroft Crescent, Don Mills, Ontario M3B 2G5

BRIAN A. GROSMAN

Born in Toronto, May 20, 1935. B.A., 1957; L.L.B., 1960 (University of Toronto); L.L.M. 1967 (McGill). Married Penny-Lynn (Cookson); son, John Shain. Assistant and associate professor of law, McGill (1966-67), professor of law at the University of Saskatchewan (1971-79). Founding Chairman of the Law Reform Commission of Saskatchewan (1974-79). Called to the Ontario bar in 1962 and in Saskatchewan in 1971. Private law practice in Toronto 1961-65 and 1979 to date.

Selected Publications:

The Prosecutor: Toronto, University of Toronto Press, 1969. ISBN 0-8020-1672-3
Police Command: Toronto, Macmillan, 1975. ISBN 0-7705-1271-2
The Executive Firing Line (Wrongful Dismissal and the Law): Toronto, Carswell/Methuen, 1982. ISBN 0-458-95450-0
New Directions in Sentencing: Toronto, Butterworths, 1980. ISBN 0-409-83460-2
Fire Power: Toronto, Viking, 1985. ISBN 0-670-80306-5

Comments: Forthcoming: Corporate Loyalty, Spring 1988 (Viking /Penguin), Toronto.
Mailing Address: Suite 1110, 390 Bay Street, Toronto, Ontario M5H 2Y2

PHYLLIS GROSSKURTH

Born in Toronto in 1924. B.A., University of Toronto; M.A., University of Ottawa; Ph.D., University of London. Taught for Worker's Education Association in London, 1963-64. Lecturer at Carleton University, 1964-65. Professor of English at the University of Toronto since 1965. Member of the National Film Board, 1967-74. Guggenheim Fellowship, 1982. Rockefeller Fellowship, 1982.

Selected Publications:

John Addington Symonds (A Biography): London, Longmans, 1964. (no ISBN)
The Woeful Victorian: New York, Holt Reinhart & Winston, 1965. ISBN 0-83303-011-5
Havelock Ellis (A Biography): New York, Knopf, 1980. ISBN 0-394-50150-0
The Memoirs of John Addington Symonds: London, Hutchinson, 1984. ISBN 0-09-154170-0
Melanie Klein (Her World and Her Work): New York, Knopf, 1986. ISBN 0-394-51342-8

Awards: University of British Columbia Award (Biography), 1965. Governor General's Award (Non-fiction), 1965. Nominated for National Book Award (U.K.), 1981.
Mailing Address: 147 Spruce Street, Toronto, Ontario M5A 2J6

DENNIS GRUENDING

Journalist, prose writer and poet. Co-host of CBC Radio Saskatchewan's Morning Edition. Have worked for three newspapers and CBC as a reporter, freelancer and producer. Articles, stories and poems have appeared in Maclean's, the Canadian Forum, This Magazine, NeWest Review and Prism International. Member of ACTRA, the Saskatchewan Writers Guild, PEN International and the Regina Central America Working Group. Honours degree in English, High Honours.

Selected Publications:

Gringo (Poems and Journals from Latin America): Regina, Coteau, 1983. ISBN 0-919926-18-5
Emmett Hall (Establishment Radical): Toronto, Macmillan, 1985. ISBN 0-7715-9689-8

Awards: City of Regina Writers' Award, 1980. Saskatchewan Writers Guild Award (Non-fiction), 1981.
Comments: "Dennis Gruending's warm, sympathetic but not totally uncritical portrait of Emmett Hall is a fascinating story about a father of medicare and a libertarian judge . . ." – Gordon Bale, *Canadian Bar Review*
"*Gringo*, in brief, is the dark side of the glossy South American travel brochures." – John Faustmann, *Vancouver Sun*
Readings, Lectures & Workshops: Will read prose and poetry for adults. Will speak on the role of media and human rights issues (emphasis on Latin America). Contact author, TWUC or Saskatchewan Writers Guild.
Mailing Address: 2830 Robinson Street, Regina, Saskatchewan S4S 1T8

CAMILLA GRYSKI

Born in Bristol, England in 1948. B.A. (Hons.) English from the University of Toronto, 1971. Montessori Primary Teaching Certificate, 1972. Master of Library Science from the University of Toronto, 1976. Now the children's librarian at Toronto's Hospital for Sick Children. Write and work, parent, serve on the executive of the Canadian Society of Children's Authors, Illustrators and Performers, the International Board on Books for Young People, and on the artistic committee of Mariposa in the Schools.

Selected Publications:

Cat's Cradle, Owl's Eyes (A Book Of String Games): Toronto, Kids Can, 1983. ISBN 0-919964-49-4
Many Stars and More String Games: Toronto, Kids Can, 1985. ISBN 0-919964-76-1

Comments: "Double and triple blessings then, on a glorious book like *Cat's Cradle, Owl's Eyes*; it is a magic open sesame that lets me back into the cave of wonders." – Michele Landsberg, *Toronto Star*
"*Many Stars* contains some very beautiful string figures as well as an impressive solo version of Cat's Cradle. Reproducing these figures gives great satisfaction, but not as much as being able to perform one of the stories at the end of the book – stories that combine the power of the spoken word with the beauty of the language of string figures." – Sylvia Funston, *Quill & Quire*
Readings, Lectures & Workshops: I enjoy sharing string games and their traditions with children and adults and have given readings, formal and informal, in schools and libraries, on front porches and at folk festivals, from O'Leary, Prince Edward Island, to Whitehorse, Yukon, and points in between.
Mailing Address: c/o TWUC, 24 Ryerson Avenue, Toronto, Ontario M5T 2P3

KRISTJANA GUNNARS

 Born in Reykjavik, Iceland, in 1948. Resident in Canada since 1969. B.A. from Oregon; M.A. from Saskatchewan; Ph.D. in progress from Manitoba. Lived in Squamish, British Columbia; Vancouver; Toronto; Regina and Winnipeg. High-school teacher in Iceland; lecturer at the University of Manitoba; editorial assistant, Iceland Review. Writer and translator since 1980. Short fiction and poetry, also journalism (features) and photo essays, casual essays and reviews. Also photographer.

Selected Publications:

Settlement Poems (Vols. I and II): Winnipeg, Turnstone, 1980. 1981. ISBN 0-88801-032-X (vol. 1)/ISBN 0-88801-051-6 (vol. 2)
One-Eyed Moon Maps: Victoria, Press Porcepic, 1981. ISBN 0-88878-178-4
Wake-Pic Poems: Toronto, Anansi, 1981. ISBN 0-88784-089-2
The Axe's Edge: Victoria, Press Porcepic, 1983. ISBN 0-88878-210-1
The Night Workers of Ragnarok: Victoria, Press Porcepic, 1985. ISBN 0-88878-239-X

Comments: "Very few poets have written, in what seems to have been a very short period of time, poems that have varied so much their poetic voice: the troll speaking as troll, the troll turning human, the human reflecting the primitive, the child, the mature and contemporary woman. With this different tuning of voices and focus, Gunnars renews her material and her possibilities." – Travis Lane, *Canadian Literature*

"Many people write verse but seldom, perhaps only once or twice in a generation, does a poet arise who has the power, like a magician, to create illusions which demand our attention. Kristjana Gunnars is one of those magicians." – W.D. Valgardson, *Iceland Review*

Mailing Address: Box 305, St. Norbert, Winnipeg, Manitoba R3V 1L6

SYLVIA GUNNERY

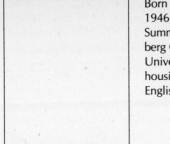

Born in Halifax, Nova Scotia, October 17,
1946, and still living there most of the year.
Summers are spent at Crescent Beach, Lunen-
berg County, Nova Scotia. B.A., 1968 (Acadia
University); B.Ed., 1969 and M.Ed., 1978 (Dalhousie University). Teaching junior high-school
English since 1969.

Selected Publications:

I'm Locker 145. Who Are You?: Toronto, Scholastic, 1984. ISBN 0-590-
   71483-X
We're Friends, Aren't We?: Toronto, Scholastic, 1986. ISBN 0-590-71619-0

   Mailing Address: c/o TWUC, 24 Ryerson Avenue, Toronto, Ontario
M5T 2P3

DAVID GURR

Born London (UK), February 5, 1936; bombed out, 1940; moved to Dorset for D-Day landings; Canada for 12th birthday. After near miss at Stage, joined RCN as a cadet in 1954, at sea to 1966, via B.Sc. (Maths/Physics) from the University of Victoria. Computer analyst to 1971. Resigned Commission. House designer-builder to 1981. First published 1979. Married, 1958, Judith, nurse/social worker/sculptor: one daughter, two sons; animals various.

Selected Publications:

Troika: Toronto, McClelland & Stewart, 1979.
A Woman Called Scylla: New York, Viking, 1981. ISBN 0-670-77775-7
The Action of the Tiger: Toronto, Seal, 1984. ISBN 0-7704-2004-4
An American Spy Story: Toronto, McClelland & Stewart, 1984. ISBN 0-7710-3663-9
On the Endangered List: Toronto, McClelland & Stewart, 1985. ISBN 0-7710-3664-7
The Ring Master: Toronto, McClelland & Stewart, 1987. ISBN 0-7710-3666-3

Mailing Address: 9170 Ardmore Drive, RR 2, Sidney, British Columbia V8L 3S1

RALPH GUSTAFSON

 Born in Lime Ridge, Eastern Townships of Quebec, August 16, 1909. Educated at Bishop's University, M.A.; Oxford, M.A.; D.C.L. (Bishop's) and D.Litt. (Mt. Allison) honoris causa; professor and poet-in-residence at Bishop's; music critic; married Elisabeth Renninger in 1958; with British Information Services 1942-46. Retired.

Selected Publications:

Flight into Darkness: New York, Pantheon, 1944.
Rivers Among Rocks: Toronto, McClelland & Stewart, 1960.
Fire on Stone: Toronto, McClelland & Stewart, 1974. ISBN 0-7710-3703-1
Landscape with Rain: Toronto, McClelland & Stewart, 1980. ISBN 0-7710-3710-4
The Moment is All (Selected Poems): Toronto, McClelland & Stewart, 1983. ISBN 0-7710-3714-7
Impromptus: Lantzville, Oolichan, 1984. ISBN 0-88982-066-X
Directives of Autumn: Toronto, McClelland & Stewart, 1984. ISBN 0-7710-3709-0

Awards: Governor General's Award (Poetry), 1974. A.J.M. Smith Award, Michigan State University.
Comments: "Authentically a poet to the vocation born." – *New York Times*
"An acknowledged master." – *Quill & Quire*
Readings, Lectures & Workshops: Read regularly throughout Canada. Poetry delegate to U.K.; U.S.S.R.; Washington, D.C.; Italy.
Mailing Address: Box 172, North Hatley, Quebec J0B 2C0

RICHARD GWYN

Born in England in 1934 and educated at Stony-hurst College and the Royal Military Academy, Sandhurst. Emigrated to Canada in 1954. After selling magazine subscriptions door to door, became a journalist in 1957 with United Press International in Halifax and have remained one for nearly three decades, except for the years 1968-1973, when I was executive assistant to the Honourable Eric Kierans and subsequently Director of Socio-Economic Planning in the federal Department of Communications. Joined the Toronto Star in 1973 as a nationally syndicated Ottawa columnist; in 1985 appointed international affairs columnist, currently based in London, England.

Selected Publications:

The Shape of Scandal (A Study of a Government in Crisis): Toronto, Clarke Irwin, 1965. (no ISBN)

Smallwood (The Unlikely Revolutionary): Toronto, McClelland & Stewart, 1968. ISBN 0-7710-3724-4

The Northern Magus (Pierre Trudeau and Canadians): Toronto, McClelland & Stewart, 1980. ISBN 0-7710-3732-5

The 49th Paradox (Canada in North America): Toronto, McClelland & Stewart, 1985. ISBN 0-7710-3733-3

Awards: National Newspaper Awards; 1980, 1984. Author of the Year, Foundation for Advancement of Canadian Letters, 1982. National Magazine Award (with Sandra Gwyn), 1984.

Readings, Lectures & Workshops: Frequent lecturer on national and international affairs. Contributor to radio and television public affairs programmes. Co-host of TV Ontario's Realities since 1982.

Mailing Address: c/o The Colbert Agency, 303 Davenport Road, Toronto, Ontario M5R 1K5

SANDRA GWYN

Born in St. John's, Newfoundland, in 1935. B.A., Dalhousie University, 1955. Married Richard Gwyn in 1958. Long apprenticeship in the writing profession as a freelance reporter-researcher, 1960-75 (CBC, Time Canada and various federal government departments and Royal Commissions). Ottawa editor of Saturday Night, 1975-80; contributing editor since 1980. Currently contributing from London, England, and researching a new book.

Selected Publications:

Women in the Arts in Canada: Ottawa, Queen's Printer, 1970. (no ISBN)
The Private Capital (Ambition and Love in the Age of Macdonald and Laurier): Toronto, McClelland & Stewart, 1984. ISBN 0-7710-3736-8

Awards: Governor General's Award (Non-fiction), 1984. Canadian Authors Association Award (Non-fiction), 1984. National Magazine Awards: Silver medal, 1978; Gold medal, 1979; Gold medal (with Richard Gwyn), 1984.

Comments: "Exemplary history that is gloriously written and wonderfully readable." – Governor General's Award Jury, 1984

Readings, Lectures & Workshops: Frequently, to groups interested in Canadian social history, especially women's social history, both in Canada and in UK.

Mailing Address: c/o The Colbert Agency, 303 Davenport Road, Toronto, Ontario M5R 1K3

JOAN HAGGERTY

Born and raised in Vancouver, British Columbia, formative years spent on the coast in cedars and salt water. B.A., University of British Columbia, English and Theatre, 1962. Travelled, taught and wrote in England, France, Spain and New York City for 11 years before returning permanently to lotus land in 1973. Taught creative writing at University of British Columbia, 1980-84. TWUC Pacific co-ordinator, 1983-86.

Selected Publications:

Please, Miss, Can I Play God?: London, Methuen, 1966. (no ISBN)
Daughters of the Moon: New York, Bobbs-Merrill, 1971. (no ISBN)

Comments: "A book to trap any teacher who reads it into the same splendid, difficult, important heresies." – Edward Blishen, *The Listener*, London (on *Please, Miss, Can I Play God?*)
"An adventure novel about childbirth set forth as hazardous and bloody, rhythmic and full and holy . . . written with a lot of intelligence and skill and a strong, vital female identity." – Marge Piercy (on *Daughters of the Moon*)
"A terrifying flight of the creative imagination . . . at once nightmarishly true and incredible." – Phyllis Webb, Critics on Air
Articles and stories: Uncoupling (The Capilano Review, Feb. 1977); Jake (McCalls' Working Mother, 1980); As the Lady Said (Journal of the Assoc. of B.C. Drama Educators, 1984); Magi (HERizons, Feb., 1985); Dancehall (Western Living, Oct. 1986).
Readings, Lectures & Workshops: Read regularly at universities, bookstores, schools, forests and beaches. Workshops in developmental drama, particularly directed to teachers who are interested in drama as a learning medium.
Mailing Address: 7-1346 Cotton Avenue, Vancouver, British Columbia V5L 3T7

GAIL HAMILTON

Born in Toronto, raised on a farm near Demorestville, Ontario. Hold a B.A. in English language and literature. Have taught high school, written advertising, travelled in Africa and Europe. Now live in the Beaches area of Toronto and write full time.

Selected Publications:

Fool's Gold: New York, Kim, 1979. ISBN 0-89772-207-8
Tears of Gold: New York, Silhouette, 1983. ISBN 0-671-57201-6
Precious Interlude: Toronto, Harlequin, 1983. ISBN 0-373-70052-0
To Catch the Wind: Toronto, Harlequin, 1985. ISBN 0-373-70118-7
Once in a Million: Toronto, Harlequin, 1985. ISBN 0-373-70169-1
Spring Thaw: Toronto, Harlequin, 1986. ISBN 0-373-25235-8
What Comes Naturally: Toronto, Harlequin, 1987.

   Awards: Air Canada Promising Young Writer Award. Lyn Harrington Diamond Jubilee Award.
   Mailing Address: Box 565, Station P, Toronto, Ontario M5S 2T1

JOHN DAVID HAMILTON

Journalist, documentary maker, editor, teacher and author. Fifth generation Canadian. Born in Manitoba. Winner of the David E. Bright Award for Foreign Correspondence (twice), the Ohio State Broadcasting Award and the U.S. Government Affairs Institute Award (Foreign Correspondence, Print). Married (twice); two daughters.

Selected Publications:

Bob Friday's Other Eye: Yellowknife, Outcrop, 1986.

Mailing Address: 253 Parkwood Avenue, Keswick, Ontario L4P 2X2

LYN HANCOCK

Born in Fremantle, Western Australia, in 1938. Taught in Australia, Africa, England and Canada. Hold teaching degrees in English, speech and drama, mime and movement, education and communication (A.S.D.A., L.S.D.A., L.T.C.L., L.R.A.M., B.Ed., M.A.). Specialise in natural history, travel and adventure. Stimulate interest by personal participation and humour. Live by the sea in Mill Bay near Victoria, British Columbia.

Selected Publications:

There's a Seal in my Sleeping Bag: Toronto, Collins, 1972. ISBN 0-00-211773-8

Pacific Wilderness/Wild Islands: Saanichton, Hancock, 1974. ISBN 0-919654-08-8

Love Affair with a Cougar: Toronto, Doubleday, 1978. ISBN 0-385-14112-2

Tell Me, Grandmother: Toronto, McClelland & Stewart, 1985. ISBN 0-7710-3809-7

Looking for the Wild: Toronto, Doubleday, 1986. ISBN 0-385-25063-0

Awards: Pacific Northwest Booksellers Award, 1973. American Express Travel Writing Awards; 1981, 1983.

Comments: *"Looking for the Wild* is excellent, gets better with every page . . . handles details and dialogue so well we feel we know her and her characters intimately." – *Roger Tory Peterson*

Readings, Lectures & Workshops: Give regular presentations, illustrated with slides and a movie.

Mailing Address: 2457 Baker View Road, Mill Bay, British Columbia V0R 2P0

ROBERT HARLOW

Born and educated in British Columbia. University of British Columbia, 1945-48 (B.A.); Iowa Writer's Workshop, 1948-50 (M.F.A.). CBC, 1951-65 (director of radio for the B.C. region). Head of the department of creative writing at UBC, 1965-77; continued as professor 1977 to present. W.W.2: pilot, Bomber Command, Discharged Flying Officer DFC.

Selected Publications:

Royal Murdoch: Toronto, Macmillan, 1962. (no ISBN)
A Gift of Echoes: Toronto, Macmillan, 1965. (no ISBN)
Scann: Victoria, Sono Nis, 1972. (no ISBN)
Making Arrangements: Toronto, McClelland & Stewart, 1978. ISBN 0-7710-4004-0
Paul Nolan: Toronto, McClelland & Stewart, 1983. ISBN 0-7710-4006-7
Felice (A Travelogue): Lantzville, Oolichan, 1985. ISBN 0-88982-086-4
Heroes in Vancouver Fiction: Winlaw, Polestar, 1985. ISBN 0-919591-05-1

Mailing Address: c/o TWUC, 24 Ryerson Avenue, Toronto, Ontario M5T 2P3

LYN HARRINGTON

Born and grew up in Sault Ste. Marie, Ontario. Graduated from the University of Toronto Library School in 1933. Married to Richard Harrington, 1942. Photo-journalist. Live in Toronto. No children. Member of the Canadian Authors Association. Author of some 2,500 articles, stories and radio talks.

Selected Publications:

Manitoba Roundabout: Toronto, Ryerson, 1951. (no ISBN)
Greece and the Greeks: Toronto, Nelson, 1962. (no ISBN)
China and the Chinese: Toronto, Nelson, 1966. (no ISBN)
The Luck of the La Verendryes: Toronto, Nelson, 1967. (no ISBN)
Australia, New Zealand and New Guinea: Toronto, Nelson, 1969. (no ISBN)
The Polar Regions: Toronto, Nelson, 1973. ISBN 0-8407-6338-7
Enchantment of Ontario: Toronto, Children's Press, 1974. ISBN 0-516-04071-5
Covered Bridges of Eastern Canada: Toronto, McGraw-Hill Ryerson, 1976. ISBN 0-07-082406-1
The Shaman's Evil Eye: Cobalt, Highway Bookshop, 1979. ISBN 0-88954-209-0
Syllables of Recorded Time: Toronto, Simon & Pierre, 1981. ISBN 0-88924-112-0

Awards: Vicky Metcalf Award, 1975
Mailing Address: 30 Beaufield Avenue, Toronto, Ontario M4G 3R3

CHRISTIE HARRIS

Born in the U.S., November 21, 1907, to parents from Ireland, I came to Canada in 1908. Raised on a British Columbia farm, I taught school and sold my first stories in the 1920s. In the 30s, 40s and 50s, I wrote radio scripts for CBC and did broadcasts and newspaper work while raising five children. At age 50 I started writing books for children and young adults. Still writing, lecturing and reading. Member of the Order of Canada.

Selected Publications:

Once Upon a Totem: Toronto, McClelland & Stewart, 1963. ISBN 0-7710-3992-1

You Have to Draw the Line Somewhere: Toronto, McClelland & Stewart, 1964. (no ISBN)

Raven's Cry: Toronto, McClelland & Stewart, 1966. ISBN 0-7710-4033-4

Mystery at the Edge of Two Worlds: Toronto, McClelland & Stewart, 1978. ISBN 0-7710-3977-8

Mouse Woman and the Muddleheads: Toronto, McClelland & Stewart, 1979. ISBN 0-7710-3984-0

The Trouble with Princesses: Toronto, McClelland & Stewart, 1980. ISBN 0-7710-3997-2

The Trouble with Adventurers: Toronto, McClelland & Stewart, 1982. ISBN 0-7710-4028-8

Awards: Pacific Northwest Booksellers' Award, 1967. Vicky Metcalf Award, 1972. Canada Council Children's Literature Award, 1981.

Readings, Lectures & Workshops: Read to children; talk to students, teachers, librarians, others, mainly on North West Coast Indian lore.

Mailing Address: 1604-2045 Nelson Street, Vancouver, British Columbia V6G 1N8

DOROTHY JOAN HARRIS

I was born in Kobe, Japan, February 14, 1931, and came to Canada in 1938. Graduated from the University of Toronto (modern languages), then taught in France and Japan. In 1955 married Alan Harris, settled in Toronto, was editor with Copp Clark. Began writing for my two children, Kim and Doug, and have gone on writing for other people's children.

Selected Publications:

The House Mouse: New York, Frederick Warne, 1973. ISBN 0-7232-6096-0

The School Mouse: New York, Frederick Warne, 1977. ISBN 0-7232-6140-7

The School Mouse and the Hamster: New York, Frederick Warne, 1979. ISBN 0-7232-6172-5

Goodnight Jeffery: New York, Frederick Warne, 1983. ISBN 0-7232-6224-1

Don't Call Me Sugarbaby!: Toronto, Scholastic, 1983. ISBN 0-590-71173-3

Comments: See also: Something About the Author (Gale Research, Detroit) and Profiles II (Canadian Library Association, Ottawa)

Readings, Lectures & Workshops: Readings and workshops for children from primary grades to grade eight may be booked through TWUC.

Mailing Address: 159 Brentwood Road North, Toronto, Ontario M8X 2C8

LORRAINE HARRIS

Born in Vancouver, British Columbia. Moved to Ocean Falls, 1918-1939. Senior matriculation; four years of writing courses. Now live in Nanaimo on Vancouver Island.

Selected Publications:

Halfway to the Goldfields: Vancouver, J.J. Douglas, 1977. ISBN 0-88894-062-9

Vancouver Once Upon a Time: Vancouver, CJOR, 1974. ISBN 0-88839-125-0

British Columbia's Own Railroad: Vancouver, Hancock, 1982. ISBN 0-88839-125-0

Barkerville (The Town that Gold Built): Vancouver, Hancock, 1984. ISBN 0-88839-152-8

Manning Park: Vancouver, Hancock, 1984. ISBN 0-88839-972-3

Fraser Canyon Highway: Vancouver, Hancock, 1984. ISBN 0-88839-182-X

Gold Along the Fraser: Vancouver, Hancock, 1984. ISBN 0-88839-157-X

Comments: Articles:
John Nilsen, B.C. Pioneer in B.C. Digest, 1966; Babysitter's Co-op in Chatelaine, 1971; The Ned McGowan War, 1967 and A.C. Elliot, Magistrate to Premier of British Columbia, 1968 in The Advocate.

Mailing Address: c/o TWUC, 24 Ryerson Avenue, Toronto, Ontario M5T 2P3

MICHAEL HARRIS

Born in Glasgow, Scotland, 1944. Educated at McGill and Concordia universities. Teach at Dawson College, Montreal. Editor, Signal Editions of Vehicule Press.

Selected Publications:

Poems From Ritual: Ransack, 1967. (no ISBN)
Text For Nausikaa: Delta Canada, 1970. (no ISBN)
Sparks: New Delta, 1976. ISBN 0-919162-45-2
Grace: New Delta, 1977. ISBN 0-919162-49-5
Miss Emily et La Mort: Montreal, VLB Editeur, 1984. ISBN 2-89005-201-X
Veiled Countries/Lives: (trans.), Montreal, Vehicule, 1984. ISBN 0-919890-54-7
In Transit: Montreal, Vehicule, 1985. ISBN 0-919890-69-5

Awards: CBC Literary Competition (Third Prize), 1985. New England Review/Breadloaf Quarterly Narrative Poetry Contest (Finalist), 1985.

Comments: "Of the handful of literary people who are 'bridging the wall of polite silence' between the two languages and cultures, Michael Harris appears to be in the forefront, both as translator and poet." — Sheila Martindale, *Canadian Author and Bookman*

Other reviews in: University of Toronto Quarterly, Canadian Literature, Matrix, The Dalhousie Review, The Antigonish Review, Books in Canada, Quarry, CV II, Open City, The Fiddlehead.

Mailing Address: 73 Chesterfield Avenue, Montreal, Quebec H3Y 2M6

KEITH HARRISON

Born in Vancouver, June 18, 1945. Grew up on the West Coast and got an Honours English degree from the University of British Columbia, and an M.A. from the University of California (Berkeley). Moved to Montreal in 1968, initially to take a Ph.D. at McGill (Dean's Honours List), later to teach and to write in Quebec.

Selected Publications:

Dead Ends: Dunvegan, Quadrant, 1981. ISBN 0-86495-010-1
After Six Days: Fredericton, Fiddlehead, 1985. ISBN 0-86492-070-9

Comments: "Harrison maintains a level of insight and tension — about the contradictions of living and writing, about some of the forms that domination can take — that's constantly high, demanding, rewarding." — Douglas Hill, *Books in Canada* (on *Dead Ends*)

"Keith Harrison's fine second novel, *After Six Days*, documents two young couples' search for a smoking gun en route to marriage breakdown . . . Harrison effectively establishes the estranged point-counterpoint positions of the couples by his use of multiple points of views. He has created four powerfully combative characters — each with a highly distinctive voice and viewpoint." — Sherie Posesorski, *Globe and Mail*

See also *Lowry's Allusions to Melville in Lunar Caustic* in Canadian Literature (No. 94 1982) and *Nelson* in Grain (No. 2 1983).

Mailing Address: c/o TWUC, 24 Ryerson Avenue, Toronto, Ontario M5T 2P3

TED HARRISON

Born in Wingate, County Durham, England, August 28, 1926. Educated at Wellfield Grammar School, Hartlepool College of Art and the University of Durham (King's College). Art Teachers Diploma, 1951. B.Ed. from the University of Alberta. Served in the British Army Intelligence Corps, 1945-48. Taught school in the U.K., Malaysia, New Zealand, Alberta and the Yukon. Married Nicky, 1960. Immigrated to Canada, 1967. One son, Charles, now at the University of British Columbia. Currently live in Whitehorse, Yukon.

Selected Publications:

Children of the Yukon: Montreal, Tundra, 1977. ISBN 0-88776-092-9
The Last Horizon: Toronto, Merritt, 1980. ISBN 0-92886-10-6
A Northern Alphabet: Montreal, Tundra, 1982. ISBN 0-88776-133-X
The Cremation of Sam McGee: (illustrations and essay), Toronto, Kids Can, 1986. ISBN 0-919964-92-3

    Awards: Child Study Association Award (Best Children's Book), 1977. IBBY Award (Illustration), 1984.
    Readings, Lectures & Workshops: In 1986, the IBBY Conference in Toronto, the Kitchener Libraries Association as well as Winnipeg, Thompson and Churchill in Manitoba, Beaver College in Glendale, Philadelphia, Ee-Yore Children's Bookstore in New York and the Children's Book Store in Toronto.
    Mailing Address: 30-12th Avenue East, Whitehorse, Yukon Y1A 4J6

NORMA HARRS

Born in Belfast, Northern Ireland, I came to Canada in my early twenties and lived in Winnipeg where my two children were born. I worked extensively for the CBC as a documentary writer and broadcaster as well as continuing in a professional acting career. Came to Toronto in 1972 and continued both acting and broadcasting besides freelancing for the Globe and Mail and several other Canadian newspapers and magazines.

Selected Publications:

A Certain State of Mind: Toronto, Virgo, ISBN 0-920528-19-8

   Comments: Available in manuscript form from the Playwrights Union (Toronto): Essential Conflict and The 40th Birthday Party.
   Mailing Address: c/o TWUC, 24 Ryerson Avenue, Toronto, Ontario M5T 2P3

ANNE HART

Born in Winnipeg, grew up in darkest rural Nova Scotia, studied at Dalhousie (Arts) and McGill (Library Science), worked for a year or two at a time in Halifax, London, England, and Kingston, Ontario, and have had the good fortune to live in St. John's, Newfoundland, for the past 23 years. A librarian at Memorial University, I devoutly believe in tax credits for literary papers and public lending right for authors. Have three children.

Selected Publications:

The Life and Times of Miss Jane Marple: New York, Dodd Mead, 1985. ISBN 0-396-08748-5

Awards: Margaret Duley Fiction Contest, 1974. Canadian Library Trustees Association Annual Merit Award (Outstanding Library Trustee), 1986.

Comments: Too many annual reports and too few poems and short stories (some anthologised).

Mailing Address: 10 Prince William Place, St. John's, Newfoundland A1B 1A5

EMILY HEARN

Born in Markham, Ontario, schooled in Kitchener and Toronto, I worked at the National Film Board, wrote children's scripts for CBC Radio and TVO television and travelled Canada finding writers for Nelson Canada reading series, to which I contribute poems and stories. Besides writing books for young children I plot the Mighty Mites for Owl Magazine, play a harpsichord and take artsy photographs.

Selected Publications:

Woosh! I Hear A Sound: Toronto, Annick, 1983. ISBN 0-920303-21-8
Good Morning Franny, Good Night Franny: Toronto, Women's Press, 1984.
   ISBN 0-88961-087-8
Race You Franny: Toronto, Women's Press, 1986. ISBN 0-88961-104-1

Readings, Lectures & Workshops: Work extensively in schools stimulating children to draw and to write their own picture books and poetry. I give library readings and workshops for teachers and librarians, write book reviews.
   Mailing Address: 905-980 Broadview Avenue, Toronto, Ontario M4K 3Y1

DORRIS HEFFRON

Born in Quebec. Childhood spent near Toronto. B.A. (Hons.) and M.A. in literature and philosophy from Queen's University, 1969. Was a tutor and lecturer for Oxford University and the Open University in England, 1970-80. Married to W.H. Newton-Smith, an Oxford philosophy don, for 12 years. Returned to Toronto in 1980, where I live with my husband, D.L. Gauer, an executive, and our four children. Forthcoming adult fiction: The Miracle Makers and The Family Man.

Selected Publications:

A Nice Fire and Some Moon Pennies: London, Macmillan, 1971. ISBN 0-333-12773-0

Crusty Crossed: London, Macmillan, 1976. ISBN 0-333-19735-6

Rain And I: London and Toronto, Macmillan, 1982. ISBN 0-333-28151-5

Comments: Have been a member of the Writers' Union since 1979. Was chairperson of the Library and School Curriculum Committees. Was Ontario Representative, 1983-85. Since 1985 the Book & Periodical Development Council representative. A founding member of PEN Canada, I serve on the executive as chair of the Visiting Writers' Committee. Was the PEN delegate to Cyprus in 1985.

Readings, Lectures & Workshops: My first four novels are particularly for high-school and junior-high students. They have been put on high-school literature courses in Europe and Canada. I give readings and lecture on novels about teenagers in schools, libraries and colleges. I have given courses on creative writing and modern literature in Canada, Europe and the Far East.

Mailing Address: 202 Riverside Drive, Toronto, Ontario M6S 4A9

WILLIAM C. HEINE

Born in Saint John, New Brunswick. Three years in the Canadian Army, followed by three years as an RCAF pilot 1939 - 1945. B.A. from the University of Western Ontario, 1949. Editor-in-chief of the London Free Press, London, 1967 - 1984. Have written hundreds of political, economic and other opinion columns in Canadian daily newspapers.

Selected Publications:

The Last Canadian: Toronto, PaperJacks, 1974.
The Swordsman: Toronto and New York, 1978.
Historic Ships of the World: London, David & Charles, 1977.
Kooks and Dukes, Counts and No-Accounts: Edmonton, Hurtig, 1986. ISBN 0-88830-302-5

Readings, Lectures & Workshops: Frequent speaker on political, military, economic and social issues. Also to high school English classes.
Mailing Address: 647 Hillcrest Drive, London, Ontario N6K 1A8

DAVID HELWIG

Born in Toronto, April 15, 1938. Now living in Kingston, Ontario. B.A.(Toronto), 1960. M.A.(Liverpool), 1962. Taught at Queen's University, 1962-74. Literary manager CBC-TV Drama, 1974-76. Taught at Queen's part-time, 1976-80. Writing full time since 1980. Author of 17 books of fiction and poetry.

Selected Publications:

Catchpenny Poems: Ottawa, Oberon, 1983. ISBN 0-88750-506-6
The Only Son: Toronto, Stoddart; New York, Beaufort, 1984. ISBN 0-7737-2019-7
The Bishop: Toronto, New York, Viking, 1986. ISBN 0-670-80746-X
Coming Attractions 5: (with Maggie Helwig), Ottawa, Oberon, 1987. ISBN 0-88750-679-8

Awards: CBC Literary Competition (Poetry), 1983
Mailing Address: 106 Montreal Street, Kingston, Ontario K7K 3E8

JAMES J. HENEGHAN

Born in Liverpool, England, October 7, 1930, and a Canadian citizen since 1957. Teach high school in Burnaby, British Columbia, but live in downtown Vancouver where I write stories for children to help support my heavy tea-drinking habit. Have a wife named Heather and four children.

Selected Publications:

Puffin Rock: (with Bruce McBay), Agincourt, Book Society, 1980. ISBN 0-7725-5070-0

Goodbye, Carleton High: (with Bruce McBay, pseudonym B.J. Bond), Toronto, Scholastic, 1983. ISBN 0-590-71124-5

Comments: Works in progress:

1. An as yet untitled novel about a Vietnamese girl who escapes from a refugee camp and is sent to Canada. To be published spring, 1988 by Grolier, Toronto.

2. The Case of the Marmalade Cat. A detective story for children.

Readings, Lectures & Workshops: Read at elementary and high schools. Conduct writing workshops for high school students.

Mailing Address: 407-527 Commodore Road, Vancouver, British Columbia V5Z 4G5

MICHAEL F. HENNESSEY

Born in Charlottetown, Prince Edward Island, May 23, 1926; returned there permanently in 1958. Spent seven years wandering the world courtesy of the Royal Canadian Navy. B.A. (English), St. Dunstan's University; B.Ed., St. Francis Xavier; Diploma in Special Ed. (Deaf), Clarke School, Northampton, Mass. Organised School for the Deaf in PEI and ran it for three years; also former teacher and guidance counsellor. Currently registrar and university secretary, University of Prince Edward Island. Married to the former Aletha Laura (Dolly) Doyle; five children: Kathleen, Maureen, Frank, Sean and Patrick.

Selected Publications:

Salt in Their Blood: Charlottetown, Irwin Printing, 1973. (no ISBN)
The Catholic Church on Prince Edward Island, 1720-1979: Charlottetown, The Roman Catholic Episcopal Corp., 1979. (no ISBN)
An Arch for the King and Other Stories: Charlottetown, Ragweed 1984.

Comments: Have written numerous opinion-type scripts for such CBC programmes as Maritime Magazine, Opinion and Cross-Canada Matinee as well as seven plays (produced) and short stories for radio and literary journals. Former stringer for Halifax Chronicle-Herald (seven years). Former sports columnist for Charlottetown Patriot (four years).

Mailing Address: 21 Greenfield Avenue, Charlottetown, Prince Edward Island C1A 3N2

JURGEN JOACHIM HESSE

Born in Germany in 1924. Grew up in Italy.
No military service. Dropped out of Grade 11.
Checkered post-war career. First novel at 25
a dismal flop. Discovered journalism at 30.
Ascending career but left for Canada in 1958.
Discovered journalism in host language. Last
proper job at Globe and Mail, 1965. Self-
employed writer and broadcaster in Vancouver.
Teach writing and broadcasting. In 1985 was
kissed by computer muse, started writing books.
Ahhhhh.

Selected Publications:

I Love You, I Love You Too: Vancouver, Creative Bullshit, 1971. (no ISBN)
The Story of ACTRA: Vancouver, Thinkware Consultants, 1985. (no ISBN)
The Mobile Retirement Handbook: Vancouver, Self-Counsel, 1987. ISBN
   0-88908-663-X
The Radio Documentary Handbook: Vancouver, Self-Counsel, 1987. ISBN
   0-88908-653-2

Awards: ACTRA Award (Radio Documentary/Public Affairs), 1982.
WILBUR Award from the Religious Public Relations Council, St. Louis,
Missouri, 1984.

Comments: "The Prime Minister (Pierre Trudeau) asked that I send you,
on his behalf, hearty congratulations on your recent ACTRA Award."
– *Office of the Prime Minister*

"The CBC is fortunate indeed to have writers of your calibre." – A.W.
Johnson, President, CBC

"I enjoyed the series very much." – Margaret Lyons, CBC

"Your acceptance was the best." – Sylvia Tait, Vancouver artist

"Jurgen Hesse got his Nellie." – Christopher Moore of ACTRA

"Who says the underdog never wins?" – Emil & Helga B., two motivated
friends

Readings, Lectures & Workshops: Recently read a chapter from magnum
opus in progress, The Hour Zero (a documentary novel), at UBC German
Department. Writing workshops at SFU/Downtown. Oodles of lectures.

Mailing Address: 307-3591 Oak Street, Vancouver, British Columbia
V6H 2M1

DORIS HILLIS

Born at Epsom, Surrey, England, in 1929. Emigrated to Canada in 1955. Taught school in Langenburg, Saskatchewan and in Winnipeg. After completing an M.A. (University of Manitoba), I lectured at the University of British Columbia while pursuing post-M.A. studies in literature. Since 1960, I've lived near Macklin, Saskatchewan, a partner in the family farm business. Also, active in adult education for many years. Have one daughter.

Selected Publications:

The Prismatic Eye: Saskatoon, Thistledown, 1985. ISBN 0-920066-98-4
Voices and Visions (Interviews with Saskatchewan Writers): Moose Jaw,
   Coteau Books, 1985. ISBN 0-919926-47-9

Awards: Alberta Poetry Contest (Short Poem), 1980. Saskatchewan Writers Guild Reading Award, 1983.

Comments: "Exacting in her choice of words and her titles sparkle in their inventiveness. Her prismatic eye offers keen insight into all that falls within its gaze." – *Canadian Book Review Annual* (on *The Prismatic Eye*)

"Attests both to her developed thoughts and her ability to express them . . . at times striking, at others poignantly apt." – *Poetry Canada Review*

"She does not depend on other critics but offers first-hand reactions to the work . . . intelligent, widely read, and equally at home discussing prose and poetry." – *Books in Canada* (on *Voices and Visions*)

Readings, Lectures & Workshops: Read regularly to elementary and high-school as well as adult audiences. Lead workshops on poetry and on interview techniques.

Mailing Address: Box 341, Macklin, Saskatchewan S0L 2C0

LEE JOHN HINDLE

Raised by wolves in Montreal, Quebec, from April 27, 1965. Packed up the family and emigrated West to graduate high school in Canmore, Alberta, where I write full time. Forthcoming novel: The Prince of Dead Man's Flats.

Selected Publications:

Dragon Fall: New York, Avon, 1984. ISBN 0-380-88468-2

Awards: Avon Books North American YA Writing Competition, 1983. Alberta Achievement Award for Excellence, 1984.

Comments: "A writer to be watched." – *Quill & Quire*

"An interview with Hindle is an interesting experience." – *Edmonton Journal*

"Very different, very sophisticated. The story is fascinating." – *Calgary Herald*

Readings, Lectures & Workshops: Read and lecture at libraries, junior-high and high schools and universities.

Mailing Address: Box 1094, Banff, Alberta T0L 0C0

GLADYS HINDMARCH

Selected Publications:

The Peter Stories: Toronto, Coach House, 1976. (no ISBN)
A Birth Account: Vancouver, New Star, 1976. ISBN 0-919888-61-5

   Comments: See: Butling, Pauline. *A Birth Account Reviewed* in Women and Words: (The Anthology): Harbour, 1984
   Butling, Pauline. Gladys Hindmarch: Pontillist Prose: Essays on Canadian Writing, Summer 1986
   (This article contains a complete bibliography of The Boat Stories.)
   Mailing Address: 1750 Parker Street, Vancouver, British Columbia V5L 2K8

JACK HODGINS

Born in 1938, in the Comox Valley, Vancouver Island. Graduated from the University of British Columbia. Married Dianne in 1960. Taught high-school English in Nanaimo, British Columbia, until 1979. Children: Shannon, Gavin and Tyler. Visiting Professor in the Creative Writing Department at the University of Ottawa. Now teaching fiction workshops in the Creative Writing Department at the University of Victoria. Living in Victoria. More fiction in progress.

Selected Publications:

Spit Delaney's Island: Toronto, Macmillan, 1976. ISBN 0-7715-9601-4

The Invention of the World: Toronto, Macmillan, 1977. ISBN 0-7705-1518-5

The Resurrection Of Joseph Bourne: Toronto, Macmillan, 1979. ISBN 0-7705-1717-X

The Barclay Family Theatre: Toronto, Macmillan, 1981. ISBN 0-7715-9597-2

The Honorary Patron: Toronto, McClelland & Stewart, 1987.

Awards: The President's Medal, University of Western Ontario, 1973. The Eaton's B.C. Book Award, 1977. The Gibson First Novel Award, 1978. The Governor General's Award for Fiction, 1980. The Canada-Australia Literary Award, 1986.

Readings, Lectures & Workshops: Workshops at the Saskatchewan Summer School of the Arts, UBC, Strathcona Lodge and Simon Fraser University. Readings and lectures in the U.S., Japan, Austria, West Germany and Norway.

Mailing Address: Dept. of Creative Writing, University of Victoria, Box 1700, Victoria, British Columbia V8V 2Y2

HELENE P. HOLDEN

Happily divorced and living in Montreal with my daughter and her boyfriend. I have an older son who lives with his father, and another son who lives with his girlfriend, his girlfriend's mother and his girlfriend's mother's boyfriend. I also have a mother who lives with the maid, and a boyfriend who lives with one of his ex-wives and two children by a previous marriage. I don't write much as I don't have time.

Selected Publications:

The Chain: Toronto, Longmans, 1969. (no ISBN)
Goodbye, Muffin Lady: New York, Curtis Books, 1974. (no ISBN)
After the Fact: Ottawa, Oberon, 1986. ISBN 0-88750-644-5

Awards: Prix de Litterature Benson & Hedges, 1977
Comments: Have published several stories in French and English, notably in Chatelaine (June 1982), 1984 Best Canadian Stories and in Les ecrits du Canada francais. Have sold TV scripts, one major film script, which I wrote with Emil Radok (who did the Laterna Magica at Expo 67). Have written and produced bilingual plays at the elementary-school level to teach French to English-speaking children. One of three founder-owners of The Double Hook, an all-Canadian book shop in Montreal.
Readings, Lectures & Workshops: Perform my own monologue, Take A Canadian Author to Bed Tonight.
Mailing Address: 471 Lansdowne, Montreal, Quebec H3Y 2V4

GREG HOLLINGSHEAD

Born in Toronto in 1947. Raised in Wood-bridge, Ontario. Studied at the Universities of Toronto and London. I did my Ph.D. on Bishop Berkeley (1974). Since 1975, I have been teaching literature and creative writing at the University of Alberta. Since 1976, I have had many short stories in literary magazines such as Canadian Fiction Magazine, Capilano Review, Descant, Malahat Review, and Matrix. I spend half the year in Edmonton and half the year in Algonquin Park, Ontario. I am married to Rosa Spricer, a psychologist, and have one son, David, born in 1984.

Selected Publications:

Famous Players: Toronto, Coach House, 1982. ISBN 0-88910-231-7

Comments: "Hollingshead specializes in assembling incomprehensible signs into stories, using such careful and clear language that you begin to think him logical." – Anne Collins, *Maclean's*

"In the end, a reviewer stands humble and perplexed." – Dennis Duffy, *Globe and Mail*

"Hollingshead's worlds may be more real than our own." – *Calgary Herald*

"Author to continue in novel and story to supersede usual world as soon as he can locate publisher with same goal." – G.H.

Readings, Lectures & Workshops: Often I read at universities, libraries and art galleries. I have taught several fiction workshops. Readings, lectures, etc. may be booked direct or through TWUC. My presence in Edmonton, Whitney (Ontario) or Montreal is uncertain at any given time.

Mailing Address: c/o TWUC, 24 Ryerson Avenue, Toronto, Ontario M5T 2P3

HAROLD HORWOOD

Born in St. John's, Newfoundland, in 1923. I now live at Annapolis Royal, Nova Scotia. Founding member of TWUC, vice-chairman of the first national council, then chairman, 1980-81. Union organizer, politician, journalist in turn during the 1940s and 50s. Writer in residence at the University of Western Ontario, 1976-77, and the University of Waterloo, 1980-83, where I founded The New Quarterly. Served third year at Waterloo as a resource person in the Integrated Studies Programme.

Selected Publications:

Tommorrow Will Be Sunday: Toronto, Doubleday, 1966. ISBN 0-7737-7083-6
The Foxes of Beachy Cove: Toronto, Doubleday, 1967.
Newfoundland: Toronto, Macmillan, 1969. ISBN 0-7705-1614-9
White Eskimo: Toronto, Doubleday, 1972. ISBN 0-7737-7043-7
Beyond the Road: Toronto, Van Nostrand Reinhold, 1976.
Bartlett: Toronto, Doubleday, 1977. (no ISBN)
Only the Gods Speak: St. John's, Breakwater, 1979. ISBN 0-919948-41-3
Tales of the Labrador Indians: St. John's, Cuff, 1981.
Pirates and Outlaws of Canada: Toronto, Doubleday, 1984.
Memories of Historic Newfoundland: Toronto, Oxford, 1986.

Awards: Beta Sigma Phi First Novel Award, 1966. Best Scientific Book of the Year, 1967. Citation, American Society for State and Local History, 1969. Order of Canada, 1980.
Comments: Other books now on press or under contract:
Remembering Summer, a novel from Pottersfield Press; Dancing on the Shore; and Bandits and Privateers (Canada in the Age of Gunpowder) from Doubleday, 1987.
Mailing Address: P.O. Box 489, Annapolis Royal, Nova Scotia B0S 1A0

JANETTE TURNER HOSPITAL

Born in Melbourne, Australia, 1942; moved to Brisbane at age seven. Went to the University of Queensland, taught high school in the far tropical north, got married. Left Australia in 1967 for Boston; librarian at Harvard for four years. Arrived in Canada in September, 1971. Received an M.A. (Queen's); taught at Millhaven maximum security penitentiary and elsewhere; went off to South India; mailed a story back to The Atlantic; life never the same since. Two teenagers; still married; still writing.

Selected Publications:

The Ivory Swing: Toronto, McClelland & Stewart, 1982. ISBN 0-7710-4220-5
The Tiger in the Tiger Pit: Toronto, McClelland & Stewart, 1983. ISBN 0-7710-4221-3
Borderline: Toronto, McClelland & Stewart, 1985. ISBN 0-7710-4222-1
Dislocations: Toronto, McClelland & Stewart, 1986. ISBN 0-7710-4219-1

Awards: Atlantic First from The Atlantic (Short Story), 1978. Seal First Novel Award, 1982. Periodical Distributors of Canada Award (Short Story), 1982. 45 Below: Canada's Ten Best Young Fiction Writers, 1986.

Comments: For years I have pined for the Queensland rainforests and beaches of my childhood, and also for Harvard Square to which I'm tied by many and long associations. Writing was a form of consolation, I guess, for the loss of those places. Finally I feel at home here, having just moved out to the country, onto the banks of the St. Lawrence. Hundreds of trees, miles of water. Peace. I may become too contented to write. – JTH

Readings, Lectures & Workshops: Writer-in-residence and lecturer in Canadian, Australian and American literature at Massachusetts Institute of Technology, Boston, 1985-86; invited back for Spring 1987. Numerous readings and workshops across Canada and the U.S.

Mailing Address: RR 1, Kingston, Ontario K7L 4V1

BLANCHE HOWARD

Born Blanche Machon, 1923. B.Sc., University of Alberta. Married Bruce Howard in 1945 and still married to him. Moved to the Okanagan Valley in British Columbia. Three children. Articled with a firm of chartered accountants and received C.A. in 1962. Husband elected to Parliament (Liberal) 1968; I began to write. Moved to North Vancouver in 1973, where I work part-time at accounting and make money, and write the other part and don't.

Selected Publications:

The Manipulator: Toronto, McClelland & Stewart, 1972. ISBN 0-7710-4239-6
Pretty Lady: Toronto, General, 1976. ISBN 0-7736-0048-5
The Immortal Soul Of Edwin Carlysle: Toronto, McClelland & Stewart, 1977. ISBN 0-7710-4245-0

Comments: Short stories have appeared in Maclean's, When every woman looked like Regina Lee (1956), in Chatelaine, So wonderful to see you (1969) and Day of Storm (1971), and in Cross-Canada Writers' Quarterly, Requiem, (1984).

Awards: Canadian Booksellers Award, 1973

Mailing Address: 3866 Regent Avenue, North Vancouver, British Columbia V7N 2C4

JAN HUDSON

Born in Calgary, Alberta. Now resident in Vancouver. B.A., University of Calgary, 1978; L.L.B., University of Alberta, 1984. Called to the Alberta bar, 1985.

Selected Publications:

Sweetgrass: Edmonton, Tree Frog Press, 1984. ISBN 0-88967-076-5
B.C. Family Law Caselaw: (ed.), Vancouver, Butterworths, 1986. ISBN 0-409-996-149

Awards: Canada Council Children's Literature Award, 1984. Canadian Library Association (Book of the Year for Children), 1984.
Comments: "Colourful and convincing . . . grittily realistic . . . language used with almost exquisite authenticity." – *Quarry*
"Told with a choice of simple words, in the native phrases and rhythms of its title character, *Sweetgrass* is a near-flawless blend of history, entertainment and story telling." – *Alberta Report*
Readings, Lectures & Workshops: Readings: Grades 6-12.
Mailing Address: c/o TWUC, 24 Ryerson Avenue, Toronto, Ontario M5T 2P3

MONICA HUGHES

Born in Liverpool, England, in 1925. Lived in Egypt. Educated in England and Scotland. Served in WRNS in World War II. Emigrated to Canada in 1952 after two years in Zimbabwe and worked at National Research Council. Settled in Edmonton in 1964 with husband Glen and four children. Began writing for young people in 1971.

Selected Publications:

Earthdark: London, Hamish Hamilton, 1977. ISBN 0-241-89544-8
The Tomorrow City: London, Hamish Hamilton, 1978. ISBN 0-241-89887-0
Guardian of Isis: London, Hamish Hamilton, 1981. ISBN 0-241-10597-8
Hunter In The Dark: Toronto, Clarke Irwin, 1982. ISBN 0-7720-1372-1
Ring Rise, Ring Set: London, Julia MacRae, 1982. ISBN 0-86203-069-2
Space Trap: London, Julia MacRae, 1983. ISBN 0-86203-135-4
My Name is Paula Popowich!: Toronto, Lorimer, 1983. ISBN 0-88862-690-8
Devil On My Back: London, Julia MacRae, 1984. ISBN 0-86203-164-8
Sandwriter: London, Julia MacRae, 1985. ISBN 0-86203-198-2
The Dream Catcher: London, Julia MacRae, 1986. ISBN 0-86203-241-5
Blaine's Way: Toronto, Irwin, 1986. ISBN 0-7725-1564-6

Awards: Vicky Metcalf Awards; 1981, 1983. Canada Council Children's Literature Awards; 1981, 1982. Alberta Culture Juvenile Novel Award, 1981. Saskatchewan Library Association Young Adult Novel Award, 1983.
Comments: "Her science is sound, but her social conscience and her understanding of the human heart is outstanding." – *Junior Bookshelf*
Readings, Lectures & Workshops: Frequently read and lead workshops for upper-elementary to adult groups.
Mailing Address: 13816-110A Avenue, Edmonton, Alberta T5M 2M9

BERNICE THURMAN HUNTER

Born and educated in Toronto, I now live in Scarborough. I have been interested in writing since childhood. At 14 I met, and read one of my stories to, my idol, L.M. Montgomery. Some of my books (the Booky Trilogy) are auto-biographical in nature.

Selected Publications:

That Scatterbrain Booky: Toronto, Scholastic, 1981. ISBN 0-590-71082-6
With Love From Booky: Toronto, Scholastic, 1983. ISBN 0-590-71220-9
A Place For Margaret: Toronto, Scholastic, 1984. ISBN 0-590-71481-3
As Ever Booky: Toronto, Scholastic, 1985. ISBN 0-590-71547-X
Margaret In The Middle: Toronto, Scholastic, 1986. ISBN 0-590-71681-6

Awards: IODE Award, 1981. Toronto Book Award Finalist, 1982. Ruth Schwartz Award Finalist, 1983.

Comments: "Hunter can recapture exactly how it felt to be a funny, spirited, naive, noticing kind of kid, scampering through Toronto's Depression years on an empty stomach and skinny legs." – Michele Landsberg, *Toronto Star*

Readings, Lectures & Workshops: Often asked to speak at schools, libraries and church groups, especially on the hungry 30s.

Mailing Address: 703-3333 Finch Avenue East, Scarborough, Ontario M1W 2R9

EDITH IGLAUER

Born in Cleveland, Ohio; moved to Canada in 1973. Now living in British Columbia in a small fishing community three hours north of Vancouver. B.A. (Wellesley); M.S. (Columbia). Articles have appeared in The Christian Science Monitor, The New York Herald Tribune, Harper's, The Atlantic, McCall's, MacLean's, Saturday Night, and most often, in The New Yorker. (Currently on the staff of The New Yorker.) During World War II worked for Office of War Information in Washington. Second marriage to the late John Heywood Daly, commercial salmon troller. In final stages of a book about fishing off the B.C. coast with him.

Selected Publications:

The New People: New York, Doubleday, 1966. (no ISBN)
Denison's Ice Road: Toronto and Vancouver, Clarke Irwin/Douglas & McIntyre, 1982. ISBN 0-88894-350-4
Inuit Journey: Vancouver, Douglas & McIntyre, 1979. ISBN 0-88894-174-9.
Seven Stones (A Portrait of Arthur Erikson, Architect): Madeira Park, B.C. and Seattle, Harbour Publishing/ University of Washington Press, 1981. ISBN 0-920080-13-8

Awards: Outdoor Science Club Selection, 1975. The Women's City Club of Cleveland Arts Prize for creative achievement in the Fine Arts of Literature, 1983.

Comments: "The unromanticised story . . . of the efforts being made by a primitive people 'to jump, literally for their lives' into the twentieth century . . . a beautiful book." – Christina McCall Newman (on *The New People* and *Inuit Journey*).

Inuit Journey contains all the material in *The New People*, plus two new chapters: an introduction assessing the Inuit cooperatives twenty years later and an epilogue, telling what happened to the people I had written about.

Mailing Address: Box 116, Garden Bay, British Columbia V0N 1S0

ANN IRELAND

Born and raised in Toronto. Attended the University of British Columbia, 1972-76 (B.F.A.). Now live in Toronto.

Selected Publications:

A Certain Mr. Takahashi: Toronto, McClelland and Stewart, 1985. ISBN 0-7710-4363-5

Awards: Seal First Novel Award, 1985
Comments: "This is a work of the highest literary merit, simply and cleanly written, yet complex in its implications." – *Calgary Herald*
"Ann Ireland has made an exciting and accomplished debut with this book." – *San Francisco Chronicle*
"This most perceptive and compassionate of fictions." – *The Observer*
Readings, Lectures & Workshops: Have read and conducted workshops in British Columbia, Ontario and Saskatchewan.
Mailing Address: c/o TWUC, 24 Ryerson Avenue, Toronto, Ontario M5T 2P3

CHARLES EDWARD ISRAEL

Born in Evansville, Indiana, November 15, 1920. Made the jump to Canadian citizenship in 1985 after only 32 years as a landed immigrant. Hold a B.A. from the University of Cincinnati and a B.H.L. from Hebrew Union College. Succumbed to the lure of full-time writing after service in the US Merchant Marine, 1943-45, and refugee work in Europe with the UN, 1946-50. With my wife, Gloria Varley, I now live and work in an elderly house in midtown Toronto.

Selected Publications:

The Mark: Toronto, Macmillan, 1958. (no ISBN)
Rizpah: Toronto, Macmillan, 1961. (no ISBN)
Shadows on a Wall: Toronto, Macmillan, 1965. (no ISBN)
The Hostages: Toronto, Macmillan, 1966. (no ISBN)
The Newcomers: (ed.), Toronto, McClelland & Stewart, 1979.

Awards: Prix Italia (Scenario) at the Prague Film Festival. First recipient of the Margaret Collier Award from the Academy of Canadian Cinema and Television, 1986.

Comments: Among some 600 radio, television and film credits, Canadian productions include The Open Grave, Let Me Count the Ways and The Diviners. Foreign and co-productions include Louisiana and Arch of Triumph. Story executive for the CTV series The Campbells, 1986-87 season. Regular, wine columnist for Toronto magazine.

Readings, Lectures & Workshops: Moderator, panel on writing, Banff Television Festival, 1985. Director, First Banff Screenwriting Workshop, 1987.

Mailing Address: 113 Howland Avenue, Toronto, Ontario M5R 3B4

FRANCES ITANI

Born in Belleville, Ontario, the middle of five children. Moved to a small village in Quebec at age four. Primary and high school education in Quebec. B.A. (Psychology), University of Alberta, 1974; M.A. (English Literature), University of New Brunswick, 1980. Taught and practised nursing (McGill) for eight years. Worked in England, Heidelberg and North Carolina. Have taught creative writing at the University of Ottawa since 1985. Married Ted Itani in 1967; two children, Russell and Sam.

Selected Publications:

No Other Lodgings: Fredericton, Fiddlehead, 1978. ISBN 0-920110-21-5
Linger by the Sea: Fredericton, Brunswick, 1979. ISBN 0-88790-108-5
Rentee Bay: Kingston, Quarry, 1983. ISBN 0-919627-06-4
Coming Attractions 3: Ottawa, Oberon, 1985. ISBN 0-88750-592-9

Awards: CBC Literary Competition, 1985

Comments: Short stories and poems have been published widely in literary journals and anthologies including 84: Best Canadian Stories. Stories From Foreign Places, a 30-minute radio feature, was broadcast on CBC State of the Arts in January 1986. Linger By The Sea was read over CBC's Morningside.

Wrote The Keepers Of The Cranes, a 60-minute play for CBC Stage in 1977. Have begun to try writing for stage; two plays have been workshopped by Ottawa theatres. Also working on a novel, which never seems to be finished.

"Frances Itani's short story, Grandmother, so loving and serene, is quite astonishing." – Ken Adachi, *Toronto Star*

"Itani is too good to need introducing: her stories are such fine examples of the genre that any writer might be proud of them." – William Connor, *The Fiddlehead*

Readings, Workshops & Lectures: Available for readings and workshops. May be contacted through TWUC.

Mailing Address: 1400 Plumber Avenue, Ottawa, Ontario K1K 4A9

BETTY E.M. JACOBS

Born and educated in England. Emigrated to Canada in 1949 with husband and two sons. Farmed for six years in British Columbia. Spent several years in England and Argentina. Returned to Canada in 1961 and in 1964 opened Jacob's Ladder Herb Farm in Sooke, on Vancouver Island. Now retired and still writing practical how-to books from personal experience.

Selected Publications:

Growing Herbs for the Kitchen: Sidney, Gray's, 1972. (no ISBN)
Profitable Herb Growing At Home: Vermont, Garden Way, 1976. ISBN
  0-88266-087-X
Growing Herbs and Plants for Dyeing: Berea, Graphicom, 1977. ISBN
  0-910458-12-X
Growing and Using Herbs Successfully: Vermont, Garden Way, 1981. ISBN
  0-88266-249-X

Comments: "One of the best and most straight forward works on growing herbs that this reviewer and zealous herb grower has read." – *New York Botanical Garden Magazine*
"A solid basic guide to herbs . . . The information the book contains doesn't intimidate, presenting cultural facts clearly and succinctly . . . without overflowing with flowery folderol." – Paul Williams, *Patriot Ledger*
"As comprehensive and readable a guide to herb culture as one is likely to find." – *Publishers Weekly*
Mailing Address: 1595 Whiffen Spit Road, RR 4, Sooke, British Columbia V0S 1N0

BETH JANKOLA

Practising, published, performing poet and graphic artist.

Selected Publications:

Jody Said: Vancouver, Press Gang, 1977. ISBN 0-88974-002-X
Sun Petals Soon to Dust: Mayne Island, Caitlin, 1981. ISBN 0-920576-09-5
Sun/Flowers: Vancouver, blewointment, 1981. ISBN 0-88911-052-X
Faceless Woman: London, Third Eye, 1985. ISBN 0-919581-26-9

  Awards: Bliss Carman Award (Poetry), 1974
  Comments: Published in Canadian Forum, Capilano Review, CVII, Poetry Canada Review, Arc, Poetry Toronto, Event, The Malahat Review, Quarry, International Prism et al.
  Dramatic reading of Slim Pickings was performed by Waterfront Theatre.
  Readings, Lectures & Workshops: Have lectured at Carleton University, University of Edmonton, Vancouver Art Gallery, Powerhouse Gallery (Montreal), Axletree (Toronto), Open Space Gallery (Victoria) et al.
  Mailing Address: Box 80644, Burnaby, British Columbia V5H 3Y1

PAULETTE JILES

Born in Dent County, Missouri, grew up in various small towns in Missouri, graduated high school in Kansas City, graduated University of Missouri in 1968, came to Canada in 1969, worked for CBC radio Public Affairs until 1973, travelled in Europe and North Africa, worked with native communications groups in the Arctic and sub-Arctic, 1973-83, taught at David Thompson University Centre in Nelson, B.C., until 1984 when it was closed down by the Social Credit government. Have lived in Nelson ever since.

Selected Publications:

Waterloo Express: Toronto, Anansi, 1973. ISBN 0-88784-129-5
Golden Hawks: Toronto, Lorimer, 1976. ISBN 0-88862-182-5
Celestial Navigation: Toronto, McClelland & Stewart, 1984. ISBN 0-7710-4421-6
Sitting In The Club Car Drinking Rum And Karma-Kola: Winlaw, Polestar, 1986. ISBN 0-919591-13-2
The Late Great Human Roadshow: Vancouver, Talon, 1986. ISBN 0-88922-239-8

Mailing Address: c/o TWUC, 24 Ryerson Avenue, Toronto, Ontario M5T 2P3

JEAN JOHNSTON

Born Jean Morton in 1910 in Hamilton, Ontario. Graduate of Victoria College, University of Toronto, where I was women's editor of Acta Victoriana and of The Varsity. Reporter or photographer for dailies in Hamilton, Woodstock and Stratford, Ontario. Contributor to many farm and garden magazines. Book reviewer, Quill & Quire and Canadian Book Review Annual. Married, 1934, to Stafford Johnston; three children, nine grandchildren. President, Armtree Inc., a tree farm.

Selected Publications:

Wilderness Women: Toronto, Peter Martin, 1973. ISBN 0-88778-084-9
Rob and the Rebels: Ottawa, Borealis, 1981. ISBN 0-88887-027-2

Comments: In progress are His Labrador Lordship, a biography of Sir Donald A. Smith, Lord Strathcona, under contract to Dundurn Press, Toronto; and Metissage, a study of White-Indian marriages and their influence on the development of a distinctively Canadian culture.
Mailing Address: RR 2, Mitchell, Ontario N0K 1N0

LEANNE MARIE JONES

Born in Kincaid, Saskatchewan, now living in
Sidney, British Columbia. A primary teacher,
trained at Brandon University, I have also
worked as a librarian in Germany and Canada.
Studied creative writing in San Miguel de
Allende, Mexico, and was influenced by two
years spent in Tokyo, Japan, as a governess.
Designed a Writing Books for Children course
for University of Victoria and currently teach
it at Camosun College. Have interviewed court-
house characters for CHEK TV. Currently freelance for Western Report news magazine and
work as a private investigator.

Selected Publications:

Hanok: Red Deer, Red Deer Press, 1979.
The Book About Nothing: Red Deer, Red Deer Press, 1980.

Readings, Lectures & Workshops: Conducted workshops sponsored by
the University of Victoria in Kelowna and Nanaimo. Also led several workshops, sponsored by the Canadian Authors Association. Visited schools all
over British Columbia with the film strip of *Hanok* to give talks and readings.
Wrote a manual for the schools entitled The Writer in the Classroom.

Mailing Address: 2516 Rothesay Avenue, Sidney, British Columbia
V8L 2B8

BESS KAPLAN

Born in Winnipeg, Manitoba, July 1, 1927. Still live there. Did a variety of writing and settled on fiction. Past-president of Manitoba Branch of the Canadian Authors Association and Penhandlers. Former editor of the Jewish Post and now its columnist. Researching a new novel. Soon. (Any day now.) Have to wash windows first. Or iron socks. Or babysit grandsons . . .

Selected Publications:

Corner Store: Winnipeg, Queenston House, 1975. ISBN 0-919866-10-7
Malke, Malke: Winnipeg, Queenston House, 1977. ISBN 0-919866-19-0
The Empty Chair: Saskatoon, WP Prairie Books, 1986. ISBN 0-88833-205-X

   Awards: Kathleen Strange Memorial Award, Manitoba Branch, CAA, 1973
   Comments: "Always fresh and agreeably idiosyncratic." – William French, *Globe and Mail*
   "A funny book; an understanding book." – Mark Trey
   "Several unpublished novels which will turn Kaplan into overnight success if and when they are published." – BK
   Readings, Lectures & Workshops: Speak on fiction techniques at writers' workshops and in schools. Give creative writing and other sessions. Readings may be booked through TWUC.
   Mailing Address: 501-15 Pipeline Road, Winnipeg, Manitoba R2P 1G9

VANCY KASPER

Only child, born and live in Toronto. Great granddaughter of Joseph Shepard, in whose living room William Lyon Mackenzie planned his 1837 Rebellion. B.A., University of Toronto. Journalist for Toronto Star for nine years. Sons Fred Jr., jazz bassist in Toronto, and Max, principal bass for the Halifax Symphony, both born on Toronto Island where I lived for 13 years. Write fiction, poetry and teach, play guitar and do poetry in performance. Summers in Haliburton at farm.

Selected Publications:

A Mighty Force in Handshakings: Toronto, Gage, 1981.
Always Ask For A Transfer: Toronto, Nelson, 1984. ISBN 0-17-602088-8
Mother, I'm So Glad You Taught Me How To Dance: Toronto, Williams-Wallace, 1986. ISBN 0-88795-054-X

Awards: First Runner Up, Max and Greta Abel Memorial Award, 1986. Best Story of the Year, JAM Magazine, 1981.

Comments: Poetry published in Fireweed, Canadian Women's Studies, Quarry, Waves and Poetry Toronto.

I Wish I Was Somebody Else Girl appeared in JAM in 1981.

In progress, an adult novel and a poetry manuscript.

Member of Writers' Union; CANSCAIP; Women's Press Club; Women's Writing Collective; Amnesty; Toronto Disarmament.

Readings, Lectures & Workshops: Read regularly at libraries, festivals, schools etc. Lead workshops for adults on the creative process. Teach creative writing and enrichment programmes to children and adults (North York, Peckham Centre, Windsor & Peel Young writers conferences and the Upper Canada Writers Workshop).

Mailing Address: 72 Briar Hill Avenue, Toronto, Ontario M4R 1H9

JOANNE KATES

Born in Toronto, live in Toronto and Algonquin Park.

Selected Publications:

Exploring Algonquin Park: Vancouver, Douglas & McIntyre, 1983. ISBN 0-88894-378-4
The Joanne Kates Cookbook: Toronto, Oxford, 1984. ISBN 0-19-540467-X
The Joanne Kates Toronto Restaurant Guide: Toronto, Methuen, 1984 (revised 1986). ISBN 0-458-80210-7
The Taste of Things: Toronto, Oxford, 1987. ISBN 0-19-540573-0

Comments: Next book will be on the relationship between feminists and men, for The Women's Press.
Mailing Address: c/o TWUC, 24 Ryerson Avenue, Toronto, Ontario M5T 2P3

WELWYN WILTON KATZ

Born in London, Ontario, June 7, 1948. B.Sc. Mathematics, Diploma in Education (University of Western Ontario, 1969, 1970). Taught secondary school math for seven years. Have been a textbook consultant and a researcher in social science, computer science and applied mathematics. Play and teach the flute. Write juvenile and young-adult fiction. Live and write in London, Ontario, with my husband and young daughter. Interested in legends, math and science of prehistory.

Selected Publications:

The Prophecy of Tau Ridoo: Edmonton, Tree Frog, 1982. ISBN 0-88967-045-5

Witchery Hill: Toronto, Groundwood, 1984. ISBN 0-88899-031-6

Sun God, Moon Witch: Toronto, Groundwood, 1986. ISBN 0-88899-041-3

Awards: First Runner Up, Canadian Library Association Book of the Year for Children, 1984

Comments: "A Canadian answer to the extraordinary Susan Cooper."
– *Children's Book News*

"Holds the reader in thrall to events she orchestrates like a maestro."
– *Publishers Weekly*

"A good storyteller who writes in a way that will appeal to teenagers and young adults alike." – *Canadian Children's Literature*

"Skilful, compelling . . . " – *ALA Book List*

"An excellent fantasy writer." – *Kids Can Read*

Readings, Lectures & Workshops: Readings or workshops may be booked through TWUC.

Mailing Address: c/o TWUC, 24 Ryerson Avenue, Toronto, Ontario M5T 2P3

DONALD ROBERT KEATING

Born on a farm in Silver Creek, Manitoba, December 9, 1925, of Socialist and Christian parents. A circuitous route through the RCAF, United Church Ministry and five years of on-the-job training through Don Benedict in Saul Alinsky's Chicago brought me to a working-class community in Toronto where the first Community Convention in Canada was held. Hold B.A., B.D. and M.E.S. degrees from Canadian universities. I now live in Toronto.

Selected Publications:

The Power To Make It Happen: Green Tree, 1975. (no ISBN)
The Future of Neighborhood Organizing in Participatory Democracy in Action: Delhi, Vikas, 1979. (no ISBN)

Readings, Lectures & Workshops: Visiting tutor for the Ontario Institute for Studies in Education's course on Community Education and Development. Workshops on community organising.

Mailing Address: 283 Booth Avenue, Toronto, Ontario M4M 2M7

JANICE KULYK KEEFER

Born in Toronto, June 2, 1952. B.A., University of Toronto, 1974; M.A., D. Phil., University of Sussex, England, 1974-83. Post-Doctoral Fellow, l'Universite Sainte-Anne, Nova Scotia, 1984-86. Now living in Annapolis Royal. Married to Michael Keefer; two children.

Selected Publications:

The Paris-Napoli Express: Ottawa, Oberon, 1986. ISBN 0-88750-624-0
White of the Lesser Angels: Charlottetown, Ragweed, 1986.
  ISBN 0-920304-60-5

Awards: First Prize, Prism International Fiction Competition, 1984. First Prize CBC Literary Competition (Fiction), 1985.

Comments: Fiction, poetry, book reviews and articles have appeared in Canadian literary journals. Have completed a critical study of Canadian Maritime fiction and am working on a book-length study of Mavis Gallant.

Mailing Address: c/o The Colbert Agency, 303 Davenport Road, Toronto, Ontario M5R 1K5

BETTY CAROL KELLER

Born in Vancouver, British Columbia, November 4, 1930. Parents: Anne Devine and Harry B. Devine. Educated in Langley, British Columbia. Teaching certificate, 1963; B.A. English, 1967. Taught high school English and Drama 1963-74. Associate in the Education Faculty of Simon Fraser University, 1975-76, 1978-79. Teacher in Numan Women's Teachers' College, Numan, Nigeria, 1977-78. Sessional lecturer in Creative Writing Dept., UBC, 1981-82, 1985.

Selected Publications:

Trick Doors and Other Dramatic Sketches: Vancouver, November House, 1974. ISBN 0-88894-053-X
Taking Off: Vancouver, November House, 1975. ISBN 0-88894-072-6
Legends of the River People: (with Norman Lerman), Vancouver, November House, 1976. ISBN 0-88894-115-3
Pauline (A Biography of Pauline Johnson): Vancouver, Douglas & McIntyre, 1982. ISBN 0-88894-322-9
Black Wolf (The Life of Ernest Thompson Seton): Vancouver, Douglas & McIntyre, 1984. ISBN 0-88894-439-X
On the Shady Side (Vancouver 1886-1914): Ganges, Horsdal & Schubart, 1986. ISBN 0-920663-04-4

Awards: Canadian Biography Award, 1982. The Gillian Lowndes Award, 1986.

Comments: In 1983, I was one of a group of writers, both professional and casual, who formed the SunCoast Writers' Forge in Sechelt, B.C. I became the group's first president and the co-ordinator of the group's annual Festival of the Written Arts. Held in mid-August each year since 1983, this event attracts nearly a thousand people to hear Canadian writers talk about their writing and read from their work.

Mailing Address: RR 1, Sandy Hook, Sechelt, British Columbia V0N 3A0

HEATHER KELLERHALS-STEWART

Grew up in Toronto, graduated from the University of Toronto. Moved to Vancouver and studied social work at the University of British Columbia. Worked with children's group and foster homes in Vancouver and Edmonton. Freelance journalism concentrating on children, women and environmental issues has appeared in the Vancouver Sun, Kinesis, Canadian Children's Annual and Magazine. Married a Swiss, Rolf Kellerhals, and have two children, Erika and Markus. Currently living on an island farm in British Columbia. Member of the British Columbia Federation of Writers.

Selected Publications:

She Shoots She Scores!: Toronto, The Women's Press, 1975. (no ISBN)
Muktu, The Backward Muskox: Vancouver, Press Gang, 1978. (no ISBN)
Rory and the Whooping Crane: Ottawa, Borealis, 1977. ISBN 0-919594-71-9
Cricket Christmas: Ottawa, Borealis, 1978. ISBN 0-919594-70-0
Stuck Fast in Yesterday: Toronto, Groundwood, 1983. ISBN 0-88899-024-3

Readings, Lectures & Workshops: Readings and storytelling in schools and libraries.
Mailing Address: Box 250, Heriot Bay, British Columbia V0P 1H0

M. T. KELLY

A native of Toronto, born November 30, 1946, I have lived in that city most of my life, although I worked as a reporter in Moose Jaw, Saskatchewan, and taught school in Northern Ontario. I am the author of four novels, a play and two books of poetry but make my living as a freelance writer. A regular contributor to the Globe and Mail Book Review section, I have made a point of reviewing books on native people as well as literary works. I have published in many magazines and journals across the country.

Selected Publications:

I Do Remember the Fall: Toronto, Simon and Pierre, 1977. ISBN 0-88924-064-7

Country You Can't Walk In: Moonbeam, Penumbra, 1979. ISBN 0-920806-00-7

The More Loving One: Windsor, Black Moss, 1980. 0-88753-069-9

The Ruined Season: Windsor, Black Moss, 1983. ISBN 0-88753-085-0

Country You Can't Walk In and Other Poems: Moonbeam, Penumbra, 1984. ISBN 0-920806-56-2

The Green Dolphin: Toronto, Playwrights Union, 1983. ISBN 0-88754-325-1

A Dream Like Mine: Toronto, General, 1987. ISBN 0-7737-2164-4

Readings, Lectures & Workshops: I have given readings and workshops across Canada and have lectured at Memorial University, Nfld.; Trent University, Peterborough, Ontario; and the University of Toronto. I am also a participant in the Ontario Arts Council Writers in the Schools programme.

Mailing Address: 60 Kendal Avenue, Toronto, Ontario M5R 1L9

NORA KELLY

Born August 29, 1945, in Paterson, New Jersey. Now living in Vancouver. B.A., University of British Columbia, 1972; Ph.D., Simon Fraser University, 1979 (History). One son, Julian, born 1977. Work in progress: The Innermost House, a book on Cape Cod.

Selected Publications:

In the Shadow of King's: Collins/Totem, 1986. ISBN 0-00-231396-0

Mailing Address: 11-2649 Quebec Street, Vancouver, British Columbia V5T 3A6

PENN(Y) KEMP

Poet, playwright, novelist and sound poet, I was raised in London, spent much of my life in Ontario and now live in Toronto between travels. After an Honours English degree from the University of Western Ontario, I taught English and creative writing for three years. Since 1974, I have been an active participant in schools, performing my poetry and plays and giving workshops for students and teachers in writing and creativity across the continent and abroad.

Selected Publications:

Bearing Down: Toronto, Coach House, 1972. (no ISBN)
Tranceform: Victoria, Soft Press, 1976. ISBN 0-919590-26-8
The Epic of Toad and Heron: Windsor, Black Moss, 1977. ISBN 0-88753-030-3
Angel Makers: Toronto, Playwrights Union, 1978. ISBN 0-88754-089-9
Toad Tales: Buffalo, White Pine, 1981. ISBN 0-934834-24-5
Animus: Mayne Island, Caitlin, 1984. ISBN 0-920576-13-3
Binding Twine: Charlottetown, Ragweed, 1984. ISBN 0-920304-32-X
Some Talk Magic: London, Ergo, 1986. ISBN 0-920516-08-4
Travelling Light: St. Catharines, Moonstone, 1986. ISBN 0-920259-10-3

Comments: "One of the most exciting Canadian poets . . . with vast experience in stimulating creativity." – Barbara Godard

"A very talented writer . . . her insights add much to our understanding. What a courageous woman." – Margaret Laurence

Readings, Lectures & Workshops: I have performed at the International Sound Poetry Festival (NYC, 1980), the Lincoln Center New Wilderness Solstice Celebration (NYC, 1981), the Great Canadian Poetry Weekend (Collingwood, 1981) and the Findhorn Arts Festival (Scotland, 1984, 85) as well as in Canadian schools and libraries.

Mailing Address: 44 Brookmount Road, Toronto, Ontario M4L 3N2

REGINALD KENDALL

Born in 1924 in England, I completed a five-year apprenticeship in a British shipbuilding yard. Served in the RAF and together with my wife, Maureen, emigrated to Canada in 1951. Was employed by Atomic Energy of Canada, Chalk River, for five years before taking up a farming career that lasted for 25 years. I hold a National Institute of Engineering certificate and a technical and commercial radio college diploma. In 1980, after retirement, my wife and I served in Papua New Guinea with CUSO.

Selected Publications:

Problem Bilong Yu: Winnipeg, Queenston House, 1986. ISBN 0-920273-08-4

Comments: "To read *Problem Bilong Yu* is to spend six or seven hours in the company of a peerless raconteur." – *London Free Press*

"In *Problem Bilong Yu* he gives a lively account of their stay in Papua New Guinea and tells a story that others with overseas development in mind would find useful." – *Western People*

"Mr. Kendall writes in a well-organized manner with each incident described being complete in itself as well as forming part of a well-rounded whole." – *C M Review Journal*

Readings, Lectures & Workshops: I enjoy giving slide presentations and lectures about Papua New Guinea to students, senior citizen groups and service clubs.

Mailing Address: 1026 Sherbourne Road, London, Ontario N6G 4C8

VALERIE KENT

Born in Tokay, Hungary, January 14, 1947. Now living in Toronto. B.F.A., Sir George Williams University, 1970; M.F.A., University of Iowa. Taught creative writing at Concordia University, McGill, Dawson College. Taught at various penitentiaries in Quebec. Owned the Canadian Language Institute and a restaurant. Did course development at George Brown College.

Selected Publications:

Polly Wants a Cracker in *The Story So Far*: Toronto, Coach House, 1971. (no ISBN)
Wheelchair Sonata: Toronto, Coach House, 1974. (no ISBN)
A Thousand Days in the Attic: Toronto, Coach House, 1976. (no ISBN)

Comments: Editor of Northern Journey magazine, 1973-76. Published in Canadian and U.S. literary magazines including Canadian Forum, Impulse and Black Swan. Married Farsad Kiani in 1983 and had a daughter, Suzanne Kiani, in 1986.

Mailing Address: c/o TWUC, 24 Ryerson Avenue, Toronto, Ontario M5T 2P3

EILEEN KERNAGHAN

Born January 6, 1939, grew up on a farm outside Grindrod, British Columbia, and have lived in Burnaby, British Columbia, since 1963. Formerly an elementary school teacher and arts administrator; now writing full time. In addition to science fiction and fantasy, I have published poetry and short stories in anthologies and literary magazines. Currently working on a fantasy novel set in bronze-age India. Forthcoming book entitled Sarsen Witch.

Selected Publications:

Journey to Aprilioth: New York, Ace, 1980. ISBN 0-441-38621-0
Songs from the Drowned Lands: New York, Ace, 1983. ISBN 0-441-772-42-0
The Upper Left-Hand Corner (A Writer's Guide for the Northwest): (3rd. ed.), Vancouver, Self-Counsel, 1986. ISBN 0-88908-631-1

Awards: PORGY Award (Original Paperback Fantasy) from the West Coast Review of Books, 1980. Canadian Science Fiction and Fantasy Award (CASPER), 1983-84.

Comments: "Kernaghan's prose is crafted with care, her plot plausible and her narrative well-balanced. Meticulous attention to geographical and historical detail imbue the fantasy with a rich depth of field." – Leslie Peterson, *Vancouver Sun*

Readings, Lectures & Workshops: Conduct workshops on writing and marketing for schools, writers' organisations, continuing education programmes, etc. Also available for readings and lectures.

Mailing Address: 5512 Neville Street, Burnaby, British Columbia V5J 2H7

SUSAN KERSLAKE

Born in Chicago in 1943. Attended Montana State University. Worked at Kroch's & Brentano's Bookstore in Chicago. Immigrated to Canada in 1966. Worked in libraries at Dalhousie University, for St. Joseph's Childrens' Centre and at the I.W.K. Hospital for Children. I live in Halifax.

Selected Publications:

Middlewatch: Ottawa, Oberon, 1976. ISBN 0-88750-206-7
The Book of Fears: Charlottetown, Ragweed, 1984. ISBN 0-920304-31-1
Penumbra: Toronto, Aya, 1984. ISBN 0-920544-40-1

Awards: Participant in 45 Below: Canada's Ten Best Young Fiction Writers
Readings, Lectures & Workshops: Readings.
Mailing Address: 304-5713 Victoria Road, Halifax, Nova Scotia B3H 2Y3

DEIRDRE KESSLER

Banned in Halifax, the first book in my series about a cat named Brupp nonetheless soon sold out its first printing. Both Brupp books have been translated into Dutch and German and will appear in French and in a mass-market edition in 1987. I live in Charlottetown, where I work as a freelance writer, editor and broadcaster. From 1981 to 1986, I was an arts reporter for CBC television and radio and host of The Story Show on CBC-FM.

Selected Publications:

The Private Adventures of Brupp: Charlottetown, Ragweed, 1983. ISBN 0-920304-25-7

Brupp on the Other Side: Charlottetown, Ragweed, 1985. ISBN 0-920304-33-8

A Child's Anne: Charlottetown, Ragweed, 1983. ISBN 0-920304-11-7

Abegweit, Land Of The Red Soil: (ed.), Charlottetown, Ragweed, 1985. ISBN 0-902304-40-0

Comments: "I'm sly as old boots, and quite handsome, too." – Brupp

Readings, Lectures & Workshops: Frequently read and perform Brupp songs in elementary and junior high schools. Workshops and lectures for teachers. University courses on writing children's books and the writing process. Readings may be booked through the Canada Council or TWUC.

Mailing Address: 29 Victory Avenue, Charlottetown, Prince Edward Island C1A 5E9

DAVID KEYHO

Born on Guernsey, the Channel Islands, in 1928. Educated in London. RAF, 1945-48. After five miserable years as a pen-pusher, I became a teacher in England. Came to Canada, 1959, and settled in Barrie, Ontario. Appointed inspector of schools (later consultant), Ontario Ministry of Education. Active in the Council of Drama in Education, specialist in the art of movement. Early retirement, 1978. Now divorced, living and writing happily in France.

Selected Publications:

Star Speak: (with Sybil Leek), New York, Arbor House, 1975. ISBN 0-87795-118-7

Comments: Articles include the Examiner series, Physical Education: This Is Your Heritage, How We Developed Our P.E. Program (School Progress), Aesthetics and Movement (Journal of Canadian Assoc. for Health, Physical Education and Recreation), Language, Movement; the Player of Parts: A Look At Movement in Dramatic Arts (CAHPER Journal); and The Teacher, The Tyrant and Me (Ontario Education Journal).

Readings, Lectures & Workshops: Travelled all over Ontario giving courses and workshops on movement in the arts between 1959 and 1978. Many lectures and demonstrations at Canadian universities – including Toronto, McMaster and Guelph – on the aesthetics of movement and movement in the arts. Lecturer in Movement, Ontario Teacher Education College, 1975-1977.

Mailing Address: Clair Matin, 74250 Viuz-en-Sallaz, Haute-Savoie, France

WILLIAM KILBOURN

Born in Toronto in 1926. B.A. (Toronto), M.A. (Oxford), Ph.D. (Harvard). Past chairman, Toronto Arts Council. Formerly on boards of Art Gallery of Ontario, UNESCO (Canada), Canada Council and executives of the City and Metropolitan Toronto and a member of the Isaacs Gallery Ensemble, a mixed media group in performing arts. Currently a member of New Music Concerts, the Toronto International Festival Board and professor of history and humanities at York University.

Selected Publications:

The Firebrand (William Lyon Mackenzie and the 1837 Rebellion): Toronto, Clarke Irwin, 1956. (no ISBN)
The Elements Combined (A History of The Steel Co. of Canada): Toronto, Clarke Irwin, 1960. (no ISBN)
The Making of the Nation: Toronto, McClelland & Stewart, 1965.
Canada (A Guide to the Peaceable Kingdom): Toronto, Macmillan, 1970. (no ISBN)
Pipeline (TransCanada and the Great Debate): Toronto, Clarke Irwin, 1970. (no ISBN)
C.D. Howe (A Biography): (with R. Bothwell), Toronto, McClelland & Stewart, 1979. ISBN 0-7710-4535-2
Toronto Remembered: Toronto, Stoddart, 1984. ISBN 0-7737-2029-4
Toronto Observed (Its Architecture, Patrons and History): Toronto, Oxford, 1986. ISBN 0-19-540508-0

Awards: University of British Columbia President's Medal for Biography, 1957. Fellow of the Royal Society of Canada, 1979. Albert B. Greg Prize of the Canadian and American Historical Associations, 1980. Toronto Historical Board Award of Merit, 1985.
Readings, Lectures & Workshops: Teaching humanities and history at York University.
Mailing Address: 66 Collier Street, #12c, Toronto, Ontario M4W 1L9

W.P. KINSELLA

Born in Edmonton, Alberta, May 25, 1935. Agent: Nancy Colbert, 303 Davenport Rd., Toronto, Ontario M5R 1K5. Graduated from the University of Victoria (B.A. 1974) and the Iowa Writers' Workshop (M.F.A. 1978). Live with wife, Ann Knight, and write full time. Member American Atheists and the Enoch Emery Society. Write primarily about Indians and baseball, though I am neither.

Selected Publications:

Dance Me Outside: Ottawa, Oberon, 1977. ISBN 0-88750-224-5
Scars: Ottawa, Oberon, 1978. ISBN 0-88750-286-5
Shoeless Joe Jackson Comes to Iowa: Ottawa, Oberon, 1980. ISBN 0-88750-343-8
Born Indian: Ottawa, Oberon, 1981. ISBN 0-88750-381-0
The Moccasin Telegraph: Toronto, Penguin, 1983. ISBN 0-14-008363-4
The Thrill of the Grass: Toronto, Penguin, 1984. ISBN 0-14-007386-8
The Iowa Baseball Confederacy: Toronto, Collins, 1986. ISBN 0-00-223046-1
The Fencepost Chronicles: Toronto, Collins, 1986. ISBN 0-00-223-118-2

Awards: Houghton Mifflin Literary Fellowship, 1982. Books in Canada First Novel Award, 1982. Writers Guild of Alberta Novel Award, 1982.

Comments: "Kinsella's horsehide epiphanies illuminate the secret soul of America – and are themselves wonderfully lit by a sweet, loony magic, a lyrical, folklorish grace." – Tom Robbins

Readings, Lectures & Workshops: Arrangements may be made directly or through TWUC. Sponsors should be able to raise a crowd of 75-100 minimum and should read Books in Canada (Field Notes), Feb. 1984, before issuing an invitation.

Mailing Address: Box 400, White Rock, British Columbia V4B 5G3

ED KLEIMAN

Born in 1932 in Winnipeg's North End. Attended St. John's High and the University of Manitoba (1949-53). Received an M.A. from the University of Toronto. Taught school in London, England, for two years (1956-58) and am currently teaching at the University of Manitoba. I am married and have four children.

Selected Publications:

The Immortals: Edmonton, NeWest, 1980. ISBN 0-920316-03-4

Comments: "*The Immortals* is a great story. It catches the expanding vitality of the North End like little I've ever seen before." – Adele Wiseman
"*The Immortals* is full of moments of luminous recognition." – Fredelle Bruser Maynard
"The stories are funny and affecting, vesting in ordinary people the nobility of kings." – David Williamson, *Winnipeg Free Press*
My work has appeared in Winnipeg Stories (Queenston House, 1974); Childhood and Youth in Canadian Literature (Macmillan); More Stories from Western Canada (Macmillan, 1980); New Voices 3 (Ginn, 1982) and Mirror of a People (Jewish Educational Publishers, 1985).
Mailing Address: 78 Queenston Street, Winnipeg, Manitoba R3N 0W5

JOY KOGAWA

Born June 6, 1935, in Vancouver, British Columbia. Now living in Toronto, Ontario.

Selected Publications:

The Splintered Moon: Fredericton, Fiddlehead, 1967. (no ISBN)
A Choice of Dreams: Toronto, McClelland & Stewart, 1974. ISBN 0-7710-4526-3
Jericho Road: Toronto, McClelland & Stewart, 1977. ISBN 0-7710-4527-1
Obasan: Toronto, Lester & Orpen Dennys, 1981. ISBN 0-919630-42-1
Woman in the Woods: Oakville, Mosaic, 1985. ISBN 0-88962-294-9
Naomi's Road: Toronto, Oxford, 1986. ISBN 0-19-540547-1

Awards: Books in Canada First Novel Award, 1981. Canadian Authors Association Book of the Year Award, 1982. Periodical Distributors Award (Fiction), 1983.

Mailing Address: 447 Montrose Avenue, Toronto, Ontario M6G 3H2

GORDON KORMAN

Born October 23, 1963, in Montreal. Now write full time. Home base is Thornhill, Ontario. Was Canada's youngest bestselling author with This Can't Be Happening at MacDonald Hall when I was 14. Hold Bachelor of Fine Arts degree from New York University (1985); major in dramatic and visual writing. Eleven juvenile and Y/A novels in print; all bestsellers.

Selected Publications:

This Can't Be Happening at MacDonald Hall: Toronto, Scholastic, 1977. ISBN 0-590-32645-7
Go Jump in the Pool: Toronto, Scholastic, 1979. ISBN 0-590-32644-9
Beware the Fish: Toronto, Scholastic, 1979. ISBN 0-590-32646-5
Who is Bugs Potter?: Toronto, Scholastic, 1980. ISBN 0-590-71036-2
I Want to Go Home: Toronto, Scholastic, 1981. ISBN 0-590-71081-8
Our Man Weston: Toronto, Scholastic, 1982. ISBN 0-590-40352-4
The War with Mr. Wizzle: Toronto, Scholastic, 1982. ISBN 0-590-32643-0
Bugs Potter Live at Nickaninny: Toronto, Scholastic, 1983. ISBN 0-590-71225-X
No Coins Please: Toronto, Scholastic, 1984. ISBN 0-590-33466-2
Don't Care High: New York, Scholastic, 1985. ISBN 0-590-40251-X
Son of Interflux: New York, Scholastic, 1986. ISBN 0-590-40163-7

Awards: Air Canada Award, 1981. Ontario Youth Medal, 1985.
Comments: "Your Bruno & Boots series novels . . . have evoked great repercussion in our country and . . . are praised to be rarely good novels." — Lu Ming, Shanghai
Readings, Lectures & Workshops: Tour extensively throughout Canada and the United States.
Mailing Address: 20 Dersingham Crescent, Thornhill, Ontario L3T 4E7

MYRNA KOSTASH

Born in 1944 in Edmonton, Alberta, I was educated at the universities of Alberta and Toronto.
In the 1970s I established myself as a full-time
writer in Toronto, then returned to Alberta in
1975 to write my first book. I now live in a
housing co-op in Edmonton and retreat to a
shack on a quarter-section in the Ukrainian
settlements of northeastern Alberta every
summer. I write full time and have survived to
tell the tale.

Selected Publications:

All of Baba's Children: Edmonton, Hurtig, 1977. ISBN 0-88830-144-8
Long Way From Home (The Story of the Sixties Generation in Canada):
  Toronto, Lorimer, 1980. ISBN 0-88862-380-1
No Kidding (Inside the World of Teenage Girls): Toronto, Douglas Gibson
  Books/McClelland & Stewart, 1987. ISBN 0-7710-4539-5

  Awards: National Magazine Award (Silver), 1985
  Comments: Contributed to Her Own Woman (Macmillan, 1975) and
Getting Here (NeWest, 1977).
  Readings, Lectures & Workshops: Often read at universities, colleges,
schools and libraries. Conduct creative writing workshops for women's
groups, prisons and junior colleges. Lecture widely on ethnicity, the women's
movement, regionalism and youth subcultures. May be booked through
TWUC.
  Mailing Address: 10415-87 Avenue, Edmonton, Alberta T6E 2P4

ELIZABETH KOUHI

Born in Lappe, Ontario, November 24, 1917. Formal education started in a one-room school house (not red) and proceeded sporadically: B.A., 1949, and OCE, 1964 (McGill). Taught in another one-room school and later in a secondary school. Married, with four children, I live in Thunder Bay, Ontario.

Selected Publications:

Jamie of Thunder Bay: Ottawa, Borealis, 1977. ISBN 0-919594-78-6
North Country Spring: Moonbeam, Penumbra, 1980. ISBN 0-920806-10-4
The Story of Philip: Winnipeg, Queenston House, 1982. ISBN 0-919866-71-9
Sarah Jane of Silver Islet: Winnipeg, Queenston House, 1983. ISBN 0-919866-87-5
Round Trip Home: Moonbean, Penumbra, 1983. ISBN 0-920806-57-0

Comments: "Anyone who has anything to do with children should take a good look at *The Story of Philip*." – Suzanne Kilpatrick, *Hamilton Spectator*
"Her style is clear and exact; she has found words to say what she wants to say, without frills or hesitation, . . . no mean accomplishment." – Robert Quickendon, *Winnipeg Free Press*
"A poet who is a pleasure to read." – Kevin Irie, *Event*
Readings, Lectures & Workshops: I give readings and workshops, for both children and adults.
Mailing Address: 224 N. Norah Street, Thunder Bay, Ontario P7C 4H2

PAT KRAUSE

Born in 1930 in Tuscaloosa, Alabama, to transplanted Saskatchewan parents. Born again, 1970, in Regina as an apprenticing foreign correspondent after attending writing workshops at the University of Regina and the Saskatchewan School of the Arts in the magical Qu'Appelle Valley. Now spend winters in Regina, summers at Lake Katepwa, and write fiction as fast as I can.

Selected Publications:

Freshie: Hamilton, Potlatch, 1981. ISBN 0-919676-29-4

Comments: "A first-rate job of portraying believable adolescents." – *Books in Canada*

"Krause has a knack for recreating universal experience with humor and pathos." – *Ottawa Citizen*

Stories have appeared in Sundogs, Saskatchewan Gold, More Saskatchewan Gold, 100% Cracked Wheat and The Old Dance, all published by Thunder Creek/Coteau.

"Best Kept Secrets show(s) good stories about prairie life don't have to be about mucking out the barn." – *Books in Canada*

"After reading Second Sight, you close the book, smile, and wait a few minutes before starting the next story." – *The Sheaf*

Founding member, Saskatchewan Writers Guild.

Director, Creative Writing Program, Saskatchewan School of the Arts, 1976-1981

Readings, Lectures & Workshops: Workshops and readings at high schools, libraries and universities. Talks on how I fulfilled a childhood dream in mid-life by becoming an apprenticing foreign correspondent. May be booked through the Saskatchewan Writers Guild, Box 3986, Regina, Saskatchewan S4P 3R9.

Mailing Address: 89 Bell Street, Regina, Saskatchewan S4S 5V2

PHILIP KREINER

I was born and raised in Timmins, Ontario. After finishing university, I taught for several years in Jamaica then worked for the Cree School Board in Fort George, James Bay. I now live in Toronto.

Selected Publications:

People Like Us in a Place Like This: Ottawa, Oberon, 1983. ISBN 0-88750-469-8
Heartlands: Ottawa, Oberon, 1984. ISBN 0-88750-557-0
Contact Prints: Toronto, Doubleday, 1987. ISBN 0-385-25102-5

Awards: Shortlisted for the Governor-General's Award (Fiction), 1983
Comments: "Taut, muscular, with the punchy immediacy of Hemingway, Kreiner's writing is direct and explosive." — Wayne Tefs, *Arts Manitoba*
"Kreiner has a keen sense of the politics of social intercourse between the races." — Barbara Black, *Montreal Gazette*
Readings, Lectures & Workshops: I have given readings in Fredericton, Regina, Timmins and Toronto (Harbourfront). I have given writing workshops in Timmins, Bradford and in Toronto (for the Toronto Board of Education).
Mailing Address: 335 Markham Street, Toronto, Ontario M6G 2K8

HENRY KREISEL

Born in Vienna in 1922. Left Austria in 1938 and went to England. To Canada in 1940. Studied at universities of Toronto and London. Since 1947 at the University of Alberta's Department of English (Professor 1959, Head 1961-67). Vice-President (Academic) 1970-75. Visiting Fellow, Cambridge University, 1975-76. Named University Professor, 1975. Since 1976 have taught in departments of comparative literature and drama.

Selected Publications:

The Rich Man: Toronto, McClelland & Stewart, 1948./New Canadian Library, 1961. ISBN 0-7710-9124-9
The Betrayal: Toronto, McClelland & Stewart, 1964./New Canadian Library, 1971. ISBN 0-7710-9177-X
The Almost Meeting: Edmonton, NeWest, 1981. ISBN 0-920316-82-4
Another Country (Writings by and about Henry Kreisel): (Shirley Neuman, ed.), Edmonton, NeWest, 1985. ISBN 0-920316-85-9

Awards: The J.I. Segal Foundation (Montreal) Award for Literature, 1983. The Sir Frederick Haultain Prize (Significant Achievement in the Fine Arts), Government of Alberta, 1986.
Comments: "Kreisel's stories . . . have a curiously delayed effect. They are likely to impress immediately, but they go on to expand and develop within the mind." – W.J. Keith, *Dalhousie Review*
Readings, Lectures & Workshops: I have given more than 100 readings and many lectures in universities, libraries and other public forums.
Mailing Address: 12516-66 Avenue, Edmonton, Alberta T6H 1Y5

ROBERT KROETSCH

Born in Alberta, 1927. Worked in the North for a number of years. Studied and taught in the U.S. for 20 years. Now teaching at the University of Manitoba.

Selected Publications:

Badlands: Toronto, General/New Press, 1981. ISBN 0-7736-7021-1
The Studhorse Man: Toronto, General/New Press, 1982. ISBN 0-7736-7033-5
What the Crow Said: Toronto, General/New Press, 1983. ISBN 0-7736-7060-2
Alibi: Toronto, General/New Press, 1984. ISBN 0-7736-7084-X
Advice to my Friends: Toronto, Stoddart, 1985. ISBN 0-7737-5021-5
Excerpts from the Real World: Lantzville, Oolichan, 1986. ISBN 0-88982-059-7

   Awards: Governor General's Award (Fiction), 1969
   Mailing Address: Dept. of English, University of Manitoba, Winnipeg, Manitoba R3T 2N2

PAUL KROPP

Born in Buffalo, New York, February 22, 1948. Completed a B.A. in English at Columbia College in 1970, just one week before emigrating to Canada. Two years spent at the University of Western Ontario brought me an M.A. and teaching credentials. I began teaching high-school in 1972, became a reading teacher at a Hamilton vocational school in 1974 and began writing for those special students in 1977. I have three children: Jason, Justin and Alexander.

Selected Publications:

Burn Out: Toronto, Collier Macmillan, 1979. ISBN 0-02-991290-3
Dope Deal: Toronto, Collier Macmillan, 1979. ISBN 0-02-991270-9
Runaway: Toronto, Collier Macmillan, 1979. ISBN 0-02-991280-6
Hot Cars: Toronto, Collier Macmillan, 1979. ISBN 0-02-991260-1
Wilted: New York, Coward McCann, 1980. ISBN 0-698-20493-X
Dead On: Toronto, Collier Macmillan, 1981. ISBN 0-02-990190-1
Dirt Bike: Toronto, Collier Macmillan, 1981. ISBN 0-02-990200-2
Fair Play: Toronto, Collier Macmillan, 1981. ISBN 0-02-990210-X
No Way: Toronto, Collier Macmillan, 1981. ISBN 0-02-990180-4
Gang War: Toronto, Collier Macmillan, 1982. ISBN 0-02-997620-0
Baby, Baby: Toronto, Collier Macmillan, 1982. ISBN 0-02-997640-5
Snow Ghost: Toronto, Collier Macmillan, 1982. ISBN 0-02-997610-3
Wild One: Toronto, Collier Macmillan, 1982. ISBN 0-02-997630-8
Amy's Wish: Toronto, Collier Macmillan, 1984. ISBN 0-02-947140-1
Micro Man: Toronto, Collier Macmillan, 1984. ISBN 0-02-947150-8
Take Off: Toronto, Collier Macmillan, 1985. ISBN 0-02-947290-3
Getting Even: Toronto, Seal, 1986. ISBN 0-7704-2112-1
Justin, Jay-Jay and the Juvenile Dinket: Toronto, Scholastic, 1986.
    ISBN 0-590-71675-1
Jo's Search: Toronto, Collier Macmillan, 1986. ISBN 0-02-947370-5
Death Ride: Toronto, Collier Macmillan, 1986. ISBN 0-02-947360-8

Readings, Lectures & Workshops: I give up to twenty creative writing workshops and school performances each year. I also lead workshops for teachers and librarians. Book through TWUC.

Mailing Address: c/o Lucinda Vardy Agency, 297 Seaton Street, Toronto, Ontario M5A 2T6

ANITA KRUMINS

Born November 15, 1946. B.A. summa cum laude; M.A., 1974 (both York University). Teacher of business and technical communication at Ryerson Polytechnic Institute in Toronto since 1975. Department Chairman, 1981-86. Have published three children's books (one of which is abridged in a McGraw-Hill Ryerson anthology) and have reviewed for CBC-TV, Writers' Quarterly and Waves.

Selected Publications:

Quillby, The Porcupine Who Lost His Quills: (with George Swede), Toronto, Three Trees, 1980. ISBN 0-88823-019-2
Who's Going to Clean Up the Mess?: Toronto, Three Trees, 1980. ISBN 0-88823-026-5
Mr. Wurtzel And the Halloween Bunny: Toronto, Three Trees, 1982. ISBN 0-88823-048-6

Comments: "Children will enjoy Mr. Wurtzel's ragings, and adults will be satisfied that the story does not have a saccharine ending." – *Books in Canada*
"Likely to be picked up by children." – *Canadian Children's Literature*
"A useful addition to children's collections." – *Quill & Quire* (on *Who's Going to Clean Up the Mess?*)
"A good selection . . . (an) amusing story." – *Winnipeg Free Press*
"(A) delightful book for youngsters." – *Canadian Materials*
Readings, Lectures & Workshops: Regularly give readings of my stories and conduct writing workshops. Book through TWUC.
Mailing Address: 70 London Street, Toronto, Ontario M6G 1N3

JOHN L. LADELL

Born in Siam (now Thailand). Schools in England, South Africa and Jamaica. Submarine officer in World War II (Royal Navy). Emigrated to Canada in 1946. Oxford University, Doctor of Philosophy, 1961. Research in forest products and consultant in agro-forestry. Became full-time writer in 1978. Now act (stage and TV) when not writing.

Selected Publications:

Inheritance (Ontario's Century Farms Past and Present): (with Monica Ladell), Toronto, Macmillan, 1979. Dundurn, 1986. ISBN 1-55002-008-0
A Farm in the Family (The Many Faces of Ontario Agriculture Over The Centuries): (with Monica Ladell), Dundurn, 1985. ISBN 1-55002-000-5

Awards: Ontario Bicentennial Award, 1985. United States Communications in Agriculture Organization Award.
Comments: "Just as we leaf through old family albums to catch a glimpse of our roots, our grandchildren will depend on the Ladells' excellent work to recall how it was and why." – Roy Bonisteel, *The Canadian Churchman* (on *Inheritance*)
"The Ladells' writing is clear and easy . . . This is a delightful book." – Dane Lanken, *Canadian Geographic* (on *A Farm in the Family*)
Have contributed articles on history, science, birds and wildlife to Quest, The Medical Post, Ontario Living, Country Property Buyer's Guide, The Loyalist Gazette, The Globe and Mail, Legacy, Bridges and Seasons. Also numerous articles co-authored with Monica Ladell.
Mailing Address: 247 Warden Avenue, Scarborough, Ontario M1N 2Z9

PATRICK LANE

Born in Nelson, British Columbia, March 1939. Wandered the world ever since. Now live in Saskatoon, teaching at the university there. No particular education. One day at a time, a poem, story, idea, which is enough. Keeping as happy as I can.

Selected Publications:

Poems (New and Selected): Toronto, Oxford, 1978. ISBN 0-19-540296-0
The Measure: Windsor, Black Moss, 1981. ISBN 0-88753-064-4
Old Mother: Toronto, Oxford, 1984. ISBN 0-19-540409-2
A Linen Crow A Caftan Magpie: Saskatoon, Thistledown. ISBN 0-920066-95-X

   Awards: Governor General's Award (Poetry), 1979
   Readings, Lectures & Workshops: Have read poetry widely in North America, Europe and Asia. Have taught English literature and creative writing at a number of universities and art schools. Am available for a fee.
   Mailing Address: c/o TWUC, 24 Ryerson Avenue, Toronto, Ontario M5T 2P3

ROSS LECKIE

Born in Lachine, Quebec, on September 17, 1953. Currently living in Toronto to complete a Ph.D. at the University of Toronto. Working on the prosaic tone in modern and contemporary American poetry. Hold an M.A. in creative writing/poetry from Concordia University supervised by Gary Geddes. I am interested in philosophy, politics, music and opera, and baseball. I love teaching.

Selected Publications:

A Slow Light: Montreal, Vehicule, 1983. ISBN 0-919890-45-8

   Comments: See also: *The Inner Ear* (Quadrant, 1982) and *Cross/Cut: Contemporary English Quebec Poetry* (Vehicule, 1982).
   Readings, Lectures & Workshops: Most recent readings have been at Harbourfront and the University of Toronto. Have taught creative writing regularly in primary schools, high schools and colleges. May be booked through TWUC.
   Mailing Address: c/o TWUC, 24 Ryerson Avenue, Toronto, Ontario M5T 2P3

SIDNEY LEDSON

Educationalist, born in London, England, 1925. Formerly a musician, painter and media writer. Now an inventor of learning systems. Founder and director of a laboratory school having the stated purpose and goal of raising children's intelligence. Live in Scarborough, Ontario.

Selected Publications:

Fundamental French Language Course: Ottawa, Campbell Printing, 1971. (no ISBN)

Grammar for People Who Hate Grammar: Ajax, Dickson Publishing, 1981. (no ISBN)

Teach Your Child to Read in 60 Days: Toronto, General, 1985. ISBN 0-7737-5031-2

Raising Brighter Children: Toronto, McClelland & Stewart, 1983. ISBN 0-7710-5205-7

Mailing Address: Sidney Ledson School, 33 Overland Drive, Don Mills, Ontario M3C 2C3

BETTY LEE

Born in Sydney, Australia, December 18, 1923. Began career as a radio script writer, then graduated to staff jobs with magazines and newspapers in Sydney, Melbourne, London, New York and Toronto. Am currently personal finance editor and columnist for Canadian Business magazine and consulting editor for Your Money magazine and Moneysworth, a television show produced by TVOntario. Live and work in downtown Toronto.

Selected Publications:

Love and Whisky (The Story of the Toronto Drama Festival): Toronto, McClelland & Stewart, 1973/Simon & Pierre, 1982. ISBN 0-88924-131-7
Lutiapik: Toronto, McClelland & Stewart, 1975/Simon & Pierre, 1982. ISBN 0-88924-132-5

Awards: Canadian Women's Press Club National Award (Spot News Reporting), 1965. National Newspaper Award (Feature Writing), 1966. Southam Fellow, 1972-73.
Mailing Address: c/o TWUC, 24 Ryerson Avenue, Toronto, Ontario M5T 2P3

DENNIS LEE

I was born in 1939 in Toronto, where I write full time. I am known for adult and children's poetry, as a song lyricist and a literary editor.

Selected Publications:

Civil Elegies and Other Poems: Toronto, Anansi, 1972. ISBN 0-88784-023-X

Alligator Pie: Toronto, Macmillan, 1974. ISBN 0-7705-1193-7

Savage Fields: Toronto, Anansi, 1977. ISBN 0-88784-058-2

Garbage Delight: Toronto, Macmillan, 1977. ISBN 0-7705-1566-5

The Gods: Toronto, McClelland & Stewart, 1979. ISBN 0-7710-5214-6

Jelly Belly: Toronto, Macmillan, 1983. ISBN 0-7715-9776-2

The New Canadian Poets, 1970-1985: (ed.), Toronto, McClelland & Stewart, 1985. ISBN 0-7710-5216-2

Awards: Governor General's Award (Poetry), 1974. CACL Bronze Medal (Canadian Children's Book Written in English) 1974, 1977. Philips Information Systems Literary Prize, 1984. Vicky Metcalf Award (Body of Work for Children), 1986.

Comments: The literary magazine Descant devoted its issue 39 (Winter, 1982) to studies of my writing and editing.

Mailing Address: c/o TWUC, 24 Ryerson Avenue, Toronto Ontario M5T 2P3

HELEN LEVI

Born in Winnipeg. Educated at Gordon Bell High School, the University of Winnipeg, University of Manitoba, Brandon University. Two children, three grandchildren, two dogs, two cats. Teach senior English, psychology and law at Glenboro Collegiate. Watercolour, needlepoint, travel when possible. Love fast cars and fast music.

Selected Publications:

A Small Informal Dance: Winnipeg, Queenston House, 1977.
ISBN 0-919866-21-2
Tangle Your Web and Dosey-Do: Winnipeg, Queenston House, 1978. ISBN 0-919866-36-0
Honour Your Partner: Winnipeg, Queenston House, 1979. ISBN 0-919866-43-3

Mailing Address: Box 54, Glenboro, Manitoba R0K 0X0

NORMAN LEVINE

Grew up in Ottawa. Went to McGill as a veteran. (In RCAF 1942-1945). On graduation, in 1949, went to England and lived in St. Ives, Cornwall . . . with visits back to Canada . . . until 1980. Since then I've lived in Toronto with visits back to St. Ives.

Selected Publications:

Canada Made Me: London, Putnam, 1958/Ottawa, Deneau, 1979. ISBN 0-88879-012-0
One Way Ticket: London, Secker & Warburg, 1961. (no ISBN)
From a Seaside Town: London, Macmillan, 1970/Deneau, 1980. ISBN 0-88879-043-0
I Don't Want to Know Anyone Too Well: London, Macmillan, 1971/Deneau, 1982. ISBN 0-88879-077-5
Selected Stories: Ottawa, Oberon, 1975. (o/p)
Thin Ice: Ottawa, Deneau, 1979. ISBN 0-88879-055-4
Why Do You Live So Far Away?: Ottawa, Deneau, 1984. ISBN 0-88879-100-3
Champagne Barn: Toronto, Penguin, 1984. ISBN 0-14-007255-1

Comments: Archival material: the University of Texas; York University.
Mailing Address: c/o TWUC, 24 Ryerson Avenue, Toronto, Ontario M5T 2P3

NORMA WEST LINDER

Born in Toronto, second of five children of Leslie and Gladys (Berry) West. Raised on Manitoulin Island. Married Toronto musician John Henry Linder. Widowed in 1982. Three children: Laureen, Karen and Jay. Attended Toronto Normal School. Taught in Muskoka Falls. Past President, Canadian Authors Association, Sarnia Branch. Conducted creative writing classes at Lambton College, Sarnia, where I have been an instructor in English as a second language since 1968.

Selected Publications:

On the Side of the Angels: Fredericton, Fiddlehead, 1971. ISBN 0-919196-63-2

Nahanni: (with H. Morritt), Toronto, Nelson Foster & Scott, 1975. ISBN 0-919324-24-X

Woman in a Blue Hat: Richmond Hill, Simon & Schuster, 1977. ISBN 0-671-80719-6

Matter of Life and Death: Brandon, Pierian. ISBN 0-920916-30-9

The Savage Blood: Sarnia, River City Press, 1987. ISBN 0-920940-10-2

Awards: First Prizes in Alberta Poetry Competition

Comments: I write articles and short stories for numerous magazines (Chatelaine, Trends, High Profile) and my work has been translated and sold abroad.

"The vivid descriptions and dialogue hold the reader's attention through this novel." – Laura Morris, *London Free Press* (on *Nahanni*)

"Although the beginning writer wants to write of great things, it is the great treatment of small things that is the most important." – N.W.L. in *Canadian Author & Bookman*

Readings, Lectures & Workshops: I have read from Manitoulin Island to Cornwall. More than a dozen short stories have been broadcast over the CBC.

Mailing Address: 1223 Willa Drive, Sarnia, Ontario N7S 1T6

ROTA HERZBERG LISTER

Born in Iserlohn, West Germany, January 9, 1928. Arrived in Canada on April 14, 1951; trilingual English, German, French. Hold a Ph.D. in English from the University of Toronto and teach English and creative writing at the University of Waterloo. I write and publish some poetry and create, direct and act in original satiric reviews. Otherwise overwhelmed with scholarly publications in Renaissance drama, Canadian drama and Canadian women writers.

Selected Publications:

A Critical Edition of John Fletcher's Comedy 'The Wild Goose Chase': New York, Garland, 1980. ISBN 0-8240-4466-5

Comments: Founding editor of Canadian Drama/L'Art dramatique canadien, 1974-80, and guest editor for *Women In Canadian Drama*: a special issue of *Canadian Drama*, 1979. (ISSN 0317-9044)
"This is an excellent and provocative issue of *Canadian Drama*, well worth anyone's time in reading it." – Moira K. Mulholland, Resources for Feminist Research/Documentation sur la recherche feministe, on *Women in Canadian Drama*
Forthcoming: Anthology of Canadian Women Writers, 1677-1987
Readings, Lectures & Workshops: Numerous public lectures on Canadian drama and Canadian women writers; poetry readings, some of my own poems.
Mailing Address: Dept. of English, University of Waterloo, Waterloo, Ontario N2L 3G1

JIM LOTZ

Born in Liverpool, England, of working-class parents. Graduated from Manchester University in 1952, then spent a year in Nigeria as a trader. Came to Canada in 1954, and took a degree in geography at McGill in 1957. Thesis based on research in the subarctic. Then served on Arctic expeditions. Worked for the federal government and taught at universities before becoming a freelance writer and community development consultant in 1973.

Selected Publications:

Northern Realities: Toronto, New Press, 1970. ISBN 0-88770-017-9
Cape Breton Island: (co-author), Newton Abbott, David and Charles. ISBN 0-7153-6072-8
Understanding Canada: Toronto, NC Press, 1977. ISBN 0-919600-53-0
Death in Dawson: Markham, PaperJacks, 1978. ISBN 0-7701-0075-9
Murder on the Mackenzie: Markham, PaperJacks, 1979. ISBN 0-7701-0112-7
Killing in Kluane: Markham, PaperJacks, 1980. ISBN 0-7701-0131-3
The Sixth of December: Markham, PaperJacks, 1981. ISBN 0-7701-0197-6
History of Canada: Greenwich, Bison, 1984. ISBN 0-86124-081-2
The Mounties: Greenwich, Bison, 1984. ISBN 0-86124-178-9
Canadian Pacific: London, Bison, 1985. ISBN 0-86124-216-5
Head, Heart and Hands: Halifax, Braemar, 1986. ISBN 0-921565-00-3

Readings, Lectures & Workshops: Available!
Mailing Address: Box 3393 (South), Halifax, Nova Scotia B3J 3J1

JACK LUDWIG

I was born in Winnipeg, attended school there and graduated from the University of Manitoba. While still in junior high (Machray School) I began editing and writing, an activity that continued through St. John's High and after. I moved to California and while there took a Degree at University of California at Los Angeles. My stories began to appear in the late 1950s and early 1960s in Tamarack Review, The Atlantic Monthly, Commentary and other periodicals. My first novel was published in 1963. I am currently associated with the Graduate Centre of the State University of New York at Stony Brook.

Selected Publications:

Recent American Novelists: Winnipeg, University of Manitoba Press, 1962. (no ISBN)
Confusions: Toronto, McClelland & Stewart, 1965. (no ISBN)
Hockey Night in Moscow: Toronto, McClelland & Stewart, 1972. (o/p)
A Woman of Her Age: Toronto, McClelland & Stewart, 1973. (o/p)
Above Ground: Toronto, McClelland & Stewart, 1974. ISBN 0-7710-9200-8
Games of Fear and Winning: Toronto, Doubleday, 1975. ISBN 0-385-11539-3
The Great American Spectaculars: Toronto, Doubleday, 1976. (o/p)
Five Ring Circus: Toronto, Doubleday, 1976. ISBN 0-385-11540-7

Comments: Short stories and novel excerpts have been frequently anthologised; numerous essays, from 1953 to the present, have appeared in the U.S., U.K. and Canadian periodicals and collections on literature, politics, culture, popular culture and sports; also numerous reviews for The New Republic, Midstream, Tamarack Review, New York Sunday Times Book Section, Partisan Review and others.

Mailing Address: c/o TWUC, 24 Ryerson Avenue, Toronto, Ontario M5T 2P3

JANET LUNN

Born Janet Louise Swoboda in Dallas, Texas, December 28, 1928. Raised in Vermont, New York and New Jersey. Came to Canada in 1946 (citizen 1963). Education: Queen's University, married Richard Lunn, five children. Children's editor, Clarke Irwin Publishers Toronto, 1972-75. Writer-in-residence at the Regina Public Library, 1982-83. Currently a reviewer, freelance editor and children's writer.

Selected Publications:

The County: (with Richard Lunn), Picton, Prince Edward County Council, 1967. (no ISBN)
Double Spell: Toronto, Penguin, 1968. ISBN 0-14-031858-5
Larger than Life: Toronto, Press Porcepic, 1979. ISBN 0-88878-097-4
The Twelve Dancing Princesses: Toronto, Methuen, 1979. ISBN 0-416-30601-2
The Root Cellar: Toronto, Lester & Orpen Dennys, 1981. ISBN 0-919630-30-8
Shadow in Hawthorn Bay: Toronto, Lester & Orpen Dennys, 1986. ISBN 0-88619-134-3

Awards: City of Toronto IODE Award (Children's Book of the Year), 1979. Canadian Library Association Award (Children's Book of the Year), 1981. Vicky Metcalf Award (For a Body of Work for Children), 1981.

Readings, Lectures & Workshops: Read regularly at schools and libraries; lecture at conferences and meetings; conduct workshops for children and for adults who write for children. Book through TWUC.

Mailing Address: RR 2, Hillier, Ontario K0K 2J0

JAKE MACDONALD

Born in St. Boniface, Manitoba, April 6, 1949.
Resided in a variety of locales from Minaki,
Ontario, to Vancouver Island before settling to
live as a full-time writer in Winnipeg, where
I divide my time among fiction, drama, journalism and summers spent in northwestern Ontario
working as a fishing guide.

Selected Publications:

Indian River: Winnipeg, Queenston House, 1981. ISBN 0-919866-61-1
The Bridge out of Town: Ottawa, Oberon, 1986. ISBN 0-88750-618-6

Awards: Manitoba Playwright Search Award
Comments: "MacDonald writes with a sense of humour that is much like
Mark Twain's." – Luis Cardoso, *New Brunswick Telegraph Journal*
"He has written a dark and compelling novel." – Len Gasparini, *Vancou-
ver Sun*
"MacDonald is the best thing to happen to Manitoba fiction since W.D.
Valgardson." – John Danakas, *Winnipeg Sun*
Readings, Lectures & Workshops: Read at bookstores, coffee shops and
colleges. Will conduct workshops in creative writing for children and adults.
Mailing Address: 950 McMillan Avenue, Winnipeg, Manitoba R3M 0V6

M.A. MACDONALD

Born in Hamilton, Ontario. Attended schools in the Canadian West, New York State and Ontario. B.A. McMaster; M.Sc. Northwestern University. Reporter on newspapers in Chicago, then Saint John, New Brunswick: police, courts, then city hall. After marriage, two children, resumed writing; articles, mostly historical, in Atlantic Advocate, Atlantic Insight and (as Jan Forster) Chatelaine. Travel in Europe, the Pacific, the Middle and Far East whenever funds and opportunity permit.

Selected Publications:

Fortune and La Tour (The Civil War in Acadia): Toronto, Methuen 1983. ISBN 0-458-95800-X
Robert Le Blant (Seminal Researcher and Historian of Early New France): Saint John, New Brunswick Museum, 1986. ISBN 0-919326-374-4

Comments: "Adroit characterisation . . . vividly presents these last, desperate years in the civil war." – *Books in Canada*
"Fine narrative and solid scholarly research . . . one would have wished it longer." – *Canadian Historical Review*
"An exciting story . . . told by a skilful writer thoroughly in charge of her material." – *Canadian Churchman*
"Creates a vivid sense of place or period with a few sharp, telling details." – *Toronto Star*
Readings, Lectures & Workshops: Lecture to groups with heritage and historical interests.
Mailing Address: Box 182, Rothesay, New Brunswick E0G 2W0

ROY MACGREGOR

I was born in 1948 in the village of Whitney, Ontario. I was educated in the public schools of Huntsville, Ontario, and graduated from Laurentian University and the University of Western Ontario. I have been a journalist since 1972, working for Maclean's, Today, The Canadian, the Toronto Star and currently as a daily columnist for the Ottawa Citizen. Married to Ellen MacGregor. We have four children: Kerry, Christine, Jocelyn and Gordon.

Selected Publications:

Shorelines: Toronto, McClelland & Stewart, 1980. ISBN 0-7710-5459-9
The Last Season: Toronto, Macmillan, 1983. ISBN 0-7715-9778-9

   Awards: ACTRA Awards (Best Dramatic Writer - Television), 1979, 1980. National Newspaper Award (Co-winner), 1983. National Magazine Awards (Gold) 1977, 1980; (Silver) 1980 Grand Prix de la Presse, Montreal Film Festival, 1979. Top Drama, Banff, 1982.
   Mailing Address: c/o The Ottawa Citizen, 1101 Baxter Road, Box 5020, Ottawa, Ontario K2C 3M4

FRANCES MACILQUHAM

Born at Rydal Bank, Ontario, October 6, 1915, youngest of six children of a pioneer lumberman in Northern Ontario. Now living in Toronto. Educated in Thessalon and Sudbury in Ontario. Drifted from office work across Ontario and Quebec into journalism (briefly). In 1960, a nostalgic fascination with outdoor life and living led to 15 years of research into fish and game cookery, resulting in two published books. Married Lloyd K. MacIlquham in 1945; one daughter, Mary Shannon Brown, and five sons, Oliver, Lloyd, Andrew, Gordon and Thomas; two grandchildren, Jonas and Amy Brown. Member of outdoor writers associations, OWAA and OWC; the Canadian Authors Association and the Women's Press Club of Toronto.

Selected Publications:

Canadian Game Cookery: Toronto, McClelland & Stewart, 1966. (no ISBN)
Fish Cookery of North America: New York, Winchester Press, 1974.

Comments: Frequent contributor to the Toronto Star.
Mailing Address: 47 Pine Crescent, Toronto, Ontario M4E 1L3

CLAIRE MACKAY

Born in Toronto in 1930. Married Jackson Mackay in 1952, three sons. Honours B.A. in political science and economics from the University of Toronto (1952). Post-grad studies in social work at the University of British Columbia, 1968-69 and in rehabilitation counselling at the University of Manitoba, 1971. Have worked as a toy painter, a waitress, a jelly powder packer, a deodorant market researcher, a medical social worker and a librarian. Full-time writer since 1978.

Selected Publications:

Mini-Bike Hero: Toronto, Scholastic, 1974. ISBN 0-590-71413-9
Mini-Bike Racer: Toronto, Scholastic, 1975. ISBN 0-590-71003-6
Exit Barney McGee: Toronto, Scholastic, 1975. ISBN 0-590-71002-8
One Proud Summer: (with Marsha Hewitt), Toronto, Women's Press, 1981.
  ISBN 0-88961-048-7
Mini-Bike Rescue: Toronto, Scholastic, 1982. ISBN 0-590-71100-8
The Minerva Program: Toronto, Lorimer, 1984. ISBN 0-88862-717-3

Awards: Toronto Star Short Story Contest (Second Prize), 1980. Ruth Schwartz Award (Best Children's Book), 1982. Vicky Metcalf Award (Body of Work for Children), 1983.

Comments: Forthcoming: The Union Book (Kids Can), Waiting for the Sunrise (Women's Press) and a sequel to *The Minerva Program*

Readings, Lectures & Workshops: School and library visits and readings, and other engagements, may be booked through TWUC.

Mailing Address: 6 Frank Crescent, Toronto, Ontario M6G 3K5

JIM MACLACHLAN

Born in St. Catharines, Ontario, July 5, 1928. B.A. Sc. in engineering physics from the University of Toronto in 1950; Ed.M. in science teaching, Harvard 1965; Ph.D. in history of science, Harvard 1972. Employed in geophysics in Alberta and Ottawa, 1950-53. Taught high school physics, 1954-68, the history of science and technology at U of T, 1969-77; Ryerson Polytechnical Institute, 1977-88; CJRT-FM Open College, 1985-87. Three children, plus Sheila's five; grandchildren Erin and Ross.

Selected Publications:

Matter and Energy (The Foundations of Modern Physics): (with K.G. McNeill and J.M. Bell), Toronto, Clarke Irwin, 1963. ISBN 0-7720-0259-2; (third ed.) ISBN 0-7725-1558-1
Matter and Energy in the Laboratory: Toronto, Clarke Irwin, 1966. (no ISBN)

Awards: Phi Delta Kappa, 1965. APEO award for contributions to the engineering profession through teaching, 1968. Honorary President, Ontario Science Teachers' Association, 1974-75.

Comments: I share my professional time between old science and new technology. Here I sit at my word processor wondering about Galileo, and whether I should upgrade to MS-DOS or Macintosh: Brecht's coldhearted cardboard-cutout Galileo cannot continue; and I shan't shrink from shelving this serious shortage of kilobytes in Kaypro's CPU. As a member and sometime chairman of the technology committee of the Book and Periodical Development Council, I'm keen to help authors take advantage of the communications revolution, which will far outshine the transfiguration Gutenberg had in mind. While the publishers capture our keystrokes, our warm hearts must remain our own.

Mailing Address: 49 Williamson Road, Toronto, Ontario M4E 1K6

HUGH MACLENNAN

Born on Cape Breton, 1907. Educated at Dalhousie, Oxford and Princeton. Teaching: Lower Canada College, McGill University. Writing from 1932. First publication 1941.

Selected Publications:

Barometer Rising: New York, Duell Sloan & Pearce, 1941. (no ISBN)
Two Solitudes: Toronto, Macmillan, 1945. (no ISBN)
The Precipice: Toronto, Collins, 1948. (no ISBN)
Cross-Country: Toronto, Collins, 1949. (o/p)
Each Man's Son: Toronto, Macmillan, 1951. (no ISBN)
Thirty and Three: Toronto, Macmillan, 1954. (no ISBN)
The Watch That Ends the Night: Toronto, Macmillan, 1959. ISBN 0-7715-9584-0
Scotchman's Return and Other Essays: Toronto, Macmillan, 1960. (o/p)
Return of the Sphinx: Toronto, Macmillan, 1967. (no ISBN)
Rivers of Canada: Toronto, Macmillan, 1974. (o/p)
Seven Rivers of Canada: Toronto, Macmillan, 1978. 0-7705-1562-2
Voices in Time: Toronto, Macmillan, 1980. 0-7715-9570-0

Awards: Governor General's Awards (Fiction), 1945, 1948, 1959; (Non-Fiction) 1949, 1954. Lorne Pearce Medal, 1951. Royal Bank of Canada Award, 1984. Nineteen Honorary Degrees.
Mailing Address: 1535 Summerhill Avenue, Montreal, Quebec H3H 1C2

ALISTAIR MACLEOD

Born in North Battleford, Saskatchewan, raised in Nova Scotia's Inverness County. Educated at Nova Scotia Teachers College (1956); St. Francis Xavier University (B.A., B.Ed., 1960); University of New Brunswick (M.A., 1961); Notre Dame University (Ph.D., 1968). Teach creative writing at the University of Windsor, Ontario. Have taught in the writing program at the Banff School of Fine Arts for seven years. Was Canada's Exchange Writer to Scotland, 1984-85.

Selected Publications:

The Lost Salt Gift of Blood: Toronto, McClelland & Stewart, 1976. ISBN 0-7710-5574-9

As Birds Bring Forth the Sun: Toronto, McClelland & Stewart, 1986. ISBN 0-7710-5566-8

Awards: Honorary Doctorate from St. Francis Xavier University, 1987

Comments: "One of North America's most promising writers." – Joyce Carol Oates

"Alistair MacLeod is one of the finest short story writers now living, or for that matter who ever lived . . ." – Hugh MacLennan

"Immensely rewarding and very beautful . . . seldom have I seen writing more movingly descriptive of the Atlantic coast . . ." – Marian Engel

"He rivals (D.H.) Lawrence in that which is said to be as rare as a phoenix, the ability to educate the feelings." – Ken MacKinnon, *Atlantic Provinces Book Review*

Stories have appeared in Best American Short Stories, 1969 and 1975; Best Modern Canadian Short Stories, 1978; Fiddlehead Greens, 1979; and Best Short Stories from the Southern Review, 1987.

Readings, Lectures & Workshops: Have given lectures and readings in the United States and Europe as well as across Canada.

Mailing Address: 231 Curry Avenue, Windsor, Ontario N9B 2B4

JACK MACLEOD

Born in Regina, Saskatchewan, in 1932. B.A. and M.A., University of Saskatchewan; Ph.D., University of Toronto. Married to Cynthia M. Smith McLeod; three children. Professor of political science at the University of Toronto. Vice President and founding member of P.O.E.T.S. Corner (piss on everything, tomorrow's Saturday).

Selected Publications:

Agenda 1970: (with T.O. Lloyd), Toronto, University of Toronto Press, 1968. ISBN 0-8020-1571-9
Essays on the Left (In Honour Of T.C. Douglas): (with L. LaPierre), Toronto, McClelland & Stewart, 1971. ISBN 0-7710-4698-7
Business and Government in Canada: (with K.J. Rea), Toronto, Methuen, 1976. ISBN 0-458-91400-2
Zinger and Me: Toronto, McClelland & Stewart, 1979. ISBN 0-7710-5576-5
Going Grand: Toronto, McClelland & Stewart, 1982. ISBN 0-7710-5563-3

Awards: Droppings, Trivial Pursuit Hon. L.W.T. (Leader of Western Thought), Prince Albert College of Journalism, Chiropractic & Upholstering, 1979
Comments: Many, pleasant, mostly wrong-headed.
Mailing Address: Dept. of Political Science, University of Toronto, 100 St. George, Toronto, Ontario M5S 1A1

DARLENE MADOTT

Born in Toronto, March 4, 1952. Middle daughter of a commercial artist. B.A. from the University of Toronto, 1975. A.R.C.T. Piano, 1973. Studied drawing and painting at the Ontario College of Art. L.L.B., Osgoode Hall Law School, 1983; Call, 1985. Practise civil litigation in Toronto. Formerly worked on editorial staffs of Saturday Night and Toronto Life magazines. Recently married.

Selected Publications:

Song and Silence: Ottawa, Borealis, 1977. ISBN 0-919594-76-X
Bottled Roses: Ottawa, Oberon, 1985. ISBN 0-88750-568-6

Awards: St. Michael's College Gold Medal, 1975
Comments: "Full of the detail of Italian-Canadian life — life that is robust, profane, warm, claustrophobic and terribly, overwhelmingly male oriented." — *Kingston Quarry*
"In the midst of vociferous, gossiping and loving families, Madott maintains an undercurrent of sensuality." — *London Press*
"Uncommon ability for investing settings with her characters' passions, melting the material world into art." — *Ottawa Citizen*
My short stories have appeared in the Toronto Star (July 11, 1985); Canadian Forum (April, 1983); Canadian Ethnic Studies (Vol. 14, No. 1, 1982); Dandelion (Vol. 9, No. 2, 1982); Event (Vol. 11, No. 2, 1982); Event (Vol. 8, No. 1, 1979); Aurora (Doubleday, 1978); Antigonish Review (Number 31, Autumn 1977); Waves (Vol. 5, Nos. 2-3, Spring, 1977) and Grain (Vol. 4, No. 3, 1976).
Libel Law, Fiction and The Charter was published in the Osgoode Hall Law Journal, Vol. 21, No. 4, 1983.
Mailing Address: 14 Glebeholme Boulevard, Toronto, Ontario M4J 1S4

JOAN MAGEE

I was born and still live in Riverside, now part of the city of Windsor. My British and European Loyalist ancestors date back to the original settlers of Nova Scotia's Annapolis Valley. I have taught Scandinavian studies at the University of Windsor, where I am now a reference librarian. In 1981, I founded the Netherlandic Press of which I am publisher.

Selected Publications:

A Dutch Heritage (200 Years of Dutch Presence in the Windsor-Detroit Border Region): Toronto, Dundurn, 1983. ISBN 0-919670-66-0
Loyalist Mosaic (A Multi-Ethnic Heritage): Toronto, Dundurn, 1984. ISBN 0-919670-84-9
A Scandinavian Heritage (200 Years of Scandinavian Presence in the Windsor-Detroit Border Region): Toronto, Dundurn, 1984. ISBN 0-919670-88-1
The Belgians in Ontario: Toronto, Dundurn, 1985. ISBN 1-55002-014-5

Comments: "Joan Magee writes as well as she researches, and the result is interesting reading." – Jerry McDonnell, *Canadian Materials*
"Joan Magee's lively and attractively presented study, *A Scandinavian Heritage*, has the possibility to quicken enthusiasm for multicultural study in any area." – Louise Dick, *Canadian Materials*
"*Loyalist Mosaic* offers well-researched biographies of Loyalist personalities, several of whom have not previously been given such treatment. The result is pleasing, refreshing, and even a bit exciting." – Terrence M. Punch, *Atlantic Provinces Book Review*
Readings, Lectures & Workshops: Will lecture on the history of ethnic groups in Canada: Scandinavians, Dutch, Swiss and Flemish.
Mailing Address: 1004 - 1176 Ouellette Avenue, Windsor, Ontario N9A 6S9

JOHN MAGOR

Born in Passaic, New Jersey, March 2, 1915, of an American mother and a Canadian father. Grew up in Montreal, now live in Duncan, British Columbia. Graduated in journalism from Columbia University with an M.S. degree. Joined Cavalcade news magazine in London, England. Later became correspondent in Washington, D.C., and Ottawa for British United Press. After service as RCAF pilot and term as CPR public relations officer, became publisher of Prince Rupert Daily News and Cowichan Leader at Duncan. Leaving newspaper business, I followed up interest in UFO mystery and for ten years was editor and publisher of the Canadian UFO Report. Also have discussed topic on radio and TV.

Selected Publications:

Our UFO Visitors: Saanichton, Hancock, 1977. ISBN 0-919654-70-3
Aliens Above, Always: Surrey, Hancock, 1983. ISBN 0-88839-969-3

Awards: Columbia University School of Journalism's 50th Anniversary Award, 1963

Comments: "A rational study and fascinating account." – Ken Spotswood, *Vancouver Province* (on *Our UFO Visiters*)

"The word fascinating comes to mind again and again. It is easy reading without a lot of useless jargon." – *Kamloops News*

"Magor's fine style and approach to his beliefs that visitors from space come here frequently make this worthwhile reading." – *Robert Barrow's Editorial Service* (on *Aliens Above, Always*)

"There is a lot of most interesting material in this book, and a good deal to be learned from it." – Brinsley Le Poer Trench, Earl of Clancarty (in the preface to *Aliens Above, Always*)

Mailing Address: Box 758, Duncan, British Columbia V9L 3Y1

KEITH MAILLARD

Born in Wheeling, West Virginia, February 28, 1942. Emigrated to Canada in 1970 and became a Canadian citizen in 1976.

Selected Publications:

Two Strand River: Erin, Press Porcepic, 1976. ISBN 0-88878-088-5 (rev. ed. General, 1982.)
Alex Driving South: New York, Dial Press, 1980. ISBN 0-8037-0196-9
The Knife in my Hands: Toronto, General, 1981. ISBN 0-7737-0057-9
Cutting Through: Toronto, Stoddart, 1982. ISBN 0-7737-2003-0

Readings, Lectures & Workshops: Readings may be booked through TWUC.

Mailing Address: c/o TWUC, 24 Ryerson Avenue, Toronto, Ontario M5T 2P3

KEVIN MAJOR

Born in Stephenville, Newfoundland, September 12, 1949. Studied science at Memorial University and graduated in 1972. Taught school in various Newfoundland communities. In 1976 gave up full-time teaching. Now reside in Sandy Cove, Bonavista Bay, with my wife, Anne Crawford. Divide my time among writing, substitute teaching and caring for two young sons.

Selected Publications:

Hold Fast: Toronto, Clarke Irwin, 1978. ISBN 0-7720-1175-3
Far From Shore: Toronto, Clarke Irwin, 1980. ISBN 0-7720-1312-8
Thirty-Six Exposures: New York, Delacorte, 1984. ISBN 0-385-29347-X

Awards: Canada Council Award for Children's Literature, 1978. Book-of-the-Year Award, Canadian Association of Childrens' Librarians, 1978. Ruth Schwartz Award, 1978. Canadian Young Adult Book Award, 1980.

Comments: "*Hold Fast* is a landmark in Canadian writing for young people." — Irma McDonough, *In Review*

"The strongest voice from the East since Lucy Maude Montgomery." — Ann Johnston, *Maclean's*

"This raw and intense novel is probably the best Canadian portrait ever drawn of seventeen-going-on-adult." — Lorri Neilsen, *Atlantic Insight* (on *Thirty-Six Exposures*)

Readings, Lectures & Workshops: Often read at junior and senior high schools across Canada; speak about and read from my work at conferences. May be booked directly or through TWUC.

Mailing Address: Sandy Cove, Bonavista Bay, Newfoundland A0G 1Z0

RUTH LOR MALLOY

 Born into a Chinese restaurant family in Brockville, Ontario, in 1932. I became a Sinophile under the influence of the University of Toronto. Graduated in 1954 and 1960. Have been a social worker, human rights activist, photographer, freelance writer, house painter, wife and mother. Have lived in Baffin Island, Mexico, Brazil, Taiwan, Philippines, Hong Kong, India, Thailand, Vietnam and the U.S. Now live in Toronto, publish a newsletter on China travel and write.

Selected Publications:

A Guide to the People's Republic of China for Travelers of Chinese Ancestry: Hong Kong, privately printed, 1973. (no ISBN)

Travel Guide to the People's Republic of China: New York, Morrow, 1975. ISBN 0-688-03690-2 (Rev. ed., 1980)

Beyond the Heights: Hong Kong, Heinemann Asia, 1980. (no ISBN)

The Morrow Travel Guide to the People's Republic of China: New York, Morrow, 1982. ISBN 0-688-01130-6

Post Guide Hong Kong: Hong Kong, South China Morning Post, 1983. ISBN 962-10-0014-9.

Gems and Jewellery in Hong Kong (A Buyer's Guide): (with Joan Reid Ahrens, G.G.), Hong Kong, South China Morning Post, 1984. ISBN 962-10-0029-7

Fielding's People's Republic of China (1987 Edition): (with Priscilla Liang Hsu), New York, Morrow, 1986. ISBN 0-688-05879-5

Hong Kong Gems and Jewelry: (with Joan Reid Ahrens, G.G.), Hong Kong, Delta Dragon, 1986. ISBN 962-10-029-7

Comments: On the Hong Kong bestseller list twice. Have hitch-hiked through Khyber Pass, slept in a Cambodian police station and been suspected of spying in Pakistan. Have flown a helicopter under fire in Vietnam, scuba-dived with poisonous sea-snakes and a shark in the Philippines and constructed stone stoves in Mexico. Visited Communist guerillas in the Philippines and attended a mediaeval war in Pennsylvania.

Mailing Address: c/o TWUC, 24 Ryerson Avenue, Toronto, Ontario M5T 2P3

CHRISTINE MANDER

Born in Canada during the Depression but, when two, accompanied parents when they returned to England, which is why I speak Canadian with an English accent. Returned, thankfully, to the land of my birth in 1952, this time accompanied by a husband. My son is a computer expert and my daughter one of the best musicians around. Write from my home in Oakville, Ontario, where I have just completed my first mystery novel.

Selected Publications:

All You Need is Enough Rope: Hamilton, Potlatch, 1971. ISBN 0-919676-30-8
Emily Murphy (Rebel): Toronto, Simon & Pierre, 1975. ISBN 0-88924-173-2

   Comments: "Emily Murphy . . . has come magically alive." – *Halifax Daily News*
   "This biography is vigorous and appealing – like its subject." – *Books in Canada*
   Readings, Lectures & Workshops: Enjoy talking to audiences on writing generally, writing specifically or reading from my own work.
   Mailing Address: c/o TWUC, 24 Ryerson Avenue, Toronto, Ontario M5T 2P3

LINDA ELIZABETH MANNING

I was born in Winnipeg, Manitoba, in 1940 and moved to Ontario in 1949. After high school and teachers' college, I taught eight grades in a one-room school near Cobourg, Ontario, for two years. I graduated with a B.A. in English from the University of Guelph in 1975 and have been writing full time since 1981. Married with three grown children, I live and write in an old farmhouse near Cobourg.

Selected Publications:

Wondrous Tales of Wicked Winston: Toronto, Annick, 1981. ISBN 0-920236-18-9

The Adventures of Freddykid and Seagull Sam: Toronto, Playwrights Union, 1982. ISBN 0-88754-307-3

Merch the Invisible Wizard: Toronto, Playwrights Union, 1983. ISBN 0-88754-378-2

The Great Zanderthon Takeover: Toronto, Playwrights Union, 1986. ISBN 0-88754-417-4

Comments: "Adds to the lore and mystery of Lake Erie . . . tales told in rhyme and verse . . . that maintains a constant rhythm." — *In Review* (on *Wondrous Tales of Wicked Winston*)

"These tales arouse the imagination of adults and children alike." — *North Toronto Herald*

"Well-written fantasy . . . amusing and exciting." — *Canadian Materials* (on *Merch the Invisible Wizard*)

Readings, Lectures & Workshops: Readings and workshops in elementary schools and libraries throughout Ontario. May be booked through TWUC and the Playwrights Union of Canada.

Mailing Address: RR 5, Cobourg, Ontario K9A 4J8

AINSLIE KERTLAND MANSON

Born on October 31 (Halloween), 1938. Childhood spent in Hudson Heights, Quebec, and
Montreal. Studied and worked at McGill University and for a Montreal-based public relations
firm before marrying David Manson in 1962.
Lived in the U.S. for eight years. Returned to
Canada in 1970 and settled in Vancouver, British Columbia. Three sons: Graeme, Murray
and Gavin, born 1965, 1967, 1971. Member
of the Canadian Society of Childrens' Authors,
Illustrators and Performers and the B.C. Writers
Federation.

Selected Publications:

Mr. McUmphie of Caulfield Cove: Winnipeg, Queenston House, 1981.
   ISBN 0-919866-72-7

   Comments: "A charming story which reads aloud well to children seven
and eight; readers nine and ten will find it a short, easy novel to read on
their own . . . Mr. McUmphie was fun to be with." – *Children's Choices of
Canadian Books*
   During the past five years, I have contributed eight 14-page series to the
education page of the Vancouver Province: Recalling Canada I: How Cana-
da's provinces got their names (1980), Recalling Canada II: How Canada's
capital cities got their names (1981),
   Trans-Canada Canoe Route: The story of Canada's exploration from east
to west (1982), Smoke Signals To Satellites: The history of various aspects of
Canadian communications (1983), Canadian Inventions from A to Z (1984),
Canadian Prime Ministers (1985) and The History of Forestry in British
Columbia (1985).
   Readings, Lectures & Workshops: Readings for grades one to four. Talks
about writing for children and newpaper writing for children grades five
to seven.
   Mailing Address: 4768 The Highway, West Vancouver, British Columbia
V7W 1J5

DAPHNE MARLATT

Born in Australia in 1941, childhood in Malaysia, arrived in Vancouver in 1951, still live here. Received a B.A. from the University of British Columbia and M.A. in comparative literature from Indiana University. Have taught numerous writing courses and workshops, co-edited several little magazines (The Capilano Review, periodics, Island, tessera) and books (Steveston Recollected, Opening Doors, Lost Language) and published a dozen volumes of poetry and one novel.

Selected Publications:

Frames of a Story: Toronto, Ryerson, 1968. ISBN 0-7700-0255-2
Zocalo: Toronto, Coach House, 1977. (no ISBN)
What Matters (Writing 1968-70): Toronto, Coach House, 1980.
   ISBN 0-88910-161-2
Selected Writing (Net Work): Vancouver, Talon, 1980. ISBN 0-88922-175-8
How Hug a Stone: Winnipeg, Turnstone, 1983. ISBN 0-88801-083-4
Touch to my Tongue: Edmonton, Longspoon, 1984. ISBN 0-919285-27-9
Steveston: Edmonton, Longspoon, 1984. ISBN 0-919285-28-7

Comments: "Arguably the most distinctive experimental voice Canadian poetry possesses." – Chris Hall, *University Of Windsor Review*
"Marlatt's method is dense, poetic, rich in association," – Marian Engel, *Toronto Star*
"*Steveston* is . . . a woman's exploration of a man's world. It shouldn't work, but Marlatt pushes her imagery, stretches her language until it does." – Charles Lilard, *Malahat Review*
"Marlatt's work is a dynamic of the self in dialogue not just with the lover, but in and through language." – Erin Moure, *Books in Canada*

Readings, Lectures & Workshops: Have given readings at colleges, universities, high schools, in galleries, bookshops across Canada, the U.S. and Australia. Given talks at conferences on contemporary Canadian poetry and feminist writing. May be booked through TWUC.

Mailing Address: 2533 West 5th Avenue, Vancouver, British Columbia V6K 1S9

JOHN MARLYN

Born in Hungary in 1912; arrived in Canada the same year. University of Manitoba (one-and-a-half years). Outside reader for Gaumont British Films, London, 1937-38. Married. Now living in Ottawa.

Selected Publications:

Under the Ribs of Death: Toronto, McClelland & Stewart, 1958.
  ISBN 0-7710-9141-9
Putzi, I Love You, You Little Square: Toronto, Coach House, 1981.
  ISBN 0-88910-234-1

Awards: English Senior Creative Writing Fellowship of the Canada Foundation, 1958. Beta Sigma Phi Award (First Novel), 1958.

Comments: "It is in this, the hungry drive toward some unattainable freedom and limitless expression, that the strength of Marlyn's work lies." — Eli W. Mandel (on *Under the Ribs of Death*)

"One of the three or four most powerful works dealing with immigrant experience in Canada." — Frank Davey

"As unconventional, delightful and insouciant as the title might indicate." — Ken Adachi, *Toronto Star* (on *Putzi, I Love You, You Little Square*)

Readings, Lectures & Workshops: Gave creative writing course at Carleton University, 1963-67. Recent readings: Carleton University, University of Ottawa, Toronto Harbourfront.

Mailing Address: c/o McClelland & Stewart, 481 University Avenue, Toronto, Ontario M5G 2E9

ANNE MARRIOTT

Born and educated in Victoria, British Columbia. Summer courses at the University of British Columbia. Wrote school broadcasts and other scripts for the CBC. Worked as a writer at the National Film Board in Ottawa, 1945-49. Women's editor of the Prince George Citizen, 1950-53. Various stints as a library assistant. Married Gerald McLellan, 1947 (died 1974). Three children. Now live and write in North Vancouver. Don't expect to stop writing!

Selected Publications:

Sandstone: Toronto, Ryerson, 1945. (no ISBN)
The Circular Coast: Oakville, Mosaic, 1981. ISBN 0-88962-128-4
A Long Way to Oregon: Oakville, Mosaic, 1984. ISBN 0-88962-240-X
Letters from Some Islands: Oakville, Mosaic, 1985. ISBN 0-88962-310-4

Awards: Governor-General's Award (Poetry), 1941. Women's Canadian Club Literary Award (with Margaret Kennedy), 1943. CBC Literary Competition (Third Prize for Fiction), 1983.

Comments: "A fine, mature story teller has made a place for herself in the space of just one book." – Barry Dempster, *Canadian Forum* (on *A Long Way to Oregon*)

"Marriott has continued to write poetry of enormous sensitivity and power." – Ronald Hatch, *Vancouver Sun* (on *Letters from Some Islands*)

Readings, Lectures & Workshops: Have given readings in B.C. and Eastern Canada. Frequently conduct poetry-writing workshops with school groups, mainly elementary and junior high.

Mailing Address: 3645 Sykes Road, North Vancouver, British Columbia V7K 2A6

TOM MARSHALL

Born in Niagara Falls, Ontario, April 9, 1938. Now living in Kingston, Ontario. B.A. in history from Queen's University in 1961; M.A. in English, Queen's, 1965. Professor of English at Queen's. Now teaching only one course per year at reduced salary, and writing fiction, poetry and criticism.

Selected Publications:

The Psychic Mariner (A Reading of the Poems of D.H. Lawrence): New York, Viking, 1970. ISBN 0-670-58190-9

Harsh and Lovely Land (The Major Canadian Poets and the Making of a Canadian Tradition): Vancouver, University of British Columbia Press, 1979. ISBN 0-7748-0107-7

The Elements: Ottawa, Oberon, 1980. ISBN 0-88750-336-5

Glass Houses: Ottawa, Oberon, 1985. ISBN 0-88750-593-7

Adele at the End of the Day: Toronto, Macmillan, 1987. ISBN 0-7715-9343-0

Comments: "The poems explore the riddles of history, pain and human redemption . . . (*The Elements*) firmly establishes Tom Marshall's claim to belong to the small circle of major Canadian poets." – K.J. Charles, *Canadian Book Review Annual*

"Told with a poet's economy of phrase, *Glass Houses* is a lively, often bawdy, thoroughly engrossing book that leaves me with only one regret: that Tom Marshall doesn't write a whole lot more fiction." – David Williamson, *Winnipeg Free Press*

Readings, Lectures & Workshops: Have read in most parts of Canada. Occasionally conduct poetry or fiction workshops. May be booked through TWUC.

Mailing Address: Dept. of English, Queen's University, Kingston, Ontario K7L 3N6

CAROL MATAS

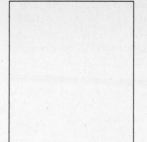

I was born in Winnipeg and after living in London, Ontario, London, England, Toronto and Montreal, I am now back in my home town. I am an actor and have been writing for children and bringing up my own. I work extensively with children in the schools, through both readings and workshops.

Selected Publications:

The D.N.A. Dimension: Toronto, Gage, 1982. ISBN 0-7715-7003-1
The Fusion Factor: Saskatoon, Fifth House, 1986. ISBN 0-920079-25-3
Zanu: Saskatoon, Fifth House, 1986. ISBN 0-920079-27-X

Comments: I write fast-paced, sci-fi adventure books for children, eight to 12. These books are very useful for teachers in schools as they can be used as a jumping off point for discussion of various issues, such as genetic engineering, nuclear war, consumer society, dictatorship and freedom. They are all set in Winnipeg, and children are delighted to see their own landscape in print.

Readings, Lectures & Workshops: Writer-in-residence, Centennial Library, Winnipeg 1986. Visiting professor, Bemidji State University 1985. Artists in the schools, Manitoba Arts Council. Canada Council Reading Tours.

Mailing Address: 465 Waterloo Street, Winnipeg, Manitoba R3N 0S9

SHIRLEE SMITH MATHESON

I was born in Winnipeg, Manitoba, and many of my short stories are set in the Birdtail Valley of the Riding Mountains. Other writing reflects experiences gained by living in the four western provinces and in Australia. Published work includes short stories, non-fiction and young-adult fiction and stage plays. I now reside in Calgary.

Selected Publications:

Youngblood of the Peace (An Authorized Biography of Father Emile Jung-bluth, OMI): Edmonton, Lone Pine, 1986. ISBN 0-919433-15-4

Awards: British Columbia Historical Federation, First Prize (Historical Writing),1983. Calgary Herald Short Story Awards, 1985 and 1986.
Comments: "*Youngblood of the Peace* gets tremendous send-off."
– *Alaska Highway News*
"With *Youngblood of the Peace* Shirlee Matheson has arrived. She's going to be around a long time." – Ken McGoogan, *Calgary Herald*
"*Youngblood of the Peace* is a fascinating chapter in the lively history of Alberta's frontier." – *Glenbow Magazine*
Work has been anthologized in: Alberta Bound (NeWest Press, 1986), Writers of the Okanagan Mainline (Okanagan Mainline Arts Council, 1984) and Treeline I And II (Northern Lights College, 1982 and 1983).
Forthcoming: A Girl Called Alien (WP Prairie Books).
Readings, Lectures & Workshops: Have given readings in British Columbia, Alberta and Manitoba.
Mailing Address: 1627 Bowness Road N.W., Calgary, Alberta T2N 3K1

CHRISTINA MCCALL

I have been a writer and editor since graduating from the University of Toronto in 1956 with an honours degree in English literature. Worked for several publications, notably Maclean's as associate editor, Saturday Night as Ottawa columnist and executive editor and the Globe and Mail as a writer on national affairs. Now working full time, in collaboration with Stephen Clarkson, on a major political study to be called The End of the Trudeau Era.

Selected Publications:

The Man from Oxbow: Toronto, McClelland & Stewart, 1967. (no ISBN)
Grits (An Intimate Portrait of the Liberal Party): Toronto, Macmillan, 1982.
  ISBN 0-7715-9573-5

Awards: President's Medal, University of Western Ontario, 1971. Southam Fellowship, University of Toronto, 1977. National Magazine Award (Gold Medal), 1983.

Comments: "A formidable illustration of how important the political writer can be to our national life." – Michael Volpe, *Globe and Mail*

"*Grits* is one of the best examples of political writing this country has yet produced." – Reginald Whitaker, *Canadian Forum*

Readings, Lectures & Workshops: Under duress (i.e. book or magazine promotion), I've been known to speak across the country and abroad (Harvard, the Free University of Berlin) on Canadian politics in general and the supine role women play in our public life in particular.

Mailing Address: 44 Rosedale Road, Toronto, Ontario M4W 2P6

DENNIS MCCLOSKEY

Born in Alberton, Prince Edward Island, in 1948 and lived with Air Force parents all over Canada and Germany. Graduated from Ryerson with a journalism degree and have earned a living since 1971 writing and editing business publications. Began freelancing in 1980 and have been published in consumer, corporate and business magazines and newspapers across the country. Began writing novels in 1983.

Selected Publications:

Manure on my Skates: Toronto, Three Trees, 1983. ISBN 0-88823-070-2
Love-15: Toronto, Three Trees, 1984. ISBN 0-88823-078-8

Comments: In 1971 I received $25 for an editorial on world hunger, which appeared in The Catholic Register. Since then I've satisfied my appetite for writing by selling a wide variety of articles such as a profile of MAD magazine publisher William Gaines (Toronto Star) and Favourite Politician's Jokes (Financial Times Magazine). Next to writing I enjoy the book tours and readings, especially in Eastern Canada. I cherish the memory of a nine-year-old girl in Charlottetown who asked me if I wrote Anne of Green Gables. Oh, how I wish!

Readings, Lectures & Workshops: The first time I addressed an audience of Young Adults was in Mississauga following the publication of my first book. I offered the sage advice that a writer should write about what he or she knows. The comment was greeted with gales of laughter which perplexed me until I realized I was holding a copy of my book, *Manure on my Skates*.

Mailing Address: 43 Tomlin Crescent, Richmond Hill, Ontario L4C 7T1

MICHAEL J. MCDONALD

I pose as a legal writer with the ability to transform seemingly complex subjects, such as the Canadian Charter of Rights, into understandable terms for the public. My real passion is to change the world, thus I am actively working on a new political ideology consonant with the 21st century. My wife would be happier if this latter-day Bethanite would turn my passion to reforming the basement of the matrimonial home!

Selected Publications:

You and the Law (What Every Small Business Owner Needs to Know):
  Toronto, Macmillan, 1978. ISBN 0-7705-1649-1
Legal First Aid: Toronto, Coles, 1978. (no ISBN)
Know Your New Rights: Toronto, Fenn, 1982. ISBN 0-919768-00-8

Mailing Address: 1941 Weston Road, Suite 203, Weston, Ontario M9N 1W8

SANDRA K. MCDONNELL

I was born in Colorado in 1952. I attended Colorado State University, obtained an MRS, then emigrated to Canada in 1972. Amid raising goats, kids (human) and bread, I took a wide range of post-secondary courses from Malaspina College and the University of British Columbia. (Avoided degrees and creative writing courses.) In 1982, I started writing romance and discovered a new skill: raising ardor. I now live near Nanaimo and write full time.

Selected Publications:

A Risky Business: (wa Sandra K. Rhoades), Toronto, Harlequin, 1986. ISBN 0-373-10917-2
Bitter Legacy: (wa Sandra K. Rhoades), Toronto, Harlequin, 1987. ISBN 0-373-10956-3
Shadows in the Limelight: (wa Sandra K. Rhodes), London, Mills & Boon, 1987.

Readings, Lectures & Workshops: Conduct lecture courses and workshops on writing romance novels and getting published for Malaspina College in Nanaimo.
Mailing Address: RR 4, Site U, 1749 Seaberg Road, Nanaimo, British Columbia V9R 5X9

JUDY MCGILLIVARY

Prairie born and raised, I have lived in nine of the provinces and have spent four years in France. I received my B.Ed. and M.F.A. from the University of British Columbia and have worked as a primary teacher, adult educator, model, court reporter and recreation specialist, all the while continuing to write prose and poetry. I am a member of the Composers, Authors and Publishers Association of Canada, Tynehead Zoological Society and the Wildlife Rescue Association.

Selected Publications:

Time Lines: Ottawa, Golden Dog, 1979. ISBN 0-919614-33-7
Deep Streets: Cornwall, Vesta, 1983. ISBN 0-919301-59-2

   Comments: "I first met Judy in 1970 in Ottawa. I was stunned by her work then and I'm so glad she is now reaching a wider audience." – Joy Kogawa
   "Sincere, brilliant, tough, tender: what do these words mean? They pale in significance as we consider Judy McGillivary." – Eugene McNamara
   "McGillivary provides intriguing and often highly individual ways of looking at a familiar world." – Christopher Levenson
   Readings, Lectures & Workshops: Read at the Ottawa Folk and Poetry Festival and, in Vancouver, at the Women in Arts Festival, the University of British Columbia, the Literary Storefront, the Billy Bishop, and on CBC and Co-op Radio.
   Mailing Address: c/o TWUC, 24 Ryerson Avenue, Toronto, Ontario M5T 2P3

AUDREY MCKIM

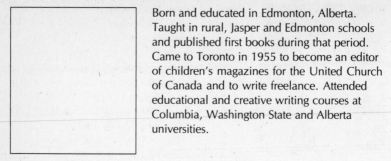

Born and educated in Edmonton, Alberta. Taught in rural, Jasper and Edmonton schools and published first books during that period. Came to Toronto in 1955 to become an editor of children's magazines for the United Church of Canada and to write freelance. Attended educational and creative writing courses at Columbia, Washington State and Alberta universities.

Selected Publications:

Here Comes Dirk: Toronto, Oxford, 1951. (no ISBN)
Lexy O'Connor: Toronto, McClelland & Stewart, 1953. (no ISBN)
Andy and the Gopher: New York, Little Brown, 1959. (no ISBN)
Lexy for Short: New York, Abingdon, 1961. (no ISBN)
Thorny's Hideaway: New York, Nelson, 1961. (no ISBN)
The Search for Uncle Joe: Toronto, Gage, 1973. ISBN 0-7715-8789-9
Pun and Fuzzles: Toronto, Scholastic, 1975. ISBN 0-590-71039-7
Alpha Diddle Riddles: Toronto, Scholastic, 1978. ISBN 0-590-71226-8
Fun Makers: (with Jennifer McKim), Toronto, Scholastic, 1985. ISBN 0-590-71509-7

Awards: Alberta IODE Fiction Award. Little Brown Canadian Children's Book Award (Honorable Mention), 1959. Vicki Metcalf Award, 1969.

Comments: Forthcoming: A biography of Jean Little, written in collaboration with Barbara Greenwood, to be published by Irwin.

Mailing Address: Apt. 307, 49 Glen Elm Avenue, Toronto, Ontario M4T 1V2

FLORENCE MCNEIL

Born and educated in Vancouver, British Columbia. M.A. in creative writing from the University of British Columbia. Had the good fortune to study with Earle Birney. Began writing as a poet; now also writing fiction, drama and non-fiction. Taught at several universities; decided to write full time in 1976. Married, live in Vancouver. Widely anthologised and broadcast in Canada and U.S.

Selected Publications:

Rim of the Park: Victoria, Sono Nis, 1972. (no ISBN)
Ghost Towns: Toronto, McClelland & Stewart, 1975. ISBN 0-7710-5821-7
A Balancing Act: Toronto, McClelland & Stewart, 1980. ISBN 0-7710-5606-0
Miss P. and Me: Toronto, Clarke Irwin, 1982. ISBN 0-7720-1374-8. (Reprinted Scholastic, 1984.)
Barkerville: Saskatoon, Thistledown, 1984. ISBN 0-920066-82-8
All Kinds of Magic: Toronto, Groundwood, 1984. ISBN 0-88899-035-9

Awards: National Magazine Award (Poetry), 1980. Macmillan Prize for Poetry, 1965.

Comments: "It is McNeil's extraordinary talent as a writer that ultimately rises up and takes the reader by storm." – *Globe and Mail*

"She has, I believe, no equal in Canada as a poet of visual metaphor." – *CV/II*

Readings, Lectures & Workshops: Readings and workshops on teaching poetry and creative writing across Canada.

Mailing Address: c/o TWUC, 24 Ryerson Avenue, Toronto, Ontario M5T 2P3

GEORGE MCWHIRTER

Born on September 26, 1939. Raised in the Shankhill Road district, Belfast. Came to Canada in 1966. B.A. and Dip. Ed., Queen's University Belfast, 1961 and 1962. M.A., University of British Columbia, 1970. Teacher at Kilkeel, Bangor, County Down, 1962-65; Language School, University of Barcelona, 1965-66; A.D.S.S., Port Alberni, 1966-68; University of British Columbia, since 1970. Professor and head of the department of creative writing, 1982. Married Angela Mairhead Coid, 1963. Two children. Live in Point Grey, Vancouver.

Selected Publications:

Catalan Poems: Ottawa, Oberon, 1971. ISBN 0-88750-041-2
Bodyworks: Ottawa, Oberon, 1974. ISBN 0-88750-100-1
Bloodlight for Malachi McNair: Vancouver/San Fransisco, Kanchenjunga, 1974. ISBN 0-913600-32-6
Queen of the Sea: Ottawa, Oberon, 1976. ISBN 0-88750-198-2
Twenty-Five: Fredericton, Fiddlehead, 1978. ISBN 0-920110-46-6
God's Eye: Ottawa, Oberon, 1981. ISBN 0-88750-394-2
Coming to Grips with Lucy: Ottawa, Oberon, 1982. ISBN 0-88750-417-5
Fire Before Dark: Ottawa, Oberon, 1984. ISBN 0-88750-503-1
Paula Lake: Ottawa, Oberon, 1985. ISBN 0-88750-536-8

Awards: Macmillan Poetry Prize, 1969; The Commonwealth Poetry Prize, 1972
Comments: Forthcoming in 1987: Cage, a novel from Oberon, and Selected Poems of Jose Emelio Pacheco, translations from New Directions. In this past 20 years I have spent four days in Ireland and would prefer to stay where I am and spend my eternity on or in Sproat Lake, Vancouver Island.
Mailing Address: c/o TWUC, 24 Ryerson Avenue, Toronto, Ontario M5T 2P3

MARY MEIGS

Born on April 27, 1917, in Philadelphia, Pennsylvania. Now live in Montreal. Education: B.A. Bryn Mawr College, 1939. Instructor of English, Bryn Mawr College 1940-42. Served as a WAVE 1942-45. Studied painting at the Art Students' League, New York City, 1945-47. Have had one-woman shows in Boston, New York, Paris and Montreal.

Selected Publications:

Lily Briscoe (A Self-Portrait): Vancouver, Talon, 1981. ISBN 0-88922-195-2
The Medusa Head: Vancouver, Talon, 1983. ISBN 0-88922-210-X

Comments: I have illustrated two novels by Marie-Claire Blais (Exile Editions, 1978). A story, *The Island*, was published in Room of One's Own (Vol. 9, Number 4, 1985). Articles and reviews have appeared in Broadside, Room of One's Own, Fireweed and The Body Politic.

Readings, Lectures & Workshops: Readings at Concordia University, the University of Toronto, Memorial University in St. John's and Women and Words. Workshops: Women and Words, Marianapolis College and the Simone de Beauvoir Institute.

Mailing Address: 427 Grosvenor Avenue, Westmount, Quebec H3Y 2S5

JOHN MELADY

Born in Seaforth, Ontario, September 12, 1938. B.A. in English and history from the University of Western Ontario. M.Ed. in educational administration from the University of Toronto. Have taught both elementary and secondary school and have been a high-school vice principal for several years. Enjoy skiing, travelling and photography. Married to Mary, also a teacher. Three sons: Paul, Mark and Tim.

Selected Publications:

Explosion: Belleville, Mika, 1980. ISBN 0-919303-50-1
Escape From Canada!: Toronto, Macmillan, 1981. ISBN 0-7715-9537-9
Korea (Canada's Forgotten War): Toronto, Macmillan, 1983. ISBN 0-7715-9780-0
Cross of Valour: Toronto, Scholastic, 1985. ISBN 0-590-71510-0
The French in Ontario in *The Shaping Of Ontario*: Belleville, Mika, 1985.

Comments: Escape From Canada! has appeared in three separate editions since 1981. The book was also one of the original titles included in the Macmillan Paperbacks series in 1986. Korea: Canada's Forgotten War was a Literary Guild and a Book-of-the-Month Club Selection. My most recent book, Cross of Valour, was listed in Emergency Librarian as one of the best Canadian paperbacks for 1985 and by the Children's Book Centre on its Our Choice list for 1986.

Articles have been published in Canadian Geographic, Reader's Digest, Financial Post Magazine, and Sentinel. For the last six years I have been a columnist for the Catholic Register.

Readings, Lectures & Workshops: I give several speeches, readings and workshops each year to school groups, professional organisations and service clubs.

Mailing Address: RR 3, Brighton, Ontario K0K 1H0

JOHN MELLOR

Born in Chester, England, October 14, 1922. Served as a naval officer in World War II and post war. Sailed the seven seas and set foot in many countries around the globe before dropping the anchor in Canada. Engineer, businessman, high-school teacher, historian, university lecturer and now full-time writer living in Kitchener, Ontario. B.A. Waterloo, M.A. Wilfrid Laurier.

Selected Publications:

Forgotten Heroes, The Canadians at Dieppe: Toronto, Methuen, 1975. ISBN 0-458-91180-1
The Dieppe Raid: London, Hodder & Stoughton, 1979. ISBN 0-340-2231-2-X
The Company Store: Toronto, Doubleday, 1983. ISBN 0-385-12812-6

Awards: Canadian Authors Association Award (Non-fiction), 1976
Comments: "Exciting . . . well done . . . *Dieppe* had to be written by somebody, and John Mellor has done it well!" – Gordon Sinclair, *CFRB*
"John Mellor has brought the Dieppe disaster to life in his book . . . to me the definitive work on a defeat Canadians should celebrate rather than forget." – Hugh Garner, *Books in Canada*
"Mr. Mellor's portrait of miners' leader Jim McLachlan is bigger than life . . . the picture that emerges is that of a martyr to the cause." – *New York Times Book Review*
Readings, Lectures & Workshops: Readings and lectures at the University of Waterloo and Wilfrid Laurier.
Mailing Address: 115 Cornell Avenue, Kitchener, Ontario N2G 3E5

GEORGE MELNYK

Raised in Winnipeg, educated in Chicago and Toronto. While living in Edmonton founded the regional journal, NeWest Review, and the publishing house, NeWest Press. I now live in Calgary, where I am the executive director of the Alberta Foundation for the Literary Arts.

Selected Publications:

Of The Spirit (The Writings of Douglas Cardinal): (ed.), Edmonton, NeWest, 1977. ISBN 0-920316-06-9

Radical Regionalism: Edmonton, NeWest, 1981. ISBN 0-920316-31-X

The Search for Community (From Utopia to a Co-Operative Society): Montreal, Black Rose, 1985. ISBN 0-920057-53-5

Mailing Address: Box 3683, Station B, Calgary, Alberta T2M 4M4

HEATHER MENZIES

Born June 17, 1949, in a Montreal suburb. Completed a B.A. at McGill University, with a formal major in sociology and an informal one in street politics. Worked as a film editor (National Cine), reporter (Report on Farming), feature writer (Edmonton Journal) and columnist (Winnipeg Tribune) before first book. Currently busy in video production, public speaking and writing, plus as parent, peace activist and feminist.

Selected Publications:

The Railroad's Not Enough (Canada Now): Toronto, Clarke Irwin, 1978. ISBN 0-7720-1226-1

Women and the Chip: Montreal, Institute for Research on Public Policy, 1981. ISBN 0-920380-88-3

Computers on the Job: Toronto, Lorimer, 1982. ISBN 0-88862-553-7

Comments: "Some of it reads like poetry." – William French, *Globe and Mail* (on *The Railroad's Not Enough*)

"One of the most organized and accessible of the books dealing with technological change." – Laurie Bildfell, *Quill & Quire* (on *Computers on the Job*)

Articles include Women's Work is Nearly Done in This Magazine (March, 1984), Back To Grandma's Place in Canadian Woman Studies/Cahiers de la femme (Fall, 1984), Transborder Data Flows: Silent Conquest in Canadian Business (April, 1982), A Chip On Her Shoulder in Broadside Magazine (June, 1984).

Readings, Lectures & Workshops: Keynote speaker at The Future Is Now conference on women and technology. Delivered a paper at the University of Edinburgh in 1986. Also addressed the Fate of the Earth Conference that year.

Mailing Address: c/o TWUC, 24 Ryerson Avenue, Toronto, Ontario M5T 2P3

JUDITH MERRIL

Born January 21, 1923, in New York City; immigrated to Canada, 1968; Canadian citizen, 1976. Usual mal-education through dropout from the City College of New York, 1940; degree in Twenty-first Century Mythology, Rochdale College, 1971. Three marriages and divorces; two daughters, Merril MacDonald and Ann Pohl; five grandchildren. Travel in England, Japan and Jamaica; now live in Jamaica November to April.

Selected Publications*:

Tesseracts: Victoria, Press Porcepic, 1985. ISBN 0-88878-242-X
Daughters of Earth and Other Stories: Toronto, McClelland & Stewart, 1985.
   ISBN 0-7710-5837-3
*Most recent

Awards: Canadian Science Fiction & Fantasy Award (Lifetime Contributions to the Field), 1983. CASPER Award (English Canada, Achievement in Editing), 1986.

Comments: Author of five collections of short fiction, four novels (two in collaboration with Cyril Kornbluth) and one book of critical writings, as well as numerous magazine articles, and radio and television documentaries. Editor of 20 anthologies of science fiction. Complete bibliography on file with TWUC.

Readings, Lectures & Workshops: Read occasionally at universities, galleries, high schools, etc. Conduct workshops, seminars, discussion groups, mainly on science fiction, general prose writing, and the future.

Mailing Address: 40 St. George, Toronto, Ontario M5S 2E4

DAVID MIBASHAN

Born in Buenos Aires, Argentina, in 1957 where I lived for almost 20 years. I then moved to Jerusalem for six years before coming to Canada in 1982. I have two loves (as far as occupation goes): I am a writer and a practising psychologist. Due to the internationality of this world most of my writing is in Spanish.

Selected Publications:

Las Vueltas a la Vida (Returns to Life): Buenos Aires, Grupo Editor Latino-
americano, 1985. ISBN 950-9432-42-3
Vida y Vuelta (Return Trip to Life): Bueno Aires, Grupo Editor Latinoameri-
cano, 1987. ISBN 950-9432-80-6

Readings, Lectures & Workshops: Participant in the North/South Encounter: Canadian and Latin American Writers, Toronto, 1987. Read regularly
for my friends and unsuspecting guests. Readings and lectures may be
booked through TWUC.
Mailing Address: 147-450 Daly Avenue, Ottawa, Ontario K1N 6H5

C.D. (DINO) MINNI

I was born in Italy and grew up in British Columbia. My short stories, articles and interviews with authors have appeared in literary magazines, anthologies and CanLit textbooks and have been heard on CBC-Radio. From 1977 to 1980, I was literary critic on the staff of Canadian Author & Bookman, and I reviewed for The Vancouver Sun for eight years. I published a short-story collection, Other Selves, in 1985 and am currently editing Ricordi.

Selected Publications:

Other Selves: Montreal, Guernica, 1985. ISBN 0-919349-54-4

Comments: Member of the literary committee at the Italian Cultural Centre in Vancouver, west coast representative for the Association of Italian Canadian Writers and an editor of the forthcoming proceedings of the first national conference of Italian Canadian Writers (Writers in Transition), held in Vancouver, September 1986.

Readings, Lectures & Workshops: Read at Soul of a City and at the first Italian Canadian Writers Conference, both in Vancouver, in 1986.

Mailing Address: 2707 Duke Street, Vancouver, British Columbia V5R 4S8

KEN MITCHELL

Born in Moose Jaw, 1940. Frequent travel since then, most recently to Tibet, in the pursuit of quality material. Now living in Regina with my wife Jeanne Shami and two children.

Selected Publications:

Wandering Rafferty: Toronto, Macmillan, 1972. ISBN 0-7705-0895-2
The Meadowlark Connection: Regina, Pile of Bones, 1975. (no ISBN)
Everybody Gets Something Here: Toronto, Macmillan, 1977. ISBN 0-7705-1495-2
Horizon: Toronto, Oxford, 1977. ISBN 0-19-540262-6
Cruel Tears: Vancouver, Talon, 1977. ISBN 0-88922-120-0
The Con Man: Vancouver, Talon, 1977. ISBN 0-88922-168-5
Davin (The Politician): Edmonton, NeWest, 1977. (no ISBN)
Chautaqua Girl: Toronto, Playwrights Union, 1982. ISBN 0-88754-322-7
Gone the Burning Sun: Toronto, Playwrights Union, 1985. ISBN 0-88754-434-7
Through the Nan Da Gate: Saskatoon, Thistledown, 1986. ISBN 0-920633-22-6

Awards: Canadian Authors Association (Best Play), 1985. Genie nomination (Best Original Screenplay), 1981.
Readings, Lectures & Workshops: In the U.S., Germany, the U.K., Mexico, China and throughout Canada.
Mailing Address: 209 Angus Crescent, Regina, Saskatchewan S4T 6N3

CHRISTOPHER MOORE

Born 1950. Raised Nelson and Vancouver, British Columbia. Educated at UBC and the University of Ottawa. Canadian citizen. Bilingual. Married. A working historian since 1972 and self-employed in that field since 1978, I now live in Toronto.

Selected Publications:

Louisbourg Portraits (Life in an Eighteenth Century Garrison Town): Toronto, Macmillan, 1982. ISBN 0-7715-9781-9

The Loyalists (Revolution, Exile, Settlement): Toronto, Macmillan, 1984. ISBN 0-7715-9702-6

New France in *The Illustrated History of Canada*: (ed. Craig Brown), Toronto, Lester and Orpen Dennys, 1987. ISBN 0-88619-1247-5

Awards: Governor General's Award (Non-fiction), 1982. Secretary of State's Prize for Excellence in Canadian Studies, 1985. Canadian Historical Association Award of Merit, 1984. Ontario Historical Society, Riddell Prize, 1984.

Comments: A professional historian who specialises in presenting historical topics to non-specialist audiences, I have written popular histories, scholarly articles, educational texts, historic sites guidebooks, newspaper and magazine articles and radio documentaries (particularly for CBC Ideas). I contributed to the Historical Atlas Of Canada, the Dictionary of Canadian Biography and the Canadian Encyclopedia.

Readings, Lectures & Workshops: Frequently lecture and speak on historical topics to university and college classes and general audiences.

Mailing Address: Care of my publishers *or* TWUC, 24 Ryerson Avenue, Toronto, Ontario M5T 2P3

ALLEN MORGAN

Born September 29, 1946. Married (Leslie) June 21, 1971. B.Ed. (ECE) from the University of British Columbia. 1974. Son (Timothy) January 5, 1979. Will accept employment as a children's book writer, playwright, storyteller, kindergarten teacher, camel consultant or territory guide.

Selected Publications:

Dropping Out in 3/4 Time: New York, Seabury, 1972. ISBN 0-8164-0234-5
Christopher and the Elevator Closet: Toronto, Kids Can, 1982. ISBN 0-919964-40-0
Molly and Mr. Maloney: Toronto, Kids Can, 1982. ISBN 0-919964-41-9
Beautiful Dreamer: Toronto, Kids Can, 1982. ISBN 0-919964-44-3
Matthew and the Midnight Tow Truck: Toronto, Annick, 1984. ISBN 0-920303-01-3
Barnaby and Mr. Ling: Toronto, Annick, 1984. ISBN 0-920236-67-7
The Kids from B.A.D.: Toronto, Scholastic, 1984. ISBN 0-590-71219-5
Christopher and the Dream Dragon: Toronto, Kids Can, 1984. ISBN 0-919964-60-5
Sadie and the Snowman: Toronto, Kids Can, 1985. ISBN 0-919964-78-8
Matthew and the Midnight Turkeys: Toronto, Annick, 1985. ISBN 0-920303-37-4
Nicole's Boat: Toronto, Annick, 1986. ISBN 0-920303-61-7
Daddy-Care: Toronto, Annick, 1986. ISBN 0-920303-59-5

Mailing Address: 38 Nina Street, Toronto, Ontario M5R 1Z4

PATRICIA MORLEY

Born May 25, 1929, to Frederick C. Marlow, M.D., and Mabel Winsland Marlow. Education: Branksome Hall, the University of Toronto (Trinity) 1951; Carleton University (M.A.,1967); University of Ottawa (Ph.D., 1970). Married Lawrence W. Morley, 1950; divorced, 1975. Children: Lawrence, Patricia, Christopher and David. Teach Canadian literature and women's studies at Concordia University (1972 ff.), where I am professor of English and Canadian studies. Freelance writer since 1968.

Selected Publications:

The Mystery of Unity (Themes and Technique in the Novels of Patrick White): Montreal, McGill-Queen's UP, 1972. ISBN 0-7735-0112-6

The Immoral Moralists (Hugh MacLennan and Leonard Cohen): Toronto, Clarke Irwin, 1972. ISBN 0-7720-0555-9

Robertson Davies: Toronto, Gage, 1976. ISBN 0-7715-5864-3

The Comedians (Hugh Hood and Rudy Wiebe): Toronto, Clarke Irwin, 1977. ISBN 0-7720-1051-X

Selected Stories of Ernest Thompson Seton: (ed. and intro.), Ottawa, University of Ottawa Press, 1977. ISBN 0-7766-4339-8

Morley Callaghan: Toronto, McClelland & Stewart, 1978. ISBN 0-7710-6470-5

Margaret Laurence: Boston, G.K. Hall, 1981. ISBN 0-8057-6433-X

Kurelek: Toronto, Macmillan, 1986. ISBN 0-7715-9748-7

Comments: Writings include essays, stories, poetry, one-act plays, literary criticism, biography and uncountable book reviews (some 600) in the Ottawa Journal, Ottawa Citizen, Birmingham News (Alabama) and in periodicals such as Journal of Canadian Fiction, Saturday Night and Canadian Literature. Work in progress includes three full-length manuscripts: biographies of poet Leo Kennedy and painter Joann Saarniit as well as a study of modern Japanese women writers. (I have a permanent love affair with Japan.) Long-range writing plans include fiction.

Mailing Address: Box 137, Manotick, Ontario K0A 2N0

ROBERTA MORRIS

Born in Windsor, Ontario, December 3, 1953, and grew up in the Detroit area before returning to Canada to attend the University of Toronto to complete a Masters programme in theology. Now live in Toronto with my husband and two children. Writing fiction, drama and reviews.

Selected Publications:

Married Sisters: Toronto, Barton, 1981. ISBN 0-919133-02-9
Vigil: Toronto, Williams-Wallace, 1986. ISBN 0-88795-049-3

Awards: Innis College Medal, 1976
Comments: "An absolute fidelity to material life which comes to stand for, and perhaps even more concretely express, felt life." – Kay Armatage
"Her nightmarish vision projects an unforgettable spectacle." – Joan McGrath, *Toronto Star*
"Morris's gift for examining major issues of belief and behavior make a provocative and timely tale." – Nancy Wigston, *Globe and Mail*
Mailing Address: 757 Manning Avenue, Toronto, Ontario M6G 2W5

HOPE MORRITT

Born in Edmonton before World War II. Hold a
B.A. in English from the University of Western
Ontario, 1979. Did post-graduate work in Irish
literature in Dublin, Ireland, with Eastern
Washington University in Cheney, 1982. Lived
in Edmonton, Whitehorse and Point Edward,
Ontario. Consider myself a Canadian writer;
neither eastern nor western Canadian. I live on
the shore of Lake Huron near Sarnia. Write full
time.

Selected Publications:

Sarah: Toronto, Hale, 1974. ISBN 0-7091-4618-3
Nahanni: (with Norma West Linder), Toronto, Hale, 1974. ISBN 0-7091-
    4794-5
Pauline: (with Norma West Linder), Sarnia, River City, 1979. ISBN
    0-920940-00-5
Land of the Fireweed: Anchorage, Alaska & Edmonds, 1986. ISBN 0-88240-
    307-9
Bohunk Road: Sarnia, River City, 1987. ISBN 0-920940-12-9

Awards: Georgia May Cook Sonnet Award, 1970. Ottawa Playwrighting
Competition (Honourable Mention), 1972. Detroit Magazine, Fiction Competition (First Prize), 1984.

Comments: "In *Nahanni*, the authors conveyed a true feeling of the north,
not only the sense of the vast physical wilderness, but the emotional impact
this can have on a person living and working there." – *Quill & Quire*

Readings, Lectures & Workshops: Read regularly at colleges, schools,
libraries; have taught creative writing at Lambton College and separate
schools in Sarnia. May be booked through TWUC.

Mailing Address: 15 Albert Street, Point Edward, Ontario N7V 1P7

DANIEL DAVID MOSES

Grew up on a farm on the Six Nations lands near Brantford, Ont. Attended the University of British Columbia on a fellowship and won the creative writing department's playwriting prize in 1977. Founded the Committee to Re-Establish the Trickster in summer 1986. President of the Association for Native Development in the Performing and Visual Arts. Treasurer of Native Earth Performing Arts, Inc. Now working on a manuscript of poetry and short fiction and plays full time. A new book of poems, The White Line, upcoming.

Selected Publications:

Delicate Bodies: blewointment, 1980. ISBN 0-88971-040-6
Post Memoriam [et al. in] *The Last Blewointment Anthology, (Vol. II)*: Nightwood, 1986. ISBN 0-88971-109-7

Comments: The Night Lights on the Farm was published in Next Exit, (No. 10) and Dandelion Salad Day appeared in This Magazine (March/April 1987).
Falling Song and *A Visit in Mid-Summer* are in First People, First Voices (University of Toronto Press, 1983, ISBN 0-8020-2515-3).
Poems published in many magazines, including the Malahat Review, Tamarack Review and the Fiddlehead. Stories soon in the Canadian Fiction Magazine and on the current Spirit Bay television series. Reviews published in Books in Canada.
Readings, Lectures & Workshops: Read regularly in Toronto. Also have read in Montreal, Boston and Vancouver in 1986.
Mailing Address: 17, 1868 Bloor Street West, Toronto, Ontario M6P 3K7

JOHN MOSS

 I was born in Blair, Ontario (Waterloo County), in 1940. I live in Bellrock, Ontario, with my wife, Virginia, in a rebuilt 19th-century log farmhouse, on an island in the middle of the Depot River. With our daughters, Julia and Laura, we travel a lot and participate in a variety of endurance sports, including marathon running and cross-country skiing. I hold a Doctorate in Canadian literature and teach at the University of Ottawa.

Selected Publications:

Patterns of Isolation: Toronto, McClelland & Stewart, 1974. ISBN 0-7710-6568-X

Modern Times (The Canadian Novel; Vol. 3): Toronto, NC Press, 1982. ISBN 0-919601-88-X

Bellrock: Toronto, NC Press, 1983. ISBN 0-919601-83-9

Beginnings (The Canadian Novel; Vol. 2): Toronto, NC Press, 1984. ISBN 0-920053-15-7

Present Tense (The Canadian Novel; Vol. 4): Toronto, NC Press, 1985. ISBN 0-919601-67-7

A Reader's Guide to the Canadian Novel (Second Edition): Toronto, McClelland & Stewart, 1987. (First Edition: ISBN 0-7710-6564-7)

Comments: Apart from Bellrock, a first-person chronicle, my books have all been in the field of literary criticism. Some, especially the Reader's Guide, are meant to provide the general reading public with wider access to the pleasures of Canadian writing. Others, such as Invisible in the House of Mirrors and the forthcoming Future Indicative: Literary Theory and Canadian Literature, are much more academic. By keeping these two functions of criticism in balance, the public and the esoteric, I endeavour to share my enthusiasm without, I hope, becoming either a promoter or a pedant.

Mailing Address: Bellrock, RR 1, Verona, Ontario K0H 2W0

CLAIRE MOWAT

Intending to be a graphic designer, I graduated from an art college. I fell into writing by accident. To assist my author-husband, I typed manuscripts, answered letters and wrote journals. It wasn't considered subversive, then, to share the workload with the guy you married. Ultimately he was the one who told me I could write well enough to do my own work. I did. The Outport People was the result. I am now working on my second book.

Selected Publications:

The Outport People: Toronto, McClelland & Stewart, 1983. ISBN 0-7710-6549-3

Mailing Address: 18 King Street, Port Hope, Ontario L1A 2R4

FARLEY MOWAT

Most of what is fit to print about my life has already been printed in my several pseudo-autobiographical books. The rest is silence until I get around to writing about that too. Biographical books include: The Dog Who Wouldn't Be (1957), Never Cry Wolf (1963) The Boat Who Wouldn't Float (1969), And No Birds Sang (1979), Owls in the Family (1961), Sibir (1970) and A Whale for the Killing (1972).

Selected Publications:

All books published in Toronto by McClelland & Stewart

People of the Deer: 1952. ISBN 0-7710-6590-6
The Regiment: 1955. ISBN 0-7710-6571-X
Lost in the Barrens: 1955. ISBN 0-7710-6639-2
Grey Seas Under: 1958. ISBN 0-7710-6595-7
The Desperate People: 1959./ Seal, 1980. ISBN 0-7704-1781-7
Ordeal by Ice: 1960. ISBN 0-7710-6626-0
The Serpent's Coil: 1961. ISBN 0-7710-6599-X
The Black Joke: 1962. ISBN 0-7710-6603-1
Westviking: 1965. ISBN 0-7710-6579-5
Curse of the Viking Grave: 1966. ISBN 0-7710-6642-2
The Polar Passion: 1967. ISBN 0-7710-6622-8
Tundra: 1973. ISBN 0-7710-6628-7
The Snow Walker: 1975. ISBN 0-7710-6630-9
Canada North Now: 1976. ISBN 0-7710-6595-5
Sea of Slaughter: 1984. ISBN 0-7710-6556-6
My Discovery of America: 1985. ISBN 0-7710-6624-4

Awards: Twenty or so, including the Governor General's Award, the Order of Canada and six honorary doctorates.

Mailing Address: c/o McClelland & Stewart, 481 University Avenue, Toronto, Ontario M5G 2E9

ROBIN LESTER MULLER

Born in Toronto, October 30, 1953. Educated at Algonquin College (fine art), George Brown College (graphic design) and the University of Toronto (arts and science). Now live in Riverdale where I write and illustrate full time.

Selected Publications:

Mollie Whuppie and the Giant: Toronto, Scholastic, 1982. ISBN 0-590-71106-7
Tatterhood: Toronto, Scholastic, 1984. ISBN 0-590-71411-2
The Sorcerer's Apprentice: Toronto, Kids Can, 1985. ISBN 0-919964-80-X

Awards: IODE Book Award, 1985. Ezra Jack Keats Memorial Award (Medalist), 1986.

Comments: "The interpretation is intelligent and by no means overindulgent, his drawing is flawless; detailed without fussiness." – *Globe and Mail*

"One of the most haunting, satisfying and talented of children's artists alive today." – *Thomson News Service*

Readings, Lectures & Workshops: Read regularly at libraries and schools. Conduct workshops on writing fairy tales.

Mailing Address: 587 Logan Avenue, Toronto, Ontario M4K 3B9

GLENN H. MULLIN

Born in 1949 in Gaspe, P.Q. Briefly studied engineering at Mt. Allison University. Lived in the U.S. and Europe for three years, then in 1972 joined the Dalai Lama's LTWA Institute in India. Remained there for 12 years. Have written and/or translated more than a dozen books on Tibet and the Dalai Lamas. Script consultant for the four-hour film documentary Tibet: A Buddhist Trilogy (UK); recording assistant and sleeve notes for the record Shedur: A Ghost Exorcism (NY); special programme adviser on CBC Man Alive production The Dalai Lama (1985).

Selected Publications:

Meditations on Arya Tara: Dharamsala, Dharmakaya Publications, 1978. (no ISBN)
Teachings at Tushita: New Delhi, Mahayana Publications, 1981. ISSN 0-861171-006-1
The Dalai Lama I (Bridging the Sutras and Tantras): New York, Snow Lion, 1981. ISBN 0-937938-27-0 (see also Dalai Lama II,III and VII)
Meditations on the Lower Tantras: Dharamsala, LTWA, 1983. (no ISBN)
Atisha and Buddhism in Tibet: New Delhi, Tibet House, 1983. ISSN 0-856497-536-0
Death and Dying (The Tibetan Tradition): Routledge & Kegan Paul, London, 1985. ISBN 1-85063-024-0

Comments: A non-academic non-fiction writer for the commercial market. I am a non-fiction addict, and believe that non-fiction will become the literary medium of the 21st century.

Readings, Lectures & Workshops: In various universities, schools etc. in Canada, the U.S. and India.

Mailing Address: c/o TWUC, 24 Ryerson Avenue, Toronto, Ontario M5T 2P3

ALICE MUNRO

Born July 10, 1931, in Wingham, Ontario.
Married James Munro in 1951. Daughters:
Sheila, Jenny and Andrea. Married Gerald
Fremlin in 1976.

Selected Publications:

Dance of the Happy Shades: Toronto, Ryerson, 1968. ISBN 0-7700-0239-0
Lives of Girls and Women: Toronto, McGraw-Hill Ryerson, 1971.
  ISBN 0-07-09-2932-7
Something I've Been Meaning to Tell You: Toronto, McGraw-Hill Ryerson,
  1974. ISBN 0-07-0777-60-8
Who Do You Think You Are: (aka The Beggar Maid) Toronto, Macmillan,
  1978. ISBN 0-7139-1317-7
The Moons of Jupiter: Toronto, Macmillan, 1982. ISBN 0-7715-9725-8
The Progress of Love: Toronto, McClelland & Stewart, 1986. ISBN 0-7710-
  6666-X

  Mailing Address: Box 1133, Clinton, Ontario N0M 1L0

ROBERT MUNSCH

Born June 11, 1945, in Pittsburgh, Pennsylvania (the fourth of nine kids). Worked in daycare for three years and then as a professor at the University of Guelph for eight years. Always told stories when working with kids. Started writing them down in 1979, now a full-time writer. Canadian citizen in 1983. Adjunct professor in family studies at the University of Guelph.

Selected Publications:

Books published in Toronto by Annick Press

Mud Puddle: 1979. ISBN 0-920236-28-6
The Dark: 1979. ISBN 0-920236-85-5
The Paper Bag Princess: 1980. ISBN 0-920236-16-2
Jonathan Cleaned Up: 1981. ISBN 0-920236-20-0
The Boy in the Drawer: 1982. ISBN 0-920236-37-7
Murmel, Murmel, Murmel: 1982. ISBN 0-920236-31-6
Angela's Airplane: 1983. ISBN 0-920236-75-8
Fire Station: 1983. ISBN 0-920236-77-4
David's Father: 1983. ISBN 0-920236-64-2
Millicent and the Wind: 1984. ISBN 0-920236-93-6
Thomas' Snowsuit: 1985. ISBN 0-920303-33-1
Mortimer: 1985. ISBN 0-920303-11-0
50 Below Zero: 1985. ISBN 0-920303-91-X
I Have To Go: 1986. ISBN 0-920303-51-X

Love You Forever: Toronto, Firefly, 1986. ISBN 0-920668-37-2

Awards: Ruth Schwartz Award, 1985
Comments: Translations in Spanish, French, Dutch, Danish, German and Swedish.
Mailing Address: Family Studies, University of Guelph, Ontario N1G 2X5

HILDA CHAULK MURRAY

Born February 3, 1934, at Maberly, Newfoundland. Received a B.A. (Ed.) in 1954; a second B.A. in 1966 and an M.A. in folklore 1972; all from Memorial University in St. John's. Taught English and mathematics in high schools in various outports and towns in Newfoundland before becoming an English instructor at the College of Trades and Technology, St.John's. Active in church and community work. Currently district commissioner, Girl Guides of Canada. Married, three children, one grandson.

Selected Publications:

More Than 50% (Woman's Life in a Newfoundland Outport, 1900-1950): St. John's, Breakwater, 1979. ISBN 0-919948-74-X

Comments: "Should become required reading for all the high schools in Newfoundland and Labrador." – Margaret Kearney, *St. John's Daily News*
  "Somewhat more than a view of woman's role in the community in old Newfoundland. She seldom divorces the role from the exquisite scenery she describes. So it's not like reading another piece of folkloristic fog."
– Gervasse Gallant, *Newfoundland Herald*
  Readings, Lectures & Workshops: Toured Newfoundland in July, 1980, giving readings in the public libraries of Clarenville, Bonavista, Gander, Grand Falls and Corner Brook. Held meeting in hometown school for the general public of Elliston and one at Port Union for the Women's Institute of Port Union/Catalina/Little Catalina. Took part in school workshop fall, 1980; university panel discussion 1985. Have been asked to visit highschools to speak on my book.
  Mailing Address: 19 First Street, Mount Pearl, Newfoundland A1N 1X7

SUSAN MUSGRAVE

Born March 12, 1951. Raised on Vancouver Island in British Columbia and have spent extended periods of time living in Ireland, England, the Queen Charlotte Islands and, most recently, in Panama and Colombia. Married Stephen Reid in 1986. Have one daughter, Charlotte Musgrave Nelson, born July 9, 1982.

Selected Publications:

The Charcoal Burners: Toronto, McClelland & Stewart, 1980. ISBN 0-7710-6650-3
Songs of the Sea-Witch: Vancouver, Sono Nis, 1970. (no ISBN)
Grave-Dirt and Selected Strawberries: Toronto, Macmillan, 1973. ISBN 0-7705-1045-0
Gullband: Vancouver, J.J. Douglas, 1974. ISBN 0-88894-058-0
A Man to Marry, A Man to Bury: Toronto, McClelland & Stewart, 1979. ISBN 0-7710-6655-4
Tarts and Muggers (Poems New and Selected): Toronto, McClelland & Stewart, 1982. ISBN 0-7710-6660-0
Cocktails at the Mausoleum: Toronto, McClelland & Stewart, 1985. ISBN 0-7710-6651-1
The Dancing Chicken: Toronto, Methuen, 1987. ISBN 0-458-81180-7

Awards: National Magazine Award (Second Prize), 1981
Comments: I was writer-in-residence at the University of Waterloo from 1983 to 1985, at the University of New Brunswick, Summer Session 1985 and the Vancouver Public Library during the National Book Festival, 1986. My poems have been broadcast on the CBC (Anthology, State of the Arts, et al.) and on Poetry Now (Radio Three, BBC London). I have given a great many radio and television interviews in connection with my work.
Readings, Lectures & Workshops: 1971: Struga Poetry Festival (Yugoslavia), 1980: Anglo-Canadian Poetry Exchange (a two-week reading tour of England, Scotland, Wales and Paris), 1983: Irish Tour (a three-week reading tour of southern Ireland), 1972-1984: numerous poetry readings across Canada.
Mailing Address: Box 2421, Sidney, British Columbia V8L 3Y3

RONALD NELSON

Born in 1942. Married in 1970. One son born in 1985. Full-time freelance writer since 1978 specialising in the outdoors. Articles, fiction and humour.

Selected Publications:

And When You Go Fishing: Lantzville, Oolichan, 1984. ISBN 0-88982-064-3

    Awards: Outdoor Writers of Canada Award (Runner up; Book Division), 1985

    Readings, Lectures & Workshops: Have read in Masset, Port Clements, Sandspit and Queen Charlotte City.

    Mailing Address: Box 598, Queen Charlotte City, British Columbia V0T 1S0

SHARON H. NELSON

Born January 2, 1948, in Montreal. B.A. (English and religion) from Sir George Williams; M.A. Concordia. Poet, occasional journalist and sometime essayist. Taught writing at Concordia and the University of British Columbia. Professional editor specialising in technical and scientific texts. Broad experience editing poetry, novels and articles. Work in theatre and with Logokinesis (dance). Active in research and reporting about our arts policy in Canada.

Selected Publications:

Sayings of my Fathers: London, Menard, 1972. ISBN 0-903400-00-6
A Broken Vessel: LaSalle, Delta, 1972. ISBN 0-919162-28-2
Seawreck: Fredericton, Fiddlehead, 1973. ISBN 0-919197-25-6
Blood Poems: Fredericton, Fiddlehead, 1978. ISBN 0-920110-15-0
Problem Solving and Computer Programming: Toronto, Addison-Welsey, 1982. ISBN 0-201-02460-8
Mad Woman and Crazy Ladies: Dewittville, Sunken Forum, 1983. ISBN 0-920208-12-6

Comments: "Extremely strong poems . . . assertive, restless, questioning, disturbing." – K.R. Tudor, *The Fiddlehead* (on *Blood Poems*)
"*Mad Women and Crazy Ladies* is a superb collection. The poems are well crafted, the words well chosen and placed. They are strong statements, mostly on the condition of women, not easily dismissed." – Ellen Pilon, *Canadian Book Review Annual 1984*
Readings, Lectures & Workshops: Readings, lectures and workshops across Canada at universities and for community organisations. Lectures about women's issues, especially women in the arts and the status of women in writing.
Mailing Address: c/o Metonymy Productions, 4125 Beaconsfield Avenue, Montreal, Quebec H4A 2H4

PETER C. NEWMAN

Born in Vienna, grew up in Czechoslovakia, immigrated to Canada in 1940. Upper Canada College (on wartime scholarship), then Master's degree at University of Toronto. Have been a working journalist for nearly four decades, including stints as Ottawa editor of both Maclean's and the Toronto Daily Star, as well as becoming editor-in-chief of both. Now live at Cordova Bay, British Columbia, writing and occasionally thinking.

Selected Publications:

Renegade in Power: Toronto, McClelland & Stewart, 1963. ISBN 0-7710-6746-1

The Distemper of our Times: Ottawa, Carleton UP, 1968. ISBN 0-7710-9813-8

The Canadian Establishment (Vol. 1): Toronto, McClelland & Stewart, 1975. ISBN 0-7710-6755-0

Bronfman Dynasty (The Rothschilds of the New World): Toronto, McClelland & Stewart, 1978. ISBN 0-7710-6758-5

The Acquisitors: Toronto, Seal, 1981. ISBN 0-7704-1779-5

The Establishment Man: Toronto, McClelland & Stewart, 1982. ISBN 0-7710-6785-2

True North – Not Strong and Free: Toronto, McClelland & Stewart, 1983. ISBN 0-7710-6798-4

Debrett's Illustrated Guide to the Canadian Establishment: (with Sir Ian Moncreiffe), Toronto, Methuen, 1983. ISBN 0-458-96790-4

Company of Adventurers: Toronto, Penguin, 1985. ISBN 0-670-80379-0

Awards: National Newspaper Award (Feature Writing), 1966. The Michener Award for Journalism, 1971. President's Medal, University of Western Ontario, 1974. Quill Award (Journalist of the Year), 1977. Canadian Authors Association Award (Non-fiction), 1986.

Mailing Address: 4855 Major Road, Cordova Bay, Victoria, British Columbia V8Y 2L8

BETTY NICKERSON

Born during a Kansas tornado in 1922. Grew up in Oregon. Attended Oregon State College; Goucher; the University of Utah, B.A. 1946 (sociology); University of Manitoba, M.A. 1967 (role of youth in social change); McGill University Ph.D. programme 1970-71 (communications). Now living on the shores of the Trincomali Channel near Ladysmith, British Columbia, and finally write full time.

Selected Publications:

How the World Grows Its Food: Toronto, McGraw-Hill Ryerson, 1965. (no ISBN)
Celebrate the Sun: Toronto, McClelland & Stewart, 1969. (no ISBN)
Chi (Letters from Biafra): Toronto, New Press, 1970. (no ISBN)
The Creative Child (Promise of the 80's): Ottawa, All About Us Books, 1980. ISBN 0-9199-70-06-0

Awards: Queen's Jubilee Medal, 1977
Comments: Founder and national co-ordinator of the All About Us/Nous Autres Foundation, 1970-1981. Producer-performer of CBC television, Winnipeg, featuring Canadian and international children's art. Designer and curator of children's art exhibitions for the Commonwealth Games, Expo 67, Habitat Vancouver, Ottawa's 150th Anniversary and Islands '86 in Duncan B.C. Commissioner for children's art and culture during International Year of the Child.
Readings, Lectures & Workshops: Present illustrated lectures and workshops on communication with children and youth based on their writings and drawings.
Mailing Address: 3012 Yellow Point Road, RR 3, Ladysmith, British Columbia V0R 2E0

NELLIE M. NIELSON

Born in Lachine, Quebec. Taken to England in 1913, at two years of age. Graduated from Hunmanby School for Girls, Yorkshire, 1930. Twenty-five years ago, after completing a writing course, launched a career that now includes a book and more than 300 short stories.

Selected Publications:

Worldwide Bloody Murders and Esp: Cobalt, Highway Book Shop, 1979. ISBN 0-88954-194-9

Comments: I have just completed writing another book, Dead People Do Tell Tales, and am engaged in the task of seeking a publisher. Many good reviews: North Bay, Stoney Creek, Hamilton Spectator. Short stories in All the Confessions, Woman's Day, Reader's Digest, Exploring the Unknown, Tomorrow and Understanding. Lately written for tabloids, most recently the National Examiner.

Readings, Lectures & Workshops: I have lectured to the Kiwanis and Optimists Clubs in Hamilton, Toronto and Burlington. I have also spoken on writing to groups in both men's and women's prisons.

Mailing Address: 233 Normanhurst Avenue, Hamilton, Ontario L8H 5N1

BARBARA J. NOVAK

Born in London, Ontario, in 1951. Graduate of the University of Western Ontario (B.A., English) and Queen's University (M.A., English). Lived in Kingston, Banff and Toronto before returning to London in 1983 where I now reside with my husband, Stephen State, and our two daughters. A former magazine editor, I have taught journalism at Fanshawe College in London. Now write full time: short fiction, children's stories and screenplays.

Selected Publications:

The Secret: Toronto, Three Trees, 1981. ISBN 0-88823-034-6

Awards: Waves Magazine Bicentennial Contest (Short Story), 1984. Health Care Public Relations Association Award.

Comments: *"The Secret* says more than some novels 10 times the length." – *London Free Press*

"The Secret deserves wide exposure." – *Quill & Quire*

Work included in the *Canadian Short Fiction Anthology II* (Vancouver, Intermedia), *The Window of Dreams* (Toronto, Methuen) and *Landscape* (Toronto, The Women's Writing Collective). Short stories published in Waves, Jewish Dialog, Branching Out, Miss Chatelaine and Who & Why.

Poems in Quarry, The NeWest ReView, Canadian Author & Bookman and Nebula.

Readings, Lectures & Workshops: Have given numerous readings at elementary and high schools throughout Ontario, as well as at libraries, community centres and restaurants. Have also led workshops in creative writing at young authors' conferences.

Mailing Address: c/o TWUC, 24 Ryerson Avenue, Toronto, Ontario M5T 2P3

SHELDON O'CONNELL

Former CBC radio announcer then manager of CBC stations in various North West Territories and Yukon locations. Later director of programming for the CBC Northern Quebec Service. B.A., Thomas Moore Institute for Adult Education, 1971. M.A., Concordia University, Montreal, 1974. Some freelance narration.

Selected Publications:

Bing, A Voice For All Seasons: Tralee, Kerryman Press, 1984. (no ISBN)
Dick Todd (King of the Juke Box): Printed in U.S.A., ISBN 0-9693023-0-4

Comments: Articles in various magazines and periodicals including Quest, Music Canada, Journal of Communication, Arctic Journal of North America, Arts and Culture of the North, Outdoors Canada, X-It Magazine, Canadian Musician, Beaver, North/Nord, Canadian Consumer, Canadian Broadcaster.

Works-in-Progress: TV situation-comedy scripts, Far North; Hollywood Lipographs (in collaboration with the former head of make-up for Columbia Pictures and 20th Century Fox, Clay Campbell, this is an analysis of lip prints and handwriting of Hollywood's most glamorous stars of the 1940s to 1960s); and a biography of songwriter Henry Tobias (Don't Sit Under the Apple Tree, Sweet and Lovely etc.).

Mailing Address: 1600 Beach Avenue, Laurier Tower 2202, Vancouver, British Columbia V6G 1Y6

PATRICK O'FLAHERTY

Born October 6, 1939, in Long Beach, Newfoundland, I live now in St. John's. Write literary criticism, fiction, journalism, history and biography. Married to theatre critic Frankie O'Flaherty, and we have three sons: Keir, Peter and Padriac.

Selected Publications

By Great Waters: (with Peter Neary), Toronto, University of Toronto Press, 1974. ISBN 0-8020-6233-4

The Rock Observed: Toronto, University of Toronto Press, 1979. ISBN 0-8020-2351-7

Part of the Main: (with Peter Neary), St. John's, Breakwater, 1983. ISBN 0-919519-27-X

Summer of the Greater Yellowlegs: St. John's, Breakwater, 1987. ISBN 0-920911-25-0

Mailing Address: 31 Carpasian Road, St. John's, Newfoundland A1B 2P9

FRANK O'KEEFFE

Born in Dublin, Ireland. Writer, storyteller and school teacher. Live with family on a quarter section of land near Edson, Alberta, and raise cattle. Hold a B.Ed. from the University of Calgary.

Selected Publications:

Guppy Love (or The Day the Fishtank Exploded): Toronto, Kids Can, 1986. ISBN 0-921103-04-2

Comments: "This book is hilarious! It starts out good and keeps getting better until at the end there's an exciting climax. It's a great book." – *Toronto Star*

Readings, Lectures & Workshops: Read and conduct writing workshops in schools and colleges.

Mailing Address: Box 213, Edson, Alberta T0E 0P0

MARTIN O'MALLEY

Born in Winnipeg, February 22, 1939. Educated at St. Paul's High School and the University of Manitoba. Reporter and editor for the Tribune, 1963-65. Reporter, religion writer, editorial board Globe and Mail, 1965-77. Globe Magazine writer, national reporter, senior op-ed writer. Freelance writer and columnist since 1977 (Saturday Night, Maclean's, Quest, Canadian Business, Toronto Life, United Church Observer, The Review, Globe and Mail, and radio and TV).

Selected Publications:

The Past and Future Land: Toronto, Peter Martin, 1976. ISBN 0-88778-137-3
Doctors: Toronto, Macmillan, 1983. ISBN 0-7715-9719-3
Hospital (Life and Death in a Major Medical Centre): Toronto, Macmillan,1986. ISBN 0-7715-9750-9

Awards: Southam Fellowship, 1972-73. National Magazine Award (Humour),1981.
Comments: "An important book, a vital book, and it has been put together with fine craftsmanship and compassion . . . a powerful book that will stir you profoundly." – *Toronto Star* (on *The Past and Future Land*)
"A gallery of characters, rich, varied and well drawn enough to people any novel . . . O'Malley produces unfailingly crisp, clear portraits." – *Winnipeg Free Press* (on *Doctors*)
"O'Malley's brilliance lies in his ability to present accurately the confluence of individual emotions and the institutional machine . . . spell-binding reading." – *Globe and Mail* (on *Hospital*)
Readings, Lectures & Workshops: Sure.
Mailing Address: 59 Golf Links Drive, Aurora, Ontario L4G 3V4

MICHAEL ONDAATJE

 Born in Sri Lanka in 1943. Came to Canada in 1962. Now live in Toronto. Teach at Glendon College, York University.

Selected Publications:

The Collected Works of Billy the Kid: Toronto, Anansi, 1970. ISBN 0-88784-118-4

Coming through Slaughter: Toronto, Anansi, 1976. ISBN 0-88784-052-3

There's a Trick with a Knife I'm Learning to Do: Toronto, McClelland & Stewart, 1980. ISBN 0-7710-6882-4

Running in the Family: Toronto, McClelland & Stewart, 1983. ISBN 0-7710-6884-0

Secular Love: Toronto, Coach House Press, 1985. ISBN 0-88910-288-0

In the Skin of a Lion: Toronto, McClelland & Stewart, 1987. ISBN 0-7710-6887-0

Mailing Address: c/o Glendon College, 2275 Bayview Avenue, Toronto, Ontario M4N 3M6

PAUL O'NEILL

Born in St. John's, Newfoundland, in 1928, I attended New York's National Academy of Theatre Arts in 1948 and was in the professional theatre, films, etc. until 1954 when I became a CBC producer. In 1986, I retired from CBC as executive producer of radio arts programming. Founding president of the Newfoundland Writers' Guild, I have served on the executives and boards of many organizations including the Writers' Union. Currently vice-president of the Newfoundland and Labrador Arts Council. I now write and act.

Selected Publications:

Spindrift and Morning Light: St. John's, Valhalla Press, 1969. (no ISBN)
The Oldest City: Erin, Press Porcepic, 1975. ISBN 0-88878-070-2
Legend of a Lost Tribe: Toronto, McClelland & Stewart, 1976. ISBN 0-7710-6878-6
Breakers: St. John's, Breakwater, 1982. ISBN 0-919519-22-9
The Seat Imperial: St. John's, Cuff, 1983. ISBN 0-919095-38-1
The Sound of Seagulls: St. John's, Creative, 1984. ISBN 0-520021-09-3
Upon this Rock: St. John's, Breakwater, 1984. ISBN 0-919519-82-2

    Awards: Newfoundland and Labrador Arts and Letters Awards (nine, including three Gold Medals). Canadian Historical Association Regional History Prize, 1970.
    Comments: "I would not argue with anyone who says he is the best writer Newfoundland ever produced." – *St. John's Daily News*
    Reading, Lectures & Workshops: Dinner speaker as well as talks, lectures and workshops.
    Mailing Address: 52 Long Pond Road, St. John's, Newfoundland A1B 1P1

BERNICE ORAWSKI

Born in Podwilk, Nowy Targ, Poland, August 12, 1936. Came to Canada with parents in 1939. Lived in Northern Ontario bush near Fryatt for three years before moving to Hamilton. Now living in Toronto. Graduate of Mohawk College, Hamilton, legal secretarial course. Now employed as secretary by Government of Ontario Temporary Services.

Selected Publications:

The Little Red Car: New York, Platt & Munk, 1978. ISBN 0-448-46527-2
If in *Under the Sea*: Toronto, Holt Rinehart & Winston, 1985.

Comments: Member of Crime Writers of Canada. Friend of Canadian Society of Children's Authors, Illustrators and Performers.
Mailing Address: Apt. 807, 25 St. Mary Street, Toronto, Ontario M4Y 1R2

P.K. PAGE (P.K. IRWIN, JUDITH CAPE)

Writer/artist. Born 1916, England. Came to Canada 1919. Attended schools in Calgary, Winnipeg and England. Worked as sales clerk, filing clerk, historical researcher and on radio. Co-editor of Preview, regional editor of Northern Review, script writer for the National Film Board. Married W. Arthur Irwin 1950. Lived in Australia, Brazil, Mexico and New York. Now live in Victoria, British Columbia.

Selected Publications:

Cry Ararat! (Poems New and Selected): Toronto, McClelland & Stewart, 1967. (no ISBN)

The Sun and the Moon and Other Fictions: Toronto, Anansi, 1973. ISBN 0-88784-429-4

P.K. Page, Poems Selected and New: Toronto, Anansi, 1974. ISBN 0-88784-132-5

Evening Dance of the Grey Flies: Toronto, Oxford, 1981. ISBN 0-19-540381-9

To Say the Least: (ed.), Victoria, Press Porcepic, 1979. ISBN 0-88878-174-1

The Glass Air: Toronto, Oxford, 1985. ISBN 0-19-540506-4

Brazilian Journal: Toronto, Lester & Orpen Dennys, 1987. ISBN 0-88619-166-1

Awards: Bertram Warr Award (Poetry). Oscar Blumenthal Award (Poetry). Governor General's Award (Poetry). Officer of the Order of Canada. D. Litt. (honoris causa) from the University of Victoria.

Readings, Lectures & Workshops: Taught at the New College Writers' Workshop for five summers and in the creative writing department, University of Victoria, for one year. Have given readings in England, Australia and the U.S. and coast to coast in Canada.

Mailing Address: c/o TWUC, 24 Ryerson Avenue, Toronto, Ontario M5T 2P3

MYRA PAPERNY

Born in Edmonton, Alberta, September 19, 1932. Oldest child of Jessie and Michael Green. Grew up in Alberta and Vancouver. Now living in Calgary. Married Maurice Paperny (1954); four children: Marina, David, Cathy and Lorne; two grandchildren. B.A. University of British Columbia; M.Sc. Columbia (1954). Reviewing for CBC radio Infotape. Taught creative writing course at the University of Calgary.

Selected Publications:

The Wooden People: Boston, Little Brown, 1976. ISBN 0-316-69040-6
Take a Giant Step: Toronto, Grolier, 1987. ISBN 0-7172-2158-X

Awards: Little, Brown Children's Award, 1975. Canada Council Children's Literature Award, 1976.

Comments: Contributor to Hiyou Muckamuck (Vancouver, CommCept, 1978), Souvenirs (Edmonton, Alberta Education, 1979) and Alberta Heritage Series (1979) as well as magazine articles and CBC radio interviews.

Readings, Lectures & Workshops: Canada Council reading tours; Alberta reading tours including Kaleidoscope; workshops (elementary, junior and high schools); lectures including Universities of Alberta and Calgary.

Mailing Address: 1224 Riverdale Avenue S.W., Calgary, Alberta T2S 0Y8

ERNA PARIS

Born in Toronto a few decades ago, I obtained a B.A.(Hons.) from the University of Toronto in philosophy and English, then a Diplome Superieur, Cours de Civilisation Francaise, from the Sorbonne. I remained in France for several years then returned to Toronto where I taught English at the high-school level. I began a full-time writing career in the early 1970s. With my husband, Professor T.M. Robinson, I live in Toronto.

Selected Publications:

Her Own Woman (Profiles of Canadian Women): Toronto, Macmillan, 1975.
   ISBN 0-7705-1275-5
Jews (An Account of their Experience in Canada): Toronto, Macmillan, 1980.
   ISBN 0-7715-9574-3
Stepfamilies: Toronto, Avon, 1984. ISBN 0-380-86405-3
Unhealed Wounds (France and the Klaus Barbie Affair): Toronto, Methuen,
   1985. ISBN 0-458-99820-6

Awards: Media Club of Canada; 1969, 1973, 1974 (two). National Magazine Award (Gold Medal), 1983.

Comments: *"Jews: An Account of Their Experience* in Canada is quite simply the best book ever written about Canadian Jews." – Larry Zolf

"Easily one of the best guides of its kind." – *Globe and Mail* (on *Stepfamilies*)

"A remarkable book." – *New York Times Book Review* (on *Unhealed Wounds*)

Readings, Lectures & Workshops: Lecture and read at schools, libraries and for private groups. Teach writing in classroom and workshop situations.

Mailing Address: 126 Felstead Avenue, Toronto, Ontario M4J 1G4

JOHN PARR

Born in Chicago, Illinois, June 18, 1928; now living in Winnipeg, Manitoba. Wife, Joan; and two children, Kristin and Louise. B.A. and Certificate in Education, University of Manitoba. English instructor, Red River Community College, Winnipeg, 1970-83. Now writing full time. Currently editing an anthology of Manitoba humour.

Selected Publications:

Speaking of Winnipeg: (ed.), Winnipeg, Queenston House, 1974.
   ISBN 0-919866-01-8
Selected Stories of Robert Barr: (ed.), Ottawa, University of Ottawa Press, 1977. ISBN 0-7766-4338-X
Jim Tweed: Winnipeg, Queenston House, 1978. ISBN 0-919866-12-3
Good Humour Man: (ed.), Winnipeg, Queenston House, 1987. ISBN 0-920273-18-1

Mailing Address: 102 Queenston Street, Winnipeg, Manitoba R3N 0W5

GEORGE PAYERLE

Born in Vancouver of Hungarian parents, August 21, 1945. Education at St. Patrick's School, Vancouver College and the University of British Columbia. Held one full-time job, as magazine editor, in 1973-74. Otherwise employed as freelance writer, editor and typographer. Currently living in Vancouver with wife Phyllis and daughter Bronwen.

Selected Publications:

Student Protest: (ed. with Gerald McGuigen and Patricia Horrobin), Toronto, Methuen, 1968. (no ISBN)
The Afterpeople: Toronto, Anansi, 1970. ISBN 0-88784-412-X
Wolfbane Fane: Vancouver, Kanchenjunga, 1977. ISBN 0-913600-43-1
Unknown Soldier: Toronto, Macmillan, 1987. ISBN 0-7715-9490-9

Comments: "Clearly, Mr. Payerle wants us to think again about the nature of experiential reality, and the impossibility of a final division between inner and outer worlds . . . (He) shows a commendable sense of adventure, the kind of readiness to experiment with form and language that . . . is much needed in Canadian writing." – Herb Rosengarten, *Canadian Literature*
   Anthologised in Contemporary Poetry of British Columbia (Sono Nis, 1970) and in Pushcart Prize, III (New York, 1978. ISBN 0-916366-03-0).
   Readings, Lectures & Workshops: Have given readings from Victoria to Charlottetown and conducted fiction workshops at the University of British Columbia. May be booked through TWUC.
   Mailing Address: 4244 West 10th Avenue, Vancouver, British Columbia V6R 2H4

KIT PEARSON

Born in Edmonton in 1947. B.A., University of Alberta, 1969; M.L.S., University of British Columbia, 1976; M.A., Simmons College Centre for the Study of Children's Literature, 1982. Worked as a children's librarian for ten years in St. Catharines, North York and Burnaby. An occasional reviewer and teacher of children's literature. I now live in Vancouver, where I work as a part-time reference librarian for Burnaby Public Library.

Selected Publications:

The Daring Game: Toronto, Penguin, 1986. ISBN 0-670-80751-6

Awards: CBC Literary Competition (Third Prize: Children's Story Division), 1984

Comments: "Reminiscent of the boarding school stories of an earlier time, *The Daring Game* has a gentle perception and understated concern as well as as interesting story to tell." – Andrea Deakin, *London Free Press*

"Pearson has shown remarkable insight into the emotional growth of young girls." – JoAnna Burns Patton, *Canadian Materials*

"There is no denying her self-assurance, a fact that bodes well for the future." – Tim Wynne-Jones, *Globe and Mail*

Readings, Lectures & Workshops: Will give readings and conduct writing workshops for children aged nine to 12.

Mailing Address: 2195 West 15th Avenue, Vancouver, British Columbia V6K 2Y4

GORDON PENROSE

I am a former teacher and elementary school master teacher who now works as Dr. Zed with Owl and Chickadee magazines and Owl TV. My interests include the learning process, simple science experiments with surprising results and the world of nature.

Selected Publications:

Dr. Zed's Brilliant Book of Science Experiments: Toronto, Greey de Pencier, 1977. ISBN 0-919872-34-4

Dr. Zed's Dazzling Book of Science Activities: Toronto, Greey de Pencier, 1982. ISBN 0-919872-78-6

Awards: Fellow of the Ontario Institute for Studies in Education, 1981

Comments: A new book is planned with the tentative title Fooling Around with Science.

Readings, Lectures & Workshops: I am prepared to present readings for schools and public libraries for eight to 12-year-old young people as well as workshops for adults in the area of simple science experiments.

Mailing Address: 14 Abbeville Road, Scarborough, Ontario M1H 1Y3

H.R. (BILL) PERCY

Born Kent, England, 1920. Joined Royal Navy as Engineering Apprentice, 1936. Saw war service in North Atlantic, Indian Ocean and far east. Joined RCN 1952: serving in HMCS Quebec, Cape Breton, Sioux, Swansea, and CFHQ Ottawa as staff officer for Training Publications. Edited Canadian Author and Bookman, 1963-65. Retired as Lieutenant Commander 1971. I now live in Granville Ferry, Nova Scotia, where my wife, Vina, and I run The Moorings guesthouse. Was founding chairman of the Writer's Federation of Nova Scotia.

Selected Publications:

The Timeless Island and Other Stories: Toronto, Ryerson, 1960.
Joseph Howe: Toronto, Fitzhenry & Whiteside, 1976. ISBN 0-88902-220-8
Flotsam: St. John's, Breakwater, 1978. ISBN 0-919948-57-X
Thomas Chandler Haliburton: Toronto, Fitzhenry & Whiteside, 1980.
    ISBN 0-88902-670-X
Painted Ladies: Toronto, Lester & Orpen Dennys, 1983. ISBN 0-88619-028-2
A Model Lover: Toronto, Stoddart, 1986. ISBN 0-7737-5052-5
Tranter's Tree: Toronto, Lester & Orpen Dennys, 1987. ISBN 0-88619-154-8

Comments: Contributor to various anthologies including *New Canadian Stories 75 and 76* (Oberon), *Beyond Time* (Pocket Books) and *Not to Be Taken at Night* (Lester & Orpen Dennys). Stories have appeared in Canadian Fiction Magazine, Queen's Quarterly, Vanity Fair (U.K.), Prism, Quarry, Wascana Review, Atlantic Insight, the New Quarterly and others.
   Awards: Nova Scotia Novel Award, 1975
   Readings, Lectures & Workshops: Available for readings through Canada Council and TWUC.
   Mailing Address: The Moorings, Granville Ferry, Nova Scotia B0S 1K0

STAN PERSKY

Selected Publications:

Wrestling the Angel: Vancouver, Talon, 1977. ISBN 0-88922-109-X
Son of Socred: Vancouver, New Star, 1979. ISBN 0-919888-89-5
The House That Jack Built: Vancouver, New Star, 1980. ISBN 0-919888-29-1
At the Lenin Shipyard: Vancouver, New Star, 1981. ISBN 0-919888-45-3
Flaunting It: (ed. with Ed Jackson), Vancouver, New Star, 1982. ISBN 0-919888-31-3
The Solidarity Sourcebook: (ed. with Henry Flam), Vancouver, New Star, 1982. ISBN 0-919573-05-3
Bennett II: Vancouver, New Star, 1983. ISBN 0-919573-11-8
America, The Last Domino: Vancouver, New Star, 1984. ISBN 0-919573-37-1

  Comments: Works-in-progress: What Do New Democrats Stand For?, The Fountain of Middle Age, The Sorrow of Sex, Buddy's and The Horses of Instruction.
  Mailing Address: c/o 2504 York Avenue, Vancouver, British Columbia V6K 1E3

MARLENE-NOURBESE PHILIP

 I am a New World writer. I was born in Crusoe's Isle (Tobago) and have lived in Canada since 1968. In a previous lifetime, I practised law for seven years in Toronto. I write full time and live with two of my three children, a husband, two cats, two Zebra finches, three goldfish and hundreds of books. Love the sun and mangoes. I am the first accredited Caucasianist (specialist in Caucasian life, affairs and culture).

Selected Publications:

Thorns: Toronto, Williams-Wallace, 1980. ISBN 0-88795-008-6
Salmon Courage: Toronto, Williams-Wallace, 1983. ISBN 0-88795-036-1

Comments: My work has appeared in *The Pushcart Prize, VI* (1983; ISBN 0-916366-12-X), *Women and Words: The Anthology* (Harbour Publishing, 1984. ISBN 0-920080-53-7), *The Penguin Book of Caribbean Verse in English* (1986; ISBN 0-14-058511-7) and Fireweed (Issue 23, 1986; ISSN 0706-3857).

Mailing Address: 173 Robina Avenue, Toronto, Ontario M6C 3Y8

EDWARD O. PHILLIPS

Born in Montreal, in 1931. B.A., McGill University, 1953. L.Ll., Universite de Montreal, 1956. A.M.T., Harvard University, 1957. M.A., Boston University, 1962. Diploma, Montreal Museum of Fine Arts School of Art and Design, 1968. Exhibitions: Studio 23, Montreal, 1969, 1970; Dorval Cultural Centre, 1971; Studio 23, St. Sauveur des Monts, 1972; and Artlanders, Montreal, 1973.

Selected Publications:

Sunday's Child: Toronto, McClelland & Stewart, 1981. ISBN 0-7710-6993-6
Where There's A Will . . . : Toronto, McClelland & Stewart, 1984.
   ISBN 0-7710-6999-4
Buried on Sunday: Toronto, McClelland & Stewart, 1986. ISBN 0-7710-6992-8

Awards: Society of Canadian Artists 5th Open Jury Exhibition, 1973. Cross-Canada Writers' Quarterly Award (Short Fiction), 1983.

Comments: "*Sunday's Child* is masterful, original, and absolutely Canadian." – Nancy Wigston, *Globe and Mail*

"And he has peopled *Where There's A Will* . . . with sharply drawn characters who virtually sputter with good, sardonic lines." – Ken Adachi, *Toronto Sun*

"His latest novel, *Buried on Sunday*, should confirm the Westmount writer as one of our premier voices of erudite wit and eccentric humour." – Michael Carin, *Montreal Gazette*

Readings, Lectures & Workshops: Readings and lectures in Montreal, Ottawa and Toronto.

Mailing Address: 487 Grosvenor Avenue, Montreal, Quebec H3Y 2S5

DAVID GOODWIN PHILPOTT

Born in White Plains, New York, August 19,1927. In 1932, moved to Toronto where I was educated and began my business career. Held senior executive positions and directorates with such companies as Trizec, Cadillac-Fairview and Mascan. Now live in Toronto, run my own business and write part time.

Selected Publications:

Dangerous Waters: Toronto, McClelland & Stewart, 1985. ISBN 0-7710-6998-7

  Comments: "A gem of a book . . . as thoughtful and moving an examination of a businessman's soul as I have ever read" – Peter Newman, *MacLean's*
  "A compelling tale of adventure and danger" – William French, *Globe and Mail*
  "A book I couldn't put down." – Larry Reid, *Toronto Star*
  "Transcends the normal adventure saga . . . " – Wayne Lilley, *Quill & Quire*
  "Immensely readable book." – John Levesque, *Hamilton Spectator*
  "David Philpott can't seem to escape success" – Ann Gibbon, *Montreal Gazette*
  Readings, Lectures & Workshops: Speak and lecture regularly on the book's theme at business seminars, conventions and luncheon clubs.
  Mailing Address: 6 Moore Avenue, Toronto, Ontario M4T 1V3

ALISON LOHANS PIROT

Born in Reedley, California. Immigrated to Canada in 1971. Hold B.A. (Music, California State Los Angeles), Diploma in Elementary Education (University of Victoria) and am now working on M.Ed. (University of Regina). Main writing interests: young adult and children's literature. Live in Regina and am actively engaged in parenting, writing and studies.

Selected Publications:

Who Cares About Karen?: Toronto, Scholastic, 1983. ISBN 0-590-71148-2
Can You Promise Me Spring?: Toronto, Scholastic, 1986. ISBN 0-590-71616-6

Awards: Canadian Author and Bookman Prize (Fiction), 1985
Readings, Lectures & Workshops: Readings and workshops primarily for grades five through nine.
Mailing Address: 2629 Garnet Street, Regina, Saskatchewan S4T 3A8

HELEN PORTER

Born May 8, 1930, at St. John's, Newfoundland, eldest child of Robert and Evelyn (Horwood) Fogwill. Still living in St. John's Metro area. Educated at Holloway School and Prince of Wales College, St. John's. In 1953 married John Porter, a teacher. John died in 1983. Four children: Kathy, Anne, John and Stephen. Writing all my life but have also worked as a secretary, library assistant and housewife. Ran four times for the NDP.

Selected Publications:

From This Place: (with Bernice Morgan and Geraldine Rubia), St. John's, Jesperson, 1977. ISBN 0-920502-02-4
Below the Bridge: St. John's, Breakwater, 1980. ISBN 0-919948-72-3

   Awards: Newfoundland and Labrador Arts and Letters Medals (Gold, silver and bronze; Dramatised Scripts, Short Stories and Poetry), 1967-72
   Comments: Writing and reading have always been very important to me and perhaps today are more so than ever. I've been publishing articles, reviews, short stories, poetry and plays since 1963 but the short story remains my favourite, both to read and to write. My novel January, February, June or July has been accepted by Breakwater and I hope to follow it up with a collection of short stories that is already complete.
   Readings, Lectures & Workshops: Creative writing teacher, Memorial University's Extension Arts Division since 1976. Regularly visit and read in schools throughout Newfoundland and Labrador.
   Mailing Address: 51 Franklyn Avenue, St. John's, Newfoundland A1C 4L2

BRUCE ALLEN POWE

Born in Edmonton, Alberta, June 9, 1925; Canadian Army overseas, 1943-45; M.A. Economics, University of Alberta. Then various jobs in journalism, government, politics (Liberals), corporate life (including Imperial Oil), ad agencies and currently vice-president of Public Affairs for the Canadian Life and Health Insurance Association. Married, live in Toronto, two offspring. Son, B.W. Powe, is also a writer and author of two books.

Selected Publications:

Expresso '67: Toronto, Peter Martin, 1966. (no ISBN)
Killing Ground (The Canadian Civil War): Toronto, PMA Books, 1968. ISBN 0-88778-021-0
The Last Days of the American Empire: Toronto, Macmillan, 1974. ISBN 0-7705-1190-2
The Aberhart Summer: Toronto, Lester & Orpen Dennys, 1983. ISBN 0-88619-013-4
The Ice Eaters: Toronto, Lester & Orpen Dennys, 1987. ISBN 0-88619-159-9

Comments: "In *The Aberhart Summer* . . . Powe has at last found solid fictional ground to stand on, superior to the melange of science fantasy and political prophecy in his previous novels." – *Canadian Forum*
With those early experiments behind me, I think I have found my voice and audience by drawing from the milieu I know best: real politics and corporate life. *The Ice Eaters* explores the theme of frontier, ranging from the Yukon to the Toronto business world against a background of the 1980-82 recession.
Mailing Address: 158 Ridley Boulevard, Toronto, Ontario M5M 3M1

DOROTHY M. POWELL

Born and educated in Toronto and have lived in Victoria, British Columbia, for the past 12 years. Depression kid who had to work after graduation from high school and technical college. Former model, secretary and accountant. Teacher of creative writing at Camosun College night classes 1974 to 1986. Member of the Canadian Authors Association and Canadian Society of Childrens' Authors, Illustrators and Performers.

Selected Publications:

The Summer of Satan's Gorge: Toronto, Scholastic, 1974. ISBN 0-590-71075-3
Captives of Cauldron Cave: Toronto, Scholastic, 1977.

Awards: Alan Sangster Award (Distinguished Service to Canadian Authors Association), 1975. Kathleen Strange Award (Service to CAA, Winnipeg Branch).

Comments: "Powells's (novels) are about teenagers and are most appropriate for adolescent readers . . . Powell deserves credit for treating intimate matters in a tasteful yet meaningful way." – *Canadian Children's Literature*

More than 80 short stories and articles have appeared in anthologies and periodicals in Canada, the U.S., the U.K., Australia and Scandinavia.

Readings, Lectures & Workshops: Reads at schools, libraries and conferences. May be booked through TWUC.

Mailing Address: c/o TWUC, 24 Ryerson Avenue, Toronto, Ontario M5T 2P3

BETTY PRATT-JOHNSON

I explore the wilderness and observe nature. My in-depth research and accurate, lively treatments of outdoor topics have appeared in many periodicals as well as books. Born in the middle west on July 16, 1930. Hold a B.Sc. from Purdue University. I now live in Vancouver close to the mountains, rivers and sea, follow my curiosity, wander the world (especially British Columbia) and write about my findings.

Selected Publications:

141 Dives in the Protected Waters of Washington and British Columbia:
  Vancouver, Soules, 1976. ISBN 0-919574-20-3
Whitewater Trips for Kayakers, Canoeists and Rafters on Vancouver Island:
  Vancouver, Soules, 1984. ISBN 0-919574-67-X
Whitewater Trips for Kayakers, Canoeists and Rafters in British Columbia:
  Vancouver, Adventure, 1986. ISBN 0-921009-03-8

Awards: Media Club of Canada (Vancouver Branch) Award (Best Magazine Feature)
Comments: "The finest guidebook to local diving we have ever seen." – *Currents* (on *141 Dives*)
"Among the best I've seen in the past year." – *Midwest Book Review* (on *Whitewater Trips/Vancouver Island*)
"Observant, enthusiastic writer . . . " – *Vancouver Sun* (on *Whitewater Trips/B.C.*)
"Paddle-by-paddle account . . . fascinating . . . " – *Vancouver Province*
"Irresistible . . . an excellent guide . . . " – *Canoeist* (U.K.)
Readings, Lectures & Workshops: Workshops and slide/talks at schools, universities, recreation centres and libraries about resources and about where to have fun in the outdoors. Readings at libraries and schools.
Mailing Address: c/o TWUC, 24 Ryerson Avenue, Toronto, Ontario M5T 2P3

ROBERT PRIEST

Born in England, came to Canada at an early age. Composer and children's writer as well as poet. A member of musical group, The Boinks, and a rock band, The Great Big Face. My rock video, Congo Toronto, can be seen on MuchMusic. The National Film Board is animating my children's book.

Selected Publications:

The Visible Man: Toronto, Unfinished Monument, 1979.
Sadness of Spacemen: Toronto, Dreadnaught, 1980.
The Man Who Broke Out of the Letter X: Toronto, Coach House, 1984.
  ISBN 0-88910-275-9
The Short Hockey Career of Amazing Jany: Toronto, Aya, 1986. ISBN
  0-920544-46-0

   Comments: "A perfect poet of the eighties." – *Poetry Canada Review*
"One of Canada's most exciting and fun young poets." – Don Harron, *Morningside*
"Unsettling New Wave writing." – *Canadian Fiction Magazine*
"Thank God someone is writing with that kind of energy." – Gwendolyn MacEwen
"Dazzling!" – Irving Layton
Recordings: Summerlong (A Children's Record) (Toronto, G-Tel Records, 1984) and The Robert Priest E.P. (Toronto, Airwave Records, 1982).
   Readings, Lectures & Workshops: Have read widely across North America, on radio and television. Have conducted workshops for all age groups, from pre-school to post-graduate.
   Mailing Address: c/o TWUC, 24 Ryerson Avenue, Toronto, Ontario M5T 2P3

JANIS RAPOPORT

Born in Toronto, June 22, 1949; educated in Canada and Switzerland. B.A. in philosophy (U.of T.). Worked in London, England, for three years as an editor. Toronto editorial positions include: associate editor, Tamarack Review (1970-82); story editor, CBC TV Drama (1973-74); and founding editor, Ethos magazine (since 1983). Write poetry, drama and short fiction. Participant in the Ontario Writers-in-Libraries Programme (January-December, 1987).

Selected Publications:

Within the Whirling Moment: Toronto, Anansi, 1967. (no ISBN)
Jeremy's Dream: Victoria, Press Porcepic, 1974. ISBN 0-88878-028-1
Winter Flowers: Toronto, Hounslow, 1979. ISBN 0-88882-028-3
Dreamgirls: Toronto, Playwrights Co-op, 1979. ISBN 0-88754-139-9
Imaginings: (with Heather Cooper and Timothy Findley), Toronto, Ethos Foundation, 1982. ISBN 0-919787-002

    Awards: New York Art Director's Club Awards of Merit, 1983 (two). American Institute of Graphic Arts Certificate for Excellence, 1983. American Poetry Association Award for Outstanding Achievement, 1986.
    Comments: "Seldom does Canadian poetry contain a fine network of felt truths. *Jeremy's Dream* does." – Mairlyn Julian, *Quarry*
    Readings, Lectures & Workshops: I give readings and workshops regularly and teach writing at Sheridan College. May be booked through TWUC.
    Mailing Address: c/o TWUC, 24 Ryerson Avenue, Toronto, Ontario M5T 2P3

FRANK RASKY

Born in Toronto, March 21, 1923, one of eight children of a Russian grocer, cantor and Hebrew scholar. Hold B.A. from the University of Toronto. Former staff writer for Variety, the Vancouver Sun and the Toronto Star. Sold first magazine article at 16 and have since written 6,000 of them for periodicals including Esquire, New York Times Sunday Magazine, Reader's Digest and Saturday Night. Still writing them, still enjoying it.

Selected Publications:

Gay Canadian Rogues (Swindlers, Goldiggers, Spies): Toronto, Nelson, 1958. (no ISBN)

Great Canadian Disasters: Toronto, Longmans, 1961. (no ISBN)

The Taming of the Canadian West: Toronto, McClelland & Stewart, 1967. (no ISBN)

The Polar Voyagers: Toronto, McGraw-Hill Ryerson, 1976. ISBN 0-07-082405-3

The North Pole or Bust: Toronto, McGraw-Hill Ryerson, 1977. ISBN 0-07-082548-3

Industry in the Wilderness (Northwestern Ontario's Heritage): Toronto, Dundurn, 1983. ISBN 0-919670-66-0

Comments: "These are great adventures, superbly told, and whet the appetite for more." — *Publishers Weekly*

"He writes so artfully that his immense research doesn't interrupt the flow of his vivid storytelling." — *Atlantic Monthly*

"Rasky gives an exciting new dimension to an old school-worn topic. The drama, pathos and comedy result in fascinating reading." — *Books in Canada*

Mailing Address: 445 Eglinton Avenue East, Toronto, Ontario M4P 1N1

ELFREIDA READ

Born in the Far East in 1920 of Estonian parents and lived in the International Settlement of Shanghai, China, during early years. Came out to Canada after the war and internment by Japanese in Shanghai. Settled in Vancouver, British Columbia, with husband, George, and daughter, Jeani. Later a son, Philip, was born. Write fiction for children, poetry for adults. Work in progress: an autobiographical account of life in China.

Selected Publications:

The Dragon and the Jadestone: London, Hutchinson, 1958. (no ISBN)
The Magic of Light: London, Hutchinson, 1959. (no ISBN)
The Enchanted Egg: London, Hutchinson, 1963. (no ISBN)
The Spell of the Chuchuchan: London, Hutchinson, 1966. (no ISBN)
Magic for Granny: Toronto, Burns & MacEachern, 1967. (no ISBN)
No One Need Ever Know: Boston, Ginn, 1971. (no ISBN)
Brothers by Choice: New York, Farrar Straus Giroux, 1974. ISBN 0-374-30996-5
The Message of the Mask: Toronto, Gage, 1981. ISBN 0-7715-6298-5
Kirstine and the Villains: Toronto, Gage, 1982. ISBN 0-7715-7001-2
Race Against the Dark: Toronto, Gage, 1982. ISBN 0-7715-7008-2
Growing Up In China: Ottawa, Oberon, 1985. ISBN 0-88750-603-8

    Awards: Canadian Centennial Contest for Children's Stories. Arts Club Poetry Contest for B.C. Junior Literary Contest.
    Readings, Lectures & Workshops: Occasional readings for children and adults.
    Mailing Address: 2686 West King Edward Avenue, Vancouver, British Columbia V6L 1T6

MALCOLM REID

My biography starts out very Canadian, and at midpoint becomes very Quebecois. I was born on July 3, 1941, and raised in Ottawa with a side trip to Madison, Wisconson, as a small boy. Then in 1960 I moved to Montreal, the Quiet Revolution began, I learned the Quebec language and the Quebec rebel spirit. This spirit has marked all my writing. I am married, have a daughter and can often be found at Bernier's restaurant in Quebec.

Selected Publications:

The Shouting Signpainters (A Literary and Political Account of Quebec Revolutionary Nationalism): New York, Monthly Review Press, 1972.
ISBN 0-85345-283-0
Salut, Gadou!: (with Rose Zgodzinski), Toronto, Lorimer, 1982.
ISBN 0-88862-575-8

Comments: "If you knock on his door you will meet a little boy who is now in his forties, and who has spent his whole career describing, in words and pictures, the day-to-day life of Quebec." – Marc Boutin, *Droit de Parole*

I used to write, now I write and draw, as people will see in my new book of labour history, Metallo. I've also begun writing about other things than Quebec, as in my novel about the peace movement in Western Europe, A Ballad for Fernando. And I'm in grave need of a photo of the late writer Irene Baird as she was in 1938.

Readings, Lectures & Workshops: When Salut, Gadou! came out, I read it to the kids at the Maison des Jeunes Saint-Jean-Baptiste, who had inspired it. I translated it into French as I read; I retold it really. I also talked to some pretty great kids in Saskatoon.

Mailing Address: 510, rue Saint-Gabriel, Quebec G1R 1W3

KATI REKAI

Born in Budapest, Hungary, October 20, 1921.
Now living in Toronto. Educated in Budapest.
Speak English, French, German, Hungarian,
some Italian. Have lived in Budapest, Paris,
Kitchener, Toronto. Married Dr. John Rekai,
surgeon, co-founder and chief of staff of Central
Hospital, Toronto, in 1941. Two daughters:
Julie, broadcaster, writer and public relations
consultant; and Judyth, a crown attorney.
Grandchildren: Christopher, Sean, Jamie and
Megan.

Selected Publications:

All books published in Toronto, by Canadian Stage and Arts

*The Adventures of Mickey, Taggy, Puppo and Cico, and how they discover
Toronto*: 1974. ISBN 0-919952-05-4
*The Adventures of Mickey, Taggy, Puppo and Cico, and how they discover
Ottawa*: 1976. ISBN 0-919952-02-X
*The Adventures of Mickey, Taggy, Puppo and Cico, and how they discover
Montreal*: 1979. ISBN 0-919952-06-2
*The Adventures of Mickey, Taggy, Puppo and Cico, and how they discover
Kingston, Brockville, The Thousand Islands*: 1979. ISBN 0-919952-11-9
*The Adventures of Mickey, Taggy, Puppo and Cico, and how they discover
Budapest*: 1979. ISBN 0-919952-08-9
*The Adventures of Mickey, Taggy, Puppo and Cico, and how they
discover The Netherlands*: 1982. ISBN 0-919952-05-4
*The Adventures of Mickey, Taggy, Puppo and Cico, and how they discover
Switzerland*: 1983. ISBN 0-919952-15-1
*The Adventures of Mickey, Taggy, Puppo and Cico, and how they discover
France*: 1986. ISBN 0-919952-23-2

Comments: "Kati Rekai, who lives in Toronto, presents folk customs with
understanding and foreign scenes with love. To understand, to make friends,
to live together in peace this is her message of her books. Could anyone
give better, more useful advice in this world so pregnant with fear?" — *Hungarian Scene*, Budapest

Readings, Lectures & Workshops: Regular workshops in schools in English
and French.

Mailing Address: 45 Nanton Avenue, Toronto, Ontario M4W 2Y8

T. F. RIGELHOF

I was born in Regina, Saskatchewan, April 24, 1944. I hold degrees in philosophy, theology and the history of religions from Saskatchewan, Ottawa and McMaster universities. Since 1973, I have lived in Westmount, Quebec, where I write novels and stories and teach at Dawson College. I am currently at work on a novel. My stories appear in Grain, Matrix, et alia.

Selected Publications:

A Beast with Two Backs: (with Mike Mason), Ottawa, Oberon, 1981. ISBN 0-88750-413-2
The Education of J.J. Pass: Ottawa, Oberon, 1983. ISBN 0-88750-463-9

   Comments: "T.F. Rigelhof has a wonderful eye . . . and a voice that is strong, meditative, wise. Worth reading." – Marian Engel, *Toronto Star*
   "*The Education of J.J. Pass* is a remarkable achievement. A lesser writer might turn his own experience into the equivalent of family films on a rainy afternoon . . . Rigelhof instead had taken his experience apart and rebuilt it into a fiction true to life, both moving and revealing. By imagining these memories, he has made our own richer and wiser." – Alberto Manguel, *Books in Canada*
   "His fiction is informed by a vision of things that preserves a sense of 'Otherness', of mystery, and which charts what Flannery O'Connor has called the invisible 'lines of spiritual motion' and the workings of grace in the characters." – William James, *Studies In Religion*
   Readings, Lectures & Workshops: May be booked through TWUC.
   Mailing Address: c/o TWUC, 24 Ryerson Avenue, Toronto, Ontario M5T 2P3

MARY WALTERS RISKIN

 Born in Wainwright, Alberta, in 1949. Lived in London, Ontario, for most of my childhood. Have a Bachelor of Education from the University of Alberta. Was executive director of the Writers Guild of Alberta from 1982 to 1987 and a member of the board of the Alberta Foundation for the Literary Arts (1984-87). Live in Edmonton, Alberta, with my two sons.

Selected Publications:

The Women Upstairs: Edmonton, NeWest, 1987. ISBN 0-920897-18-5

   Comments: "With this novel, Riskin has served notice that she has the fictional techniques to make a significant contribution." — Ken McGoogan, *Calgary Herald*
     Readings, Lectures & Workshops: Reads to senior high school and adult audiences.
     Mailing Address: 280 Hillcrest Place, Edmonton, Alberta T5R 5X6

KEN ROBERTS

A storyteller whose tales involve visual elements, I won a CanPro award for children's television writing, co-wrote a comic murder mystery, Suspect: A Game of Murder, that played at Vancouver's City Stage for three months and am a regular lecturer on teaching imaginative skills. A librarian, I will soon be Storyteller in Residence for the Vancouver School Board.

Selected Publications:

Crazy Ideas: Toronto, Groundwood, 1984. ISBN 0-88899-028-6
Pop Bottles: Toronto, Groundwood, 1987. ISBN 0-88899-059-6

   Comments: "Perfect summer reading." – Andrea Daikin, *Vancouver Sun* (on *Crazy Ideas*)
   "*Crazy Ideas* . . . is a must for the paperback rack." – *Canadian Materials*
   "Suspect mingles improvisation with the set script so successfully that it is often difficult to tell where one begins and the other leaves off."
– *Vancouver Province*
   "An exhilarating spoof." – *The Vancouver Sun*
   Readings, Lectures & Workshops: Available for workshops and lectures on topics such as storytelling, teaching imagination and creating stories for oral telling.
   Mailing Address: c/o TWUC, 24 Ryerson Avenue, Toronto, Ontario M5T 2P3

KENNETH G. ROBERTS

Born in Toronto, April 1, 1922, and educated in Toronto schools. Joined RCAF in 1942 and completed tour of operations with Bomber Command. Earned a B.A. from the University of Toronto in 1946 and a B.J. at Carleton in 1947. Freelanced until hired by the Moncton Times Transcript in 1948. Assistant editor, Saturday Night, 1948-52. Rejoined RCAF in PR, 1952. Managing editor, Sentinel Magazine, 1962-69. DND public servant 1969-72: director of exhibitions and displays and ministers' speech writer. Retired in 1972.

Selected Publications:

The Canoe: (with Philip Shackleton), Toronto, Macmillan, 1983. ISBN 0-7715-9582-4

Awards: Distinguished Flying Cross, CD, 1939-45 Star, France and Germany. Star, Defense Medal, War Medal, CVSM and Clasp, Operational Wings. Canadian Industrial Editors Association, Award of Merit, 1969. Canadian Public Relations Society, Award of Excellence, 1975. Canadian Recreational Canoeing Association, Award of Merit, 1984.

Comments: Accredited member, Canadian Public Relations Society.

Mailing Address: Suite 1208, 370 Metcalfe Street, Ottawa, Ontario K2P 1S9

KEVIN ROBERTS

I was born in Australia, did my B.A. at Adelaide and came to Canada in 1966, where I finished an M.A. at Simon Fraser University in 1968. Since then I've taught at Malaspina College, run a commercial salmon boat and lived as a writer in Devon, Greece and South Australia. Writing to me is the fascination of discovering the marvellous; the intricacy of the imagined snowflake of language, ever-changing and unique; full of the integrity and wonder of the only absolute, the imagination.

Selected Publications:

Cariboo Fishing Notes: Devon, Beau Gest, 1972. (no ISBN)
West Country: Lantzville, Oolichan, 1974.
Deep Line: Madeira Park, Harbour, 1976.
Sney'mos: Lantzville, Oolichan, 1978. ISBN 0-88982-023-6
Stonefish: Lantzville, Oolichan, 1979. ISBN 0-88982-033-3
Flash Harry: Medeira Park, Harbour, 1980. ISBN 0-920080-11-1
Nanoose Bay Suite: Lantzville, Oolichan Books, 1983. ISBN 0-88982-068-6
Black Apples: Burnaby, West Coast Review Books/SFU, 1982. (no ISBN)
Picking the Morning Colour: Lantzville, Oolichan, 1984.

Mailing Address: Box 55, Lantzville, British Columbia V0R 2H0

PHILIP DAVIES ROBERTS

Born October 9, 1938, in Sherbrooke, Quebec. Educated at Magog High School, l'Institut Feller, Acadia University (B.A. 1959), Oxford University (B.A. 1962, M.A. 1966) and the University of Sydney, Australia (B.Mus. 1979). Have worked in England as a teacher, Fleet Street sub-editor and P.R. consultant; in Australia as publisher and university lecturer; and in Costa Rica as a journalist. Live in Annapolis Royal, Nova Scotia, where I work as a writer and musician. Two daughters, Rachael and Megan.

Selected Publications:

Just Passing Through: Ladysmith, Ladysmith Press, 1969. (no ISBN)
Crux: Ladysmith, Ladysmith Press, 1973. ISBN 0-919556-17-5
Will's Dream: Queensland UP, 1975. ISBN 0-7022-1044-7
Selected Poems: Sydney, Island, 1978. ISBN 0-909771-19-7
How Poetry Works: Toronto, Penguin, 1986. ISBN 0-14-022584-6
Plain English: Toronto, Penguin, 1987. ISBN 0-14-008407-X

Comments: "Roberts's modernism is jokey, raunchy, and sometimes quite dazzling. Amid the youth language and the hip jargon, Roberts speaks poignantly of some old worries." – Peter Porter, *The Times Literary Supplement*
"A poet of the very first rank." – Robert Adamson, *The Australian*
"(*How Poetry Works*) is not primarily intended to teach anyone to write poetry, not to read it . . . but first of all to listen to it . . . Down-right exhilarating, even astonishing." – Alex Hamilton, *The Guardian*
Readings, Lectures & Workshops: Have given readings, lectures and poetry workshops in Australia, England, India, Israel, the U.S. and Canada. Interests: the language of poetry, recent Commonwealth poetry, English usage, printing and publishing, music. Executive member of the Writers Federation of Nova Scotia.
Mailing Address: Box 557, Annapolis Royal, Nova Scotia B0S 1A0

IRENE J. ROBINSON

Born and educated in California. Tested the job market from crop picker to airlines employee to writing speeches for U.S. congressmen until I settled in Vancouver, British Columbia, to raise three sons and write plays (radio and television) for the CBC. Returned to San Francisco (worked on a 13-week series for PBS), Los Angeles and Europe. Settled again in Vancouver and am currently working on a collection of short stories.

Selected Publications:

Cherished Destiny: (wa Jo Manning), Worldwide Library, 1981. ISBN 0-373-70015-6

Comments: Twenty-two original dramas or adaptations for radio and television have been produced by the CBC. *Cherished Destiny* has been translated into German, Portugese, Spanish, Dutch, Japanese, Italian and Swedish and published in 24 countries.

Readings, Lectures & Workshops: Have given workshops on successfully writing the popular novel in Prince Edward Island, Halifax, Penticton, Burnaby and Vancouver, and in Singapore. Have given workshops on Feminism and the Romantic novel in Montreal, Vancouver, San Francisco and Athens, Georgia.

Mailing Address: 303-1695 West 10th Avenue, Vancouver, British Columbia V6J 2A2

LINDA ROGERS

I have a B.A. from the University of British Columbia in theatre, fine arts and English and have taught drama, painting, literature and creative writing. Currently I teach creative writing at the University of Victoria. I write criticism for various journals and am West Coast editor for Poetry Canada Review.

Selected Publications:

Queens of the Next Hot Star: Lantzville, Oolichan, 1981. ISBN 0-88982-032-5

Witness: Victoria, Sono Nis, 1985. ISBN 0-919203-60-4

Singing Rib: Lantzville, Oolichan, 1986. ISBN 0-88982-067-8

Awards: Pat Lowther Award (Runner-up), 1982. Burnaby Writers Award, 1985. Cross-Canada Writers' Quarterly Award, 1985.

Comments: "*Witness* is an impressive pot pourri of tightly controlled and vastly descriptive language. There is a calm thoughtful sense of irony juxtaposed with a relentless curiosity in her work." – J. Rekai, *Canadian Book Review Annual*

Readings, Lectures & Workshops: Have toured and given workshops for Canada Council, National Book Festival and the League of Canadian Poets. School readings a specialty.

Mailing Address: RR 1, Chemainus, British Columbia V0R 1K0

LEON ROOKE

Born in 1934, I have lived in Victoria, British Columbia, since 1969. Short story writer, playwright and novelist.

Selected Publications:

Fat Woman: New York, Knopf, 1981./Toronto, General, 1982. ISBN 0-7736-7026-2

Shakespeare's Dog: Toronto, Stoddart, 1983. ISBN 0-7737-2011-1

Sing Me No Love Songs I'll Say You No Prayers: New York, Ecco, 1984. ISBN 0-88001-036-3

A Bolt of White Cloth: Toronto, Stoddart, 1985. ISBN 0-7737-5011-8

Awards: Canada-Australia Literary Prize, 1981. Author's Award (Paperback Novel of the Year), 1982. Governor General's Award (Fiction), 1983. Author's Award (Short Story of the Year), 1986.

Comments: "The current darling of Canadian literature." – *Canadian Book Review Annual, 1982*

"Not so much post-modern as post-mortem." – George Galt, *Books in Canada*

"One couldn't ask for more." – Michael Mirolla, *Calgary Herald*

Readings, Lectures & Workshops: Give workshops and perform regularly across Canada and U.S.

Mailing Address: 1019 Terrace Avenue, Victoria, British Columbia V8S 3V2

JOE ROSENBLATT

Born in Toronto, December 26, 1933. I lived in Toronto most of my life until I moved out to Vancouver Island in the fall of 1980. A peripatetic poet, I have abided my time equally between Toronto and Qualicum Beach, British Columbia. Author of 12 volumes of poetry and a memoir on my childhood in Toronto in the late 1940s, Escape from the Glue Factory. Now working on a 50s autobiographical sequel, The Kissing Gold Fish of Siam. Favourite pastimes: Fishing, cat fancier and sketching.

Selected Publications:

The Winter of the Luna Moth: Toronto, Anansi, 1968. (no ISBN)
Bumble Bee Dithyramb: Toronto, Press Porcepic, 1972. ISBN 0-88878-006-0
Blind Photographer: Erin, Press Porcepic, 1973. ISBN 0-88878-008-7
Virgins and Vampires: Toronto, McClelland & Stewart, 1975. ISBN 0-7710-7720-3
Loosely Tied Hands: Windsor, Black Moss, 1979. ISBN 0-88753-042-7
The Sleeping Lady: Toronto, Exile, 1980. ISBN 0-920428-10-X
Brides of the Stream: Lantzville, Oolichan, 1983. ISBN 0-88982-048-1
Poetry Hotel (Selected Poems): Toronto, McClelland & Stewart, 1985. ISBN 0-7710-7721-1
Escape from the Glue Factory: Toronto, Exile, 1986. ISBN 0-920428-72-X

Awards: Governor General's Award for Poetry, 1976. British Columbia Book Prize for Poetry, 1986.
Readings, Lectures & Workshops: University of Victoria, York University, Saskatchewan School for the Arts, Ganaraska Writers' Colony, University of Alabama.
Mailing Address: c/o TWUC, 24 Ryerson Avenue, Toronto, Ontario M5T 2P3

VERONICA ROSS

 Born in Hanover, West Germany, January 7, 1946, came to Canada as a child, grew up in Montreal. For a long time, lived in the Maritimes where much of my fiction is set. Now writing full time in Kitchener, Ontario, where I live with husband, Richard O'Brien, a journalist.

Selected Publications:

Goodbye Summer: Ottawa, Oberon, 1980. ISBN 0-88750-348-9
Dark Secrets: Ottawa, Oberon, 1983. ISBN 0-88750-473-6
Fisherwoman: Porter's Lake, Pottersfield, 1984. ISBN 0-919001-19-X

Awards: Benson-Hedges Magazine Writing Award, 1977. Periodical Distributors of Canada Award, 1980 and 1984.

Comments: "A careful disciplined craftsman, she gives eloquent expression to half-truth and hypocrisy." – *Montreal Gazette*

"Subtle, smooth, and powerful." – *Canadian Materials*

"The writing is so assured, the prose so completely believable." – *Winnipeg Free Press*

Readings, Lectures & Workshops: Have read in schools, libraries, workshops, etc. Was Writer-in-Community in S.W. Nova Scotia and have taught creative writing. Readings and workshops, etc., may be booked through TWUC.

Mailing Address: c/o TWUC, 24 Ryerson Avenue, Toronto, Ontario M5T 2P3

CLAYTON C. RUBY

National Council, Amnesty International. Bencher, Law Society of Upper Canada. Director, Criminal Lawyers Association.

Selected Publications:

Sentencing: Toronto, Butterworths, 1980. (3rd edition, 1987) ISBN 0-409-86421-8

Comments: Editor of Canadian Rights Reporter (Butterworths) and associate editor of Criminal Law Quarterly (Canada Law Book Co.).
Mailing Address: 11 Prince Arthur Avenue, Toronto, Ontario

JANE RULE

Born in New Jersey in 1931, grew up in California, Illinois and Missouri. B.A. from Mills College, California; graduate studies at University College, London, England, and Stanford, California. Taught at Concord Academy in Massachusetts 1954-56. Moved to Canada in 1956. Assistant director of International House at the University of British Columbia, intermittent instructor in English there until 1973. Canadian citizen. For the last ten years a resident of Galiano Island, British Columbia.

Selected Publications:

Desert of the Heart: Vancouver, Talon, 1964. ISBN 0-88922-131-6
Theme for Diverse Instruments: Vancouver, Talon, 1975. ISBN 0-88922-060-3
Lesbian Images: New York, Doubleday, 1975. ISBN 0-385-04255-8
The Young in One Another's Arms: Naiad, 1977. ISBN 0-930044-53-3
Contract with the World: Naiad, 1980. ISBN 0-930044-28-2
Outlander: Naiad, 1981. ISBN 0-930044-17-7
Inland Passage: Toronto, Lester & Orpen Dennys, 1985. ISBN 0-88619-075-4
A Hot-Eyed Moderate: Toronto, Lester & Orpen Dennys, 1985. ISBN 0-88619-077-0
Memory Board: Toronto, Macmillan, 1987. ISBN 0-7715-9529-8

Awards: Canadian Authors Association (Novel), 1978. Canadian Authors Association (Short Story), 1978. Gay Academic Union USA Award for Literature, 1978. The Fund for Human Dignity Award USA, 1983.

Readings, Lectures & Workshops: I have given writing workshops in Montreal, Winnipeg, Saskatoon, Edmonton, Calgary, Victoria and Nelson. I don't give readings or lectures.

Mailing Address: The Fork, Route 1, Galiano, British Columbia V0N 1P0

RONALD RUSKIN

I was born in the old Mount Sinai Hospital on Yorkville Avenue in Toronto on October 16, 1944. My mom said when my father took me home he told her I'd be a doctor. Twenty-five years later I got my M.D. from Queen's University and then went off to study art in Aix-en-Provence. I always wanted to be an artist, a writer. I wrote for the Queen's journal, did poetry, managed to get through medical school and later went to McGill to specialise in psychiatry. I was fascinated by history and mythology as a child. I became a psychoanalyst.

Selected Publications:

The Last Panic: Toronto, Seal, 1979. ISBN 0-7704-1534-2

Comments: Poems have appeared in Quarry (vol. 18, No.4, 1969 and vol. 19, No. 3, 1970) and The Canadian Forum (March 1970). A short story, Night of Sighs, was published in Queen's Quarterly (Summer, 1986). A novel, Duck Lake, is currently with New York agent, H. Morrison. Articles include A Manual to Medical Martyrdom in Canadian Doctor (Dec. 1974) and The Age of Conspiracy in the Montreal Star (July 1974).

Two plays in progress are Dadabar and Up North.

Readings, Lectures & Workshops: I give papers and lectures at the Wellesley Hospital where I am a senior staff psychiatrist. We have a regular group that studies literature and psychoanalytic criticism. For the past two years I have spoken at our annual movie night on Diva and Modern Times.

Mailing Address: 223A St. Clair Avenue West, Toronto, Ontario M4V 1R3

ESTELLE SALATA

Born in Hamilton, Ontario, July 11, 1926. B.A. Religion, McMaster University, 1976; married Ben Salata 1948; four children, Michael, Paula, Kathy and Mark; five grandchildren at this moment in time. Member of the Canadian Authors Association and the Canadian Society of Children's Authors, Illustrators and Performers. Teach creative writing part time at Sheridan College in Oakville and Burlington.

Selected Publications:

Mice at Centre Ice: Toronto, Nelson, 1984. ISBN 0-17-602086-1

Awards: Writing for Young Canada Award from Gage, 1964. Centennial Story Writing Competition (First Prize, Ontario), 1967. Vicky Metcalf Award (Short Story), 1979. CommCept's Canadian KidLit Contest (Third Prize), 1979.

Comments: Tales of the Mouse Hockey League: adapted script for television, Marmalade Animation, half-hour CBC feature cartoon, Spring 1987.

Short stories and articles have been published in 25 anthologies including *Nunny Bag 3* (Gage, 1964); *My Home, My Native Land* (Olympus Publishing, 1967); *Accent on Reading* (Holt, Rinehart & Winston, 1968); *Canadian Children's Annual* (1975, 1976, 1980, 1984 and 1985); *Leapfrog* (Gage, 1977); *Zap Music* (Fitzhenry & Whiteside, 1977); *What if?* (Ginn, 1977); *The Seasons of Childhood* (Simon & Pierre, 1979); *Time Enough* (Holt, Rinehart & Winston, 1979) and *Invitations* (McGraw-Hill Ryerson, 1985).

Readings, Lectures & Workshops: School readings up to and including grade eight. Workshops in creative writing for children and adults.

Mailing Address: 96 Reid Avenue South, Hamilton, Ontario L8K 3V1

JOHN RALSTON SAUL

Born in Ottawa, June 19, 1947. Educated in
Calgary, Rivers (Manitoba), Kingston and Oakville, Ontario. B.A. (Honours) McGill 1969.
Ph.D. King's College, London (with Science Po.
Paris) 1972. Directeur General investment
company, Paris 1972-75. Assistant to chairman
of Petro Canada from its creation, Calgary,
1976-78; Toronto 1978-82. Extended periods
in North Africa and Far East. Paris 1982-86.

Selected Publications:

The Birds of Prey: Toronto, Macmillan, 1977. (Current paperback edition/
   Grafton, ISBN 0-586-059-563)
Baraka: Toronto, Grafton, 1983. ISBN 0-246-122-293
The Next Best Thing: Toronto, Collins, 1986. ISBN 0-00-223043-7

   Mailing Address: c/o Nancy Colbert, 303 Davenport Road, Toronto,
Ontario M5R 1K5

CANDACE SAVAGE

Born December 1949 in Grande Prairie, Alberta. Granddaughter of pioneers and daughter of school teachers, which, in summary, accounts for who I am. Honours graduate of the University of Alberta in 1971. Write poetry, children's stories and non-fiction. Full-time writer and editor for ten years. Currently live in Yellowknife with my young daughter, work for the Government of the Northwest Territories, and write in my "spare" time(!).

Selected Publications:

A Harvest Yet To Reap (A History of Prairie Women): Toronto, Women's Press, 1976. ISBN 0-88961-029-0

Our Nell (A Scrapbook Biography of Nellie L. McClung): Saskatoon, WP Prairie Books, 1979. ISBN 0-88833-033-2

Wild Mammals of Western Canada: Saskatoon, WP Prairie Books, 1981. ISBN 0-88833-078-2

The Wonder of Canadian Birds: Saskatoon, WP Prairie Books, 1985. ISBN 0-88833-136-3

Comments: "An intelligent, lively writer." – William French, *Globe and Mail*

"The beauty of Savage's work is its readability . . . She breathes life into her subjects." – Brian Christmas, *Hamilton Spectator*

"Just as the writer herself is an unusual specimen, her book is very much out of the ordinary. It is written with passion and a grand human sensitivity to the processes of life." – Patrick Tivy, *Calgary Herald*

Readings, Lectures & Workshops: Give readings and illustrated lectures, mostly in schools. Also available for storytelling and will work with students and teachers to stimulate creative writing, particularly among the very young.

Mailing Address: 46 Calder Crescent, Yellowknife, North West Territories X1A 3B1

JOHN SAWATSKY

Born in Winkler, Manitoba, May 8, 1948, but grew up in British Columbia's Fraser Valley. Graduated from Simon Fraser University in 1974 with a B.A. (Hon.) in political science. Joined the Vancouver Sun as a reporter in 1970 and became parliamentary correspondent in Ottawa in 1975. I have been a freelance journalist and author since 1979 and continue as a member of the Parliamentary Press Gallery in Ottawa.

Selected Publications:

Men in the Shadows (The RCMP Security Service): Toronto, Doubleday, 1980. ISBN 0-385-14682-5

For Services Rendered (Leslie James Bennett and the RCMP Security Service): Toronto, Doubleday, 1982. ISBN 0-385-17660-0

Gouzenko (The Untold Story): Toronto, Macmillan, 1984. ISBN 0-7715-9812-2

Awards: Michener Award for Public Service Journalism, 1976. Periodical Distributors of Canada/Foundation for the Advancement of Canadian Letters Award (Non-fiction Paperback), 1983. Outstanding Alumni Award for Professional Achievement, Simon Fraser University Alumni Association, 1985.

Mailing Address: 475 Bay Street, Ottawa, Ontario K1R 6A7

LIBBY SCHEIER

Born in 1946, New York City. Also lived in France, California and Israel. Settled in Toronto, 1975. B.A., philosophy and French, Sarah Lawrence College; M.A., English, State University of New York/Stony Brook. Published two books of poetry; short-story collection in preparation. Poetry in several anthologies. Sometime freelance critic/journalist for the Globe and Mail, This Magazine, Canadian Forum, Quarry, Status of Women News, other publications.

Selected Publications:

The Larger Life: Windsor, Black Moss, 1983. ISBN 0-88753-099-0
Second Nature: Toronto, Coach House, 1986. ISBN 0-88910-297-X

Awards: Prism International Poetry Contest (Third Prize), 1986
Comments: "Striking honesty . . . Scheier is determined to convey . . . the violence and anger in life as well as the tenderness . . . uncompromising poems, about as far from the hearts and flowers school of feminine poetry as one can get." – John Oughton, *Now* (on *Second Nature*)
"A quite terrific poet." – Robert Fulford, *Toronto Star*
"Read this book! You women whose bodies are restless, read this book. You men of pleasure and insouciance, read this book . . . You men and women whose gentleness is suffocated by the politicians, read this book. These are tough poems. They are poems from the mouth of love, directed against the dangerous." – Erin Moure, *Kinesis* (on *The Larger Life*)
Readings, Lectures & Workshops: Give readings and workshops often. Specialise in talks on women's writing, aesthetics, criticism and censorship.
Mailing Address: B-165 Riverdale Avenue, Toronto, Ontario M4K 1C4

BILL SCHERMBRUCKER

Born in Eldoret, Kenya, in 1938. Have lived in Vancouver since 1964. A founding member of Capilano College and former editor of The Capilano Review. Have co-authored a political mystery. Currently working on a book of historical fiction, recreating a woman's life in Africa. A travel memoir is also in progress.

Selected Publications:

The Aims and Strategies of Good Writing: North Vancouver, Capilano College, 1976. (no ISBN)
Chameleon and Other Stories: Vancouver, Talon, 1983. ISBN 0-88922-208-8

Awards: CBC Literary Competition (Second Prize, Memoir), 1980
Comments: "It's an impressive debut; the stories (in *Chameleon and Other Stories*) are deceptively subtle and finely crafted, and they illuminate a period of British Imperialism that was not the empire's finest hour." – William French, *Globe and Mail*
"His father-and-son relationships are unique in Canadian short fiction. Schermbrucker's prose has a sense of authority and assurance that keeps his autobiographical fiction from wallowing in sentimental nostalgia." – Geoff Hancock, *Toronto Star*
"A spellbinding series of short stories that draw their strength from the tension between fiction and fact." – *Books in Canada*
Mailing Address: 1826 East 35th Avenue, Vancouver, British Columbia V5P 1B6

ANDREAS PETER SCHROEDER

Born to a Mennonite family in Germany, 1946. Emigrated to Canada 1951. Attended the University of British Columbia 1965-71 (B.A./M.A. comparative literature and creative writing). Travelled North America, Europe, the Middle East, Asia, then settled in a mountaintop tower near Mission, British Columbia. Enthusiastic public reader/lecturer. Have been writer-in-residence at the Regina Public Library (1981), University of Winnipeg (1983), Fraser Valley Public Library (Clearbrook and Port Coquitlam) in 1984 and 1985.

Selected Publications:

The Ozone Minotaur: Vancouver, Sono Nis, 1969. (no ISBN)
File of Uncertainties: Vancouver, Sono Nis, 1971. (no ISBN)
UNIverse: Vancouver, MASSage, 1971. (no ISBN)
The Late Man: Vancouver, Sono Nis, 1972. (no ISBN)
Shaking It Rough: Toronto, Doubleday, 1976. ISBN 0-385-12310-8
Toccata In "D": Lantzville, Oolichan, 1985. ISBN 0-88982-070-8
Dust Ship Glory: Toronto, Doubleday, 1986. ISBN 0-385-25038-X

Awards: Woodward Memorial Award for Prose, 1969. National Film Board Award, 1970. Canadian Film Development Corporation Award, 1971. Governor General's Award (Short List, Non-fiction), 1977.

Comments: If youth is the time to try everything, and middle age the time to staighten out the resulting chaos (La Rochefoucault), then I've probably reached middle age. A decade ago I was producing radio documentaries, directing films, writing a weekly literary column, teaching creative writing in both universities and prisons and hosting a weekly literary TV talk show. Today I just breathe normally and concentrate on writing fiction.

Mailing Address: Box 3127, Mission, British Columbia V2V 4J3

SAM SELVON

Born in Trinidad in 1923. Lived and wrote in England for 28 years before moving to Canada in 1978. Now a Canadian citizen.

Selected Publications:

Turn Again Tiger: London, Heinemann, 1979. ISBN 0-435-98780-1
Moses Ascending: London, Heinemann, 1984. ISBN 0-435-98750-X
Moses Migrating: London, Longmans, 1983. ISBN 0-582-78580-4
The Plains of Caroni: Toronto, Williams-Wallace, 1985. ISBN 0-88795-046-9
A Brighter Sun: London, Longmans, 1985. ISBN 0-582-64265-5
Ways of Sunlight: London, Longmans, 1985. ISBN 0-582-64261-2
The Lonely Londoners: London, Longmans, 1985. ISBN 0-582-64264-7

Awards: Creative Writing Fellow, Iowa University, 1981. Hon. Doctorate (D. Litt.), University of the West Indies, 1985.

Readings, Lectures & Workshops: Read, conduct workshops, talk. Never lecture.

Mailing Address: 4031 Charleswood Drive, Calgary, Alberta T2L 2E1

PHILIP SHACKLETON

Born in Fort Erie, Ontario, November 30, 1923.
In no hurry to be remaindered.

Selected Publications:

The Furniture of Old Ontario: Toronto, Macmillan, 1973. ISBN 0-7705-1046-9

The Canoe: (with K.G. Roberts), Toronto, Macmillan, 1983. ISBN 0-7715-9582-4

Comments: Contributed to *The Book of Canadian Antiques* (Toronto, McGraw-Hill Ryerson, 1974, ISBN 0-07-082140-2).

Mailing Address: Box 280, Manotick, Ontario K0A 2N0

MERLE SHAIN

Born in Toronto, October 14, 1935. University of Toronto, B.A. 1957; B.SW. 1959. I live in Toronto with my son, Shain Grosman. Collect antique furniture and clothes. Have appeared in all types of media as guest, interviewer, panelist, editor and hostess. Columnist for Toronto Life Fashion and the Toronto Sun.

Selected Publications:

Some Men Are More Perfect Than Others: Toronto, McClelland & Stewart, 1973. ISBN 0-7704-1595-4

When Lovers Are Friends: Toronto, McClelland & Stewart, 1978. ISBN 0-7710-8134-0

Hearts That We Broke Long Ago: Toronto, McClelland & Stewart, 1983. ISBN 0-7710-8135-9

Comments: Appointed to Board of Trustees of the National Film Board of Canada. Subject of half-hour TV special Take 30 (CBC). Profiled in Chatelaine, Financial Post Magazine and Playgirl. Aide to Pierre Trudeau in campaign for leadership of Liberal Party. Design consultant to Ralph Lauren.

Readings, Lectures & Workshops: Have addressed the Connecticut Psychiatric Association, the University of Missouri Medical School, the State of Virginia Welfare Council and the Calgary Status of Women Action Committee.

Maling Address: 50 Chestnut Park Road, Toronto, Ontario M4W 1W8

JOAN FERN SHAW

Born April 29, 1938, in Toronto, I have lived in various towns and cities in Ontario, Nova Scotia and Germany. B.A. in English from Queen's and teaching certificate from Peterborough Teachers' College. I commute daily from my home in Willowdale to Sharon, Ontario, where I am school librarian. Became fiction editor of Waves in 1986. Married, two daughters.

Selected Publications:

Raspberry Vinegar: Ottawa, Oberon, 1985. ISBN 0-88750-565-1

Awards: Federation of Women Teachers' Associations of Ontario Writer's Award, 1985. Gerald Lampert Award, 1986.

Comments: "To find equivalents for the quality of this first book one has to think of such parallels as Alice Munro." – *Canadian Literature*

I began writing in 1978 when I turned 40. My first story appeared in The Fiddlehead in 1979. Since then I have had 27 stories and numerous poems published in little magazines across Canada. Three stories appeared in *Coming Attractions 2*, edited by David Helwig and Sandra Martin (Ottawa, Oberon, 1984).

Readings, Lectures & Workshops: Have given readings at various libraries, schools and at Harbourfront.

Mailing Address: c/o TWUC, 24 Ryerson Avenue, Toronto, Ontario M5T 2P3

SARAH SHEARD

Born in Toronto, February, 1953. Graduated from York University, 1976. Editor at the Coach House Press since 1979. Currently working as Ontario co-ordinator for the National Book Festival. Living in Toronto with David Young and our son Benn and writing my second novel.

Selected Publications:

Almost Japanese: Toronto, Coach House, 1985. ISBN 0-88910-277-5

Awards: 45 Below: Canada's Ten Best Young Fiction Writers
Comments: Almost Japanese has been published by Scribner's in the U.S., Faber & Faber in the U.K. and Uniboek in The Netherlands.
Represented by Lee Davis-Creal, Lucinda Vardey Agency, Toronto.
Readings, Lectures & Workshops: Have taught creative writing in high schools since 1980. Readings in Toronto, the Prairies and Vancouver.
Mailing Address: 34 Marchmount Road, Toronto, Ontario M6G 2A9

ROBERT G. SHERRIN

 Born in Ottawa in 1951. Have lived in Alberta, Ontario and West Germany. Now reside and work in Vancouver where I am active as a writer, visual artist, photographer and teacher.

Selected Publications:

The Black Box: Vancouver, November House, 1976. ISBN 0-88894-114-5

Comments: Short Stories have appeared in Prism International, Canadian Fiction Magazine, The Capilano Review, Descant, Grain and 2Plus2 (Switzerland). Some of these stories have been anthologised: *The Canadian Short Fiction Anthology, Prism International: 25th Anniversary Retrospective*, and *Best Stories 1985*.

Readings, Lectures & Workshops: Readings in Vancouver, Vienna and Graz. One lecture at the University of Vienna.

Mailing Address: 2218 Blenheim Street, Vancouver, British Columbia V6K 4J3

MURPHY ORLANDO SHEWCHUK

Born in Hamilton, Ontario, September 14, 1943, to parents of Ukrainian/Hungarian background. Raised in Saskatchewan and British Columbia and trained in Quebec and Ontario. Certified Electronics Technician with B.C. Hydro. Specialise in photo-illustrated magazine articles and books on outdoor travel, regional history and biography. Live in Merritt, B.C., with wife Katharine, where I practise in electronics, writing and photography.

Selected Publications:

Fur, Gold and Opals (A Guide to the Thompson River Valleys): Surrey, Hancock, 1975. ISBN 0-919654-36-3

Exploring the Nicola Valley: Vancouver, Douglas & McIntyre, 1981. ISBN 0-88894-307-5

The Craigmont Story: Surrey, Hancock, 1983. ISBN 0-88839-980-4

Backroads Explorer (Vol.1 Thompson-Cariboo): Vancouver, Maclean Hunter,1985. ISBN 0-88896-151-0

Awards: Outdoor Writers of Canada Award of Merit (Newspaper Writing), 1974. Macmillan-Bloedel Newspaper Journalism Award, 1975. OWC Award of Merit (Photography), 1984 and 1985. OWC Award of Merit (Magazine Writing), 1986.

Comments: "Murphy Shewchuk knows his province, and his latest publication, *Thompson Cariboo*, shows it." — *Vancouver Province*

Readings, Lectures & Workshops: Conduct workshops on photography, wordprocessing and the business of writing at writers' conferences.

Mailing Address: Box 400, Merritt, British Columbia V0K 2B0

CAROL SHIELDS

Born in Oak Park, Illinois, in 1935 and immigrated to Canada in 1957. Hold a B.A. from Hanover College and an M.A. from the University of Ottawa. Now live in Winnipeg, teach at the University of Manitoba and write novels, short fiction and plays.

Selected Publications:

Others: Ottawa, Borealis, 1972. ISBN 0-919594-08-5
Intersect: Ottawa, Borealis, 1974. ISBN 0-919594-27-1
Susanna Moodie (Voice and Vision): Ottawa, Borealis, 1975. ISBN 0-919594-46-8
Small Ceremonies: Toronto, McGraw-Hill Ryerson, 1976.
The Box Garden: Toronto, McGraw-Hill Ryerson, 1977.
Happenstance: Toronto, McGraw-Hill Ryerson, 1980./Penguin, 1981. ISBN 0-14-005891-5
A Fairly Conventional Woman: Toronto, Macmillan, 1982. ISBN 0-7715-9724-X
Various Miracles: Toronto, Stoddart, 1985. ISBN 0-7737-5036-3
Swann: Toronto, Stoddart, 1987. ISBN 0-7737-2092-8

Awards: CBC Young Writers Award, 1965. Canadian Authors Association Award, 1976. CBC National Drama Award (First Prize), 1983. CBC Literary Competition (Short Story), 1984. National Magazine Awards, 1984 and 1985.

Readings, Lectures & Workshops: Lectures on concepts of fiction, readings at universities and for other groups, short workshops. May be booked through TWUC.

Mailing Address: 701-237 Wellington Crescent, Winnipeg, Manitoba R3M 0A1

MICHEL M.J. SHORE

Born in Paris, France, March 9, 1948. Arrived in Montreal as a child of three. Fluent in English and French, working knowledge of Hebrew, German, Polish (Slavic languages). Hold a B.A. (Classics) from College Notre-Dame (University of Montreal); M.A. in philosophy from McGill University (thesis: Cultural Dialogue); LL.L (Law degree) from the University de Montreal; elected to Who's Who in American Universities for Ph.D. work in philosophy.

Selected Publications:

Jerusalem Breezes: New York, Shengold, 1981. ISBN 0-88400-079-6
O Canada, Canada: Sherbrooke, Editions Naaman, 1983. ISBN 2-89040-247-9
The Tempest: Sherbrooke, Editions Naaman, 1986. ISBN 2-89040-373-4

Comments: "I want to share your hope that our potential as a nation will emerge from dream to reality." — Prime Minister Pierre Elliot Trudeau

"A most welcome addition to our Canadiana Library." — Governor General Ed Schreyer

"I like it. I found reverberations . . . They reflect (Shore's) anguish and (his) fervour." — Elie Wiesel

"Shore doesn't preach. His serious messages peak through the many-coloured coats of his impressionistic prose . . . Shore bares his heart on issues most vital to Canadians and all other human beings." — Burt Heward, *Ottawa Citizen*

Readings, Lectures & Workshops: Read regularly and lecture on the human condition through literature.

Mailing Address: 2030 Delmar Court, Ottawa, Ontario K1H 5R6

SHARON SIAMON

Born in Saskatoon, Saskatchewan, I was educated in Ontario and have lived in Uganda, California and Kirkland Lake, Ontario. I have been writing for children since 1979, a career I have combined with teaching, editing and being the mother of Amy, Kate and Becky.

Selected Publications:

Strange Lake Adventure: Toronto, Gage. ISBN 0-7715-5982-8
A Puli Named Sandor: Toronto, Gage. ISBN 0-7715-6272-1
Ski for Your Mountain: Toronto, Gage, 1983. ISBN 0-7715-7007-4
Dirt Bikes at Hangman's Clubhouse: Toronto, Gage, 1984. ISBN 0-7715-7013-9
Log House Mouse: Toronto, Gage. ISBN 0-7715-6783-9
The Secret of Sunset House: Toronto, Gage. ISBN 0-7715-6870-3

Awards: Federation of Women Teacher's Association of Ontario Author's Award, 1979
Readings, Lectures & Workshops: I have led numerous workshops with children in schools and libraries across Canada.
Mailing Address: 148 Dorset Road, Scarborough, Ontario M1M 2T4

MAGGIE SIGGINS

Born in Toronto in 1942. Bachelor of Journalism 1965. Began career as a rookie reporter for the Toronto Telegram. Also worked as a magazine writer and political columnist, television reporter and producer and journalism professor. In 1984 moved to sunny Saskatchewan. Currently spending two years researching a book in China.

Selected Publications:

How to Catch a Man: (with Ben Wicks), Toronto, Trojan, 1969. (no ISBN)
Bassett, A Biography: Toronto, Lorimer, 1979. ISBN 0-88862-284-8
Brian and the Boys, A Story of Gang Rape: Toronto, Lorimer, 1984. ISBN 0-88862-659-2
A Canadian Tragedy, Joann and Colin Thatcher (A Story of Love and Hate): Toronto, Macmillan, 1986. ISBN 0-7704-2139-3

Awards: Southam Fellowship, 1974-75. Arthur Ellis Award, Crime Writers of Canada, 1986.

Comments: "Siggins . . . reveals the talents of a firm storyteller weaving incident and character back and forth across decades and the Prairies with the dexterity of a Russian novelist." – Peter Calamai, *Southam News*

"A Canadian Tragedy is . . . entirely, irresistibly engrossing." – Jack Batten, *Books in Canada*

Readings, Lectures & Workshops: Have lectured extensively on journalism and other issues. Currently teach journalism to the first class of graduate students at the Broadcast Institute, Beijing, China.

Mailing Address: c/o TWUC, 24 Ryerson Avenue, Toronto, Ontario M5T 2P3

REG SILVESTER

An Albertan writer with strong ties to Saskatchewan, where I was born (Moose Jaw, 1945) and raised (North Battleford). Trained as a journalist (Carleton B.J. 1971), I began writing fiction after courses at the Saskatchewan School of the Arts in the mid-70s. Now in Edmonton, I work half time as editor of a legal education magazine and continue to write short stories.

Selected Publications:

Fish-Hooks: Moose Jaw, Coteau, 1984. ISBN 0-919926-31-2

Comments: "Creates the world of consciousness as a narrative line which has no more authority over the natural world than the fishing line has power into new depths." – Keith Louise Fulton, *NeWest Review*

"Evocative but concise, moving quickly between the mundane and the mysterious." – Carolyn Fleming, *Calgary Herald*

"Stephen King with a comic twist." – Ian Adam, *Foothills Magazine*

"The stories are . . . poignant, definitive translations of our prairie consciousness." – Carol Hlus, *Edmonton Journal*

Readings, Lectures & Workshops: Have read in libraries, bookstores and bistros. Give combined readings/lectures at high schools and junior highs. Teach introduction to creative writing and short-story workshops through the University of Alberta, Faculty of Extension. Available for readings and lectures and writing courses on request.

Mailing Address: 10134-88th Street, Edmonton, Alberta T5H 1P1

ROBIN SKELTON

Born in Yorkshire, October 12, 1925. Self-educated at Cambridge and Leeds universities and in the RAF. Joined the University of Victoria, 1963. Co-founder of The Malahat Review, 1967. Founding chairman of the creative writing department, 1973. Editor, Sono Nis Press, 1976-1983. Author, compiler or editor of more than 60 books and 20 chapbooks (as well as broadsides) of poetry, fiction, biography, drama, history, criticism, translations and occult lore. Chairman of TWUC, 1982-83.

Selected Publications:

The Collected Shorter Poems, 1947-1977: Victoria, Sono Nis, 1981. ISBN 0-919462-79-0

Limits: Erin, Porcupine's Quill, 1981. ISBN 0-88984-041-5

Zuk: Erin, Porcupine's Quill, 1982. ISBN 0-88984-068-7

The Man Who Sang in His Sleep: Erin, Porcupine's Quill, 1984. ISBN 0-88984-053-9

The Collected Longer Poems, 1947-1977: Victoria, Sono Nis, 1985. ISBN 0-919203-72-8

Talismanic Magic: York Beach, Samuel Weiser, 1985. ISBN 0-87728-553-5

Awards: F.R. Scott Award (Literary Translation), 1985

Comments: See also Who's Who, Who's Who in Canada, Who's Who in Canadian Literature, The Oxford Companion to Canadian Literature (1983), The Dictionary of Literary Biography, Contemporary Authors Autobiography Series (Gale Research Co.) and Skelton at Sixty edited by Barbara Turner (Porcupine's Quill).

Readings, Lectures & Workshops: Readings, workshops and lectures have been given at colleges and universities in Canada, Ireland, Sweden, England and the U.S.

Mailing Address: 1255 Victoria Avenue, Victoria, British Columbia V8S 4P3

JOSEF SKVORECKY

Born September 27, 1924, in Nachod, Bohemia, Czechoslovakia. During WWII worked in an aircraft factory. Ph.D. (philosophy) 1951 from Charles University, Prague. After confiscation and banning of my novel *The Cowards* in 1959, I became one of the most popular Czech novelists, a popularity enhanced by further bannings of novels *The Tank Corp, The End of the Nylon Age, Miss Silver's Past,* and after leaving the country in 1969 by the blacklisting of my entire oeuvre. In Canada since 1969, citizen since 1976. Professor, University of Toronto.

Selected Publications:

All the Bright Young Men and Women: Toronto, PMA, 1971. ISBN 0-88778-110-1
The Cowards: London, Penguin, 1972. ISBN 0-14-003511-7
The Mournful Demeanour of Lt. Boruvka: London, Gollancz, 1973. ISBN 0-575-01755-4
Miracle en Boheme: Paris, Gallimard, 1978. (no ISBN)
Tankovy Prapor: Toronto, Sixty-Eight, 1980. ISBN 0-88781-000-4
The Swell Season: Toronto, Lester & Orpen Dennys, 1982. ISBN 0-88619-038-X
Jiri Menzel and the History of the Closely Watched Trains: Boulder, 1982. ISBN 0-88033-011-2
The Engineer of Human Souls: Toronto, Lester & Orpen Dennys, 1984. ISBN 0-919630-17-0
Miss Silver's Past: New York, Ecco Press, 1985. ISBN 0-88001-074-6
Dvorak in Love: Toronto, Lester & Orpen Dennys, 1986. ISBN 0-88619-122-X

Awards: Neustadt International Prize for Literature, 1980. City of Toronto Book Award, 1984. Governor General's Award (Fiction), 1984.
Comments: "The finest fiction ever written about jazz." – *The Village Voice* (on *The Bass Saxophone*)
"So this is what the novel has been! So this is what the novel can still be!" – *Time* (on *The Engineer of Human Souls*)
Readings, Lectures & Workshops: Many lectures and readings all across Canada and the U.S.
Mailing Address: 487 Sackville Street, Toronto, Ontario M4X 1T6

IAN SLATER

Born in Australia in 1941. Worked in Canberra for the Navy, External Affairs and the Joint Intelligence Bureau. Was marine geology technician with the New Zealand and University of British Columbia's Institutes of Oceanography. Ph.D. in political science, 1977, UBC. As author and lecturer, I have taught a wide variety of courses in the humanities and am currently teaching at UBC. Married; two children.

Selected Publications:

Firespill: Toronto, Seal, 1977. ISBN 0-7704-1504-0
Sea Gold: Toronto, Seal, 1979. ISBN 0-7704-1525-3
Air Glow Red: Toronto, Seal, 1983. ISBN 0-7704-1799-X
Orwell (The Road to Airstrip One): New York, Norton, 1985. ISBN 0-393-01908-X

Comments: "It is doubtful that any book provides a better foundation for a full understanding of Orwell's unique and troubling vision." — *Washington Post*

"Perhaps it is because Ian Slater is a Canadian, removed from what he is writing about by a continent as well as his own youth, that he looks at familiar material so freshly." — *Times Literary Supplement*

"*Air Glow Red* is a hot page-turning novel of power politics and the devastating misuse of the sun's tremendous energy." — *Toronto Star*

Readings, Lectures & Workshops: I give regular workshops on writing (novels and non-fiction) and on negotiating with publishers. May be booked through TWUC.

Mailing Address: 4074 West 17th Avenue, Vancouver, British Columbia V6S 1A6

REUBEN SLONIM

Born in Winnipeg, Manitoba, February 27, 1914. Education: Illinois Institute of Technology, Chicago, B.S.A.S. 1933; ordained rabbi, teacher and preacher by the Jewish Theological Seminary, New York City, M.H.L. 1937; Albany Law School, N.Y. 1945-47. Rabbi of three Toronto congregations from 1937 to 1983; President, Association for the Living Jewish Spirit. Former co-chairman, Interfaith Committee of Metropolitan Toronto Community Chest. Member of the World Society of Skippers of the Flying Dutchmen. Former chaplain, Variety Club, Toronto.

Selected Publications:

In the Steps of Pope Paul: Montreal, Palm, 1965. (no ISBN)
Both Sides Now: Toronto, Clarke Irwin, 1972. ISBN 0-7720-0575-3
Family Quarrel: Toronto, Clarke Irwin, 1977. ISBN 0-7720-1092-7
Grand To Be An Orphan: Toronto, Clarke Irwin, 1983. ISBN 0-7720-1389-6
To Kill A Rabbi: Toronto, ECW Press, 1987. ISBN 0-920763-99-5

Readings, Lectures & Workshops: Appear on radio and TV. Lecture on contemporary issues: political, philosophical and religious. May be booked through TWUC.

Mailing Address: 625 Roselawn Avenue, Suite 1105, Toronto, Ontario M5N 1K7

CAROLYN SMART

Born in England, March 16, 1952, and live on a farm near Sydenham, Ontario. I have previously lived in Ottawa, Winnipeg, Toronto, England and Mexico. I hold an Hon. B.A. from the University of Toronto and have worked as an editor for publishing houses, as a civil servant, as a salesperson, as a teacher, as a housewife and mother, and consistently as a writer.

Selected Publication:

Swimmers in Oblivion: Toronto, York, 1981. ISBN 0-920424-27-9
Power Sources: Fredericton, Fiddlehead, 1982. ISBN 0-86492-018-0
Stoning the Moon: Ottawa, Oberon,1986. ISBN 0-88750-658-5

Comments: Works appear in *Full Moon: An Anthology of Canadian Women Poets* (Quadrant, 1983. ISBN 0-86495-028-4), *Anything is Possible: A Selection of 11 Women Poets* (Mosaic, 1984. ISBN 0-88962-251-5) and Fireweed (1986. ISSN 0706-3857).

"Smart creates for her readers a world ennobled by her poetic understanding." – Rhea Tregebov, *Kingston Whig-Standard*

"Smart makes whole poems whose emotional acuity sticks in the mind. *Power Sources* is a book whose power is grounded in Smart's intense awareness of the ways our emotions affect us moment to moment." – Doug Barber, *Quarry*

"*Power Sources* is a remarkable book in many ways. Smart's writing is strong; she manipulates language and imagery with skill." – Carroll Klein, *Broadside*

"(Smart) is possessed of an engaging tone and melancholy . . . more good things to come from this quarter." – Rosemary Aubertubt, *Quill & Quire*

Mailing Address: c/o TWUC, 24 Ryerson Avenue, Toronto, Ontario M5T 2P3

IAN SMILLIE

After graduating from McGill in 1967, I worked four years in West Africa and subsequently held posts in Ottawa and at the University of Western Ontario. Between 1972 and 1974, I managed a large reconstruction project in Bangladesh, and in 1975 founded Inter Pares, today a respected international development organisation. In 1979, I became executive director of CUSO and since 1983 have worked as a writer and international development consultant.

Selected Publications:

The Land of Lost Content: Toronto, Deneau, 1985. ISBN 0-88879-125-9
No Condition Permanent: London, Intermediate Technology, 1986. ISBN 0-946688-32-X

Comments: "The writing is quick and fresh, the anecdotes and emphasis on people exactly right." – *Calgary Herald*
"An intelligent and entertaining style." – *London Free Press*
"Smillie . . . is a member of that small brigade of international Canadians who bridge the huge gap between our smug and opulent society and the Third World." – *Toronto Star*
"The flair of a good adventure writer." – *Canadian Churchman*
"Smillie's feeling for events and his power of description make for absorbing and . . . entertaining reading." – *International Perspectives*
Readings, Lectures & Workshops: Frequent professional and university lectures in Canada and Britain on economic and international development topics. Related appearances on Canadian and British television and radio. Contributor to newspapers and journals on development issues.
Mailing Address: 618 Melbourne Avenue, Ottawa, Ontario K2A 1X1

JIM SMITH

Born September 17, 1951, in Niagara Falls, Ontario. B.A. in English (Queen's 1977); M.A. in English and creative writing (Concordia 1981). Poet, editor, reviewer, interviewer, translator (Spanish), social critic. Chair: Writers and Artists Action Committee for Nicaragua and Chile. Editor: Front Press Publications. Union organiser and administrator of national co-op housing association. Reside in Toronto. Mother: Ella Margaret Smith.

Selected Publications:

Surface Structures: Kingston, St. Lawrence College, 1979. (no ISBN)
Virus: Toronto, Underwhich, 1983. (no ISBN)
One Hundred Most Frightening Things: Toronto, blewointment, 1985. ISBN 0-88971-102-X
Convincing Americans: Toronto, Proper Tales, 1986. ISBN 0-920467-03-2

Awards: McIlquham Prize in Creative Writing, Queen's University, 1973
Comments: *The Inner Ear*: (ed. Gary Geddes). Major selection (16pp). Centrespread feature – WHAT Magazine, Toronto, Vol 1, #7 1986. Pirhana #3 – feature spread, Toronto, 1986.

"The key word in describing Smith's writing is adventurous. Everything from hypereconomic prose to contemporary epic poetry. His prose pieces are deceptively simple, his poetry daring and complex. His instincts are almost infallible, his essential morality above reproach." – Kevin Connolly, *What Magazine*

"He will add something refreshing to Canadian poetry." – *Canadian Literature*

"An intensly personal poetry." – Alan Brown, *Kingston Whig-Standard*
Mailing Address: Box 177, Station G, Toronto, Ontario M4M 3G7

RAY SMITH

Although born December 12, 1941, in Inverness, as the hospital is there, I am from Mabou, Cape Breton, and am the twenty-third most famous person from this tiny, remarkable, beautiful village. Early life in Halifax (Dalhousie,1963); since 1968 Montreal (teach at Dawson College). Wife, Anja, born Netherlands, quadrilingual flight attendant. Son Nicholas, born 1985, exemplary child.

Selected Publications:

Cape Breton is the Thought Control Centre of Canada: Toronto, Anansi, 1969. ISBN 0-88784-402-2
Lord Nelson Tavern: Toronto, McClelland & Stewart, 1974. ISBN 0-7710-8195-2
Century: Toronto, Stoddart, 1986. ISBN 0-7737-5076-2

Awards: New Press Award (Short Fiction), 1985
Comments: "A brilliant stylist . . . *Cape Breton* and *Lord Nelson Tavern* are clearly within the tradition of post-modernist fiction . . . They are elaborately crafted, playful, self-referential." – Constance Rooke, *Oxford Companion to Canadian Literature*
"(A) writer like Ray Smith defies easy categories. There is no critical vocabulary precise enough to describe the forms and functions of his new work." – Lawrence Garber (on *Lord Nelson Tavern*)
"The stories are so different from most Canadian short fiction that they seem like a foreign art film, caught by enjoyable surprise on a rainy afternoon." – Geoff Hancock, *Toronto Star* (on *Century*)
Readings, Lectures & Workshops: A member of The Montreal Storytellers (with Blais, Fraser, Hood and Metcalf). Readings across Canada, in the U.S. and in Europe.
Mailing Address: c/o TWUC, 24 Ryerson Avenue, Toronto, Ontario M5T 2P3

BARBARA C. SMUCKER

 Born in Newton, Kansas, in 1915. Educated at the State University in journalism and English. As a newspaper reporter, met and married Donovan Smucker, Mennonite minister and professor. Three children. Moved to Canada in 1969. Became children's librarian at Kitchener (Ontario) Public Library and later a reference librarian at Renison College, Waterloo. Wrote for newspapers, periodicals and an encyclopedia until I published my first juvenile fiction in 1955.

Selected Publications:

Henry's Red Sea: Scottsdale, Herald, 1955. ISBN 0-8361-1372-1
Wigwam in the City: New York, Dutton, 1966. (no ISBN)
Underground to Canada: Toronto, Clarke Irwin, 1977. ISBN 0-7720-1111-7
Days of Terror: Toronto, Clarke Irwin, 1979. ISBN 0-7720-1280-6
Amish Adventure: Toronto, Clarke Irwin, 1983. ISBN 0-7720-1391-8
White Mist: Toronto, Irwin, 1985. ISBN 0-7725-1542-5

Awards: Canada Council Children's Literature Award, 1980. Ruth Schwartz Award, 1980. All-Japan Juvenile Book Review Contest, Tokyo, 1981. Doctor of Letters, University of Waterloo, May 1986.

Comments: My books have been translated into seven languages.

Readings, Lectures & Workshops: Have given workshops and lectures on children's literature at teachers' conferences in Hamilton, Halifax, Calgary and Philadelphia.

Mailing Address: 57 McDougall Road, Waterloo, Ontario N2L 2W4

LOLA SNEYD

A poet, short-story writer and journalist who grew up in the West but has been a Torontonian for many years. A former public-health nurse, I have written about and for all ages. I enjoy working with children and adults, encouraging them to be creative. Memberships: Canadian Authors Association (president, Toronto Branch 1978-80, 1982; national vice-president [Ont.] 1980-82), Canadian Society of Children's Authors, Illustrators and Performers (Recording Secretary, 1980-82).

Selected Publications:

The Asphalt Octopus: Toronto, Simon & Pierre, 1983. ISBN 0-88924-130-9
The Concrete Giraffe: Toronto, Simon & Pierre, 1984. ISBN 0-88924-140-6
Ringette is Fun: Cobalt, Highway Book Shop, 1985. ISBN 0-88954-331-9
Nature's Big Top: Toronto, Simon & Pierre, 1987. ISBN 0-88924-200-3

Awards: Lyn Harrington Award, Canadian Authors Association, 1983
Comments: "Originality of perceptions augmented by a keen sense of humour." – Gudrun Wright, *Canadian Materials*
"Gives age-old themes a fresh and newly minted flavour." – Helen M. Dobie, *Canadian Book Review Annual*
Readings, Lectures & Workshops: Have taught creative writing and writing for children to students (in elementary and high schools as well as in university) and adult groups in Ontario and Alberta. Book through TWUC.
Mailing Address: 7 Wheeler Avenue, Toronto, Ontario M4L 3V3

GLEN SORESTAD

I was born in Vancouver in 1937 but have lived most of my life in Saskatchewan. I taught school in Saskatoon until 1981 when I quit to write full time. A founder of Thistledown Press in 1975, I remain active in its publishing activities. I hold an M.Ed. from the University of Saskatchewan. I have lived in Saskatoon with my wife, Sonia, and our four children since 1967.

Selected Publications:

Pear Seed in My Mouth: Windsor, Sesame, 1977. ISBN 0-9690464-9-9
Ancestral Dances: Saskatoon, Thistledown, 1979. ISBN 0-920066-25-9
Jan Lake Poems: Madeira Park, Harbour, 1984. ISBN 0-920080-82-0
Hold the Rain in Your Hands: Moose Jaw, Coteau, 1985. ISBN 0-919926-41-X

Comments: "In national terms Glen Sorestad may seem peripheral; he is not mentioned in the Oxford Companion; he does not appear in Atwood's New Oxford Book of Canadian Verse. But he has a name in his own region, and what he produces is regional writing near its best." – *Canadian Literature*
"Sorestad presents a photo album of Alberta and Saskatchewan with the viscera and sprirt still intact. I understand his Canadians better than my own neighbours." – Nancy Lenau, *Pocket Poetry #10* (Florida)
Readings, Lectures & Workshops: Read regularly in schools, colleges and universities across Canada and the U.S. Conduct workshops in poetry, short fiction and publishing. May be booked directly or through TWUC.
Mailing Address: 668 East Place, Saskatoon, Saskatchewan S7J 2Z5

MURRAY SOUPCOFF

Born in Toronto, February 15, 1943. Education: B.A., M.A., Phil. M., University of Toronto. Former writer and producer with the CBC. Founding partner of Ian Sone & Associates and former senior associate of The Sutcliffe Group. Contributing writer to several computing publications, including Epson Today, Epsonlink, Lifeboat and Canada Computes. Currently living in Toronto with wife, Bonnie, and greatest kid in the world, daughter Marni.

Selected Publications:

Good Buy Canada: (with Gary Dunford and Rick Salutin), Toronto, Lorimer, 1975. ISBN 0-88862-089-6
Canada 1984: Toronto, Lester & Orpen Dennys, 1979.

Comments: "Satire – biting, blatant – but never blase." – *The Albertan*
"Resembles less the inspired grotesquerie of Monty Python than the good-natured nastiness of that wonderful English rag, Private Eye." – *Toronto Star*
"Satire is alive and well in Canada." – *Globe and Mail*
"A brilliant spoof." – Peter C. Newman, *Maclean's*
"Managed to almost succeed in producing the impossible, a book that's not only undeniably Canadian, but funny as well." – *Quill & Quire*
"It's a funny book. A very funny book. And interesting and topical to boot." – *Windsor Star*
"The best satire always cuts to the bone . . . Let's hear it for Murray Soupcoff." – *Skyword*
Mailing Address: 79 Castle Knock Road, Toronto, Ontario M5N 2J8

EDNA STAEBLER

Born in Kitchener, Ontario, now living at Sunfish Lake, near Waterloo. B.A. Toronto, 1929; Ontario College of Education, 1931. Married Keith Staebler; divorced 1962. Member: Toronto Heliconian Club, Toronto Women's Press Club, Media Club of Canada, Canadian Authors Association for 23 years. Trustee Kitchener Library Board. Past president Kitchener-Waterloo Women's Canadian Club and K-W Confederation of University Women.

Selected Publications:

Food That Really Schmecks: Toronto, Ryerson, 1968. ISBN 07-077392-0
Sauerkraut and Enterprise: Toronto, McClelland & Stewart, 1969.
   ISBN 0-7710-8298-4
Cape Breton Harbour: Toronto, McClelland & Stewart, 1972. ISBN 0-7710-8288-6
More Food That Really Schmecks: Toronto, McClelland & Stewart, 1979.
   ISBN 0-7710-8295-9
Whatever Happened to Maggie: Toronto, McClelland & Stewart, 1983.
   ISBN 0-7710-8299-1

Comments: "Edna Staebler shares in the ability of great writers to universalize the particular. During her twenty years as a magazine writer her careful and artistic articulations of the quality of life in smaller communities from coast to coast have been quoted in scholarly articles throughout the Commonwealth. She has been justly commended for her 'wit, warmth and insight.' When she is not traveling she lives in a cottage at Sunfish Lake where she reads, writes, swims and feeds hundreds of birds, two cats and many friends." – Honorary L.L.D. citation, Wilfrid Laurier University

Readings, Lectures & Workshops: Read and speak at many luncheons, dinners, banquets, workshops, universities, libraries, art galleries, secondary and elementary schools etc. Arranged directly.

Mailing Address: RR 3, Waterloo, Ontario N2J 3Z4

SARA STAMBAUGH

I was born and raised in Lancaster County, Pennsylvania. I received my B.A. from Beaver College in Philadelphia and my M.A. and Ph.D. from the University of Minnesota. From 1966 to 1969 I taught at Towson State College in Baltimore. Since then, I have lived in Edmonton, where I teach English at the University of Alberta.

Selected Publications:

I Hear the Reaper's Song: Intercourse, Good Books, 1984. ISBN 0-934672-24-5 (Distributed by Raincoast)

Comments: "A beautifully told lesson for the contemporary reader in how any community adapts to a changing world, and how values endure." – *Publishers Weekly*

"A fine performance by a writer of considerable ability and accomplishment." – George Core, *Washington Post*

"An historical novel with deep personal resonance, it is a model for the value of the past in each of our lives." – Jane Rule, *Herizons*

"A quiet achievement, a pastoral novel that rings true." – Alberto Manguel, *Books in Canada*

"Stambaugh's touch is sure: her narrative is without flab; . . . her account of the central event is riveting." – John Moore, *Quill & Quire*

"A novel for sleepwalkers. I would have thought it unpublishable; it was for me, with its one-note technique, close to unreadable." – Leon Rooke, *Books in Canada*

I Hear the Reaper's Song was shortlisted for the Books in Canada First Novel Award. Verse, stories and articles have appeared in Descant, Fiddlehead, Event, Dandelion, Nineteenth-Century Fiction, Mosaic, Scandinavica.

Mailing Address: Dept. of English, University of Alberta, Edmonton, Alberta T6G 2E5

JOHN STARNES

Born in Montreal, February 5, 1918. Bishop's University B.A. 1939. Canadian Army 1939-44; Canadian delegate to U.N. 1948-50; NATO Secretariat 1956-58; Canadian ambassador to UAR and Sudan 1966-67; Assistant Under Secretary External Affairs 1967-70; Director General, RCMP Service 1970-73; Council, International Institute Strategic Studies, London, 1977-85; Director, Themadel Foundation of New Brunswick since 1980.

Selected Publications:

Deep Sleepers: Ottawa, Balmuir, 1981. ISBN 0-919511-04-X
Scarab: Ottawa, Balmuir, 1982. ISBN 0-919511-11-2
Orion's Belt: Ottawa, Balmuir, 1983. ISBN 0-919511-17-1
The Cornish Hug: Ottawa, Balmuir, 1985. ISBN 0-919511-29-5

Awards: Bishop's University, DCL (Honoris Causa), 1975.
Comments: "Take a pinch of George Smiley, a little bit of 'M', a soupcon of *Tinker, Tailor, Soldier, Spy* and you're still a long way from catching the flavour of John Starnes, Canada's best-known ex-spymaster." – Val Sears, *Toronto Star*
"Starnes raises the spy thriller's focus from the spooks and shadows to the chess master's manoeuvres." – Burt Heward, *Ottawa Citizen*
Mailing Address: Apt. 9-100 Rideau Terrace, Ottawa, Ontario K1M 0Z2

TED STAUNTON

Born, raised and still living in Toronto, I did my B.A. and B.Ed. at, you guessed it, the University of Toronto, where I also wrote my first book. At various times a teacher, musician, worker in children's programmes and civil servant, I now combine writing with readings and workshops in schools and libraries.

Selected Publications:

Puddleman: Toronto, Kids Can, 1983. ISBN 0-919964-51-6
Taking Care of Crumley: Toronto, Kids Can, 1984. ISBN 0-919964-55-9
Simon's Surprise: Toronto, Kids Can, 1986. ISBN 0-919964-97-4
Maggie and Me: Toronto, Kids Can, 1986. ISBN 0-921103-00-X

Readings, Lectures & Workshops: Readings for grades K to eight that combine stories, music, imagining and a question-and-answer session with manuscripts, proofs, art, etc. Available through TWUC. Workshops (four sessions, one per week) for grades four to eight. Students write stories, peer edit and create their own books.
Mailing Address: 46 Ward Street, Port Hope, Ontario L1A 1A5

J.J. STEINFELD

Short-story writer, novelist and playwright living in Charlottetown, Prince Edward Island. A former teacher with a B.A. from Case Western Reserve University in Ohio and an M.A. from Trent University in Ontario, I abandoned graduate school after two years in a Ph.D. programme at the University of Ottawa, and in 1980 moved to P.E.I., where I have lived and written ever since.

Selected Publications:

The Apostate's Tattoo: Charlottetown, Ragweed, 1983. ISBN 0-920304-28-1
Our Hero in the Cradle of Confederation: Porters Lake, Pottersfield, 1987.
  ISBN 0-919001-37-8

Awards: Norma Epstein Award, 1979. Okanagan Short Fiction Award from Canadian Author and Bookman, 1984. Great Canadian Novella Competition, 1986. Theatre Prince Edward Island's Playwriting Competition, First Prize, 1984,85,86; Second Prize, 1985,87.

Comments: "Steinfeld has a gift for humour, wit, and ironic social comment which is rare in our fiction . . . His stories show . . . that he sees the absurdities of life, and understands the jokes that fate plays on almost everyone." – Miriam Waddington, *Canadian Literature*

"He's a competent craftsman with a rich imagination, obsessively recording every experience touching him . . . Blessed with an imagination as dark as Franz Kafka's." – Sharon Drache, *Globe and Mail*

"The writing is brisk, assured, fresh . . . These are profound stories about complex situations." – Veronica Ross, *Books in Canada* (on *The Apostate's Tattoo*)

Mailing Address: Apt. 28, 1 Harbourside, Charlettetown, Prince Edward Island C1A 8R4

FRED STENSON

Born in Pincher Creek, Alberta, in 1951. Raised on a farm in the Waterton area. Received a B.A. in economics from the University of Calgary in 1972. Live and work in Calgary as a full-time freelance writer.

Selected Publications:

Lonesome Hero: Toronto, Macmillan, 1974. ISBN 0-7705-1173-2
Three Times Five: Edmonton, NeWest Press, 1984. ISBN 0-920316-86-7
Waste to Wealth: Calgary, C.G.P.A., 1985. ISBN 0-88925-583-0
Rocky Mountain House: Toronto, NC Press, 1985. ISBN 0-920053-48-3
Alberta Bound: (ed.), Edmonton, NeWest, 1986. ISBN 0-920897-04-5

Awards: Canadian Authors Association Silver Medal (Fiction), 1975. Alberta Motion Picture Industry Association Award, 1984.

Comments: "The finest novel about alienation and growing up to appear in some time." – *Canadian Author & Bookman* (on *Lonesome Hero*)

"There is a warmth and reality in all Stenson's stories." – Janice Macdonald, *Edmonton Journal*

Readings, Lectures & Workshops: Readings to adult audiences as well as junior and senior high schools; workshops; college and library residencies.

Mailing Address: c/o TWUC, 24 Ryerson Avenue, Toronto, Ontario M5T 2P3

MARYLEE STEPHENSON

Combine a professional career as a sociologist specialising in women's studies with a very active parallel vocation as an amateur natural historian, bird watcher, nature photographer and research consultant in recreational and environmental issues. I have written the only guide to Canada's National Parks, which includes nearly 200 of my own photographs. I travel extensively and have written on my experiences in the Galapagos Islands, Cuba and – most recently – the Okefenokee Swamp.

Selected Publications:

Canada's National Parks (A Visitor's Guide): Toronto, Prentice-Hall, 1983.
  ISBN 0-13-113977-0

Comments: "Thorough and well presented; a necessity for travel writers, conservationists and tourists." – Margaret Atwood
"Whether for amateur botanists or birders, hikers or the casual visitor to our National Parks, there's something here for everyone. An overdue, and most useful introduction." – Graeme Gibson
"Contains the nuts-and-bolts information that park visitors need . . . is extremely handy . . . a worthwhile investment for anyone planning to visit several of the parks over the next few years . . . She is an enthusiastic writer with a good feel for nature . . . " – Ian Darragh, *Quill and Quire*
(*Canada's National Parks* has been published in French, by Editions du Trecarre, and in German, by Conrad Stein Verlag.)
Readings, Lectures & Workshops: Have appeared regularly on radio to discuss the National Parks and other nature-related topics. Frequent guest speaker, with slide presentation, for associations, universities, etc. Contact at mailing address.
Mailing Address: 171 Dalhousie, Ottawa, Ontario K1N 7C7

HILARY STEWART

Born in St. Lucia, West Indies, November 3, 1924, mainly educated in England. Four years in the WAAF. Graduated from St. Martin's School of Art, London. Came to Canada in 1951, discovered the west coast, loved it, moved there. Worked 16 years in TV design, gave it up to write and illustrate a major book on coast archaeology – my first love – and never looked back. Live in Vancouver; write, illustrate and lecture on early Northwest Indian art and culture, full time.

Selected Publications:

Indian Artifacts of the Northwest Coast: Seattle, University of Washington Press, 1973. ISBN 0-88894-332-6

Indian Fishing (Early Methods on the Northwest Coast): Vancouver, J.J. Douglas, 1977. ISBN 0-88894-332-6

Robert Davidson, Haida Printmaker: Vancouver, Douglas & McIntyre, 1979. ISBN 0-88894-242-7

Looking at Indian Art of the Northwest Coast: Vancouver, Douglas & McIntyre, 1981. ISBN 0-88894-229-X

Cedar (Tree of Life to the Northwest Coast Indians): Vancouver, Douglas & McIntyre, 1987. ISBN 0-88894-437-3

John R. Jewitt, Captive of Maquinna: Vancouver, Douglas & McIntyre, 1987. ISBN 0-88894-554-X

Awards: Pacific Northwest Booksellers Award, 1980. British Columbia Book Prizes (two), 1985.

Comments: "Stewart finds her way close to the centre of the old life, and she takes the reader along." – *Scientific American*

Readings, Lectures & Workshops: Frequently give lectures, workshops and demonstrations of native technologies.

Mailing Address: 2986 Point Grey Road, Vancouver, British Columbia V6K 1B1

KATHY STINSON

 Toronto born and raised. Former elementary-school teacher and instructor of pre-school programmes. Mother of two; my children often appear in my books. Red Is Best and Big or Little? were two of the first books published in Canada for pre-schoolers. Now earn my living in Toronto as a full-time writer of books for children of all ages.

Selected Publications:

Red Is Best: (with Robin Baird Lewis), Toronto, Annick, 1982. ISBN 0-920236-24-3
Big Or Little?: Toronto, Annick, 1983. ISBN 0-920236-30-8
Mom and Dad Don't Live Together Any More: (with Nancy Lou Reynolds), Toronto, Annick, 1984. ISBN 0-920236-92-8
Those Green Things: (with Mary McLoughlin), Toronto, Annick, 1985. ISBN 0-920303-40-4
The Bare Naked Book: (with Heather Collins), Toronto, Annick, 1986. ISBN 0-920303-52-8

Awards: IODE Award
Comments: "Either has a total recall for her own early years or else she is a sensitive observer of toddler behaviour." – *Quill & Quire*
"Perfect book on . . . human dignity, humour, self-reliance, thoughtfulness, and the struggle of a young child to see where he fits into the world . . . 250 words well spent." – *Mudpie*
Readings, Lectures & Workshops: May be booked through TWUC.
Mailing Address: c/o TWUC, 24 Ryerson Avenue, Toronto, Ontario M5T 2P3

GERTRUDE STORY

Saskatchewan born, September 19, 1929 (A Year of the Snake). I consider cute and clever biographies interesting but unessential. Dislike writing; have a passion for the search for spirit. Was invaded by Joan of Arc voices some years ago but refused to ride off on a white charger to save Saskatchewan for my monarch. Penance: take dictation from The Writer Inside for nine more ("holy") years.

Selected Publications:

The Book of Thirteen: Saskatoon, Thistledown, 1981. ISBN 0-920066-52-6
The Way to Always Dance: Saskatoon, Thistledown, 1983. ISBN 0-920066-66-6
It Never Pays to Laugh Too Much: Saskatoon, Thistledown, 1984. ISBN 0-920066-86-0
The Need of Wanting Always: Saskatoon, Thistledown, 1985. ISBN 0-920633-00-5
Black Swan: Saskatoon, Thistledown, 1986. ISBN 0-920633-20-X

Awards: CBC Literary Competition (Short Fiction), 1980. President's Medal, University of Saskatchewan, 1981.

Comments: "There is more intensity and undiluted meaning in these short 130 pages than there is in most 500-page blockbusters. It is a terrific story, and well told." – *Arts Manitoba*

Readings, Lectures & Workshops: A "charismatic" teacher, reader, lecturer, after-dinner speaker. School visits a specialty. Love rural audiences. Book directly, or through TWUC or through Thistledown.

Mailing Address: 203-2218C St. Charles Avenue, Saskatoon, Saskatchewan S7M 5A7

JUDY STUBBS

I was born on March 4, 1949, the youngest of four girls, in Hamilton, Ontario. After graduating from Hamilton Teachers College in 1968, I moved to Guelph where I still reside with my husband and two children. I spend my summers at the family cottage in Honey Harbour where I find reading and writing science fiction and fantasy books for young adults very exciting.

Selected Publications:

Giants from the Sky: Ottawa, Borealis, 1980. ISBN 0-88887-067-1
Terror of the Cocoons: Ottawa, Borealis, 1983. ISBN 0-88887-960-1

Mailing Address: 1 Stirling Place, Guelph, Ontario N1H 6W1

PETER SUCH

Poetry begins it; novels carry it through; screen-writing, drama, opera keep me in touch with the vital Canadian creative world. I live on the Island, the last anarchist, tribal community in North America. I'm 47.

Selected Publications:

Fallout: Toronto, Anansi, 1968. (reprinted by NC Press, Toronto, 1977. ISBN 0-919600-96-4)
Soundprints: Toronto, Clarke Irwin, 1972. ISBN 0-7720-0564-8
Riverrun: Toronto, Clarke Irwin, 1973. ISBN 0-7720-1010-3
Vanished Peoples: Toronto, NC Press, 1978. ISBN 0-919600-84-0
Dolphins Wake: Toronto, Macmillan, 1981.

Comments: "It is one of the best novels to come out of Canada – or anywhere – in some time and establishes Peter Such as one of the best creative writers we have." – *Calgary Herald*
"Hauntingly powerful, totally absorbing." – *Canadian Reader*
"A truly fine book, skilfully sensuous, insightful and unfalteringly rhythmic." – *London Free Press*
"A psychological thriller of great depth and power." – *Globe and Mail*
"One of the four best novels written in Canada." – *Toronto Star*
See entries in *Oxford Companion to Canadian Literature*, *Dictionary of Literary Biography* and *ACTRA Screenwriters' Guide (Who's Who in Film)*.
Mailing Address: 14 4th Street, Wards Island, Toronto, Ontario M5J 2B5

ROSEMARY SULLIVAN

Born in Montreal, August 29, 1947. Now living in Toronto. B.A. McGill; Ph.D. University of Sussex. Lived in Europe seven years; academic post in France; also taught in India. Travelled throughout Latin America. Co-ordinated The Writer and Human Rights Conference (1981) in aid of Amnesty International. Currently teach English at the University of Toronto.

Selected Publications:

Theodore Roethke (The Garden Master): Seattle, University of Washington Press, 1975. ISBN 0-295-95429-9

Elements of Fiction (Canadian Edition): (ed. with Robert Scholes), Oxford, 1982, 1986. ISBN 0-19-540539-0

The Pool in the Dessert (Sara Jeannette Duncan): (ed.), Toronto, Penguin, 1984. ISBN 0-14-007457-0

Stories by Canadian Women: (ed.), Toronto, Oxford, 1984. ISBN 0-19-540468-8

The Space a Name Makes: Windsor, Black Moss, 1986. ISBN 01-87437-147-4

Comments: "Lean vigorous work with the colloquial directness of a documentary film . . . a poet who bears watching." – *Books in Canada* (on *The Space a Name Makes*)

"Poems are accessible, firmly rooted in landscape, in the Amazon gathering orchids or watching crazies on Bloor Street." – *Kingston Whig Standard*

Readings, Lectures & Workshops: Lectured on modern literature in universities in Canada, the U.S., Britain, France, Puerto Rico and India. Workshop in Canadian literature, University of Karnataka, six weeks, 1982.

Mailing Address: 665 Manning Avenue, Toronto, Ontario M6G 2W3

MERNA SUMMERS

I grew up on a farm in Alberta, worked for eight years as a reporter for the Edmonton Journal and did freelance journalism and radio work before turning to fiction.

Selected Publications:

The Skating Party: Ottawa, Oberon, 1974. ISBN 0-88750-123-0
Calling Home: Ottawa, Oberon, 1982. ISBN 0-88750-448-5

Awards: Writers Guild of Alberta Award for Short Fiction, 1982. Katherine Anne Porter Award for Fiction, 1979. Ohio State Award for Educational Broadcasting, 1968.

Comments: Forthcoming: North of the Battle, a collection of short fiction (Douglas & McIntrye).

Mailing Address: 14615 - 91 Avenue, Edmonton, Alberta T5R 4Y7

SUSAN SWAN

A novelist, poet, journalist, critic, playwright and performance artist, my work includes the theatre piece Queen of the Silver Blades, an examination of the adulation of Barbara Ann Scott; Down and In, a performance on self-pity; and True Confessions of the Female Organs. My novel, *The Biggest Modern Woman of the World*, was a 1983 Governor General's Award finalist.

Selected Publications:

Unfit for Paradise: Toronto, Dingle Editions, 1982. ISBN 0-9690923-0-X
The Biggest Modern Woman of the World: Toronto, Lester & Orpen Dennys, 1983. ISBN 0-88619-043-6

Awards: National Magazine Award (Silver, Fiction), 1977. Books in Canada First Novel Award (Finalist), 1985.
Comments: I teach fiction and interdisciplinary art at York University.
Readings, Lectures & Workshops: I teach for a living and have travelled extensively, giving talks and performances in Canada and the U.S. (New York, Detroit, Calgary, Halifax, Charlottetown et al.).
Mailing Address: 21 Bellwoods Avenue, Toronto, Ontario M6J 2P5

CAROLYN SWAYZE

Born in Grimsby, Ontario, March 10, 1945. Moved to the British Columbia interior in 1953. Married to C.J. Moyer 1961-1985; children, David (1963) and Natalie (1967). Left school at 15 to work as a waitress, secretary, jail matron, advertising sales rep, counselling co-ordinator, employment counsellor, columnist, freelance writer and perpetual student. Graduated from the University of Victoria (1984) with a law degree, failed to become bilingual and settled down to write in White Rock, B.C., a small seaside town.

Selected Publications:

The Secret of Bourke's Mansion: (wa Carolyn Moyer), New York, Bavregy, 1977. ISBN 0-685-75642-4
Hard Choices (A Life of Tom Berger): Vancouver, Douglas & McIntyre, 1987. ISBN 0-88894-522-1

Comments: Short fiction and essays (as Carolyn Moyer) contributed to A Room of One's Own, Readers' Choice, Happenings!, Western Producer and The Advocate. Work in progress: Hawk Mountain, a prison novel. Represented by the Bella Pomer Agency, Toronto.
   Mailing Address: 14889 Beach View Avenue, White Rock, British Columbia V4B 1N8

GEORGE SWEDE

Born November 20, 1940. B.A., University of British Columbia, 1964. M.A., Dalhousie University, 1965. Teacher of psychology at Ryerson Polytechnical Institute in Toronto since 1968. Publications include more than 30 books and appearances in almost 500 periodicals. Formerly on the executive of Canadian Society of Children's Authors, Illustrators and Performers and now an editor for Writers' Quarterly.

Selected Publications:

Tell-Tale Feathers: Fredericton, Fiddlehead, 1978. ISBN 0-920110-56-8
A Snowman, Headless: Fredericton, Fiddlehead, 1979. ISBN 0-920110-84-3
Missing Heirloom: Toronto, Three Trees, 1980. ISBN 0-88823-027-3
Downhill Theft, Toronto: Toronto, Three Trees, 1982. ISBN 0-88823-049-4
Night Tides: London, Southwest Ont. Poetry, 1984. ISBN 0-919139-19-1
Dudley and the Birdman: Toronto, Three Trees, 1985. ISBN 0-88823-102-4
High Wire Spider: Toronto, Three Trees, 1986. ISBN 0-88823-111-3

> **Comments:** "Crystal clear, sensible, but magical too." – *Toronto Star*
> "Superbly evocative poems." – *Canadian Children's Literature*
> "Wonderful, upbeat." – *The Reviewing Librarian*
> "Versatile and inventive." – *The New York Times*
> **Readings, Lectures & Workshops:** Regularly give readings in schools, public libraries and other venues. Also conduct writing workshops. Book through TWUC.
> **Mailing Address:** Box 279, Station P, Toronto, Ontario M5S 2S8

ALASTAIR SWEENY

Born in Toronto, August 15, 1946. Attended St. Andrew's College, University of Toronto (B.A.); Trinity College, Dublin (Ph.D.). Freelance writer, researcher, editor and consultant. Recent clients: Peter C. Newman, Richard Gwyn, Jeffery Simpson, Douglas Fullerton, David Slater. Also Magna International, Sony of Canada, Business Council on National Issues, Ministry of International Trade, Carleton University, Public Archives of Canada. Tel: (613) 828-5235

Selected Publications:

George-Etienne Cartier (A Biography): Toronto, McClelland & Stewart, 1976. ISBN 0-7710-8363-7

Canadians All: Toronto, Methuen, 1986. ISBN 0-458-80030-9

Mailing Address: Box 2821, Station D, Ottawa, Ontario K1P 5W8

GEORGE SZANTO

Born in Northern Ireland in 1940, educated in the U.S., France and Germany, and came to Canada in 1974. Ph.D. from Harvard University in comparative literature. Chairman, Playwrights Canada, 1980-81. At McGill University, professor of comparative literature and communications.

Selected Publications:

Narrative Consciousness: Austin, University of Texas Press, 1972. ISBN 0-292-75500-7

After the Ceremony: Toronto, Playwrights Canada, 1978. ISBN 0-88754-112-7

Sixteen Ways to Skin a Cat: Vancouver, Intermedia, 1978. ISBN 0-88956-042-0

Theater and Propaganda: Austin, University of Texas Press, 1978. ISBN 0-292-78020-6

Not Working: Toronto, Macmillan, 1983. ISBN 0-312-57962-4

Narrative Taste and Social Perspective (The Matter of Quality): New York, St. Martin's, 1986. ISBN 0-312-55934-8

Comments: "Szantos handles literary problems with real virtuosity." – *New York Times* (on *Not Working*)

"It has a wonderfully literate surface, and its perfect pacing gives it real emotional impact." – *Books in Canada*

"A brilliant, provocative and important book." – *World Literature Today* (on *Theatre and Propaganda*)

"A masterly reading, uniformly clarifying and helpful." – *Modern Fiction Studies* (on *Narrative Consciousness*)

Readings, Lectures & Workshops: May be booked through TWUC.

Mailing Address: c/o TWUC, 24 Ryerson Avenue, Toronto, Ontario M5T 2P3

CHARLES TAYLOR

Born in Toronto, February 13, 1935. B.A., Queen's University, 1955. As a journalist, worked in some 50 countries for the Toronto Telegram, Reuters, the CBC, the Globe and Mail. Contributor to numerous magazines and journals. President, Windfields Farm Limited. Past chairman, The Writers' Union of Canada.

Selected Publications:

Reporter in Red China: New York, Random House, 1966. (no ISBN)

Snow Job (Canada, the United States and Vietnam, 1954-1973): Toronto, Anansi, 1974. ISBN 0-88784-619-X

Six Journeys (A Canadian Pattern): Toronto, Anansi, 1977. ISBN 0-88784-057-4

Radical Tories (The Conservative Tradition in Canada): Toronto, Anansi, 1982. ISBN 0-88784-096-5

China Hands (The Globe and Mail in Peking): (ed.), Toronto, McClelland & Stewart, 1984. ISBN 0-7710-8436-6

Mailing Address: 208 Heath Street West, Toronto, Ontario M4V 1V5

LEONARD WILFRED TAYLOR

Born in London, England. Canadian resident since 1913. Reporter, sports editor, Woodstock (Ont.) Sentinel Review 1927-41. Canadian Army 1941-45. Senior Canadian field press censor SHAEF 1944-45. Reporter, editorial writer, Kitchener-Waterloo Record 1946-68. Sports editor 1951-62. Reporter, business writer, editorial writer, Vancouver Province 1968-76. Public relations account executive (MacFarland, Morris, Peacock) Vancouver 1977-83. Canadian correspondent for Stadion (Prague) and Le Semaine Sportif (Geneva). Married; five children.

Selected Publications:

Vertical Ascent: (with Charles O. Weir), Saanichton, Hancock, 1977.
    ISBN 0-919654-74-2
The Sourdough and the Queen: Toronto, Methuen, 1983. ISBN 0-458-96810-2

Comments: Recently completed two manuscripts, Passed as Censored and Days of Real Sport. Former president, Ontario Sports Writers and Sportscasters Association.

Mailing Address: 202-1368 Foster Street, White Rock, British Columbia V4B 3X4

BARBARA THAL-HODES

I came to Canada from the United States in 1973 and became a citizen. I have worked at the Royal Ontario Museum, at a Jewish day school and for Grolier. My book, *Puzzling Canada*, was published in 1979. A short story, Bonded, appeared in Room of One's Own in 1982. I have travelled in Ontario, Quebec and New Brunswick giving programmes based on my book. I live in Toronto with my husband and three sons.

Selected Publications:

Puzzling Canada: Toronto, Dundurn, 1979. ISBN 0-919670-45-8

   Comments: "No one can make Canadian history as interesting and exciting as Barbara can." – *Oshawa Times*
   "*Puzzling Canada*, a book that makes learning about Canada fun."
– *Book Times*, The Children's Book Centre
   Readings, Lectures & Workshops: Workshops in creative ways to learn and write about Canadian history for children in grades three to ten and adults in or out of the field of education.
   Mailing Address: 21 Glencedar Road, Toronto, Ontario M6C 3E9

AUDREY G. THOMAS

 Born in Binghamton, New York, in 1935. B.A., Smith College, M.A., University of British Columbia. Three daughters: Sarah, Victoria and Claire. Immigrated to Canada, August 1959. Canadian citizen. Member of PEN, Amnesty International and the North Galiano Community Association. Write novels, stories and radio plays. Writer-in-residence, Concordia, Simon Fraser University, David Thompson University Centre and the University of Ottawa.

Selected Publications:

Mrs. Blood: Vancouver, Talon, 1970. ISBN 0-88922-079-4
Blown Figures: Vancouver, Talon, 1974. ISBN 0-88922-074-3
Ladies and Escorts: Ottawa, Oberon, 1977. ISBN 0-88750-219-9
Ten Green Bottles: Ottawa, Oberon, 1977. ISBN 0-88750-215-6
Latakia: Vancouver, Talon, 1979. ISBN 0-88922-167-7
Two in the Bush and Other Stories: Toronto, McClelland & Stewart, 1981. ISBN 0-7710-9306-3
Real Mothers: Vancouver, Talon, 1982. ISBN 0-88922-191-X
Intertidal Life: Toronto, Stoddart, 1984. ISBN 0-7737-2028-6
Goodbye Harold, Good Luck: Toronto, Penguin, 1986. ISBN 0-670-81058-4

Awards: CBC Literary Competition (two, Seconds). National Magazine Award Chatelaine Literary Competition. Canada-Scotland Literary Fellow.

Readings, Lectures & Workshops: Extensive readings and workshops throughout Canada and in Great Britain, Scandinavia, Holland and elsewhere.

Mailing Address: RR 2, Galiano, British Columbia V0N 1P0

CLARA THOMAS

Born in Strathroy, Ontario, in 1919. Educated at the University of Western Ontario B.A. 1941, M.A. 1944 University of Toronto, Ph.D., 1962. Professor emeritus, York, since 1984, before that at York since 1961. Married Morley Thomas, 1942. Two sons, Stephen and John.

Selected Publications:

Canadian Novelists, 1920-1945: Toronto, Longmans, 1946. (no ISBN)
Love and Work Enough (The Life of Anna Jameson): Toronto, University of Toronto Press, 1967. (no ISBN)
Margaret Laurence: Toronto, McClelland & Stewart, 1969. (no ISBN)
Ryerson of Upper Canada: Toronto, Ryerson, 1969. ISBN 0-7700-0268-4
Our Nature Our Voices: Toronto, New Press, 1972. (no ISBN)
The Manawaka World of Margaret Laurence: Toronto, McClelland & Stewart, 1975. ISBN 0-7710-9231-8
William Arthur Deacon (A Canadian Literary Life): (with John Lennox), Toronto, University of Toronto Press, 1982. ISBN 0-8020-5593-1

Awards: Fellow Royal Society of Canada. D.Litt., York University, 1986.
Mailing Address: c/o TWUC, 24 Ryerson Avenue, Toronto, Ontario M5T 2P3

KENT THOMPSON

I usually live in Fredericton, New Brunswick, where I teach at the university and write short stories and novels and sometimes radio plays and commentary for the CBC.

Selected Publications:

The Tenants Were Corrie and Tennie: Toronto, Macmillan, 1973.
ISBN 0-7705-1001-9
Across from the Floral Park: New York, St. Martin's, 1974.
Shotgun and Other Stories: Fredericton, NB Chapbooks, 1979.
ISBN 0-920084-04-4
Shaking Up: Ottawa, Oberon, 1980. ISBN 0-88750-375-6
A Local Hanging: Fredericton, Goose Lane, 1984. ISBN 0-86492-037-7
Leaping Up Sliding Away: Fredericton, Goose Lane, 1986. ISBN 0-86492-080-6

Awards: CBC Literary Competition (Second Prize, Short Story), 1981
Comments: Everything pertains and no one escapes.
"Thompson observes . . . self-deceptions and cravings and the stunted spirits of all his characters with great compassion . . . " – *John Mills*, Simon Fraser University
Readings, Lectures & Workshops: Read frequently at universities and high schools; lead workshops in creative writing.
Mailing Address: Dept. of English, University of New Brunswick, Fredericton, New Brunswick E3B 5A3

MARK THURMAN

Born in Toronto, September 27, 1948. Still live there. Illustrator, author, painter and teacher. Member of Canadian Society of Children's Authors, Illustrators and Performers and ACTRA. Went to Toronto Island School, Lord Dufferin Public School and Central Technical High School. Wanted to be an artist from age six, thought I was an artist at ten, became a professional artist at 18, didn't know what an artist was at 28, still not sure at 38.

Selected Publications:

All books published in Toronto by NC Press

The Elephant's Cold: 1979. ISBN 0-920053-68-8
The Elephant's New Bicycle: 1980. ISBN 0-920053-66-1
The Lie That Grew and Grew: 1981. ISBN 0-920053-54-8
The Birthday Party: 1981. ISBN 0-920053-56-4
Two Pals on an Adventure: 1981. ISBN 0-920053-52-1
City Scrapes: 1983. ISBN 0-920053-50-5
You Bug Me: 1985. ISBN 0-920053-55-6
Old Friends, New Friends: 1985. ISBN 0-920053-58-0
Two Stupid Dummies: 1986. ISBN 0-920053-94-7
Who Needs Me?: 1981. ISBN 0-919601-58-8
Cabbagetown Gang: 1986. ISBN 0-920053-98-X

   Comments: I recently completed my first juvenile novel, *Cabbage Town Gang*, in which I draw from my childhood in Toronto's Regent Park. I also illustrate and co-author the Mighty Mites adventures in Owl Magazine.
   Readings, Lectures & Workshops: For the past six years, I have been conducting school workshops, encouraging children of all ages to write and illustrate their own picture books.
   Mailing Address: c/o TWUC, 24 Ryerson Avenue, Toronto, Ontario M5T 2P3

EVA TIHANYI

Born in Budapest, Hungary, in 1956 and came
to Canada when I was six. Lived in Windsor,
Ontario, for many years. Completed an M.A. in
English and creative writing at the University
of Windsor in 1978. Have resided for the past
six years in Toronto, where I teach Canadian
literature and business communication at
Seneca College.

Selected Publications:

A Sequence of the Blood: Toronto, Aya, 1983. ISBN 0-920544-29-0
Prophecies Near the Speed of Light: Saskatoon, Thistledown, 1984.
   ISBN 0-920066-84-4

Awards: Cross-Canada Writers' Quarterly Poetry Competition (First Prize),
1985
Comments: "A strong collection and certainly one of the most satisfying
books by a new poet I have read in a long time." – Cathy Matyas (on
Prophecies Near the Speed of Light)
   "Taut and sensually intricate." – Gillian Russell, *Quarry*
   "A promising and interesting book . . ." – Christopher Wiseman,
Canadian Literature
Readings, Lectures & Workshops: Have read in various places across
Canada but readings are currently restricted to Toronto area due to teaching
commitments.
Mailing Address: 68 Appleton Avenue, Toronto, Ontario M6E 3A5

HAMILTON BAIRD TIMOTHY

Born in Irvine, Scotland. M.A. B.D. dist. (Glasgow), B.A. Hons. (London, UK), Ph.D. (Edinburgh), Ph.D. (Saskatchewan). Assistant professor, near eastern languages, and lecturer on the psychology of religion, University College, Winnipeg; associate professor, Classics (philosophy specialist) and resident Galt scholar (University of Western Ontario); on the Faculty of Letters: research assistant to Professor Dr. C.J. de Vogel, at the Filosofisch Instituut (Utrecht). Professor of Humanities, associate dean of arts and sciences (humanities) and acting head of English department (University of Saskatchewan). Professor of humanities and director of religious studies (University of Regina).

Selected Publications:

The Early Christian Apologists and Greek Philisophy: Assen, Netherlands, Van Gorcum, 1973. ISBN 90-232-0979-6

The Tenets of Stoicism (Assembled and Systematised, from the Works of L. Annaeus Seneca): Amsterdam, Hakkert, 1973. ISBN 90-256-0649-0

The Collected Poems of John Galt: (ed.), 2 vols, London & Regina, privately published; 1969 & 1982. (no ISBN)

The Galts (A Canadian Odyssey) (Vol.1) John Galt 1779-1839: Toronto, McClelland & Stewart, 1977. ISBN 0-7710-8457-9. *(Vol. 2) Alexander Tilloch Galt 1850-1928*: Toronto, McClelland & Stewart, 1984. ISBN 0-7710-8454-4

Ukrainian Folk Stories by Marko Vovchok: (ed.), Saskatoon, WP Prairie Books, 1983. ISBN 0-88833-103-7

John Galt, Alexander Tilloch Galt and Elliot Torrance Galt in Canada: Irvine, Irvine Herald Press.

Comments: Now retired from the University of Regina with the rank of professor emeritus of humanities. My research material is now in the University of Guelph archives. Work in progress: The case for the John Galt authorship of The Canadian Boat Song.

Mailing Address: 14282 Vine Avenue, White Rock, British Columbia V4B 2S8

MARIA TIPPETT

Born in Victoria, British Columbia, in 1944; educated at Victoria High, Simon Fraser University (B.A. Honours, History) and University College, University of London (Ph.D.). Have taught as a part-time sessional instructor at Simon Fraser University, the University of British Columbia and The Emily Carr College of Art from 1976-85. Now the Robarts Professor of Canadian Studies at York University for the 1986-87 academic year.

Selected Publications:

From Desolation to Splendour (Changing Perceptions of the British Columbia Landscape): (with Douglas Cole), Toronto, Clarke Irwin, 1977.
Emily Carr (A Biography): Toronto, Oxford, 1979./Penguin, 1982. ISBN 0-14-006457-5
Phillips in Print (Selected Writings of Walter J. Phillips): (with Douglas Cole), Winnipeg, Manitoba Records Society, 1982.
Art at the Service of War (Canada, Art and the Great War): Toronto, University of Toronto Press, 1984. ISBN 0-8020-2541-2

Awards: Eatons' British Columbia Book Award, 1978. Sir John A. Macdonald Prize for Canadian History, 1979. Governor General's Award (Non-fiction), 1979.

Comments: Articles have also been written for such journals as BC Studies, Pacific Northwest Quarterly, Journal of Canadian Art History, The Canadian Collector, Canadian Literature and The Canadian Historical Review.

Readings, Lectures & Workshops: I have lectured extensively in Canada, the U.S. and abroad.

Mailing Address: Bowen Island, British Columbia V0N 1G0

KEN TOLMIE

Born in Halifax, September 18, 1941; graduated with a B.F.A. from Mount Allison University, 1962. Lived and travelled in England and Spain, across Canada from coast to coast. Currently living in Cabbagetown in downtown Toronto. Full-time artist for the past 25 years. Owner of the Tolmie Gallery in Bridgetown, Nova Scotia. Work held in the National Gallery of Canada, the Montreal Museum of Fine Arts and many public, corporate and private collections.

Selected Publications:

A Tale of an Egg: Ottawa, Oberon, 1975. ISBN 0-88750-155-9
A Rural Life: Ottawa, Oberon, 1986. ISBN 0-88750-620-8

Comments: "Tolmie writes as engagingly as he paints . . . I am always delighted to encounter works of art with staying power." – Joan Weir, *Atlantic Provinces Book Review*
"A delight to every harried city-dweller who dreams of a return to the simpler life of small-town Canada." – *Montreal Gazette*
"A very special feeling for words produced A Tale of an Egg, one of the best picture books to appear on the Canadian publishing scene in many years." – *In Review: Canadian Books for Children*
Documentary Films: Profile of Ken Tolmie a CBC-TV documentary for the series Seeing It Our Way (1981); Ken Tolmie, CBC-TV, for the programs Newsday, Profile, Take Thirty, and View from the Atlantic (1981), half-hour documentary; The Human Link, TVOntario, for their series Visions, Artists and the Creative Process (1982), half-hour documentary; The Massive Mirror, TVOntario, for their series, Visions, the Critical Eye (1983), half-hour documentary.
Mailing Address: 81 Langley Avenue, Toronto, Ontario M4K 1B4

JAN TRUSS

Born in Stoke-on-Trent in the industrial Midlands of England, May 3, 1925. Immigrated to rural Alberta, 1957. Graduate of Goldsmith's College, University of London, University of Alberta, and University of Calgary. First vocation and career — which lasted 25 years — educator, in dockside schools, reform schools, prairie schools and at the University of Calgary. Member of Playwrights Union of Canada, ACTRA, Canadian Society of Children's Authors, Illustrators and Performers.

Selected Publications:

Bird at the Window: Toronto, Macmillan, 1974. ISBN 0-7705-1175-9
A Very Small Rebellion: Edmonton, LeBel, 1977. ISBN 0-920008-02-X
Ooomerahgi Oh! & A Very Small Rebellion: Toronto, Playwrights Canada, 1978. ISBN 0-88754-063-5
The Judgement of Clifford Sifton: Toronto, Playwrights Canada, 1979. ISBN 0-88754-142-9
Jasmin: Toronto, Groundwood, 1982. ISBN 0-88899-014-6
Rocky Mountain Symphony: Calgary, GB Publishing, 1983. ISBN 0-919029-08-6

Awards: Search for a New Alberta Novelist Competition (First Winner). Ruth Schwartz Award for Children's Literature.
Comments: Am also known to write short stories, poetry, librettos.
Readings, Lectures & Workshops: I do.
Mailing Address: Box 8, Water Valley, Alberta T0M 2E0

ALAN TWIGG

Born in Vancouver, 1952. Married (Tara) 1973. Son (Jeremy) 1975. Son (Martin) 1984. Live in Vancouver with my family. Journalist. Brother (John) also a journalist.

Selected Publications:

All books published in Madeira Park, B.C., by Harbour Publishing

For Openers (Conversations with 24 Canadian Writers): 1981. ISBN 0-920080-07-3
Hubert Evans (The First Ninety-Three Years): 1985. ISBN 0-920080-88-X
Vancouver and Its Writers: 1986. ISBN 0-920080-77-4
Vander Zalm (From Immigrant to Premier): 1986. ISBN 0-920080-30-8

   Mailing Address: 3516 West 13th Avenue, Vancouver, British Columbia V6R 2S3

PABLO URBANYI

Conceived in Czechoslovakia, I was born in Hungary in 1939, in the same bed. In 1948 I immigrated to the Argentine. There I grew up and studied, published my first books and worked as a journalist (no computer) on the newspaper La Opinion of Buenos Aires. In 1977 I immigrated to Canada. I live in Ottawa. I teach Spanish. I have a wife (the original one), two children and no dog or cat. But everything could have happened any other way too.

Selected Publications:

Night of the Revolutionaries: Buenos Aires, Centro Editor, 1972. (no ISBN)
A Revolver for Mack: Buenos Aires, Editorial Corregidor, 1974. (no ISBN)
The Nowhere Idea: Toronto, Williams-Wallace, 1982. ISBN 0-88795-015-9
No Name: Buenos Aires, Editorial Legasa, 1986. (no ISBN)

Comments: "What an idiot! Writing instead of learning about diesel motors." — My father, in the kitchen, in 1955 before the arrival of the atomic motors.

"Not believing in words like 'experience', 'new', 'really', 'nice', you leave today's man without a vocabulary. You are a pessimist, and worse still, you try to explain the reason why and only create disorder. You will not go far this way!" — A writer friend in a pub.

Readings, Lectures & Workshops: Since I stutter while reading, I invented the abominable arguments that reading is something private and intimate, a communion with the spirit. I say that nobody listens at public readings, but that everybody waits for the session to end and rushes to the wine and cheese table. Since I am slightly deaf, I know this from experience.

Mailing Address: 104 - 2650 Southdale Crescent, Ottawa, Ontario K1B 4S9

JANE URQUHART

Born in Geraldton, Ontario, in 1949. Spent my late childhood and teenage years in Toronto where I attended Havergal College. I hold a B.A. in art history and English from the University of Guelph. I now live in Wellesley, Ontario, with my husband, artist Tony Urquhart, and our daughter Emily.

Selected Publications:

I Am Walking in the Garden of his Imaginary Palace: Toronto, Aya, 1982.
ISBN 0-920544-25-8
False Shuffles: Victoria, Porcepic, 1982. ISBN 0-88878-204-7
The Little Flowers of Madame de Montespan: Erin, Porcupine's Quill, 1983.
ISBN 0-88984-049-0
The Whirlpool: Toronto, McClelland & Stewart, 1986. ISBN 0-7710-8655-5
Storm Glass: Erin, Porcupine's Quill, 1987. ISBN 0-88984-106-3

Comments: "Urquhart is the kind of writer who makes us wonder, with a sense of pleasurable anticipation, what in the world she'll do next."
– William French, *Globe and Mail*
"A courageous stylist with a unique vision." – Timothy Findley, *Books in Canada*
"Urquhart combines the poet's passionate feeling for language and the material world with nearly a classicist's sense of form." – Ken Adachi, *Toronto Star*
Readings, Lectures & Workshops: Have given readings for universities and writers' groups and at Harbourfront. Have taught short-story workshops. May be booked through TWUC.
Mailing Address: Box 208, Wellesley, Ontario N0B 2T0

GEOFFREY URSELL

I was born in Moose Jaw, Saskatchewan, in 1943, and grew up in various prairie cities. I studied at the University of Manitoba and the University of London, where I received my Ph.D. I write fiction, poetry, songs and drama for stage, radio and television. I also edit anthologies of short stories and of writing for children. I live in Saskatoon, where I write full time.

Selected Publications:

Prairie Jungle (An anthology of prairie writing for children): (ed. with Wenda McArthur), Moose Jaw, Coteau, 1985. ISBN 0-919926-45-2
Perdue, or How the West Was Lost: Toronto, Macmillan, 1984. ISBN 0-7715-9870-X
Trap Lines: Winnipeg, Turnstone, 1982. ISBN 0-88801-080-X
The Running of the Deer: Toronto, Playwrights Canada, 1981. ISBN 0-88754-235-2
Superwheel: (with Rex Deverell), Moose Jaw, Coteau, 1979. ISBN 0-919926-07-X

Awards: Books in Canada First Novel Award, 1984. Persephone Theatre National Playwriting Award, 1981. Clifford E. Lee National Playwriting Award, 1977.

Comments: "An ambitious, visionary book." – Wayne Tefs, *Arts Manitoba* (on *Perdue*)

"Ursell's conception is a daring one, and the language is carefully crafted, beautifully sculptured." – Leon Rooke

Readings, Lectures & Workshops: Readings and workshops at universities, libraries, schools and conferences across Canada.

Mailing Address: 1516B Hilliard Street East, Saskatoon, Saskatchewan S7J 0G4

W.D. VALGARDSON

Born in 1939. Raised in Gimli, Manitoba. B.A. (1961, United College); B.Ed. (1965, University of Manitoba); M.F.A. (1969, University of Iowa). Professor and chairman of the creative writing department at the University of Victoria since 1982.

Selected Publications:

Bloodflowers: Ottawa, Oberon, 1973. ISBN 0-88750-086-2
God Is Not a Fish Inspector: Ottawa, Oberon, 1975. ISBN 0-88750-149-4
Red Dust: Ottawa, Oberon, 1978. ISBN 0-88750-260-1
Gentle Sinners: Ottawa, Oberon, 1980. ISBN 0-88750-330-6
A Carpenter of Dreams: Victoria, Skaldhus, 1986. ISBN 0-9692455-0-5
In the Gutting Shed: Winnipeg, Turnstone, 1986.

Awards: President's Medal (Fiction), 1971. CBC Literary Competition (First Prize), 1980. Books in Canada (First Novel Award), 1981. Canadian Authors Association Award (Drama), 1983.

Comments: Ten radio drama productions (CBC). Two stage plays. Five stories adapted for film or TV. One original screenplay.

Readings, Lectures & Workshops: Numerous workshops in creative writing, readings, speeches concerning education, particularly the teaching of writing.

Mailing Address: 3221 Doncaster Drive, Victoria, British Columbia V8P 3V3

ARITHA VAN HERK

Born in Alberta in 1954 and grew up just a few miles from the Battle River. Have been a secretary, hired hand, bush-cook, teacher and editor. Hold an M.A. in English from the University of Alberta; currently associate professor of English at the University of Calgary. Live in Calgary, divide my time between writing and teaching.

Selected Publications:

Judith: Toronto, McClelland & Stewart, 1978. ISBN 0-7710-8700-4
The Tent Peg: Toronto, McClelland & Stewart, 1981. ISBN 0-7710-8702-0
No Fixed Address: Toronto, McClelland & Stewart, 1986. ISBN 0-7710-8701-2

Awards: Miss Chatelaine Short Fiction Contest, 1976. Seal First Novel Award, 1978. 45 Below: Canada's Ten Best Young Fiction Writers, 1986.

Comments: I have always inhabited multiple worlds. I am interested in the unexplored areas of human myth. A dedicated regionalist. I harbour a desire to become a balloonist.

Readings, Lectures & Workshops: Read regularly at universities and high schools. Teach creative writing. May be booked through TWUC.

Mailing Address: Dept. of English, University of Calgary, Alberta T2N 1N4

GLORIA ISABEL VARLEY

Born in Toronto, March 31, 1932. Hold a diploma in journalism from the Ryerson Polytechnical Institute and a B.A. from the University of Toronto. Following staff jobs with CBC Radio in Montreal, an ad agency in Miami and a book publisher in Toronto, I turned to freelance writing in 1965. With my husband, Charles Israel, I now live and work in an elderly house in midtown Toronto.

Selected Publications:

To Be a Dancer: Toronto, Peter Martin, 1971. ISBN 0-88778-053-9

Comments: Contributor to Peter Gzowski's Spring Tonic (Hurtig, 1979). Have written for numerous publications and broadcast services in Canada and the U.S. A regular contributor to Rotunda (the Royal Ontario Museum magazine) and Toronto Life. Magazine work now shares time with scriptwriting and children's stories, among other projects.

Professional affiliations: Periodical Writers Association of Canada, the Independent Wine Education Guild, the Wine Writer's Circle, the Toronto Culinary Guild, the American Institute of Wine and Food and the Royal Horticultural Society.

Mailing Address: 113 Howland Avenue, Toronto, Ontario M5R 3B4

PAUL VASEY

Born in Toronto in 1945, I was raised in Owen Sound, Ontario, where I started a career in newspapers that has spanned two decades. A graduate of the University of Windsor (philosophy), I was awarded a Southam Fellowship in 1980 and studied at Toronto's Massey College. I live in Windsor with my wife and two children and devote most of my time to writing.

Selected Publications:

All books published in Windsor by Black Moss

The Sufferer Kind: 1978. ISBN 0-88753-048-6
Lord, Lord: 1980. ISBN 0-88753-066-4
The Great Train Ride: 1981. ISBN 0-88753-081-0

Awards: Southam Fellowship, 1980-81
Comments: Forthcoming: The Inland Seas (A Journey Through The Great Lakes) will be published by Key Porter Books. A novel, Last Man In, is in progress.
Readings, Lectures & Workshops: Lecture occasionally on both journalism and fiction; read and conduct workshops in elementary and secondary schools and community colleges. May be booked through TWUC.
Mailing Address: 2305 Chilver Road, Windsor, Ontario N8W 2V6

ELIZABETH VERKOCZY

Born in Budapest, educated in Hungary and England, joined the Hungarian National Children's Newspaper at the age of 15, the youngest journalist in the country. I escaped to England in 1956 and continued my writing with technical articles in the medical research field. Emigrated to Canada in 1966, and as a hobby, I returned to fiction writing in 1978. I became the newsletter editor of the Canadian Authors Association for 1980-81, and the markets editor of the Canadian Author and Bookman for 1980-82. Member of the Crime Writers of Canada. Now living in Toronto.

Selected Publications:

White Tulips for Lena: Toronto, Simon & Pierre, 1983. ISBN 0-88924-117-1

Comments: *The Haunted Realm of the Humber River* and *Stanislaw's Clocks* have appeared in Black Cat Mystery Magazine (ISSN 0710-2844, Vol.1. Nos. 2 and 3). Major works in progress: A Letter to God (Vol.1) and A Letter From God (Vol.II), novels.

Mailing Address: c/o TWUC, 24 Ryerson Avenue, Toronto, Ontario M5T 2P3

FRED WAH

Have lived in the West Kootenays of southeastern British Columbia for most of my life. I was born in Swift Current, Saskatchewan, in 1939. A founding editor of the poetry newsletter, TISH, in the early 1960s in Vancouver and of the recent electronic literary magazine, Swift-Current, I have been an editor of a number of magazines in the U.S. and Canada. At present I teach in the writing and publishing programme at Selkirk College.

Selected Publications:

Lardeau: Toronto, Island, 1965. (no ISBN)
Mountain: Buffalo, Audit, 1967. (no ISBN)
Among: Toronto, Coach House, 1972. (no ISBN)
Tree: Vancouver, Vancouver Community Press, 1972. (no ISBN)
Earth: Canton, Institute of Further Studies, 1974. (no ISBN)
Pictograms from the Interior of B.C.: Vancouver, Talon, 1975. ISBN 0-88922-099-9
Loki is Buried at Smoky Creek (Selected Poetry): Vancouver, Talon, 1980. ISBN 0-88922-177-4
Owners Manual: Lantzville, Island Writing Series, 1981. ISBN 0-919479-04-9
Breathin' My Name With a Sigh: Vancouver, Talon, 1981. ISBN 0-88922-188-X
Waiting for Saskatchewan: Winnipeg, Turnstone, 1985. ISBN 0-88801-096-9

Awards: Governor General's Award for Poetry, 1985
Readings, Lectures & Workshops: Poetry readings and workshops in poetry and editing. Lectures in contemporary poetry and poetics and in the use of data communications and electronic literary databases in teaching writing. May be booked through TWUC or through home address.
Mailing Address: Box 75, South Slocan, British Columbia V0G 2G0

BRONWEN WALLACE

Born and educated in Kingston, Ontario. B.A. (Hons.) and M.A., English, Queen's University, 1967 and 1969. Have worked as a secretary, civil servant, bookstore clerk, housewife, mother, teacher and counsellor in a shelter for abused women and children. Currently teach creative writing at Queen's and occasionally at St. Lawrence College. One son, Jeremy Baxter.

Selected Publications:

Bread and Chocolate/Marrying Into the Family: (with Mary di Michele), Ottawa, Oberon, 1980. ISBN 0-88750-370-5
Signs of the Former Tenant: Ottawa, Oberon, 1983. ISBN 0-88750-483-3
Common Magic: Ottawa, Oberon, 1985. ISBN 0-88750-570-8
The Stubborn Particulars of Grace: Toronto, McClelland & Stewart, 1987. ISBN 0-7710-8790-X

Awards: DuMaurier Award for Poetry, 1980. Red Ribbon, American Film Festival, 1982. Pat Lowther Award for Poetry, 1984.
Comments: Contributor to *The New Canadian Poets, 1970-85* (McClelland & Stewart, 1985) and *Anything is Possible* (Mosaic, 1984). Co-director, with Chris Whynot, of two documentary films: All You Have to Do (1982) and That's Why I'm Talking (1984).
Readings, Lectures & Workshops: Writer-in-residence (short term), Scarborough College, 1986. Instructor, Upper Canada Writers Workshop, Kingston, summer, 1986. Numerous workshops for elementary and high-school students in Ontario. Readings all over Canada.
Mailing Address: 32 Gibson Avenue, Kingston, Ontario K7L 4R2

IAN WALLACE

A native of Niagara Falls, Ontario, and Honours graduate of the Ontario College of Art 1973, I began my career working with Kids Can Press 1974-76. Realising the need to stabilise my financial situation, I joined the staff of the Art Gallery of Ontario while continuing to write and illustrate. In 1981 I made the professional leap to producing picture books full time.

Selected Publications:

The Sandwich: (with Angela Wood), Toronto, Kids Can, 1975.
  ISBN 0-919964-02-8
Chin Chiang and the Dragon's Dance: Toronto, Groundwood, 1984.
  ISBN 0-88899-020-0
The Sparrow's Song: Toronto, Penguin, 1986. ISBN 0-670-81453-9

  Awards: Amelia Francis Howard-Gibbon Award, 1985. IODE Award, 1985.
  Comments: Illustrated *Very Last First Time* (Groundwood, 1985). *Chin Chiang and the Dragon's Dance* was also an exhibition at the Art Gallery of Ontario, February 1986.
  "A distinguished contribution from a talented artist and sensitive writer." – *Quill & Quire* (on *The Sparrow's Song*)
  "The total impact of *Dragon's Dance* is compelling and vivid." – *School Library Journal*
  Readings, Lectures & Workshops: To date I have met approximately 100,000 school children and have given workshops to thousands of librarians, teachers and other writers.
  Mailing Address: c/o TWUC, 24 Ryerson Avenue, Toronto, Ontario M5T 2P3

RONALD R. WALLINGFORD

Born in Ottawa, September 13, 1933. Ran around in circles there until the University of Michigan offered athletic scholarship. Graduated from Michigan, zoology, 1956. Taught at North Toronto Collegiate for three years before moving to McMaster University to teach exercise physiology. Masters and Doctorate degrees from the University of Buffalo in part-time and sabbatical studies. Currently combine writing with other responsibilities at Laurentian University.

Selected Publications:

Portrait of a Runner: Cobalt, Highway Book Shop, 1985. ISBN 0-88954-310-0

   Comments: "What is amazing in this book is that Wallingford offers his literal earnest view of the world, and because he is a decent and honest man, his book does what literature does; it allows a reader to know another human being, to feel, to see, to experience." – *Kingston Whig-Standard*
   "His main purpose – to illustrate the difficult path a young runner must follow to eventually achieve success at the national or international level. *Portrait* not only meets this objective but tells an interesting story along the way." – Tom Jewiss, *The Front Runner*
   Readings, Lectures & Workshops: Lectures on coaching distance running and on exercise physiology.
   Mailing Address: Site 12, Box 33 SS 1, Sudbury, Ontario P3E 4S8

BETSY WARLAND

Born December 27, 1946. Immigrated to Canada from the United States in 1972. Initiator and a co-ordinator of the Women and Words/ Les femmes et les mots conference in 1983. Poet, freelance writer, editor and literary organiser. Make my home on the edge, in Vancouver, British Columbia.

Selected Publications:

A Gathering Instinct: Toronto, Williams-Wallace, 1981. ISBN 0-88795-007-8
open is broken: Edmonton, Longspoon, 1984. ISBN 0-919285-26-0

Comments: "She takes language and the poetic line out into open territory." – *Toronto Star*
"Warland's words are an archaeology of women-speech, of her language, of her unabashed eroticism." – *B.C. Library Association Reporter*
"Drawing on the original meanings of commonly exploited words, she sifts etymologies, fracturing and re-forming the language." – *Herizons*
Readings, Lectures & Workshops: Frequently read at educational and community centres; lecture on experimental women writers in Canada and Quebec; teach poetry workshops with an emphasis on language. May be booked directly or through TWUC.
Mailing Address: 2533 West 5th Avenue, Vancouver, British Columbia V6K 1S9

BETTY WATERTON

Born in Oshawa, Ontario, August 31, 1923. Seventh generation Canadian (U.E.L.). Migrated west in the 1930s, because father, Eric W. Wrightmeyer, was the Western Canada representative for the Toronto Star Weekly. Married an RCAF pilot, 1942. Raised three children and studied art. Worked (briefly!) as a retoucher on the Vancouver Sun, television animator and portrait painter. Now living in Sidney, on Vancouver Island. Friend of Canadian Society of Children's Authors, Illustrators and Performers.

Selected Publications:

A Salmon for Simon: Vancouver, Douglas & McIntyre, 1978. ISBN 0-88894-168-4

Pettranella: Vancouver, Douglas & McIntyre, 1980. ISBN 0-88894-237-0

Mustard: Toronto, Scholastic, 1983. ISBN 0-590-71175-X

Orff, 27 Dragons (and a Snarkel!): Toronto, Annick, 1984. ISBN 0-920303-02-1

The White Moose: Toronto, Ginn, 1984. ISBN 0-7702-1153-4

Quincy Rumpel: Toronto, Groundwood,1984. ISBN 0-88899-036-7

Starring Quincy Rumpel: Toronto, Groundwood, 1986. ISBN 0-88899-048-0

Awards: Amelia Frances Howard-Gibbon Award, 1978. Canada Council Children's Literature Award (Illustration), 1978.

Comments: *A Salmon for Simon* and *Pettranella* have been published in the United States, Scandinavia and Germany.

Readings, Lectures & Workshops: Readings in schools and libraries.

Mailing Address: 10135 Tsaykum Road, Sidney, British Columbia V8L 3R9

DAVID WATMOUGH

Born in London, England, in 1926 of Cornish background. Educated at Coopers' School, King's College, London, 1945-1949; Paris and Lyons, France, 1949-1952. New York City and San Francisco, 1952-1960. Moved to Vancouver, British Columbia, in 1960. Became a Canadian citizen in 1969. Worked as critic (music, visual arts, theatre) and literary journalist for N.Y. Times, Vancouver Sun, the Province, CBC-TV, CBC-Radio, San Francisco Examiner, Opera, The Beaver and Connoisseur, NYC. For further references see: the Oxford Companion to Canadian Literature (1983), the Dictionary of Literary Biography (1986) and Canadian Who's Who (1986).

Selected Publications:

A Church Renascent: London, S.P.C.K., 1951. (no ISBN)
Ashes for Easter: Vancouver, Talon, 1972. ISBN 0-88922-042-5
Love and the Waiting Game: Ottawa, Oberon, 1975. ISBN 0-88750-170-2
No More Into the Garden: Toronto, Doubleday, 1978. ISBN 0-385-13452-5
Fury: Ottawa, Oberon, 1984. ISBN 0-88750-542-2
The Connecticut Countess: New York, Crossing, 1984. ISBN 0-89594-125-2
The Unlikely Pioneer: Oakville, Mosaic, 1986. ISBN 0-88962-286-8
Vibrations in Time: Oakville, Mosaic, 1986. ISBN 0-88962-339-2

Awards: Novel of the Year (Giovanni's Room, Philadelphia), 1978
Comments: "What astonishes and delights in Watmough's fiction, apart from the unusally stylish and uncluttered prose, is a sensibility that is not bound by age, class, education, or sex." – *Vancouver Sun*
"David Watmough is a very good writer." – *Globe and Mail*
"One of the most skilful and one of the best fiction writers in Western Canada." – George Woodcock, *The World of Writing*
Mailing Address: 3358 West First Avenue, Vancouver, British Columbia V6R 1G4

HELEN WEINZWEIG

Born in Poland in 1915, came to Toronto at the age of nine. Had to leave school during the Depression, the rest of my education came from extensive reading. Began writing age 45.

Selected Publications:

Passing Ceremony: Toronto, Anansi, 1973. ISBN 0-88784-325-5
Basic Black With Pearls: Toronto, Anansi, 1980. ISBN 0-88784-079-5

Awards: CBC Literary Competition (Third Prize), Short Story, 1979. City of Toronto Book Award (Fiction), 1981.

Readings, Lectures & Workshops: Numerous readings across Canada. Readings and public lectures in conjunction with workshops. Fiction workshops: Maritime Writers Workshop (Fredericton, New Brunswick) and Upper Canada Writers Workshop (Kingston, Ontario).

Mailing Address: 107 Manor Road East, Toronto, Ontario M4S 1R3

JOAN WEIR

Author of both juvenile fiction and adult non-fiction. Born in Calgary, now live in Kamloops, British Columbia. B.A. degree from the University of Manitoba. Started writing for radio and children's television, then moved into juvenile novels. Now combines writing for young readers with researching and writing adult non-fiction. Instructor of English and creative writing at Cariboo College, Kamloops.

Selected Publications:

Exile at the Rocking Seven: Toronto, Macmillan, 1977. ISBN 0-7705-1517-7
Career Girl: Edmonton, Tree Frog, 1979. ISBN 0-89967-032-3
So, I'm Different: Vancouver, Douglas & McIntyre, 1981. ISBN 0-88894-320-2
Secret at Westwind: Toronto, Scholastic, 1984. ISBN 0-590-71091-5
Walhachin: Vancouver, Hancock, 1984. ISBN 0-88839-982-0
Canada's Gold Rush Church: Vancouver, Anglican Church, 1986. ISBN 0-9692-467-0-6
Go for the Gold: Toronto, Scholastic, 1987.
Backdoor to the Klondike: Toronto, Boston Mills, 1987.

Comments: Experienced teacher of creative writing. Have conducted writing workshops for both adults and children in centres across Canada, including Winnipeg, Calgary, Lethbridge, Vancouver, Terrace, Quesnel, Williams' Lake and Kamloops. In 1985 conducted ten-day Canada Council sponsored writer-in-residence program in public libraries throughout the Cariboo-Thompson-Nicola Library System.

Readings, Lectures & Workshops: Available for readings, lectures and workshops.

Mailing Address: 463 Greenstone Drive, Kamloops, British Columbia V2C 1N8

MERRILY WEISBORD

Conceived in Montreal in time for the great, new post-war world. Studied modern dance. Seduced, at McGill, from Wedelyn to literature by writers from other realms. Work in media and film while writing stories, poems, non-fiction. Live in Montreal and in the foothills of the Laurentians.

Selected Publications:

The Strangest Dream (Canadian Communists, The Spy Trials and the Cold War): Toronto, Lester & Orpen Dennys, 1983.

Comments: "A generation of radicals comes to life in their own words and feelings as passionate, complicated, frequently attractive and certainly compelling human beings." – Rick Salutin, *This Magazine*
"For a couple of hundred pages Weisbord makes us dream along with them – the dream of a fair world no longer dreamable here on the brink." – David Homel, *Books in Canada*
"The result is a beautifully written, evocative and often moving account of the betrayal of a generation's hope." – J.L. Granatstein, *Maclean's*
"This is a haunting tale." – Douglas Fisher, *Legion*
Story editor on Women, CBC-TV. Co-writer, Blacklist, The Journal. Co-writer, Margaret Atwood, NFB feature documentary. Numerous radio documentaries. Short stories and poems in literary journals like Branching Out and Erotics.
Readings, Lectures & Workshops: Reading and workshop, Jewish Public Library, Montreal. Montreal Writes, Concordia Faculty Club, Montreal.
Mailing Address: 3635 Henri Julien, Montreal, Quebec H2X 3H4

CYRIL WELCH

Californian by birth (1939), now Canadian citizen. Educated at ten different schools (two in Switzerland) and numerous summer camps, then five different colleges or universities (one in Germany). Ph.D. in philosophy from Pennsylvania State University (1964). Taught at several colleges and universities before settling at Mount Allison University (1967) to read and write and talk.

Selected Publications:

The Sense of Language: The Hague, Martinus Nijhoff, 1973. ISBN 90-247-1340-4

Emergence (Baudelaire, Mallarme, Rimbaud): (with Liliane Welch), Pennsylvania State College, Bald Eagle, 1973. (no ISBN)

Address (Rimbaud, Mallarme, Butor): (with Liliane Welch), Victoria, Sono Nis, 1982. ISBN 0-919203-10-8

The Art of Art Works: Victoria, Sono Nis, 1982. ISBN 0-919203-10-8

Mailing Address: c/o TWUC, 24 Ryerson Avenue, Toronto, Ontario M5T 2P3

LILIANE WELCH

Born in Luxembourg, 1937. Studied in Europe and the United States. Hold a Ph.D. from Penn State University and have taught French literature for the past 20 years at Mount Allison University in Sackville, New Brunswick. An emigrant continental Celt, I return to Europe each summer with my husband-philosopher Cyril, to write and study in the north and to go mountain climbing in the Alps and Dolomites.

Selected Publications:

Assailing Beats: Ottawa, Borealis, 1979. ISBN 0-88887-998-6
October Winds: Fredericton, Fiddlehead, 1981. ISBN 0-920110-97-5
From the Songs of the Artisans: Fredericton, Fiddlehead, 1983. ISBN 0-86492-040-7
Manstorna (Life on the Mountains): Charlottetown, Ragweed, 1985. ISBN 0-920304-45-1
Unrest Bound: Brandon, Pierian, 1985. ISBN 0-920916-38-4

Awards: Writers Federation of New Brunswick Past President's Award, 1986
Comments: "Sexual morality, ecology, and political rights are explored profoundly, and related coherently (in *Brush and Trunks*)." – R.J. Merrett, *Canadian Book Review Annual*
"From the Songs of the Artisans, a major achievement in recent Maritime poetry." – Richard Lemm, *Atlantic Provinces Book Review*
Readings, Lectures & Workshops: Read regularly at universities in Canada and abroad. Lecture on poetics, wilderness and aesthetics.
Mailing Address: Box 246, Sackville, New Brunswick E0A 2C0

PATIENCE WHEATLEY

Born at Bourne End, Bucks, England, in 1924. Came to Canada at the age of 15 in 1940. Went to McGill for three years then joined the CWAC and went overseas. Went back to McGill in 1946, received a degree, took a graduate year in English. Married a Canadian Rhodes Scholar in 1948. Lived in Oxford, then Montreal 1949-81. After much frustration returned to writing seriously in early seventies. Now live in Kingston with retired husband and steamboat.

Selected Publications:

A Hinge of Spring: Fredericton, Fiddlehead, 1986. ISBN 0-86492-076-5
Mr. MacKenzie King in *Fiddlehead Greens*: Ottawa, Oberon, 1979.
   ISBN 0-88750-304-7

Readings, Lectures & Workshops: Kingston Public Library, April 1986. Double Hook Book Store, Greene Avenue, Montreal, October 1986. Thomas More Institute for Adult Education, Montreal, November 1986. The Book Shop, Princess Street, Kingston, November 1986. Ban Righ Women's Centre, Queen's University, Kingston, February 1986.
   Mailing Address: 36 Simcoe Street, Kingston, Ontario K7L 2S6

FLO WHYARD

Born in London, Ontario, 1917. Daughter of newsman Bill Elliot. After B.A. (University of Western Ontario) news and public relations in London, Toronto, Fort Erie, Ottawa and WRCNS, Naval Information. Married Jim Whyard, 1944. Three children, five grandchildren. Freelanced from Yellowknife and Whitehorse which has been home since 1954. Editor, Whitehorse Star; Canadian editor, Alaska Northwest Publishing Company. Member of the Yukon Legislative Assembly 1974-78. Mayor of Whitehorse 1981-83. Now retired, researching/writing northern history, biography full time.

Selected Publications:

My Ninety Years: Edmonds, Alaska Northwest, 1976. ISBN 0-88240-062-2
Canadian Bush Pilot Ernie Boffa: Edmonds, Alaska Northwest, 1984. ISBN 0-88240-264-1
A Yukon Colouring Book: (illustrated by Cathy Deer), Whitehorse, Beringian, 1986. ISBN 0-9692744-0-8

Awards: Member, Order of Canada, 1984
Readings, Lectures & Workshops: Readings and lectures at conferences, in schools, on Martha Louise Black, who climbed the Chilkoot Trail in 1898, became second woman elected to Canadian Parliament. (I wear a replica of the costume worn by Martha Louise when travelling to the Klondike.)
Mailing Address: 89 Sunset Drive North, Whitehorse, Yukon Y1A 3G5

RUDY WIEBE

Born near Fairholme, Saskatchewan, in 1934, I now live in Edmonton, Alberta. I was educated at the Coaldale Mennonite High School, the universities of Alberta, Tuebingen (W. Germany), Manitoba and Iowa, and am at present professor of English at the University of Alberta. I have served on the Federal Cultural Policy Review Committee (1980-82), on the Alberta Foundation for the Literary Arts (since 1985), and the Advisory Committee on the Status of the Artist (since 1987).

Selected Publications:

Peace Shall Destroy Many: Toronto, McClelland & Stewart, 1962. ISBN 0-7710-9182-6

First and Vital Candle: Toronto, McClelland & Stewart, 1966. ISBN 0-7710-8979-3

The Blue Mountains of China: Toronto, McClelland & Stewart, 1970. ISBN 0-7710-9208-3

The Temptations of Big Bear: Toronto, McClelland & Stewart, 1973. ISBN 0-7710-9222-9

Where Is the Voice Coming From?: Toronto, McClelland & Stewart, 1974. ISBN 0-7710-8987-2

The Scorched-Wood People: Toronto, McClelland & Stewart, 1977. ISBN 0-7710-9294-6

The Mad Trapper: Toronto, McClelland & Stewart, 1980. ISBN 0-7710-8975-9

The Angel of the Tar Sands: Toronto, McClelland & Stewart, 1982. ISBN 0-7710-9308-X

My Lovely Enemy: Toronto, McClelland & Stewart, 1983. ISBN 0-7710-8989-9

A Voice in the Land: (essays, edited by W.J. Keith), Edmonton, NeWest, 1981. ISBN 0-920316-07-7

War in the West: (with B. Beal), Toronto, McClelland & Stewart, 1985. ISBN 0-7710-8973-2

Awards: Governor General's Award, 1973. Periodical Distributors of Canada Award (Short Story), 1978. D. Litt. (Winnipeg), 1986. Lorne Pierce Medal, 1987.

Mailing Address: English Dept., University of Alberta, Edmonton T6G 2E5

BARBARA WILLIAMS

Born near Chester, England (English, Irish, Scottish, Welsh origin). B.A., Sheffield. Certificate in Education, Bristol. M.A., University of Guelph. Creative writing, York University (1983-84). Taught high school, United Kingdom and Canada. Moved to Canada, mid-1960s. Toronto since 1982. Grown son, Matthew; daughter Sophie. Helped establish Veterinary Microbiology business. Writing two books on pioneer woman-artist Anne Langton (non-fiction and poetry) and other poetry sequences. Wrote as Barbara Wilson until 1985.

Selected Publications:

ABC et/and 123: Victoria, Press Porcepic, 1980. ISBN 0-88878-165-2
Anne Langton (Pioneer Woman and Artist): Peterborough, Peterborough Historical Society, 1986. ISBN 0-9692621-4-0

Awards: Cross-Canada Writers' Quarterly Competition (Children's Poem and Collection of Children's Poems), 1980
Comments: Columnist on Australian poetry for Poetry Canada Review, since 1984. Frequent contributor to Canadian, American and Australian periodicals (adult and children's literature): articles, essays, interviews and profiles (of other authors), poems, reviews, short fiction. Anthologised poems and short fiction: Canada and United States (trade and education).
Readings, Lectures & Workshops: Readings include voice-portrait presentation (period costume) on Anne Langton (my poems and journal extracts from Anne Langton). Lectures on Anne Langton (with slides of her artwork). Workshops on poetry and on the creative-writing process.
Mailing Address: c/o TWUC, 24 Ryerson Avenue, Toronto, Ontario M5T 2P3

DAVID WILLIAMS

Born in Souris, Manitoba, June 22, 1945.
Returned after the war to Lac Vert, Saskatchewan. Studied at Briercrest Bible Institute, the
University of Saskatchewan and Oxford University. Refused to become a Toronto Argonaut.
Hold a Ph.D. in English from the University of
Massachusetts. Taught since 1972 at the University of Manitoba. Married to Darlene Olinyk
in 1967. With our sons, Jeremy and Bryan,
we live in an old house beside the Red River.

Selected Publications:

The Burning Wood: Toronto, Anansi, 1975. ISBN 0-88784-435-9
The River Horsemen: Toronto, Anansi, 1981. ISBN 0-88784-086-8
Eye of the Father: Toronto, Anansi, 1985. ISBN 0-88784-144-9
Faulkner's Women (The Myth and the Muse): Montreal, McGill-Queen's
 UP, 1977. ISBN 0-7735-0257-2

Comments: "*The River Horsemen* ought to be proclaimed instantly as one
of English Canadian literature's finer exercises in the modernist mode, in
the sort of fiction we associate with Faulkner and Lowry."– *Queen's
Quarterly*

"An epic in itself, straight out of Norse mythology in its intensity and
rhythm." – *Kingston Whig-Standard* (on *Eye of the Father*)

"The Lacjardin Trilogy is a major accomplishment and should be required
reading for anyone interested in the fiction of prairie Canada." – Geoff
Hancock, *Toronto Star*

Readings, Lectures & Workshops: Read regularly in libraries, high schools
and universities. Have toured Scandinavia for External Affairs. Taught fiction
writing at Saskatchewan Summer School of the Arts in Fort San.

Mailing Address: Dept. of English, St. Paul's College, University of Manitoba, Winnipeg R3T 2M6

DAVID RICARDO WILLIAMS

Born in Kamloops, British Columbia, formerly practised law (I became a Queen's Counsel in 1969) in Duncan, British Columbia,where I live but now work full time as an author and historical researcher. Since 1980 I have been adjunct professor and writer-in-residence at the faculty of law at the University of Victoria. I try to keep trim by playing squash.

Selected Publications:

The Man for a New Country (Sir Matthew Baillie Begbie): Victoria, Gray's, 1977. ISBN 0-88826-068-7
Trapline Outlaw (Simon Peter Gun-a-noot): Victoria, Sono Nis, 1982. ISBN 0-919462-97-9
Duff (A Life in the Law): Vancouver, University of British Columbia Press, 1984. ISBN 0-7748-0203-0
Mayor Gerry (The Remarkable Gerald Grattan McGeer): Vancouver, Douglas & McIntyre, 1986. ISBN 0-88894-504-3

Awards: University of British Columbia Medal (Canadian Biography), 1978. Association of Canadian Studies Biography Award, 1979. British Columbia Book Prize (Non-fiction), 1985.
Comments: "His biographies of noteworthy B.C. characters are well researched and written in a highly readable entertaining style."
– *The Advocate*
"Possesses a prose style that flows with grace and clarity." – *Globe and Mail*
Readings, Lectures & Workshops: Workshop leader at international biography conference, Vancouver, British Columbia, March 1981. Speak frequently.
Mailing Address: 170 Craig Street, Duncan, British Columbia V9L 1W1

DAVID WILLIAMSON

Dean of business and general education at Red River Community College, Winnipeg, by day; novelist, playwright and critic by night. Born in Winnipeg, 1934. Have B.A. and B.Ed. from University of Manitoba. Was in advertising management with The Bay. Went into education field in 1966. Teach creative writing; review fiction for Winnipeg Free Press. President, Manitoba Writers' Guild, 1986-87. Married (wife, Janice) with four children.

Selected Publications:

The Bad Life: Winnipeg, Queenston House, 1975. ISBN 0-919866-06-9
Shandy: Winnipeg, Queenston House, 1980. ISBN 0-919866-50-6
The Nocturnal Jogger et al. in Manitoba Stories: Winnipeg, Queenston House, 1981. ISBN 0-919866-40-9

Comments: "A good book with a broad appeal; a high-spirited burlesque of young love and rebellion, of artists and bohemians, Fifties style, written with a deft comic touch." – John Robert Colombo (on *The Bad Life*)
"An extraordinarily sexy little page-turner." – Anne Montagnes, *Globe and Mail* (on *Shandy*)
"It is the humour and gentle irony which makes this book so enjoyable." – Ingrid Haase, Canadian Materials
Adapted *The Nocturnal Jogger* for CBC-TV: shown nationally in November, 1986.
Readings, Lectures & Workshops: In 1986, gave readings in Vancouver, Red Deer, Fort Smith, Moorhead (Minnesota) and Winnipeg. Held workshop on novel-writing (for Canadian Authors Association) and book-reviewing (for Writers' Guild). Lectures on general fiction and humour.
Mailing Address: 53 Cormorant Bay, Winnipeg, Manitoba R2J 2V8

MONCRIEFF WILLIAMSON

Born in 1915. Became Canadian citizen 1962. Former museum director. Worked on documentary films. Studied at Edinburgh College of Art. Poet. Biographer. Novelist. Art critic. Extensive bibliography articles and art-catalogues. Lived for long periods in Belgium, France and three and a half years in the United States. World War II army intelligence corps. Married to Pam. Our son Tim works in theatre. Working on memoirs since 1973 with other books in progress.

Selected Publications:

The Fluid Idol: Glasgow, William McLellan, 1951. (no ISBN)
Robert Harris (An Unconventional Biography): Toronto, McClelland & Stewart, 1970. ISBN 0-7710-9010-2
Robert Harris (1849-1915): Ottawa, National Gallery of Canada, 1973. ISBN 0-88884-4-245-7
Death in the Picture: Toronto, Musson, 1982. ISBN 0-77370-062-5
Island Painter: Charlottetown, Ragweed, 1983. ISBN 0-920304-24-9

Awards: LL.D., University of Prince Edward Island, 1972. Order of Canada (Member), 1976. Diplome d'Honneur, Canadian Conference of the Arts, 1975. Royal Canadian Academy Medal, 1976. Gold Medal, Glenbow, 1986.

Readings, Lectures & Workshops: Have given poetry readings Saint John, New Brunswick, and Truro, Nova Scotia. Fiction readings in schools in Prince Edward Island. Lectures and talks in Victoria, Calgary, Regina, Oshawa, Ottawa, Halifax and Charlottetown.

Mailing Address: 14 Churchill Avenue, Charlottetown, Prince Edward Island C1A 1Y8

BUDGE WILSON

Born in 1927 in Nova Scotia and lived there 33 years. Educated, Dalhousie University and University of Toronto. Degree in philosophy and psychology. Did graduate work in English and education. Taught school and worked as editor and freelance photographer and artist, illustrating three books for University of Toronto Press. Married since 1953 to Alan Wilson. Two daughters. Have taught fitness classes in Peterborough for 17 years. Have been writing fiction for ten years.

Selected Publications:

The Best Worst Christmas Present Ever: Toronto, Scholastic, 1984, 1985. ISBN 0-590-71430-9

A House Far From Home: Toronto, Scholastic, 1986. ISBN 0-590-71679-4

Mr. John Bertrand Nijinsky and Charlie: Halifax, Nimbus, 1986. ISBN 0-920852-57-2

Awards: CBC Literary Competition (Short Story), 1981. Chatelaine Short Story Contest (Second) 1983. Atlantic Writing Competition (Short Fiction), 1986.

Comments: Short stories have appeared in Chatelaine (February, 1983 and October, 1983), Atlantis (Fall, 1985), Dinosaur Review (1986) and Herizons (January/February, 1987). Children's stories published in *Magook 2* (1977) and *Canadian Children's Annual (1983)*. About 20 articles in Canadian and American journals. Wrote a weekly column on child care for the Globe and Mail during the 60s.

Readings, Lectures & Workshops: Available for readings of adult stories, and for readings and workshops with elementary-school children.

Mailing Address: September 1 to June 1: 672 Stannor Drive, Peterborough, Ontario K9J 4S7

June 1-September 1: NW Cove, RR 1, Hubbards, Nova Scotia B0J 1T0

ERIC WILSON

Began writing for the reluctant readers in my grade eight classroom in White Rock, British Columbia, in 1970 and have since produced many mysteries for ages nine and up. The Eric Wilson Mystery Club has more than 12,000 members world wide.

Selected Publications:

Murder on The Canadian: Toronto, Collins, 1976. ISBN 0-00-222632-4
Vancouver Nightmare: Toronto, Collins, 1978. ISBN 0-00-222631-6
Susie-Q: Toronto, Scholastic, 1978. ISBN 0-590-71042-7
Terror in Winnipeg: Toronto, Clarke Irwin, 1979. ISBN 0-7736-7043-2
Lost Treasure of Casa Loma: Toronto, Clarke Irwin, 1980. 0-7736-7044-0
Ghost of Lunenburg Manor: Toronto, Collins, 1980. ISBN 0-00-222629-4
Disneyland Hostage: Toronto, Collins, 1982. ISBN 0-00-222637-5
The Kootenay Kidnapper: Toronto, Collins, 1983. ISBN 0-00-222842-4
Vampires of Ottawa: Toronto, Collins, 1984. ISBN 0-00-222858-0
Summer of Discovery: Toronto, Collins, 1984. ISBN 0-00-222850-5
Spirit in the Rainforest: Toronto, Collins, 1985. ISBN 0-00-223029-6
The Unmasking of 'Ksan: Toronto, Collins, 1986. ISBN 0-00-223116-6

Comments: Work in progress: The Green Gables Detectives. Free membership for all ages in the Eric Wilson Mystery Club available by writing Collins Publishers.

Readings, Lectures & Workshops: Available for readings at schools, workshops at Young Authors Conferences, and seminars for adults interested in writing for children.

Mailing Address: c/o Collins Publishers, 100 Lesmill Road, Don Mills, Ontario M3B 2T5

CATHERINE WISMER

The result of a night spent in post-war London by a Canadian naval officer and his bride. Brought over on a banana boat, born in Waterloo and raised in Oakville, Ontario. A graduate from the University of Western Ontario, found work as a photojournalist on the staff of Toronto Life and Maclean's, and served as editor of Miss Chatelaine. Freelance broadcaster/writer and a mother, married with one child. Active in PEN and former second vice-chair of the Writers' Union.

Selected Publications:

Come See My Garden: Toronto, Martlet, 1969. Limited Edition
Faces Of The Old North: Toronto, McGraw-Hill Ryerson, 1974. ISBN 0-07-077774-8
Sweethearts (The Builders, the Mob and the Men): Toronto, James Lorimer, 1980. ISBN 0-88862-384-4

Comments: "*Sweethearts* which I found excellent and fascinating reading." – Graham Greene
Mailing Address: c/o TWUC, 24 Ryerson Avenue, Toronto, Ontario M5T 2P3

WILLIAM HAROLD WOLFERSTAN

Born in Vancouver, British Columbia, July 28, 1942. Now living in Victoria, British Columbia. B.Sc., University of British Columbia, 1964. M.A., Simon Fraser University, 1972. Lieutenant, Royal Canadian Signal Corps, 1964-67. Geography master, Ringwood Grammar School, Bournemouth, United Kingdom, 1967-68. Director, Wetlealdath Environmental and Recreational Consultants, 1972-73. Research officer, British Columbia Government since 1973. Director, SALT Society since 1983.

Selected Publications:

All Cruising Guides to British Columbia published in Vancouver by Maclean-Hunter/Special Interest Publications

Volume I; Gulf Islands and Vancouver Islands from Sooke to Courtenay: 1976 ISBN 0-969057-47-0
Volume II; Desolation Sound and the Discovery Islands: 1980 ISBN 0-969057-41-5
Volume III; Sunshine Coast – Vancouver and Fraser Estuary to Jervis Inlet: 1982 ISBN 0-969057-42-3
The Pacific Swift (Building and Sailing a Traditional Tall Ship): (ed.), Vancouver, Sail and Life Training Society, 1986. ISBN 0-9692482-0-2

Readings, Lectures & Workshops: Slide-lecture presentations on British Columbia coast to universities, colleges, yacht clubs, power squadrons and other interested groups.

Mailing Address: 1322 Clover Avenue, Victoria, British Columbia V8S 1A6

GEORGE WOODCOCK

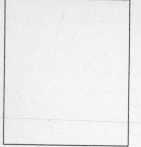

Born in Winnipeg, 1912. Taken to England in infancy, spent childhood there, and adulthood until 1949, when I returned to Canada. Began writing as an English Thirties poet, edited NOW in London, 1940-47, also edited Freedom, an anarchist paper. Taught at universities seven years to escape poverty. Founded Canadian Literature, 1959, edited to 1977. Travelled the world.

Selected Publications:

Pierre-Joseph Proudhon: London, Routledge & Kegan Paul, 1956. (no ISBN)
Incas and Other Men: London, Faber, 1959. (no ISBN)
Anarchism: Cleveland, Meridian, 1962. (no ISBN)
Faces of India: London, Faber, 1964. (no ISBN)
The Crystal Spirit: London, Jonathan Cape, 1967. (no ISBN)
Gabriel Dumont: Edmonton, Hurtig, 1975. ISBN 0-88830-095-6
Peoples of the Coast: Edmonton, Hurtig, 1977. ISBN 0-88830-136-7
Thomas Merton, Monk and Poet: Vancouver, Douglas & McIntyre, 1978. ISBN 0-88894-189-7
The World of Canadian Writing: Vancouver, Douglas & McIntyre, 1980. ISBN 0-88894-286-6
Letter to the Past: Don Mills, Fitzhenry & Whiteside, 1982. ISBN 0-88902-715-3
Collected Poems: Victoria, Sono Nis, 1983. ISBN 0-919203-40-X

Mailing Address: c/o TWUC, 24 Ryerson Avenue, Toronto, Ontario M5T 2P3

ELIZABETH WOODS

Born in Prince George, British Columbia, on January 10, 1940, now residing in Victoria after many years' voluntary exile in Toronto. B.A., University of British Columbia, 1961, plus two years' post-graduate study in experimental psychology at Queen's and UBC. Jobs include gofering at CBC and hot-walking Thoroughbreds at Woodbine and Fort Erie. Also a member of the League of Canadian Poets; former chair of Copyright Committee and Book and Periodical Development Council's Freedom of Expression Committee.

Selected Publications:

The Yellow Volkswagon: Toronto, Simon & Schuster, 1971. ISBN 0-671-77338-0
Gone: Ladysmith, Ladysmith Press, 1972. ISBN 0-919556-13-2
Men: Fredericton, Fiddlehead, 1979. ISBN 0-920110-49-5
The Amateur: Toronto, PaperJacks, 1980. ISBN 0-7701-0141-0

   Comments: A Way of Loving, The Colour Between Us, Fool's Paradise and Maya have been broadcast on CBC radio.
   Readings, Lectures & Workshops: Storytelling – *Betsy's Dream* and *Wandering a Way Home* – and writing workshops for elementary-school children. Poetry readings and writing workshops for high-school students, and adults. Readings for all ages at libraries. Workshops include: Creating An Alien; Five Senses Exercize; Word Lottery; and Adding a Verse – to one of the songs in *Betsy's Dream*, or *Wandering a Way Home*. Lectures on: Copyright and the Creator; The Benefits to the User of a Reprography Collective; and The Usefulness of Free Speech to the Community. May be booked through TWUC.
   Mailing Address: 7A Vickery Road, Victoria, British Columbia V9B 1M3

SHIRLEY EDWARDS WOODS

Born in Ottawa in 1934. Educated at Port Hope and Lennoxville. Served three years as a subaltern in the Royal Canadian Regiment. Married Sandrea Ogilvie of Montreal in 1957. Three daughters: Victoria, Julia and Penelope. Present occupation and most of business career has been spent as a stock broker. Fellow of the Royal Society of Arts and a director of the Canadian Writers' Foundation.

Selected Publications:

Gunning for Upland Birds and Wildfowl: New York, Winchester, 1976. 0-87691-219-6
Angling for Atlantic Salmon: Goshen, 1976. Limited Edition
The Squirrels of Canada: Ottawa, National Museums of Canada, 1980. ISBN 0-660-10344-3
Ottawa (The Capital of Canada): Toronto, Doubleday, 1980. ISBN 0-385-23146-6
The Molson Saga 1763-1983: Toronto, Doubleday, 1983. ISBN 0-385-17863-8
The Money Labyrinth: Toronto, Doubleday, 1984. ISBN 0-385-19651-2
Her Excellency Jeanne Sauve: Toronto, Macmillan, 1986. ISBN 0-7715-9899-8

Readings, Lectures & Workshops: Have spoken on a variety of subjects to professional associations, service clubs and adult education classes.
Mailing Address: 545 Montagu Place, Ottawa, Ontario K1M 0J2

ERIC WRIGHT

Married; two daughters.

Selected Publications:

The Night the Gods Smiled: Toronto, Collins, 1983. ISBN 0-00-231695-1
Smoke Detector: Toronto, Collins, 1984. ISBN 0-00-231415-0
Death in the Old Country: Toronto, Collins, 1985. ISBN 0-00-231970-5
A Single Death: Toronto, Collins, 1986. ISBN 0-00-223053-4

Awards: John Creasey Award, 1983. Crime Writers of Canada Awards, 1983 and 1985. City of Toronto Book Award, 1983.
Mailing Address: c/o Collins, 100 Lesmill Road, Don Mills, Ontario M3B 2T5

L.R. (BUNNY) WRIGHT

Born in Saskatoon, June 5, 1939. Now living in Vancouver. Two daughters. Was a journalist with the Calgary Herald for several years, and freelanced for several more. Began writing fiction in 1976.

Selected Publications:

Neighbours: Toronto, Macmillan, 1979. ISBN 0-7705-1791-9
The Favorite: Toronto, Doubleday, 1982. ISBN 0-385-17624-4
Among Friends: Toronto, Doubleday, 1984. ISBN 0-385-18403-4
The Suspect: New York, Viking Penguin, 1985. ISBN 0-670-80596-3
Sleep While I Sing: Toronto, Doubleday, 1986. ISBN 0-385-25042-8

Awards: Alberta First Novel Award, 1979. Mystery Writers of America Edgar Allan Poe Award (Best Novel), 1985.

Comments: Member of the British Columbia Federation of Writers, the Crime Writers of Canada and the Authors Guild (United States).

Readings, Lectures & Workshops: Have done all three.

Mailing Address: 6695 Hersham Avenue, Burnaby, British Columbia V5E 3K7

RONALD WRIGHT

Born in England, 1948; educated at Cambridge University (M.A., 1973). First came to Canada in 1970; citizenship 1978. Formerly an archaeologist (excavations in Britain, Canada, Africa and Latin America); now a writer and broadcaster. Have also recorded and produced records of indigenous music from the Andes, Alberta and Northwest Territories. Now living in Toronto.

Selected Publications:

Cut Stones and Crossroads (A Journey in the Two Worlds of Peru): New York, Viking, 1984. ISBN 0-670-69381-2
On Fiji Islands: Toronto, Viking Penguin, 1986. ISBN 0-670-80634-X

Awards: Canadian Science Writers Association Award, 1985
Comments: "*Cut Stones and Crossroads* is absolutely superlative." – *Plain Dealer*
"There is so much to praise about this excellent book." – *Washington Post*
"Extraordinarily perceptive." – *Times Literary Supplement*
"*On Fiji Islands* is a model of clarity and grace." – *Plain Dealer*
"Persuasive and evocative." – *New York Times Book Review*
"Graceful prose and intimate knowledge . . . (a) rich evocation of Fiji's wild, mountainous beauty and of a society that preserves many tribal customs with confidence and dignity." – *Maclean's*
Readings, Lectures & Workshops: May be booked through TWUC.
Mailing Address: Bella Pomer Agency, PH2, 22 Shallmar Boulevard, Toronto, Ontario M5N 2P3

BETTY JANE WYLIE

I bill myself as "Canada's professional widow," write self-help books to support playwriting habit. Born and educated in Winnipeg (M.A. from University of Manitoba). Stranded in the East where dual career began. *Beginnings: A Book for Widows* published in six English-speaking countries as well as Denmark. Live and write in a Muskoka cabin when not travelling, speaking or workshopping new plays.

Selected Publications:

Beginnings (A Book for Widows): Toronto, McClelland & Stewart, 1977.
  ISBN 0-7710-9057-9
A Place on Earth: Toronto, Playwrights Union, 1982. ISBN 0-88754-319-7
The Book of Matthew: Toronto, McClelland & Stewart, 1984. ISBN 0-7710-9059-5
Everywoman's Money Book: (with Lynne MacFarlane), Toronto, Key Porter, 1985. ISBN 0-91949-15-7
Successfully Single: Toronto, Key Porter, 1986. ISBN 1-55103-007-1

  Awards: Smile Company Contests, First Prize, 1982; Third Prize, 1983
  Comments: "She is a playwright, a journalist unafraid to get her hands dirty, an author who keeps six publishers busy, a mother, a survivor, and every bit the Renaissance woman she claims to be." – *Kingston Whig-Standard*
  Readings, Lectures & Workshops: I read regularly at universities, high schools, libraries and elementary schools (especially my puppet plays for the latter). May be booked through TWUC.
  Mailing Address: c/o TWUC, 24 Ryerson Avenue, Toronto, Ontario M5T 2P3

TIM WYNNE-JONES

Born in 1948 in a house called Ravensheugh in Cheshire, England. Some months short of four I was moved to Kitimat, British Columbia, and thence forth to Vancouver and Ottawa. I moved myself to Waterloo and received a B.A. in fine arts at the university and, later, an M.F.A. in visual arts at York University. I am married to Amanda West Lewis. We have three children: Xan, Maddy and Lewis.

Selected Publications:

Odd's End: Toronto, McClelland & Stewart, 1980. ISBN 0-7710-9052-8
The Knot: Toronto, McClelland & Stewart, 1982. ISBN 0-7710-9051-X
Zoom at Sea: Toronto, Groundwood, 1983. ISBN 0-88899-021-9
Zoom Away: Toronto, Groundwood, 1985. ISBN 0-88899-042-1
Mischief City: Toronto, Groundwood, 1986. ISBN 0-88899-049-9
I'll Make You Small: Toronto, Groundwood, 1986. ISBN 0-88899-045-6
St. Anthony's Man in Fingerprints: Toronto, Irwin, 1984.

Awards: Seal First Novel Award, 1980. IODE Award (Toronto Chapter), 1984. Ruth Schwartz Award, 1984.

Comments: Short stories in Descant (Fall 1985), Now (no. 47, 1986) and the University of Waterloo Courier (Sept. 1986). Profile of Playwright George F. Walker in Books in Canada (April 1985). Fact into Fiction appeared in the Banff letters (Spring 1986). Designed several vault toilet outhouses for the Ontario Department of Lands and Forests. Sung and played electric baseball bat in a Spadina bar band.

Mailing Address: 142 Winona Drive, Toronto, Ontario M6G 3S9

PAUL YEE

Born in Spalding, Saskatchewan, in 1956, but moved to Vancouver shortly thereafter to grow up in and near Chinatown. Hold an M.A. in Canadian history from the University of British Columbia and now work as an archivist for the City of Vancouver. Have done volunteer work with Vancouver's Chinese community since 1975.

Selected Publications:

Teach Me to Fly, Skyfighter and other Stories: Toronto, Lorimer, 1983. ISBN 0-88862-646-0
The Curses of Third Uncle: Toronto, Lorimer, 1986. ISBN 0-88862-910-9

Readings, Lectures & Workshops: Read and discuss writing at elementary schools.

Mailing Address: 2021 York Avenue, Vancouver, British Columbia V6J 1E4

SHULAMIS YELIN

Born in Montreal, April 12, 1913. Permanent resident except for years studying at Columbia University Teachers College and teaching at Hebrew University, Jerusalem. Hold first class teaching diploma from the McGill School for Teachers. B.A., Sir George Williams College (now Concordia University). M.A., Magna cum Laude from the University of Montreal. Now retired, write full time, with excursions into freelance lecturing in Jewish and comparative literature. Winter in south.

Selected Publications:

Seeded in Sinai: New York, Reconstructionist, 1975. ISBN 0-91808-03-0
Shulamis (Stories From a Montreal Childhood): Montreal, Vehicule, 1983.
 ISBN 0-919890-52-0
Many Mirrors Many Faces: London, South Western Ontario Poetry, 1986.
 ISBN 0-919193-27-3

 Awards: La Med Literary Award, American Foundation for Jewish Culture (New York), 1963
 Comments: "Marks out new areas of experience, rediscovering forgotten riches of language." – Eli Mandel (on *Seeded in Sinai*)
 "Yelin's stories are brief yet rich with real insight," – *Montreal Gazette* (on *Shulamis*)
 "The world through Yelin's eyes is gentle and warm, yet not without its moments of pathos." – *Quill & Quire*
 Readings, Lectures & Workshops: Enjoy giving readings. Have read across Canada, on CBC and other stations, in universities, libraries, community centres, high schools, etc.
 Mailing Address: 15-4865 Queen Mary Road, Montreal, Quebec H3W 1X1

DAVID YOUNG

Born in Oakville, Ontario, July 17, 1946. Educated University of Western Ontario (Class of '67). Editor at the Coach House Press since 1972. Wrote many episodes of Fraggle Rock (children's televsion) and two plays (with Paul Le Doux): *Love is Strange* and *Fire*. Live in Toronto with Sarah Sheard and son Benn.

Selected Publications:

Agent Provocateur: Toronto, Coach House, 1976. (no ISBN)
Incognito: Toronto, Coach House, 1981. ISBN 0-88910-204-X

Awards: Gemini Award, 1985
Comments: Is this as tall as I get?
Readings, Lectures & Workshops: Founded the For/Words Foundation in 1972 to establish creative writing programmes in Ontario high schools. Taught the Dream Class (a programme for gifted kids) since 1979.
Mailing Address: 34 Marchmount Road, Toronto, Ontario M6G 2A9

CARMEN ZIOLKOWSKI (nee LAURENZA)

Born in an old convent in Italy on a stormy February night. Studied nursing science at the Policlinico in Rome. Learned English in England and received further education in medical field, earning diploma in obstetrics. After coming to Canada in 1956, took journalism courses at Port Huron Junior College and Wayne State University. Now live in Sarnia with husband Bruno and sons Robin and Jim. Write full time.

Selected Publications:

Roses Bloom at Dusk: Cornwall, Vesta, 1976. ISBN 0-919806-12-0
The House of Four Winds: Sarnia, River City, 1987. ISBN 0-920940-08-0

Awards: Esposizione Italiana – Arte e Letteratura (Drama) 1969 and (Poetry) 1970

Comments: Short stories and poetry published in Canada, Italy, United States, and England. Writing makes me feel that I have wings . . . I can fly to any height and there are no boundaries to my adventures.

Readings, Lectures & Workshops: Sarnia Poetry in the Park, 1976-77. London Poetry in the Park, many times. Ital-Canada festival, Ottawa, Ontario, 1978. Sarnia Public Library, 1982 and 1986. Host on TV channel 6 for three years (Italian programme).

Mailing Address: 1066 Parsons Street, Sarnia, Ontario N7S 1S3

MEGUIDO ZOLA

I was completely unknown until 1939. Then I was born. Even then, I continued to be known to just a select few. Today, though, I am seldom mistaken for anyone else. The name, Meguido, is Hebrew for 'storyteller', and I take pride in being a former child. When I look back on it all, though, I feel that after peaking at about the age of seven, it has been more or less downhill all the way. Seven is the beginning of the end.

Selected Publications:

A Dream of Promise: Toronto, Kids Can, 1980. ISBN 0-919964-31-1
Only the Best: London, Julia MacRae, 1981. ISBN 0-86203-047-1
Gretzky! Gretzky! Gretzky!: Toronto, Grolier, 1982. ISBN 0-7172-1826-0
Moving: London, Julia MacRae, 1983. ISBN 0-86203-115-X
Nobody: Winnipeg, Pemmican, 1983. ISBN 0-919143-38-5
Karen Kain (Born to Dance): Toronto, Grolier, 1983. ISBN 0-7172-1839-2
Sharon, Lois & Bram: Toronto, Grolier, 1984. ISBN 0-7172-1839-2
Terry Fox: Toronto, Grolier, 1984. ISBN 0-7172-1843-0
My Kind of Pup: Winnipeg, Pemmican, 1985. ISBN 0-919143-19-9

Comments: "I wanted to write to someone who is still living, that's why I picked you" — EMF, Moncton
"Do you write books just out of your head? Or do you use a kit or something? I'D LIKE TO KNOW!" — PSB, Montreal
"I read Moving and have nothing I dislike about it." — AC, Ottawa

Readings, Lectures & Workshops: For children and adults: on writing, storytelling, reading aloud and all aspects of literature for childhood. Complimentary ice-creams. Free pony rides.

Mailing Address: Faculty of Education, Simon Fraser University, Burnaby, British Columbia V5A 1S6

(DEBORAH) MELANIE ZOLA

Choices, choices – Life is 31 flavours, and I like the taste: writing, alone or with someone else; teaching and giving workshops in drama, writing, reading and music; and generally having fun being a mom. Young Writers' Conferences are my favourite times for working with writers who, however short, are tall in aspirations to sample the elusive, yet delicious, satisfaction of writing and touching the lives of others.

Selected Publications:

Alligators: Toronto, Grolier, 1986. ISBN 0-7172-1906-2
Peanut Butter Is Forever: Toronto, Nelson, 1984. ISBN 0-17-602089-6
Sharon, Lois and Bram: Toronto, Grolier, 1983. ISBN 0-7172-1849-X
Terry Fox: Toronto, Grolier, 1984. ISBN 0-7172-1843-0

Awards: David C. Cook Award for Children's Writing, 1978. Dr. S. O'Connell Scholarship in Children's Literature, 1986.

Comments: Numerous short stories, poems and articles have appeared in the Impressions reading series, Holt, Rinehart & Winston of Canada; the Hiyou series, Commcept Publishing; and the Vancouver Province newspaper. *The Champ* was published in *Magook*: Toronto, McClelland & Stewart, 1980.

Readings, Lectures & Workshops: For children and adults, in the areas of language arts (writing, reading, speaking), drama, music and movement, and French.

Mailing Address: 5-1019 Gilford Street, Vancouver, British Columbia V6G 2P1

FURTHER MEMBERS

Lloyd Abbey
Don Abrams
Sue Ann Alderson
Ted Allan
Keith Alldritt
Alexandre L. Amprimoz
Martin Avery
Zina Barnieh
Jo Anne Williams Bennett
Earle Birney
Arthur Black
Michael Bliss
Joan Bodger
Roy Bonisteel
Paulette Bourgeois
Pleuke Boyce
Harry Boyle
Chris Brookes
Jean Bruce
Edward Butts
Morley Callaghan
    (honorary member)
Jock Carpenter
Peter A. Charlebois
Marion Crook
Barry Dickson
Anne Konrad Dyck
Nancie Erhard
Judith Ariana Fitzgerald
Simon Fodden
Madeline Freeman
Northrop Frye
Robert Fulford
Mavis Gallant
Sally Gibson
Aubrey Golden
Carolyn Gossage
Rabbi Meir Uri Gottesman
Arthur Hailey
Marilyn Halvorson
Alice Hamilton

Don Harron
Elisabeth Harvor
Terrence Heath
Maye Preston Hill
Marion Hoffman
Simma Holt
Clyde Hosein
Mary Howarth
Victor Jerrett-Enns
Paul Jeune
Simon Johnston
Margaret Keith
Nora Hickson Kelly
Betty Kennedy
Fred Kerner
Crawford Kilian
G. Doug Killam
Madeline Kronby
Donn J. Kushner
Hal Lawrence
Alma Lee (honorary member)
Terry Leeder
Jean Little
Dorothy Livesay (life member)
Douglas Long
Alex Macdonald
Richard Mackie
Joan Maloney
David Margoshes
Robin Mathews
Bruce McBay
John A.B. McLeish
John Mellor
W.O. Mitchell
Gloria Montero
Edward J. Mulawka
John A. Munro
Norman Newton
Dorothy O'Connell
Eleanor O'Donnell
Carlie Oreskovich

E.G. Perrault
Gordon Pinsent
Ted Plantos
Ellen Powers (honorary member)
Thomas H. Raddall
    (honorary member)
Mordecai Richler
Charles Ritchie
Erika Ritter
Paul Roazen
Heather Robertson
Ajmer Rode
Gary Ross
Sinclair Ross (honorary member)
Helen J. Rosta
William N. Rowe
Andy Russell
Jeanne Scargall
Diane Schoemperlen
Lois Simmie

Leo Simpson
Donna E. Smyth
Ken Stange
David Lewis Stein
Brian Jeffrey Street
Sukhinder
Anne Szumigalski
Janice Tyrwhitt
Guy Vanderhaeghe
Jean Veevers
Katherine Vlassie
Miriam Waddington
Clarke Wallace
Norman Ward
Robert Weaver (honorary member)
Clifton Whiten
Garrett Wilson
Richard T. Wright
Scott Young
Larry Zolf

THE NATIONAL COUNCILS

The Union's National Council consists of the chair, the first and second vice-chairs, and nine other members of whom five are regionally tied. The efforts of the volunteer members who have served on National Councils through the years have provided the Union with strong leadership in advancing the status of the writer in Canada.

First National Council – elected at the inaugural meeting, November 3, 1973:
Marian Engel (chair), Harold Horwood (vice-chair), Rudy Wiebe (vice-chair), Graeme Gibson, Robert Harlow, Terrence Heath, John Metcalf, George Payerle, Heather Robertson, Andreas Schroeder, Ray Smith, Kent Thompson.

Second – elected October, 1974:
Graeme Gibson (chair), Harold Horwood (vice-chair), Robert Harlow (vice-chair), Cassie Brown, Silver Donald Cameron, Terrence Heath, Helene Holden, Robert Kroetsch, Margaret Laurence, John Metcalf, Ken Mitchell, Andreas Schroeder.

Third – elected October, 1975:
David Lewis Stein (chair), Andreas Schroeder (vice-chair), Silver Donald Cameron (vice-chair), Cassie Brown, Sylvia Fraser, Terrence Heath, Helene Holden, Robert Kroetsch, John Metcalf, Herbert T. Schwarz, Audrey Thomas, Kent Thompson.

Fourth – elected April, 1976:
Andreas Schroeder (chair), Sylvia Fraser (vice-chair), Kent Thompson (vice-chair), Cassie Brown, Silver Donald Cameron, Helene Holden, Gerald Lampert, Ken Mitchell, John Peter, Herbert T. Schwartz, Ray Smith, Betty Wilson.

Fifth – elected May, 1977:
Timothy Findley (chair), Charles Taylor (first vice-chair), June Callwood (second vice-chair), Silver Donald Cameron, Charlotte Fielden, Edith Fowke, Joan Haggerty, Helene Holden, Judith Merril, Don Sawatsky, Leo Simpson, Rudy Wiebe.

Sixth — elected May, 1978:

Charles Taylor (chair), June Callwood (first vice-chair), Rudy Wiebe (second vice-chair), Marie-Claire Blais, Harry Boyle, Myrna Kostash, Joyce Marshall, Paul O'Neill, H.R. Percy, George Szanto, David Watmough, David Williams.

Seventh — elected May, 1979:

June Callwood (chair), Harold Horwood (first vice-chair), Janet Lunn (second vice-chair), Ann Charney, Susan Crean, Trevor Ferguson, Jack Hodgins, Myrna Kostash, Keith Maillard, Paul O'Neill, H.R. Percy, Bill Repka.

Eighth — elected May, 1980:

Harold Horwood (chair), Margaret Atwood (first vice-chair), Keith Maillard (second vice-chair), James Bacque, Jamie Brown, June Callwood, Jan Drabek, Frances Duncan, Robert Kroetsch, Janet Lunn, Kevin Major, Leo Simpson, Elizabeth Woods.

Ninth — elected May, 1981:

Margaret Atwood (Chair), Robin Skelton (first vice-chair), Susan Crean (second vice-chair), Joyce Barkhouse, Jamie Brown, Anne Innis Dagg, Jan Drabek, Jeffrey Holmes, Robert Kroetsch, David Watmough, David Young.

Tenth — elected May, 1982:

Robin Skelton (chair), Eugene Benson (first vice-chair), Matt Cohen (second vice-chair), Edna Alford, Doris Anderson, Bruce Armstrong, Helene Holden, Jeffrey Lewis, Jack MacLeod, Erna Paris, Merna Summers, Richard T. Wright.

Eleventh — elected May, 1983:

Eugene Benson (chair), Janet Lunn (first vice-chair), Audrey Thomas (second vice-chair), Edna Alford, Bruce Armstrong, Edith Fowke, Michael A. Gilbert, Dorris Heffron, Heather Menzies, Ted Phillips, Irene Robinson, Richard T. Wright.

Twelfth — elected May, 1984:

Janet Lunn (chair), Matt Cohen (first vice-chair), Merna Summers (second vice-chair), Bruce Armstrong, Michael A. Gilbert, Reshard Gool, Dorris Heffron, Heather Menzies, Irene Robinson, Candace Savage, Robert Sherrin, Audrey Thomas.

Thirteenth – May, 1985:

Matt Cohen (chair), Rudy Wiebe (first vice-chair), Catherine Wismer (second vice-chair), Beverly Allinson, Gregory M. Cook, Frances Duncan, Bill Freeman, Michael A. Gilbert, Dennis Gruending, Myrna Kostash, Donna E. Smyth, Thomas York.

Fourteenth – elected May, 1986:

Rudy Wiebe (chair), Pierre Berton (first vice-chair), Jane Rule (second vice-chair), Robert Bringhurst, Gregory M. Cook, Jan Hudson, Patricia Morley, Bruce Powe, Libby Scheier, Fred Stenson, Merrily Weisbord, Betty Jane Wylie.

Fifteenth – elected May, 1987:

Pierre Berton (chair), Betty Jane Wylie (first vice-chair), Daphne Marlatt (second vice-chair), Joan Clark, Bill Freeman, Sylvia Gunnery, Patricia Morley, George Payerle, Libby Scheier, Robert Sherrin, Fred Stenson, Merrily Weisbord.

INFORMATION SOURCES

Association of Canadian Publishers
260 King Street East
Toronto, Ontario M5A 1K3
(416) 361-1408

Book and Periodical Development
  Council
200-34 Ross Street
Toronto, Ontario M5T 1Z9
(416) 595-9967

Canadian Book Information Centre
260 King Street East
Toronto, Ontario M5A 1K3
(416) 362-6555

Canadian Book Publishers
  Council
701-45 Charles Street East
Toronto, Ontario M4Y 1S2
(416) 964-7231

Canadian Booksellers
  Association
301 Donlands Avenue
Toronto, Ontario M4J 3R8
(416) 467-7883

Childrens' Book Centre
229 College Street, 5th Floor
Toronto, Ontario M5T 1R4
(416) 597-1331

THE WRITERS' UNION OF CANADA AUTHORS ON TOUR

With funding assistance of the Canada Council and the Ontario Arts Council, The Writers' Union of Canada is able to arrange public readings by its members. The programmes available through our Tour Office are as follows:

The National Reading Programme

The National Reading Programme is funded through the assistance of the Canada Council. The readings must be open to the public, and take place in a location accessible to all residents of the community, such as an art gallery, public library, theatre, or community centre.

The host organization is responsible for accommodation and meals for the author and an administration fee payable The Writers' Union of Canada.

Host organizations may also apply directly to the Canada Council for readings. There is no administration fee for this service.

Contact: Public Readings, Canada Council, P.O. Box 1047, Ottawa, Ontario K1P 5V8

Writers-in-the-Schools

The Writers-in-the-Schools programme is funded through the assistance of the Ontario Arts Council. This programme is an opportunity for schools throughout Ontario to have an author visit the classroom.

The authors receive an honorarium and all daily and travel costs, within the province of Ontario, are covered under this programme.

The cost to the host school, based on a half-day or a full-day visit, is payable to the author on the day of the visit.

The popularity of public readings by Canadian authors necessitates that these programmes operate on a first come, first served basis. Requests that are received after the year's funds have been allocated will be put on a waiting list. A host organization or school also has the option of arranging a private booking.

Private Booking

When it is not possible to have a funding-assisted reading, the Tour Office can arrange a private booking with the author selected. The host organization or school is then responsible for all costs, including the author's honorarium, which is usually based on the fees paid in either programme, as well as all daily and travel costs.

Requests for readings must be made IN WRITING to:

The Tour Office
The Writers' Union of Canada
24 Ryerson Avenue
Toronto, Ontario   M5T 2P3

(416) 868-6914

PHOTO CREDITS